Foundations of
Data Quality Management

Synthesis Lectures on Data Management

Editor
M. Tamer Özsu, *University of Waterloo*

Synthesis Lectures on Data Management is edited by Tamer Özsu of the University of Waterloo. The series will publish 50- to 125 page publications on topics pertaining to data management. The scope will largely follow the purview of premier information and computer science conferences, such as ACM SIGMOD, VLDB, ICDE, PODS, ICDT, and ACM KDD. Potential topics include, but not are limited to: query languages, database system architectures, transaction management, data warehousing, XML and databases, data stream systems, wide scale data distribution, multimedia data management, data mining, and related subjects.

Foundations of Data Quality Management
Wenfei Fan and Floris Geerts
2012

Business Processes: A Database Perspective
Daniel Deutch and Tova Milo
2012

Data Protection from Insider Threats
Elisa Bertino
2012

Deep Web Query Interface Understanding and Integration
Eduard C. Dragut, Weiyi Meng, and Clement T. Yu
2012

P2P Techniques for Decentralized Applications
Esther Pacitti, Reza Akbarinia, and Manal El-Dick
2012

Query Answer Authentication
HweeHwa Pang and Kian-Lee Tan
2012

Declarative Networking
Boon Thau Loo and Wenchao Zhou
2012

Full-Text (Substring) Indexes in External Memory
Marina Barsky, Ulrike Stege, and Alex Thomo
2011

Spatial Data Management
Nikos Mamoulis
2011

Database Repairing and Consistent Query Answering
Leopoldo Bertossi
2011

Managing Event Information: Modeling, Retrieval, and Applications
Amarnath Gupta and Ramesh Jain
2011

Fundamentals of Physical Design and Query Compilation
David Toman and Grant Weddell
2011

Methods for Mining and Summarizing Text Conversations
Giuseppe Carenini, Gabriel Murray, and Raymond Ng
2011

Probabilistic Databases
Dan Suciu, Dan Olteanu, Christopher Ré, and Christoph Koch
2011

Peer-to-Peer Data Management
Karl Aberer
2011

Probabilistic Ranking Techniques in Relational Databases
Ihab F. Ilyas and Mohamed A. Soliman
2011

Uncertain Schema Matching
Avigdor Gal
2011

Fundamentals of Object Databases: Object-Oriented and Object-Relational Design
Suzanne W. Dietrich and Susan D. Urban
2010

Advanced Metasearch Engine Technology
Weiyi Meng and Clement T. Yu
2010

Web Page Recommendation Models: Theory and Algorithms
Sule Gündüz-Ögüdücü
2010

Multidimensional Databases and Data Warehousing
Christian S. Jensen, Torben Bach Pedersen, and Christian Thomsen
2010

Database Replication
Bettina Kemme, Ricardo Jimenez-Peris, and Marta Patino-Martinez
2010

Relational and XML Data Exchange
Marcelo Arenas, Pablo Barcelo, Leonid Libkin, and Filip Murlak
2010

User-Centered Data Management
Tiziana Catarci, Alan Dix, Stephen Kimani, and Giuseppe Santucci
2010

Data Stream Management
Lukasz Golab and M. Tamer Özsu
2010

Access Control in Data Management Systems
Elena Ferrari
2010

An Introduction to Duplicate Detection
Felix Naumann and Melanie Herschel
2010

Privacy-Preserving Data Publishing: An Overview
Raymond Chi-Wing Wong and Ada Wai-Chee Fu
2010

Keyword Search in Databases
Jeffrey Xu Yu, Lu Qin, and Lijun Chang
2009

Copyright © 2012 by Morgan & Claypool

All rights reserved. No part of this publication may be reproduced, stored in a retrieval system, or transmitted in any form or by any means—electronic, mechanical, photocopy, recording, or any other except for brief quotations in printed reviews, without the prior permission of the publisher.

Foundations of Data Quality Management

Wenfei Fan and Floris Geerts

www.morganclaypool.com

ISBN: 9781608457779   paperback
ISBN: 9781608457786   ebook

DOI 10.2200/S00439ED1V01Y201207DTM030

A Publication in the Morgan & Claypool Publishers series
SYNTHESIS LECTURES ON DATA MANAGEMENT

Lecture #29
Series Editor: M. Tamer Özsu, *University of Waterloo*
Series ISSN
Synthesis Lectures on Data Management
Print 2153-5418   Electronic 2153-5426

Foundations of
Data Quality Management

Wenfei Fan
University of Edinburgh

Floris Geerts
University of Antwerp

SYNTHESIS LECTURES ON DATA MANAGEMENT #29

MORGAN & CLAYPOOL PUBLISHERS

ABSTRACT

Data quality is one of the most important problems in data management. A database system typically aims to support the creation, maintenance, and use of large amount of data, focusing on the quantity of data. However, real-life data are often dirty: inconsistent, duplicated, inaccurate, incomplete, or stale. Dirty data in a database routinely generate misleading or biased analytical results and decisions, and lead to loss of revenues, credibility and customers. With this comes the need for data quality management. In contrast to traditional data management tasks, data quality management enables the detection and correction of errors in the data, syntactic or semantic, in order to improve the quality of the data and hence, add value to business processes.

This monograph gives an overview of fundamental issues underlying central aspects of data quality, namely, data consistency, data deduplication, data accuracy, data currency, and information completeness. We promote a uniform logical framework for dealing with these issues, based on data quality rules. The text is organized into seven chapters, focusing on relational data. Chapter 1 introduces data quality issues. A conditional dependency theory is developed in Chapter 2, for capturing data inconsistencies. It is followed by practical techniques in Chapter 3 for discovering conditional dependencies, and for detecting inconsistencies and repairing data based on conditional dependencies. Matching dependencies are introduced in Chapter 4, as matching rules for data deduplication. A theory of relative information completeness is studied in Chapter 5, revising the classical Closed World Assumption and the Open World Assumption, to characterize incomplete information in the real world. A data currency model is presented in Chapter 6, to identify the current values of entities in a database and to answer queries with the current values, in the absence of reliable timestamps. Finally, interactions between these data quality issues are explored in Chapter 7. Important theoretical results and practical algorithms are covered, but formal proofs are omitted. The bibliographical notes contain pointers to papers in which the results were presented and proven, as well as references to materials for further reading.

This text is intended for a seminar course at the graduate level. It is also to serve as a useful resource for researchers and practitioners who are interested in the study of data quality. The fundamental research on data quality draws on several areas, including mathematical logic, computational complexity and database theory. It has raised as many questions as it has answered, and is a rich source of questions and vitality.

KEYWORDS

data quality, data consistency, data deduplication, data accuracy, information completeness, data currency, data dependencies, dependency discovery, rule validation, error detection, data repairing, master data, certain fixes

In memory of my mother (1933–2009)

Wenfei Fan

Contents

Acknowledgments		**xv**
1	**Data Quality: An Overview**	**1**
	1.1 Data Quality Management	1
	1.2 Central Issues of Data Quality	3
	1.2.1 Data Consistency	3
	1.2.2 Data Deduplication	4
	1.2.3 Data Accuracy	4
	1.2.4 Information Completeness	5
	1.2.5 Data Currency	6
	1.2.6 Interactions between Data Quality Issues	7
	1.3 Improving Data Quality Using Rules	8
	1.4 Background	10
	Bibliographic Notes	10
2	**Conditional Dependencies**	**13**
	2.1 Conditional Dependencies	13
	2.1.1 Conditional Functional Dependencies	14
	2.1.2 Conditional Inclusion Dependencies	17
	2.2 Static Analyses of Conditional Dependencies	21
	2.2.1 Satisfiability	21
	2.2.2 Implication	25
	2.2.3 Finite Axiomatizability	28
	2.2.4 Dependency Propagation	31
	Bibliographic Notes	36
3	**Cleaning Data with Conditional Dependencies**	**39**
	3.1 Discovering Conditional Dependencies	39
	3.1.1 The CFD Discovery Problem	39
	3.1.2 Discovering Constant CFDs	41
	3.1.3 Discovering General CFDs	44
	3.2 Error Detection	47

		3.2.1 Checking a Single CFD with SQL 47
		3.2.2 Validating Multiple CFDs 48
	3.3	Data Repairing 52
		3.3.1 The Data Repairing Problem 53
		3.3.2 Repairing Violations of CFDs and CINDs 55
		Bibliographic Notes 65

4 Data Deduplication 69
4.1	Data Deduplication: An Overview 69
4.2	Matching Dependencies 72
4.3	Reasoning about Matching Dependencies 78
4.4	Relative Keys for Record Matching 80
4.5	Matching Dependencies for Data Repairing 86
	Bibliographic Notes 89

5 Information Completeness 93
5.1	Relative Information Completeness 93
	5.1.1 Partially Closed Databases 94
	5.1.2 A Model for Relative Information Completeness 95
	5.1.3 Relative Completeness and Data Consistency 98
5.2	Determining Relative Completeness 100
5.3	Representation Systems for Possible Worlds 106
5.4	Capturing Missing Tuples and Missing Values 109
5.5	The Complexity of Fundamental Problems 111
	Bibliographic Notes 116

6 Data Currency 119
6.1	Data Currency: An Overview 119
6.2	A Data Currency Model 121
6.3	Reasoning about Data Currency 125
6.4	Incorporating Copy Functions 130
	6.4.1 The Data Currency Model Revisited 130
	6.4.2 Currency Preserving Copy Functions 132
6.5	Determining Currency Preservation 135
	Bibliographic Notes 137

7 Interactions between Data Quality Issues ... 139
7.1 Finding Certain Fixes ... 139
7.1.1 Certain Fixes: An Introduction ... 140
7.1.2 Editing Rules ... 142
7.1.3 Certain Fixes and Certain Regions ... 144
7.1.4 A Framework for Finding Certain Fixes ... 147
7.1.5 Fundamental Problems for Certain Fixes ... 149
7.2 Unifying Data Repairing and Record Matching ... 151
7.2.1 Interaction of CFDs and MDs: An Introduction ... 152
7.2.2 The Data Cleaning Problem and Cleaning Rules ... 154
7.2.3 A Framework for Data Cleaning ... 156
7.2.4 Static Analyses of Data Cleaning with CFDs and MDs ... 160
7.3 Resolving Conflicts ... 163
7.3.1 Conflict Resolution: An Overview ... 163
7.3.2 A Model for Conflict Resolution ... 165
7.3.3 A Framework for Conflict Resolution ... 168
7.3.4 Fundamental Problems for Conflict Resolution ... 169
7.4 Putting Things Together ... 171
Bibliographic Notes ... 173

List of Symbols ... 177

Bibliography ... 179

Authors' Biographies ... 201

Acknowledgments

This book is an account of recent research and development in the area of data quality. Our first debt of gratitude is to Philip Bohannon, Loreto Bravo, Gao Cong, Michael Flaster, Xibei Jia, Anastasios Kementsietsidis, Laks V.S. Lakshmanan, Jianzhong Li, Shuai Ma, Heiko Müller, Rajeev Rastogi, Nan Tang, Jef Wijsen, Ming Xiong, and Wenyuan Yu, for working with us on the subject. The joint work with them has served as the basis of this book. We are also grateful to our colleagues at our home institutions for their unfailing support: the Database Group at the University of Edinburgh and the ADReM Research Group at the University of Antwerp.

We are grateful to Tamer Özsu for the thorough reading of the book and for his valuable comments. We would also like to thank Peter Buneman, Leopoldo Bertossi, Jan Chomicki, Ting Deng, and Scott Weinstein for their comments on a first version of this book.

Tamer Özsu and Diane Cerra guided us through the materialization and publication of this monograph. It was a pleasure to work on this project with them.

Part of the book was written when Wenfei was visiting Harbin and Shenzhen, China. He would like to thank Chong Chen and Huan Tu for the facilities and help they provided.

We would also like to thank EPSRC (029213/1), the 973 Program (2012CB316200), and NSFC (61133002) of China, the RSE-NSFC Joint Project Scheme, and IBM, for their support of our research on the subject.

Finally, Wenfei would like to thank his daughter, Grace (Nuonuo), for her patience, understanding, and love for all these years.

Wenfei Fan and Floris Geerts
July 2012

CHAPTER 1

Data Quality: An Overview

Database texts typically teach us how to design databases, formulate queries, and speed up query evaluation. We are led to believe that as long as we get a query right, then our database management system (DBMS) will find the correct answer to the query, and *voilà!* Unfortunately, this may not happen. In the real world, data are often dirty. Given dirty data in a database, we are not warranted to get accurate, complete, up-to-date or even correct answer to our query, no matter how well we write our query and how efficient our DBMS is. These highlight the need for improving *the quality of the data*.

This chapter identifies central issues in connection with data quality, and introduces a uniform logical framework to deal with these issues, based on data quality rules.

1.1 DATA QUALITY MANAGEMENT

Traditional database systems typically focus on *the quantity of data*, to support the creation, maintenance, and use of large volumes of data. But such a database system may not find correct answers to our queries if the data in the database are "dirty," i.e., when the data do not properly represent the real world entities to which they refer.

To illustrate this, let us consider an employee relation residing in a database of a company, specified by the following schema:

employee(FN, LN, CC, AC, phn, street, city, zip, salary, status) .

Here each tuple specifies an employee's name (first name FN and last name LN), office phone (country code CC, area code AC, phone phn), office address (street, city, zip code), salary, and marital status. An instance D_0 of the employee schema is shown in Figure 1.1.

Consider the following queries posted on relation D_0.

(1) Query Q_1 is to find the number of employees working in the NYC office (New York City). A DBMS will tell us that the answer to Q_1 in D_0 is 3, by counting tuples t_1, t_2, and t_3. However, the answer may not be correct, for the following reasons. First, the data in D_0 are *inconsistent*. Indeed, the CC and AC values of t_1, t_2, and t_3 have conflicts with their corresponding city attributes: when CC = 44 and AC = 131, the city should be Edinburgh (EDI) in the UK, rather than NYC in the U.S.; and similarly, when CC = 01 and AC = 908, city should be Murray Hill (MH) in the U.S. It is thus likely that NYC is not the true city value of t_1, t_2, and t_3. Second, the information in D_0 may be *incomplete* for employees working in NYC. That is, some tuples representing employees working in NYC may be *missing* from D_0. Hence, we cannot trust 3 to be the answer to Q_1.

1. DATA QUALITY: AN OVERVIEW

	FN	LN	CC	AC	phn	street	city	zip	salary	status
t_1:	Mike	Clark	44	131	null	Mayfield	NYC	EH4 8LE	60k	single
t_2:	Rick	Stark	44	131	3456789	Crichton	NYC	EH4 8LE	96k	married
t_3:	Joe	Brady	01	908	7966899	Mtn Ave	NYC	NJ 07974	90k	married
t_4:	Mary	Smith	01	908	7966899	Mtn Ave	MH	NJ 07974	50k	single
t_5:	Mary	Luth	01	908	7966899	Mtn Ave	MH	NJ 07974	50k	married
t_6:	Mary	Luth	44	131	3456789	Mayfield	EDI	EH4 8LE	80k	married

Figure 1.1: An employee instance.

(2) Query Q_2 is to find the number of distinct employees with FN = Mary. In D_0 the answer to Q_2 is 3, by enumerating tuples t_4, t_5, and t_6. Nevertheless, the chances are that t_4, t_5, and t_6 actually refer to the same person: all these tuples were once the true values of Mary, but some have become obsolete. Hence, the correct answer to Q_2 may be 1 instead of 3.

(3) Query Q_3 is to find Mary's current salary and current last name, provided that we know that t_4, t_5, and t_6 refer to the same person. Simply evaluating Q_3 on D_0 will get us that salary is either 50k or 80k, and that LN is either Smith or Luth. However, it does not tell us whether Mary's current salary is 50k, and whether her current last name is Smith. Indeed, reliable timestamps for t_4, t_5, and t_6 may not be available, as commonly found in practice, and hence, we cannot tell which of 50k or 80k is more current; similarly for LN.

This example tells us that when the data are dirty, we cannot expect a database system to answer our queries correctly, no matter what capacity it provides to accommodate large data and how efficiently it processes our queries.

Unfortunately, real-life data are often *dirty*: inconsistent, duplicated, inaccurate, incomplete, and out of date. Indeed, enterprises typically find data error rates of approximately 1–5%, and for some companies it is above 30% [Redman, 1998]. In most data warehouse projects, data cleaning accounts for 30–80% of the development time and budget [Shilakes and Tylman, 1998], for improving the quality of the data rather than for developing the systems. When it comes to incomplete information, it is estimated that "pieces of information perceived as being needed for clinical decisions were missing from 13.6% to 81% of the time" [Miller Jr. et al., 2005]. When data currency is concerned, it is known that "2% of records in a customer file become obsolete in one month" [Eckerson, 2002]. That is, in a database of 500,000 customer records, 10,000 records may go stale per month, 120,000 records per year, and within two years about 50% of all the records may be obsolete.

Why do we care about dirty data? Data quality has become one of the most pressing challenges to data management. It is reported that dirty data cost U.S. businesses 600 billion dollars annually [Eckerson, 2002], and that erroneously priced data in retail databases alone cost U.S. consumers $2.5 billion each year [English, 2000]. While these indicate the daunting cost of dirty data in the U.S., there is no reason to believe that the scale of the problem is any different in any other society that is dependent on information technology.

These highlight the need for *data quality management*, to improve the quality of the data in our databases such that the data consistently, accurately, completely, timely, and uniquely represent the real-world entities to which they refer.

Data quality management is at least as important as traditional data management tasks for coping with the quantity of data. There has been increasing demand in industries for developing data quality management systems, aiming to effectively detect and correct errors in the data, and thus to add accuracy and value to business processes. Indeed, the market for data quality tools is growing at 16% annually, way above the 7% average forecast for other IT segments [Gartner, 2011]. As an example, data quality tools deliver "an overall business value of more than 600 million GBP" each year at British Telecom [Otto and Weber, 2009]. Data quality management is also a critical part of big data management, master data management (MDM) [Loshin, 2009], customer relationship management (CRM), enterprise resource planning (ERP), and supply chain management (SCM), among other things.

1.2 CENTRAL ISSUES OF DATA QUALITY

We highlight five central issues in connection with data quality, namely, data consistency, data deduplication, data accuracy, information completeness, and data currency.

1.2.1 DATA CONSISTENCY

Data consistency refers to the validity and integrity of data representing real-world entities. It aims to detect inconsistencies or conflicts in the data. In a relational database, inconsistencies may exist within a single tuple, between different tuples in the same relation (table), and between tuples across different relations.

As an example, consider tuples t_1, t_2, and t_3 in Figure 1.1. There are discrepancies and conflicts within each of these tuples, as well as inconsistencies between different tuples.

(1) It is known that in the UK (when CC = 44), if the area code is 131, then the city should be Edinburgh (EDI). In tuple t_1, however, CC = 44 and AC = 131, but city $\neq$ EDI. That is, there exist inconsistencies between the values of the CC, AC, and city attributes of t_1; similarly for tuple t_2. These tell us that tuples t_1 and t_2 are erroneous.

(2) Similarly, in the U.S. (CC = 01), if the area code is 908, the city should be Murray Hill (MH). Nevertheless, CC = 01 and AC = 908 in tuple t_3, whereas its city is not MH. This indicates that tuple t_3 is not quite correct.

(3) It is also known that in the UK, zip code uniquely determines street. That is, for any two tuples that refer to employees in the UK, if they share the same zip code, then they should have the same value in their street attributes. However, while $t_1[CC] = t_2[CC] = 44$ and $t_1[zip] = t_2[zip]$, $t_1[street] \neq t_2[street]$. Hence, there are conflicts between t_1 and t_2.

Inconsistencies in the data are typically identified as violations of *data dependencies* (a.k.a. integrity constraints [Abiteboul et al., 1995]). As will be seen in Chapter 2, errors in a single relation can be detected by intrarelation constraints such as extensions of functional dependencies, while errors across different relations can be identified by interrelation constraints such as extensions of inclusion dependencies.

1.2.2 DATA DEDUPLICATION

Data deduplication aims to identify tuples in one or more relations that refer to the same real-world entity. It is also known as entity resolution, duplicate detection, record matching, record linkage, merge-purge, and object identification (for data with complex structures).

For example, consider tuples t_4, t_5, and t_6 in Figure 1.1. To answer query Q_2 given earlier, we want to know whether these tuples refer to the same employee. The answer is affirmative if, for instance, there exists another relation that indicates that Mary Smith and Mary Luth have the same email account and hence, are the same person.

The need for studying data deduplication is evident: for data cleaning it is needed to eliminate duplicate records; for data integration it is to collate and fuse information about the same entity from multiple data sources; and for master data management it helps us identify links between input tuples and master data. The need is also highlighted by payment card fraud, which cost $4.84 billion worldwide in 2006 [SAS, 2006]. In fraud detection it is a routine process to cross-check whether a credit card user is the legitimate card holder. As another example, there was a recent effort to match records on licensed airplane pilots with records on individuals receiving disability benefits from the U.S. Social Security Administration. The finding was quite surprising: there were 40 pilots whose records turned up in both databases (cf. [Herzog et al., 2009]).

No matter how important it is, data deduplication is nontrivial. As will be seen in Chapter 4, tuples pertaining to the same object may have different representations in various data sources with different schemas. Moreover, the data sources may contain errors. These make it hard, if not impossible, to match a pair of tuples by simply checking whether their attributes are pairwise equal to each other. Worse still, it is often too costly to compare and examine every pair of tuples from large data sources.

1.2.3 DATA ACCURACY

Data accuracy refers to the closeness of values in a database to the true values of the entities that the data in the database represent. Consider, for example, a person schema:

$$\text{person(FN, LN, age, height, status)},$$

where a tuple specifies the name (FN, LN), age, height, and marital status of a person. A person instance is shown Figure 1.2.3, in which s_0 presents the "true" information for Mike. From these we can conclude that s_1[age, height] are more accurate than s_2[age, height] as they are closer to the true values of Mike, while s_2[FN, status] are more accurate than s_1[FN, status].

1.2. CENTRAL ISSUES OF DATA QUALITY

	FN	LN	age	height	status
s_0:	Mike	Clark	14	1.70	single
s_1:	M.	Clark	14	1.69	married
s_2:	Mike	Clark	45	1.60	single

Figure 1.2: A person instance.

It is more challenging, however, to determine the *relative accuracy* of s_1 and s_2 when the reference s_0 is unknown, as commonly found in practice. In this setting, it is still possible to find that for certain attributes, the values in one tuple are more accurate than the other by an analysis of the semantics of the data, as follows.

(1) Suppose that we know that Mike is still going to middle school. From this, we can conclude that s_1[age] is more accurate than s_2[age]. That is, s_1[age] is closer to Mike's true age value than s_2[age], although Mike's true age may not be known. Indeed, it is unlikely that students in a middle school are 45 years old. Moreover, from the age value (s_1[age]), we may deduce that s_2[status] may be more accurate than s_1[status].

(2) If we know that s_1[height] and s_2[height] were once correct, then we may conclude that s_1[height] is more accurate than s_2[height], since the height of a person is typically monotonically increasing, at least when the person is young.

1.2.4 INFORMATION COMPLETENESS

Information completeness concerns whether our database has complete information to answer our queries. Given a database D and a query Q, we want to know whether Q can be completely answered by using only the data in D. If the information in D is incomplete, one can hardly expect its answer to Q to be accurate or even correct.

In practice, our databases often do not have sufficient information for our tasks at hand. For the entities that the data in our database intend to represent, both attribute values and tuples may be missing from our databases. For instance, the value of t_1[phn] in the relation D_0 of Figure 1.1 is missing, as indicated by null. Worse still, tuples representing employees may also be missing from D_0. As we have seen earlier, for query Q_1 given above, if some tuples representing employees in the NYC office are missing from D_0, then the answer to Q_1 in D_0 may not be correct. Incomplete information introduces serious problems to enterprises: it routinely leads to misleading analytical results and biased decisions, and accounts for loss of revenues, credibility and customers.

How should we cope with incomplete information? Traditional work on information completeness adopts either the Closed World Assumption (CWA) or the Open World Assumption (OWA), stated as follows (see, for example, [Abiteboul et al., 1995]).

- The CWA assumes that a database has collected all the tuples representing real-world entities, but the *values* of some attributes in those tuples are possibly *missing*.

- The OWA assumes that in addition to missing values, some *tuples* representing real-world entities may also be *missing*. That is, our database may only be a proper subset of the set of tuples that represent those real-world entities.

Database theory is typically developed under the CWA. Unfortunately, in practice, one often finds that not only attribute values but also tuples are missing from our database. That is, the CWA often does not hold. On the other hand, under the OWA, we can expect few sensible queries to find complete answers.

As will be seen in Chapter 5, neither the CWA nor the OWA is quite appropriate in emerging applications such as master data management. In other words, databases in the real world are *neither* entirely closed-world *nor* entirely open-world. These databases are actually "partially closed." The good news is that we often find that partially closed databases have complete information to answer our queries at hand.

1.2.5 DATA CURRENCY

Data currency is also known as *timeliness*. It aims to identify the current values of entities represented by tuples in a database, and to answer queries with the current values.

The question of data currency would be trivial if all data values carried valid timestamps. In practice, however, one often finds that timestamps are unavailable or imprecise [Zhang et al., 2010]. Add to this the complication that data values are often copied or imported from other sources [Berti-Equille et al., 2009; Dong et al., 2010, 2009a,b], which may not support a uniform scheme of timestamps. These make it challenging to identify the "latest" values of entities from the data in our database.

For example, recall query Q_3 and the employee relation D_0 of Figure 1.1 given above. Assume that tuples t_4, t_5, and t_6 are found pertaining to the same employee Mary by using data deduplication techniques [Elmagarmid et al., 2007]. As remarked earlier, in the absence of reliable timestamps, the answer to Q_3 in D_0 does not tell us whether Mary's current salary is 50k or 80k, and whether her current last name is Smith or Luth.

Not all is lost. As will be seen in Chapter 6, it is often possible to deduce currency orders from the semantics of the data, as illustrated below.

(1) While we do not have reliable timestamps associated with Mary's salary, we may know that the salary of each employee in the company does *not* decrease, as commonly found in the real world. This tells us that t_6[salary] is more current than t_4[salary] and t_5[salary]. Hence, we may conclude that Mary's current salary is 80k.

(2) We know that the marital status can only change from single to married and from married to divorced, but not from married to single. In addition, employee tuples with the most current marital status also contain the most current last name. Therefore, t_6[LN] = t_5[LN] is more current than t_4[LN]. That is, Mary's current last name is Luth.

1.2. CENTRAL ISSUES OF DATA QUALITY 7

	CC	AC	phn	street	city	zip
t_{m1}:	44	131	3456789	Mayfield	EDI	EH4 8LE
t_{m2}:	01	908	7966899	Mtn Ave	MH	NJ 07974

Figure 1.3: An example office master data relation.

1.2.6 INTERACTIONS BETWEEN DATA QUALITY ISSUES

To improve data quality we often need to deal with each and every of the five central issues given above. Moreover, these issues interact with each other, as illustrated below.

As we have observed earlier, tuples t_1, t_2, and t_3 in the relation D_0 of Figure 1.1 are inconsistent. We next show how data deduplication may help us resolve the inconsistencies. Suppose that the company maintains a master relation for its offices, consisting of consistent, complete, and current information about the address and phone number of each office. The master relation is denoted by D_m and given in Figure 1.3. It is specified by schema:

$$\text{office(CC, AC, phn, street, city, zip)},$$

As will be seen in Chapter 7, we may "repair" t_1, t_2, and t_3 as follows.

(1) If the values of attributes CC and AC of these tuples are confirmed accurate, we can safely update their city attributes by letting $t_1[\text{city}] = t_2[\text{city}] := \text{EDI}$, and $t_3[\text{city}] := \text{MH}$, for reasons remarked earlier. This yields t_1', t_2', and t_3', which differ from t_1, t_2, and t_3, respectively, only in their city attribute values.

(2) We know that if an employee tuple $t \in D_0$ and an office tuple $t_m \in D_m$ agree on their address (street, city, zip), then the two tuples "match," i.e., they refer to the same address and phone. Hence, we can update $t[\text{CC, AC, phn}]$ by taking the corresponding master values from t_m. This allows us to change $t_2'[\text{street}]$ to $t_{m1}[\text{street}]$. That is, we repair $t_2'[\text{street}]$ by matching t_2' and t_{m1}. This leads to tuple t_2'', which differs from t_2' only in the street attribute.

(3) We also know that for employee tuples t_1 and t_2, if they have the same address, then they should have the same phn value. In light of this, we can augment $t_1'[\text{phn}]$ by letting $t_1'[\text{phn}] := t_2''[\text{phn}]$, and obtain a new tuple t_1''.

One can readily verify that t_1'', t_2'', and t_3' are consistent. In the process above, we "interleave" operations for resolving conflicts (steps 1 and 3) and operations for detecting duplicates (step 2). On one hand, conflict resolution helps deduplication: step 2 can be conducted only after $t_2[\text{city}]$ is corrected. On the other hand, deduplication also helps us resolve conflicts: $t_1'[\text{phn}]$ is enriched only after $t_2'[\text{street}]$ is fixed via matching.

There are various interactions between data quality issues, including but not limited to the following.

- Data currency can be improved if more temporal information can be obtained in the process for improving information completeness.

- To determine the current values of an entity, we need to identify tuples pertaining to the same entity, via data deduplication. For instance, to find Mary's LN in the relation D_0 of Figure 1.1, we have to ask whether tuples t_4, t_5, and t_6 refer to the same person.

- To resolve conflicts in tuples representing an entity, we often need to determine whether the information about the entity is complete, and only if so, we can find the true value of the entity from the available data residing in our database.

These suggest that a practical data quality management system should provide functionality to deal with each and every one of the five central issues given above, and moreover, leverage the interactions between these issues to improve data quality.

1.3 IMPROVING DATA QUALITY USING RULES

We have seen that real-life data are often dirty, and that dirty data are costly. In light of these, effective techniques have to be in place to improve the quality of our data. But how?

Errors in real-life data. To answer this question, we first classify errors typically found in the real world. There are two types of errors, namely, syntactic errors and semantic errors.

(1) Syntactic errors: violations of domain constraints by the values in our database. For example, name = 1.23 is a syntactic error if the domain of attribute name is string. Another example is age = 250 when the range of attribute age is [0, 120].

(2) Semantic errors: discrepancies between the values in our database and the true values of the entities that our data intend to represent. All the examples we have seen in the previous sections are semantic errors, related to data consistency, deduplication, accuracy, currency, and information completeness.

While syntactic errors are relatively easy to catch, it is far more challenging to detect and correct semantic errors. In this book we focus on semantic errors.

Dependencies as data quality rules. A central question concerns how we can tell whether our data have semantic errors, i.e., whether the data are dirty or clean. To this end, we need data quality rules to detect semantic errors in our data, and better still, fix those errors by using the rules. But what data quality rules should we adopt?

A natural idea is to use data dependencies (integrity constraints). Dependency theory is almost as old as relational databases themselves. Since Codd [1972] introduced functional dependencies, a variety of dependency languages, defined as various classes of first-order logic sentences, have been proposed and studied. There are good reasons to believe that dependencies should play an important role in data quality management systems. Indeed, dependencies specify a fundamental part of the semantics of data, in a declarative way, such that errors emerge as violations of the dependencies. Furthermore, inference systems, implication analysis, and profiling methods for dependencies have shown promise as a systematic method for reasoning about the semantics of the data. These help us deduce and discover rules for improving data quality, among other things. In addition, as will be seen later, all five central aspects of data quality—data consistency, deduplication, accuracy, currency, and information completeness—can be specified in terms of data dependencies. This allows us to treat various data quality issues in a uniform logical framework, in which we can study their interactions.

Nevertheless, to make practical use of dependencies in data quality management, classical dependency theory has to be extended. Traditional dependencies were developed to improve *the quality of schema* via normalization, and to optimize queries and prevent invalid updates (see, for example, [Abiteboul et al., 1995]). To *improve the quality of the data*, we need new forms of dependencies, by specifying patterns of semantically related data values to capture data inconsistencies, supporting similarity predicates to accommodate data errors in data deduplication, enforcing the containment of certain information about core business entities in master data for reasoning about information completeness, and by incorporating temporal orders to determine data currency.

When developing dependencies for improving data quality, we need to balance the tradeoff between expressive power and complexity, and revisit classical problems for dependencies such as the satisfiability, implication, and finite axiomatizability analyses.

Improving data quality with rules. After we come up with the "right" dependency languages for specifying data quality rules, the next question is how to effectively use these rules to improve data quality. In a nutshell, a rule-based data quality management system should provide the following functionality.

Discovering data quality rules. To use dependencies as data quality rules, it is necessary to have efficient techniques in place that can *automatically discover* dependencies from data. Indeed, it is often unrealistic to rely solely on human experts to design data quality rules via an expensive and long manual process, and it is typically inadequate to count on business rules that have been accumulated. This suggests that we learn informative and interesting data quality rules from (possibly dirty) data, and prune away trivial and insignificant rules based on a threshold set by the users.

Validating data quality rules. A given set Σ of dependencies, either automatically discovered or manually designed by domain experts, may be dirty itself. In light of this we have to identify "consistent" dependencies from Σ, i.e., those rules that make sense, to be used as data quality rules. Moreover, we need to deduce new rules and to remove redundancies from Σ, via the implication analysis of those dependencies in Σ.

Detecting errors. After a validated set of data quality rules is identified, the next question concerns how to effectively catch errors in a database by using these rules. Given a set Σ of data quality rules and a database D, we want to *detect inconsistencies* in D, i.e., to find all tuples in D that violate some rule in Σ. We may also want to decide whether D has complete and current information to answer an input query Q, among other things.

Repairing data. After the errors are detected, we want to automatically localize the errors, fix the errors, and make the data consistent, as illustrated in Section 1.2.6. We also need to identify tuples that refer to the same entity, and for each entity, determine its latest and most accurate values from the data in our database. When attribute values or tuples are missing, we need to decide what data we should import and where to import from, so that we will have sufficient information for the tasks at hand. As remarked earlier, these should be carried out by exploring and capitalizing on the interactions between processes for improving various aspects of data quality.

1.4 BACKGROUND

We focus on the quality of relational data in this monograph. Data consistency will be covered in Chapters 2 and 3, followed by data deduplication, information completeness, and data currency in Chapters 4, 5, and 6, respectively. We study their interactions in Chapter 7.

We assume that the reader is familiar with the relational data model and the standard notions of schemas, instances, data dependencies and query languages (see [Abiteboul et al., 1995]). We also assume the knowledge of complexity theory (see, for example, [Papadimitriou, 1994]). In particular, we use the following notations.

(1) A database is specified by a relational schema $\mathcal{R}$, which consists of a collection of relation schemas $(R_1, \ldots, R_n)$. Each relation schema R_i is defined over a set of attributes, denoted by $\text{attr}(R)$. For each attribute $A \in \text{attr}(R)$, its domain is specified in R, denoted by $\text{dom}(A)$. We use A, B, C and X_i, Y_i to range over attributes in $\text{attr}(R)$, and W, X, Y, Z to range over sets (or lists) of attributes.

(2) We consider the following query languages (see [Abiteboul et al., 1995] for details):
- conjunctive queries (CQ), built up from atomic formulas with constants and variables, i.e., relation atoms in database schema $\mathcal{R}$ and built-in predicates ($=, \neq, <, \leq, >, \geq$), by closing under *conjunction* $\wedge$ and *existential quantification* $\exists$;
- union of conjunctive queries (UCQ) of the form $Q_1 \cup \cdots \cup Q_r$, where for each $i \in [1, r]$, Q_i is in CQ;
- positive existential FO queries ($\exists \text{FO}^+$), built from atomic formulas by closing under $\wedge$, *disjunction* $\vee$ and $\exists$;
- first-order logic queries (FO) built from atomic formulas using $\wedge, \vee$, *negation* $\neg, \exists$ and *universal quantification* $\forall$; and
- datalog queries (FP), defined as a collection of rules $p(\bar{x}) \leftarrow p_1(\bar{x}_1), \ldots, p_n(\bar{x}_n)$, where each p_i is either an atomic formula (a relation atom in $\mathcal{R}$, =, $\neq$) or an IDB predicate. In other words, FP is an extension of $\exists \text{FO}^+$ with an *inflational fixpoint operator*.

BIBLIOGRAPHIC NOTES

Data quality has been a longstanding issue for decades, and the prevalent use of the Web has increased the risks, on an unprecedented scale, of creating and propagating dirty data. There have been several books on various topics in connection with data quality [Batini and Scannapieco, 2006; Bertossi, 2011; Herzog et al., 2009; Naumann and Herschel, 2010].

1.4. BACKGROUND

The need for studying the quality of relational schemas was already recognized when Codd [1970] introduced the relational model. Starting with keys [Codd, 1970], functional dependencies [Codd, 1972], and inclusion dependencies [Fagin, 1981], a variety of integrity constraints have been studied, including equality-generating dependencies and tuple-generating dependencies [Beeri and Vardi, 1984] (see [Abiteboul et al., 1995; Maier, 1983; Vardi, 1987] for a historical account and surveys).

To improve the quality of data, rather than schemas, Fellegi and Holt [1976] introduced the concept of *edits* to detect and repair inconsistent census data. The use of integrity constraints in improving the consistency of relational data was first formalized by Arenas et al. [1999], which introduced two approaches: *repair* is to find another database that is consistent and minimally differs from the original database, and *consistent query answer* is to find an answer to a given query in every repair of the original database. We consider data repairing in this book, and refer the reader to [Bertossi, 2011] for a comprehensive lecture on consistent query answering.

There has also been a host of work on data deduplication. We refer the interested reader to [Elmagarmid et al., 2007; Herzog et al., 2009; Naumann and Herschel, 2010].

The subject of information completeness has also received much attention; see, for example, [Abiteboul et al., 1995; Grahne, 1991; Imieliński and Lipski Jr, 1984; van der Meyden, 1998] for surveys.

The temporal database community has studied how to incorporate temporal information into the relational model, in terms of timestamps; see, for example, [Chomicki and Toman, 2005; Snodgrass, 1999; van der Meyden, 1997] for surveys.

The study of data accuracy is still in its infancy, and its formal treatment is not yet in place. This issue will be briefly discussed in Chapter 7.

Much more extensive bibliographic comments will be provided in the subsequent chapters.

Beyond the relational model, there has also been work on improving the quality of XML data (e.g., [Flesca et al., 2005; Weis and Naumann, 2005]) and the quality of results returned in searches (e.g., [Cafarella et al., 2009; Dong et al., 2009a; Galland et al., 2010; Yin et al., 2008]). These are beyond the scope of this book.

CHAPTER 2
Conditional Dependencies

As we saw earlier, there are often conflicts and discrepancies in real-life data. The study of data consistency aims to detect inconsistencies in our data, and better still, repair the data by fixing the errors. To tell whether our data are inconsistent, we need data dependencies such that inconsistencies in the data emerge as violations of the dependencies. But what dependencies should we use? As will be seen shortly, traditional dependencies such as functional dependencies and inclusion dependencies often fail to catch errors commonly found in practice. This is not surprising: traditional dependencies were developed for improving the quality of *schema*, rather than for improving the quality of *data*.

In this chapter, we introduce conditional dependencies, which extend functional dependencies and inclusion dependencies by specifying constant patterns (conditions), to circumvent limitations of those traditional dependencies in their ability to capture inconsistencies in real-life data. We first present conditional functional dependencies (CFDs) and conditional inclusion dependencies (CINDs), which are intrarelation and interrelation constraints, respectively, to help us determine whether our data are dirty or clean (Section 2.1). Extending traditional dependency theory, we then study the satisfiability, implication, finite axiomatizability, and propagation of conditional dependencies (Section 2.2).

2.1 CONDITIONAL DEPENDENCIES

One of the central issues in connection with data consistency concerns how to determine whether our data are dirty or clean. As remarked earlier, here we need to use dependencies as data quality rules to capture semantic errors in the data. However, traditional dependencies may not be able to detect conflicts and discrepancies commonly found in real-life data.

Example 2.1 Consider the schema employee defined in Section 1.1. Recall functional dependencies (FDs) covered in most database textbooks (see, for example, [Abiteboul et al., 1995]). Functional dependencies defined on employee relation include the following:

$$\text{fd}_1 : [\text{CC, AC, phn}] \rightarrow [\text{street, city, zip}],$$
$$\text{fd}_2 : [\text{CC, AC}] \rightarrow [\text{city}].$$

That is, an employee's phone number uniquely determines her address (fd_1). In other words, for any two employee tuples t and t', if $t[\text{CC, AC, phn}] = t'[\text{CC, AC, phn}]$, then it must be the case that $t[\text{street, city, zip}] = t'[\text{street, city, zip}]$. Similarly, the country code and area code uniquely determine the city (fd_2).

14 2. CONDITIONAL DEPENDENCIES

	FN	LN	CC	AC	phn	street	city	zip	salary	status
t_1:	Mike	Clark	44	131	7966899	Mayfield	NYC	EH4 8LE	60k	single
t_2:	Rick	Stark	44	131	3456789	Crichton	NYC	EH4 8LE	96k	married
t_3:	Joe	Brady	01	908	7966899	Mtn Ave	NYC	NJ 07974	90k	married

Figure 2.1: An example employee relation.

Now consider an instance D_1 of employee given in Figure 2.1. Then D_1 satisfies fd_1 and fd_2. That is, there exists no violation of fd_1 or fd_2 in D_1. Hence, if we use fd_1 and fd_2 as data quality rules to specify the consistency of employee data, then no inconsistencies are found by these rules in D_1, and as a consequence, one may conclude that D_1 is clean. □

As we observed in Section 1.2, however, none of the tuples in D_1 is error-free. That is, those FDs fd_1 and fd_2 fail to detect the errors and hence, are not appropriate data quality rules. Indeed, FDs were developed for schema design, not for data cleaning.

This calls for a new form of dependency for capturing inconsistencies in real-life data. In response to the need, we present conditional dependencies, which are extensions of traditional functional dependencies and inclusion dependencies.

2.1.1 CONDITIONAL FUNCTIONAL DEPENDENCIES

To capture the inconsistencies in D_1, we may use the following dependencies:

$$cfd_1 : ([CC = 44, zip] \rightarrow [street]),$$
$$cfd_2 : ([CC = 44, AC = 131, phn] \rightarrow [street, city = EDI, zip]),$$
$$cfd_3 : ([CC = 01, AC = 908, phn] \rightarrow [street, city = MH, zip]).$$

Here, cfd_1 asserts that for employees in the UK (when CC = 44), zip code uniquely determines street. In other words, cfd_1 is an "FD" that holds on the *subset* of tuples that satisfies the pattern "CC = 44," i.e., $\{t_1, t_2\}$ in D_1. It is not a traditional FD since it is defined with constants, and it is not required to hold on the entire employee relation D_1 (in the U.S., for example, zip code does not uniquely determine street).

The last two constraints refine the FD fd_1 given earlier: cfd_2 states that for any two UK employees, if they have the same area code 131 and the same phn, then they must share the same street and zip, and moreover, the city *must* be EDI; similarly for cfd_3.

When we use these dependencies as data quality rules, we find that they catch each and every tuple in D_1 as a violation; that is, each tuple in D_1 is inconsistent. Indeed, tuples t_1 and t_2 in D_1 violate cfd_1: they refer to employees in the UK and have the same zip, but they differ in their street attributes. In addition, while D_1 satisfies fd_1, each of t_1 and t_2 in D_1 violates cfd_2, since CC = 44 and AC = 131, but city $\neq$ EDI. Similarly, t_3 violates cfd_3.

This motivates us to introduce the following dependencies. Consider a relation schema R defined over a set $attr(R)$ of attributes. For an instance, I of R and a tuple $t \in I$, we use $t[A]$ to

2.1. CONDITIONAL DEPENDENCIES

(a) $\varphi_1 = ([\text{CC, zip}] \to [\text{street}], T_1)$, where T_1 is

CC	zip ‖ street
44	– ‖ –

(b) $\varphi_2 = ([\text{CC, AC, phn}] \to [\text{street, city, zip}], T_2)$, where T_2 is

CC	AC	phn ‖ street	city	zip
–	–	– ‖ –	–	–
44	131	– ‖ –	EDI	–
01	908	– ‖ –	MH	–

(c) $\varphi_3 = ([\text{CC, AC}] \to [\text{city}], T_3)$, where T_3 is

CC	AC ‖ city
–	– ‖ –

Figure 2.2: Example CFDs defined on employee.

denote the projection of t onto A; similarly, for a sequence X of attributes in attr(R), $t[X]$ denotes the projection of t onto X.

Definition 2.2 A *conditional functional dependency* (CFD) defined on a relation schema R is a pair $R(X \to Y, T_p)$, where

1. $X \to Y$ is a standard FD, referred to as the FD *embedded in* φ; and
2. T_p is a tableau with attributes in X and Y, referred to as the *pattern tableau* of φ.

Here $X \subseteq \text{attr}(R)$, $Y \subseteq \text{attr}(R)$, and for each attribute $A \in X \cup Y$ and for each pattern tuple $t_p \in T_p$, $t_p[A]$ is either a constant "a" in dom(A), or an unnamed (yet marked) variable "_" that draws values from dom(A).

If an attribute A occurs in both X and Y, we use $t[A_X]$ and $t[A_Y]$ to indicate the occurrence of A in X and Y, respectively. We separate the X and Y attributes in a pattern tuple with "‖". We write φ as $(X \to Y, T_p)$ when R is clear from the context. □

Example 2.3 All the constraints we have encountered so far in this chapter can be expressed as the CFDs shown in Figure 2.2 (φ_1 for cfd$_1$, φ_2 for fd$_1$, cfd$_2$, and cfd$_3$, and φ_3 for fd$_2$). Note that each tuple in a pattern tableau indicates a constraint. For instance, φ_2 actually defines three constraints, each by a pattern tuple in T_2. □

2. CONDITIONAL DEPENDENCIES

Semantics. To formalize the semantics of CFDs, we define an operator $\asymp$ on constants and the symbol "_": $\eta_1 \asymp \eta_2$ if either $\eta_1 = \eta_2$, or one of η_1 and η_2 is "_". The operator $\asymp$ naturally extends to tuples. For example, (Mayfield, EDI) $\asymp$ (_, EDI) but (Mayfield, EDI) $\not\asymp$ (_, NYC).

Definition 2.4 An instance I of schema R *satisfies* a CFD $\varphi = R(X \to Y, T_p)$, denoted by $I \models \varphi$, if for *each* tuple t_p in the pattern tableau T_p of φ, and for *each pair* of tuples t_1 and t_2 in I, if $t_1[X] = t_2[X] \asymp t_p[X]$, then $t_1[Y] = t_2[Y] \asymp t_p[Y]$. □

Intuitively, each tuple t_p in the pattern tableau T_p of φ is a constraint defined on the subset $I_{t_p} = \{t \mid t \in I, t[X] \asymp t_p[X]\}$ of I, such that for all tuples $t_1, t_2 \in I_{t_p}$, if $t_1[X] = t_2[X]$, then (a) $t_1[Y] = t_2[Y]$, and (b) $t_1[Y] \asymp t_p[Y]$. Here, condition (a) enforces the semantics of the FD embedded in φ, and condition (b) assures the binding between the *constants* in $t_p[Y]$ and the *constants* in $t_1[Y]$. This constraint is defined on the subset I_{t_p} of I identified by $t_p[X]$, rather than on the entire relation I.

Example 2.5 While the instance D_1 of employee satisfies the CFD φ_3 given in Figure 2.2, it satisfies neither φ_1 nor φ_2, or in other words, it *violates* φ_1 and φ_2. Indeed, tuple t_1 alone violates the pattern tuple $t_p = (44, 131, \_ \| \_, \text{EDI}, \_)$ in the tableau T_2 of φ_2: $t_1[\text{CC, AC, phn}] = t_1[\text{CC, AC, phn}] \asymp (44, 131, \_)$, but $t_1[\text{street, city, zip}] \not\asymp (\_, \text{EDI}, \_)$ since $t_1[\text{city}]$ is NYC instead of EDI; similarly for t_2. In addition, as remarked earlier, for pattern tuple $t'_p = (44, \_ \| \_)$ in the tableau T_1 of φ_1, $t_1[\text{CC}] = t_2[\text{CC}] = 44$ and $t_1[\text{zip}] = t_2[\text{zip}]$, but $t_1[\text{street}] \neq t_2[\text{street}]$. That is, t_1 and t_2 violate φ_1 when they are taken together. □

In contrast to FDs, CFDs specify patterns of semantically related *constants*. In other words, CFDs are FDs reinforced by patterns of semantically related data values. Equipped with patterns, conditional functional dependencies are able to capture more errors than their traditional counterparts can detect. In practice, dependencies that hold conditionally may arise in a number of domains. In particular, when integrating data, dependencies that hold only in a subset of sources will hold only conditionally in the integrated data.

Observe that while it takes two tuples to violate an FD, a single tuple may violate a CFD. For example, tuple t_1 alone violates the CFD φ_2, as shown by Example 2.5.

We say that an instance I of R *satisfies* a set Σ of CFDs defined on R, denoted by $I \models \Sigma$, if $I \models \varphi$ for each $\varphi \in \Sigma$.

Special cases. We next identify several special cases of CFDs. As will become evident in the subsequent chapters, these special cases have found various applications in practice.

Functional dependencies. Traditional FDs are a special case of CFDs, in which the pattern tableau consists of a single tuple that contains "_" only. For instance, CFD φ_3 expresses the traditional FD fd_2.

Normal form. A CFD $\varphi = (X \to Y, T_p)$ is said to be *in normal form* if

- T_p consists of a single pattern tuple t_p, and

2.1. CONDITIONAL DEPENDENCIES 17

- Y consists of a single attribute A.

We write φ simply as $(X \to A, t_p)$, and denote X and A as $\text{LHS}(\varphi)$ and $\text{RHS}(\varphi)$, respectively.

A CFD $\varphi = (X \to Y, T_p)$ can be expressed as a set Σ_φ of CFDs such that each CFD of Σ_φ is in normal form. More specifically, $\Sigma_\varphi = \{(X \to A, t_p) \mid A \in Y, t'_p \in T_p, t_p = t'_p[X, A]\}$. One can readily verify that $\{\varphi\}$ and Σ_φ are "equivalent," after the notion of equivalence is introduced in the next section.

Example 2.6 The CFDs φ_1 and φ_3 given in Figure 2.2 are in normal form, while φ_2 can be expressed as a set of CFDs of the form ([CC, AC, phn] $\to$ [A], t_p), where A ranges over street, city and zip. When A is city, the pattern tuple t_p is one of $(\_, \_, \_ \parallel \_)$, $(44, 131, \_ \parallel \text{EDI})$, and $(01, 908, \_ \parallel \text{MH})$; similarly for t_p when A is street or zip. □

Constant and variable CFDs. Consider a CFD $(X \to A, t_p)$ in the normal form. It is called a *constant* CFD if its pattern tuple t_p consists of constants only; that is, $t_p[A]$ is a constant and for all attributes $B \in X, t_p[B]$ is a constant. It is called a *variable* CFD if $t_p[A] = \text{"}\_\text{"}$; that is, the righthand side (RHS) of its pattern tuple is the unnamed variable "_".

Example 2.7 The CFDs φ_1 and φ_3 given in Figure 2.2 are variable CFDs. An example constant CFD is ([CC, AC] $\to$ [city], t_p), where $t_p = (44, 131 \parallel \text{EDI})$. □

Constant CFDs help us detect inconsistencies between attributes of the same tuple, and variable CFDs are used to catch conflicts between different tuples in the same relation.

Coping with null values. The attributes in a tuple may be null. To cope with null we adopt the simple semantics of the SQL standard for null [SQL Standard, 2003]: $t_1[X] = t_2[X]$ evaluates to true if either one of them contains null. In contrast, when matching a data tuple t and a pattern tuple $t_p, t[X] \not\asymp t_p[X]$ if $t[X]$ contains null. That is, CFDs only apply to those tuples that precisely match a pattern tuple. Note that null does not occur in pattern tuples.

2.1.2 CONDITIONAL INCLUSION DEPENDENCIES

Conditional functional dependencies are intrarelation constraints that allow us to catch errors in a single relation. To detect inconsistencies between tuples across different relations, we need to use interrelation dependencies. However, traditional interrelation dependencies, such as inclusion dependencies (INDs), are not up to the job, as illustrated below.

Example 2.8 Consider the two schemas below, referred to as the source schema and the target schema, respectively:

$$\begin{array}{ll} \text{Source}: & \text{order(asin, title, type, price)} \\ \text{Target}: & \text{book(isbn, title, price, format)} \\ & \text{CD(id, album, price, genre).} \end{array}$$

2. CONDITIONAL DEPENDENCIES

	asin	title	type	price
t_7:	a23	Snow White	CD	7.99
t_8:	a12	Harry Potter	book	17.99

(a) Example order data

	isbn	title	price	format
t_9:	b32	Harry Potter	17.99	hard-cover
t_{10}:	b65	Snow White	7.99	soft-cover

(b) Example book data

	id	album	price	genre
t_{11}:	c12	J. Denver	7.94	country
t_{12}:	c58	Snow White	7.99	a-book

(c) Example CD data

Figure 2.3: Example order, book, and CD relations.

The source database contains a single relation order, specifying items of various types such as books, CDs, and DVDs ordered by customers. The target database has two relations, namely, book and CD, specifying customer orders of books and CDs, respectively. An example source and target instance D_2 is shown in Figure 2.3.

To detect errors across these databases, or to find schema mappings from the source schema to the target schema, one might be tempted to use INDs such as:

$$\text{ind}_1 : \text{order(title, price)} \subseteq \text{book(title, price)},$$
$$\text{ind}_2 : \text{order(title, price)} \subseteq \text{CD(album, price)}.$$

These INDs, however, do not make sense: one cannot expect that a book item in the order table can find a corresponding CD tuple such that their title and price attributes pairwise match; similarly for CD items in the order table to find a match in the book table. □

There indeed exist inclusion dependencies from the source to the target, as well as on the target instances, but these dependencies make sense only under certain conditions:

$$\text{cind}_1 : (\text{order(title, price, type = book)} \subseteq \text{book(title, price)}),$$
$$\text{cind}_2 : (\text{order(title, price, type = CD)} \subseteq \text{CD(album, price)}),$$
$$\text{cind}_3 : (\text{CD(album, price, genre = a-book)} \subseteq \text{book(title, price, format = audio)}).$$

Here, cind_1 states that for each order tuple t, if its type is "book," then there must exist a book tuple t' such that t and t' agree on their title and price attributes; similarly for cind_2. Constraint cind_3 asserts that for each CD tuple t, if its genre is "a-book" (audio book), then there must be a book tuple t' such that the title and price of t' are identical to the album and price of t, and moreover, the format of t' must be "audio." Like CFDs, these constraints are required to hold only on a subset of tuples satisfying certain patterns. They are specified with constants (data values), and hence cannot be expressed as standard INDs.

2.1. CONDITIONAL DEPENDENCIES 19

$\varphi_4 = (\text{order}(\text{title}, \text{price}; \text{type}) \subseteq \text{book}(\text{title}, \text{price}), T_4)$

$\varphi_5 = (\text{order}(\text{title}, \text{price}; \text{type}) \subseteq \text{CD}(\text{album}, \text{price}), T_5)$

$\varphi_6 = (\text{CD}(\text{album}, \text{price}; \text{genre}) \subseteq \text{book}(\text{title}, \text{price}; \text{format}), T_6)$

type
book

T_4

type
CD

T_5

genre	format
a-book	audio

T_6

Figure 2.4: Example CINDs.

While the database D_2 of Figure 2.3 satisfies cind_1 and cind_2, it violates cind_3. Indeed, tuple t_{12} in the CD table has an "a-book" genre, but it cannot find a match in the book table with "audio" format. Note that book tuple t_{10} is not a match for t_{12}: while t_{12} and t_{10} agree on their album (title) and price, the format of t_{10} is "soft-cover" rather than "audio."

To capture such inclusion relationships, we extend INDs by incorporating patterns of semantically related constants, along the same lines as CFDs. Consider two relation schemas, R_1 and R_2, with attributes $\text{attr}(R_1)$ and $\text{attr}(R_2)$, respectively.

Definition 2.9 A *conditional inclusion dependency* (CIND) ψ defined on relation schemas R_1 and R_2 is a pair $(R_1[X; X_p] \subseteq R_2[Y; Y_p], T_p)$, where

1. (X, X_p) and (Y, Y_p) are lists of attributes of $\text{attr}(R_1)$ and $\text{attr}(R_2)$, respectively, such that X and X_p (resp. Y and Y_p) are disjoint;
2. $R_1[X] \subseteq R_2[Y]$ is a standard IND, referred to as the IND *embedded in* ψ; and
3. T_p is a tableau with attributes in X_p and Y_p, referred to as the *pattern tableau* of ψ, such that for each pattern tuple $t_p \in T_p$ and each attribute B in X_p (or Y_p), $t_p[B]$ is a constant in $\text{dom}(B)$, i.e., pattern tuples in CINDs consist of constant only.

If an attribute A occurs in both X_p and Y_p, we use $t[A_X]$ and $t[A_Y]$ to denote the occurrence of A in X_p and Y_p, respectively. We separate X_p and Y_p in a pattern tuple with '∥'. □

Example 2.10 Constraints cind_1, cind_2 and cind_3 can be expressed as CINDs φ_4, φ_5, and φ_6 shown in Figure 2.4, respectively, in which T_4–T_6 are their pattern tableaux. Observe that in φ_6, X is [album, price], Y is [title, price], X_p is [genre], and Y_p is [format]. The standard IND embedded in ψ_6 is CD[album, price] $\subseteq$ book[title, price]. □

Semantics. We next give the semantics of CINDs.

Definition 2.11 An instance (I_1, I_2) of (R_1, R_2) *satisfies* a CIND $\psi = (R_1[X; X_p] \subseteq R_2[Y; Y_p], T_p)$, denoted by $(I_1, I_2) \models \psi$, if for *each* tuple t_p in the pattern tableau T_p and for

20 2. CONDITIONAL DEPENDENCIES

each tuple t_1 in the relation I_1, if $t_1[X_p] = t_p[X_p]$, then *there must exist* a tuple t_2 in I_2 such that $t_1[X] = t_2[Y]$ and moreover, $t_2[Y_p] = t_p[Y_p]$. □

That is, each pattern tuple t_p in T_p is a constraint defined on the subset $I_{(1,t_p)} = \{t_1 \mid t_1 \in I_1, t_1[X_p] = t_p[X_p]\}$ of I_1, such that: (a) the IND $R_1[X] \subseteq R_2[Y]$ embedded in ψ is defined on $I_{(1,t_p)}$, not on the entire I_1; (b) for each $t_1 \in I_{(1,t_p)}$, there exists a tuple t_2 in I_2 such that $t_1[X] = t_2[Y]$ as required by the standard IND, and moreover, $t_2[Y_p]$ must be equal to the pattern $t_p[Y_p]$. Intuitively, X_p identifies those R_1 tuples on which ψ is defined, and Y_p enforces the corresponding R_2 tuples to have a certain constant pattern.

Example 2.12 The database D_2 of Figure 2.3 satisfies CINDs φ_4 and φ_5. Note that while these CINDs are satisfied, their embedded INDs do not necessarily hold. For example, while φ_4 is satisfied, the IND ind_1 embedded in φ_4 is not. The pattern X_p in φ_4 is used to identify the order tuples over which φ_4 has to be enforced, i.e., those book tuples; similarly for φ_5.

On the other hand, φ_6 is *violated* by D_2, as we have seen earlier. Indeed, for CD tuple t_{12}, there exists a pattern tuple t_p in T_6 such that $t_{12}[\text{genre}] = t_p[\text{genre}]$ = "a-book" but there exists no tuple t in the book table such that $t[\text{format}]$ = "audio," $t[\text{title}] = t_{12}[\text{title}]$ = "Snow White", and $t[\text{price}] = t_{12}[\text{price}] = 7.99$. Here, the genre pattern is to identify those CD tuples on which φ_6 is applicable, while the format pattern is a *constraint* defined on the book tuples that match those CD tuples via the IND embedded in φ_6. □

We say that an instance (I_1, I_2) of (R_1, R_2) *satisfies* a set Σ of CINDs defined on R_1 and R_2, denoted by $(I_1, I_2) \models \Sigma$, if $(I_1, I_2) \models \psi$ for each $\psi \in \Sigma$.

When null is present in the instances, we define the semantics of CINDs in precisely the same way as its CFD counterpart (see Section 2.1.1).

Special cases. We highlight two special cases of CINDs.

Inclusion dependencies. Traditional INDs are a special case of CINDs, in which X_p and Y_p are empty lists, denoted by nil, and their pattern tableaux T_p consist of a single unit tuple ( ), referred to as the empty pattern.

Normal form. A CIND $\psi = (R_1[X; X_p] \subseteq R_2[Y; Y_p], T_p)$ is *in normal form* if T_p consists of a single pattern tuple t_p only. We write ψ as $(R_1[X; X_p] \subseteq R_2[Y; Y_p], t_p)$.

For instance, CINDs φ_4, φ_5, and φ_6 are already in normal form.

Along the same lines as CFDs, a CIND $\psi = (R_1[X; X_p] \subseteq R_2[Y; Y_p], T_p)$ can be expressed as a set $\Sigma_\psi = \{(R_1[X; X_p] \subseteq R_2[Y; Y_p], t_p) \mid t_p \in T_p\}$ of CINDs in the normal form. One can verify that Σ_ψ is *equivalent* to $\{\psi\}$, after the notion of equivalence is introduced for CINDs in the next section.

2.2 STATIC ANALYSES OF CONDITIONAL DEPENDENCIES

We have introduced conditional dependencies by extending traditional functional and inclusion dependencies. Recall that classical dependency theory investigates several fundamental problems associated with traditional dependencies: satisfiability, implication, finite axiomatizability, and propagation via views (see, for example, [Abiteboul et al., 1995; Fagin and Vardi, 1984]). To improve data quality using conditional dependencies, these fundamental questions also have to be settled. That is, we need to revise the classical dependency theory for conditional dependencies. In this section we provide an account of results on classical decision problems associated with CFDs and CINDs. We show that these revised dependencies introduce new challenges. That is, the increased expressive power of CFDs and CINDs comes at the price of a higher complexity for reasoning about these dependencies.

We focus on finite database instances. In particular, by implication we mean finite implication, although most of the results of this section for CFDs and CINDs taken alone remain intact for unrestricted implication (formal discussions about finite and unrestricted implication can be found in [Abiteboul et al., 1995; Fagin and Vardi, 1984]).

2.2.1 SATISFIABILITY

To detect errors and inconsistencies in real-life data with conditional dependencies, the first question we have to answer concerns whether a given set of CFDs (resp. CINDs) has conflicts and inconsistencies, i.e., whether the data quality rules are "dirty" themselves. If the dependencies are not satisfiable (or in other words, inconsistent), then there is *no need* to validate them against the data at all. Furthermore, the satisfiability analysis can help the users find out what goes wrong in their data quality rules. Formally, this can be stated as the *satisfiability problem* for CFDs (resp. CINDs).

- INPUT: A set Σ of CFDs (resp. CINDs) defined on a relational schema $\mathcal{R}$.
- QUESTION: Does there exist a nonempty database instance D of $\mathcal{R}$ such that $D \models \Sigma$?

CFDs . Recall that for traditional dependencies, one can specify arbitrary FDs and INDs without worrying about their satisfiability. That is, any set of FDs and INDs is satisfiable. Unfortunately, this is no longer the case for CFDs.

Example 2.13 Consider a CFD $\varphi = R([A] \to [B], T_0)$, where its pattern tableau T_0 consists of two pattern tuples (_ || b) and (_ || c), with $b \neq c$. Then no nonempty instance I of R can possibly satisfy φ. Indeed, assume that there were such an instance I. Then for any tuple t in I, while the first pattern tuple says that $t[B]$ must be b no matter what value $t[A]$ has, the second pattern tuple requires $t[B]$ to be c.

As another example, consider two CFDs $\psi_1 = R'([A] \to [B], T_1)$ and $\psi_2 = R'([B] \to [A], T_2)$, where dom($A$) is bool (the Boolean domain), the pattern tableau T_1 has two pattern tuples (true || b_1), (false || b_2), T_2 contains (b_1 || false) and (b_2 || true), and b_1 and b_2 are distinct constants. Then although each of ψ_1 and ψ_2 is satisfiable separately, there exists no nonempty instance

I of schema R' such that $I \models \{\psi_1, \psi_2\}$. Indeed, assume that such an I existed. Then for any tuple t in I, no matter what value $t[A]$ has, ψ_1 and ψ_2 together force $t[A]$ to take the other value from the finite domain bool. □

It turns out that the satisfiability problem for CFDs is intractable, as opposed to its trivial counterpart for traditional FDs.

Theorem 2.14 The satisfiability problem is NP-complete for CFDs. □

Crux. An NP algorithm can be developed to check whether a given set Σ of CFDs is satisfiable. The algorithm is based on the following *small property* of the satisfiability problem for CFDs. For any set Σ of CFDs defined on a schema R, there exists a nonempty instance I of R such that $I \models \Sigma$ if and only if there exists an instance I_u of R such that $I_u \models \Sigma$ and moreover, I_u consists of a single tuple. For the lower bound, one can verify that the problem is NP-hard by reduction from the non-tautology problem, which is known to be NP-complete (cf. [Garey and Johnson, 1979]). □

Recall the notion of constant CFDs from Section 2.1.1. One might think that for constant CFDs the satisfiability analysis would be simpler. Unfortunately, this is not the case. Indeed, the intractability proof of Theorem 2.14 uses constant CFDs only. We refer the interested reader to [Fan et al., 2008b] for detailed proofs.

Corollary 2.15 *The satisfiability problem remains NP-complete for constant CFDs.* □

Approximation. The intractability of the satisfiability problem for CFDs tells us that it is beyond reach in practice to determine whether a set Σ of CFDs is satisfiable, to validate a given set of data quality rules. As an immediate consequence, one can readily verify that it is also intractable to compute a maximum satisfiable subset $\Sigma_{\max}$ of Σ. To see this, assume by contradiction that there exist a polynomial time (PTIME) algorithm for computing $\Sigma_{\max}$. This implies a PTIME algorithm for determining whether Σ is satisfiable. Indeed, one can first compute $\Sigma_{\max}$ and then simply check whether $\Sigma_{\max} = \Sigma$.

Not all is lost. There exists an efficient approximation algorithm that, given a set Σ of CFDs, finds a satisfiable subset Σ_m of Σ such that $|\Sigma_m| \geq (1 - \epsilon)|\Sigma_{\max}|$. Here $|S|$ denotes the cardinality of a set S, and ϵ is a constant in $[0, 1)$. That is, while we cannot compute $\Sigma_{\max}$ in PTIME, we can efficiently compute Σ_m that cannot go too wrong. This allows us to identify valid data quality rules from a given set of (possibly inconsistent) CFDs. We refer the interested reader to [Fan et al., 2008b] for the details of the approximation algorithm.

Special cases. Better still, there are special cases of CFDs for which the satisfiability analysis is in PTIME. Below we identify three such cases. We encourage the reader to consult [Fan et al., 2008b] for the proofs of the results presented below. In the sequel we consider CFDs in normal form, without loss of generality.

2.2. STATIC ANALYSES OF CONDITIONAL DEPENDENCIES

(1) *CFDs with no constants in their* RHS. One can readily verify that a set Σ of CFDs is not satisfiable only if it contains a CFD with a constant RHS, i.e., a CFD of the form $R(X \to A, (t_p \| a))$ for some constant $a \in \text{dom}(A)$. Indeed, let Σ_c be the set of all CFDs in Σ with a constant RHS. Then Σ is satisfiable if and only if Σ_c is satisfiable. Clearly, if Σ is satisfiable then obviously so is Σ_c. Conversely, let I be an instance of R such that $I \models \Sigma_c$. Select a single tuple $t \in I$ and define $J = \{t\}$. Clearly, $J \models \Sigma_c$. Let Σ_v be the subset of CFDs in Σ of the form $R(Y \to B, (s_p \| \_))$. Then for all $\varphi \in \Sigma_v$, φ is trivially satisfied by single-tuple instances, including J. That is, $J \models \Sigma$. This tells us the following.

Proposition 2.16 *For any set Σ of CFDs that contains no CFDs with a constant* RHS, *Σ is satisfiable.* □

(2) *CFDs without finite domain attributes.* Recall that the domains of attributes involved in dependencies are typically not considered in classical dependency theory. In contrast, Example 2.13 demonstrates that for the satisfiability analysis of CFDs, one may have to consider whether or not the attributes of those CFDs have a finite domain, such as bool. This is because CFDs are defined in terms of constants drawn from certain domains, and may interact with domain constraints. More specifically, given a set Σ of CFDs, let $\text{attr}(\Sigma)$ denote the set of attributes in $\text{attr}(R)$ that appear in the CFDs in Σ. Clearly, $|\text{attr}(\Sigma)| \le |\text{attr}(R)|$. Then one can readily verify the following by developing a PTIME decision algorithm.

Proposition 2.17 *For any set Σ of CFDs defined on a schema R, the satisfiability of Σ can be determined in $O(|\Sigma|^2 |\text{attr}(\Sigma)|)$ time if all the attributes in $\text{attr}(\Sigma)$ have an infinite domain.* □

In particular, if Σ has no finite-domain attributes and, moreover, if it satisfies certain syntactic restrictions, Σ is always satisfiable. More specifically, a CFD is said to be *total* if it is of the form $R(X \to A, (t_p \| a))$, where t_p consists of "_" only. It says that each tuple in a relation must take the same value "a" in the A attribute. Then the absence of total CFDs and the absence of finite-domain attributes simplify the satisfiability analysis.

Proposition 2.18 *For any set Σ of CFDs defined on a schema R, if no CFD in Σ is total and if all attributes in $\text{attr}(\Sigma)$ have an infinite domain, then Σ is satisfiable.* □

(3) *CFDs defined on a fixed schema.* Denote by $\text{finattr}(R)$ the set of attributes in $\text{attr}(R)$ that have a finite domain. Obviously $|\text{finattr}(R)| \le |\text{attr}(R)|$. Assume, without loss of generality, that there exists a unique finite domain, denoted by fdom. Then one can verify that for CFDs defined on a fixed schema, their satisfiability analysis is in PTIME. In practice, the schema is often predefined and fixed, but one often writes dependencies in stages: dependencies are added incrementally when new requirements are discovered.

Proposition 2.19 *For any set Σ of CFDs defined on a fixed schema R, determining whether Σ is satisfiable is in $O(|\Sigma|^2)$ time.* □

Remarks. One might want to adopt a stronger notion of satisfiability, as suggested by the following example. Consider a CFD $\psi_0 = R([A] \to [B], T)$, where T consists of pattern tuples $(a \parallel b)$ and $(a \parallel c)$, while $b \neq c$. If dom(A) contains constants distinct from a, then there obviously exists a nonempty instance I of R that satisfies ψ_0. However, the conflict between the pattern tuples in ψ_0 becomes evident if I contains a tuple t with $t[A] = a$. Indeed, the first pattern tuple forces $t[B]$ to be b while the second pattern tuple requires $t[B]$ to be c. In light of this one might want to ensure that every CFD in Σ does not conflict with the rest of Σ no matter what instances of R are considered. This can be achieved by requiring for each CFD $\varphi = R(X \to A, (t_p \parallel a)) \in \Sigma$ the existence of an instance $I_\varphi \models \Sigma$ such that I_φ contains a tuple t with $t[X] \asymp t_p$.

This stronger notion of satisfiability is actually equivalent to the notion of satisfiability given earlier. Indeed, one can check the strong satisfiability of a set Σ of CFDs as follows. For each $\varphi \in \Sigma$, define a set $\Sigma \cup \{R([C] \to [C], (\_ \parallel t_p[C])) \mid C \in X_{(c,\phi)}\}$, by including total CFDs. Here $X_{(c,\phi)}$ denotes the set of attributes in X (i.e., LHS(φ)) for which the pattern tuple of φ has a constant value. It is easy to verify that Σ is strongly satisfiable if and only if all these sets are satisfiable. For example, for $\Sigma = \{\psi_0\}$, since $\Sigma \cup \{R([A] \to [A], (\_ \parallel a))\}$ is not satisfiable, it follows that Σ is not strongly satisfiable. Therefore, there is no need to consider the stronger notion of satisfiability for CFDs.

CINDs. In contrast to CFDs, the satisfiability analysis of CINDs is as trivial as their IND counterpart, despite the increased expressive power of CINDs [Bravo et al., 2007].

Theorem 2.20 *Any set of CINDs is satisfiable.*

Crux. This can be verified by a constructive proof: given any set Σ of CINDs defined on a relational schema $\mathcal{R}$, a nonempty instance D of $\mathcal{R}$ can be constructed such that $D \models \Sigma$. Here D is defined in terms of constants from "active domains," which are finite sets of values taken from constants that appear in Σ or from the domains of attributes in $\mathcal{R}$. □

CFDs and CINDs put together. To improve data consistency, it is often necessary to use both CINDs and CFDs. We have seen that CINDs do not make the satisfiability analysis harder than its traditional IND counterpart. However, the satisfiability problem becomes far more intriguing when CINDs and CFDs are taken together. Indeed, it is undecidable to determine, given a set Σ consisting of both CFDs and CINDs defined on a database schema $\mathcal{R}$, whether there exists a nonempty instance D of $\mathcal{R}$ such that D satisfies all the dependencies in Σ. It remains undecidable even in the absence of finite-domain attributes (see [Bravo et al., 2007] for a proof). In contrast, FDs and INDs together are trivially satisfied.

Theorem 2.21 *The satisfiability problem is undecidable for CFDs and CINDs put together, in the absence or in the presence of finite-domain attributes.*

Crux. The undecidability is verified by reduction from the implication problems for traditional FDs and INDs taken together, which is known to be undecidable (cf. [Abiteboul et al., 1995]). The reduction does not use any finite-domain attributes. □

2.2.2 IMPLICATION

Another fundamental issue associated with dependencies concerns the implication analysis. A set Σ of dependencies defined on a database schema $\mathcal{R}$ *implies* another dependency φ defined on $\mathcal{R}$, denoted by $\Sigma \models \varphi$, if for each instance D of $\mathcal{R}$ such that $D \models \Sigma$, we also have that $D \models \varphi$. The *implication problem* for CFDs (resp. CINDs) is stated as follows.

- INPUT: A Σ of CFDs (resp. CINDs) and a single CFD (resp. CIND) φ defined on a relational schema $\mathcal{R}$.
- QUESTION: Does $\Sigma \models \varphi$?

Effective implication analysis allows us to remove redundancies from a given set of data quality rules (CFDs and CINDs), among other things. More specifically, we say that two sets Σ_1 and Σ_2 of dependencies are *equivalent*, denoted by $\Sigma_1 \equiv \Sigma_2$, if for each $\varphi_1 \in \Sigma_1$, $\Sigma_2 \models \varphi_1$, and moreover, for each $\varphi_2 \in \Sigma_2$, $\Sigma_1 \models \varphi_2$. One can remove redundancies from a set Σ of data quality rules by finding a minimal cover Σ_{mc} of Σ, such that $\Sigma_{mc} \equiv \Sigma$ and moreover, there exists no $\psi \in \Sigma_{mc}$ such that $\Sigma_{mc} \setminus \{\psi\} \models \psi$. Since CFDs (CINDs) tend to be larger than their traditional counterparts due to their pattern tableaux, the impact of redundancies is far more evident on the performance of inconsistency detection and repairing processes than traditional dependencies, as will be seen in the next chapter.

We next study the implication problem for CFDs, for CINDs, and for CFDs and CINDs put together.

CFDs. Recall that for traditional FDs, the implication problem is in linear time [Abiteboul et al., 1995; Fagin and Vardi, 1984]. We have seen that the satisfiability problem for CFDs is more intriguing than for FDs. When it comes to the implication analysis, CFDs also make our lives harder. Nevertheless, in the absence of finite-domain attributes or when the schema is predefined and fixed, the implication problem is in PTIME (see [Fan et al., 2008b] for detailed proofs). These are consistent with the observations of Propositions 2.17 and 2.19 for the satisfiability analyses.

Theorem 2.22 The implication problem for CFDs is coNP-complete, but it is in:
- $O(|\Sigma|^2 |attr(\Sigma)|)$ time if no attributes in $attr(\Sigma)$ have a finite domain; and
- $O(|\Sigma|^2)$ time if schema R is fixed,

for deciding whether $\Sigma \models \varphi$ given Σ and φ defined on a relation schema R.

Crux. (1) Consider a set Σ of CFDs and another CFD φ defined on a relation schema R. The implication problem is to determine whether $\Sigma \models \varphi$. It is equivalent to the complement of the problem for deciding whether there exists a nonempty instance I of R such that $I \models \Sigma$ and $I \models \neg\varphi$.

Thus, it suffices to show that the satisfiability problem for $\Sigma \cup \{\neg\varphi\}$ is NP-hard, again by reduction from the non-tautology problem. The reduction uses constant CFDs only. In contrast to the proof of Theorem 2.14, here we need to deal with $\neg\varphi$.

The satisfiability problem for $\Sigma \cup \{\neg\varphi\}$ has the following *small model property*: there exists a nonempty instance I of R such that $I \models \Sigma \cup \{\neg\varphi\}$ if and only if there exists an instance I_w of R consisting of two tuples such that $I_w \models \Sigma \cup \{\neg\varphi\}$. From this an NP algorithm for deciding the satisfiability of $\Sigma \cup \{\neg\varphi\}$ can be easily developed.

(2) For the two special cases, decision algorithms can be readily developed for the implication analysis, with the desired complexity. □

CINDs. For INDs, the implication problem is: PSPACE-complete [Abiteboul et al., 1995; Fagin and Vardi, 1984]. When it comes to CINDs, the problem remains PSPACE-complete for CINDs without finite-domain attributes. Nevertheless, it becomes EXPTIME-complete in the presence of finite-domain attributes [Bravo et al., 2007]. This tells us that the implication analysis of CFDs is harder than its counterpart for INDs, as opposed to the satisfiability problem. Moreover, the presence of finite-domain attributes also complicates the implication analysis of CINDs. This is consistent with its counterpart for CFDs.

Theorem 2.23 The implication problem is:
- EXPTIME-complete for CINDs; and
- PSPACE-complete for CINDs in the absence of finite-domain attributes.

Crux. (1) One can verify that the problem is EXPTIME-hard by reduction from the two-player game of corridor tiling problem, which is EXPTIME-complete [Chlebus, 1986]. An EXPTIME decision algorithm can be developed for the implication analysis of CINDs.

(2) In the absence of finite-domain attributes, one can show that the implication problem for CINDs is PSPACE-hard by reduction from the implication problem for traditional INDs, which is PSPACE-complete (cf. [Abiteboul et al., 1995]). In this setting, the decision algorithm for the implication analysis is down to PSPACE from EXPTIME. □

CFDs and CINDs put together. When CFDs and CINDs are taken together, the implication problem becomes undecidable. This is not surprising: the implication problem is already undecidable for FDs and INDs put together [Abiteboul et al., 1995; Fagin and Vardi, 1984], and CFDs (resp. CINDs) subsume FDs (resp. INDs). Furthermore, the problem remains undecidable even in the absence of finite-domain attributes.

Corollary 2.24 *The implication problem is undecidable for CFDs and CINDs put together, in the absence or in the presence of finite-domain attributes.* □

Finite implication and unrestricted implication. We have so far studied finite implication, simply referred to as implication, when only finite instances of database schema are considered. One

2.2. STATIC ANALYSES OF CONDITIONAL DEPENDENCIES   27

might also be interested in *unrestricted implication*, when infinite databases instances are also allowed [Abiteboul et al., 1995; Fagin and Vardi, 1984]. More specifically, given a set Σ of dependency and a single dependency φ defined on a database schema $\mathcal{R}$, we say that Σ entails φ via unrestricted implication, denoted by $\Sigma \models_{\mathsf{unr}} \varphi$, if for each instance D of $\mathcal{R}$ such that $D \models \Sigma$ and D is either finite or infinite, $D \models \varphi$. The *unrestricted implication problem* is to decide, given Σ and φ, whether $\Sigma \models_{\mathsf{unr}} \varphi$.

Along the same lines, one might also want to study the *unrestricted satisfiability* problem for CFDs (resp. CINDs), to determine whether there exists a (possibly infinite) nonempty database instance that satisfies a given set of CFDs (resp. CINDs). In contrast, the satisfiability problem (also known as the finite satisfiability problem) we have seen earlier is to decide whether there exists a nonempty finite database instance that satisfies a given set of CFDs (resp. CINDs).

For CFDs and CINDs taken alone, unrestricted implication (resp. unrestricted satisfiability) and implication (resp. satisfiability) coincide.

Corollary 2.25

- *For any set $\Sigma \cup \{\varphi\}$ of CFDs (resp. CINDs), $\Sigma \models \varphi$ if and only if $\Sigma \models_{\mathsf{unr}} \varphi$.*
- *For any set Σ of CFDs (resp. CINDs) defined on a schema $\mathcal{R}$, there exists a nonempty (possibly infinite) instance D of $\mathcal{R}$ such that $D \models \Sigma$ if and only if there exists a nonempty finite instance D' of $\mathcal{R}$ such that $D' \models \Sigma$.*

Crux. For CFDs, this follows from the small model properties of their satisfiability and implication problems. When it comes to CINDs, the satisfiability problem is trivial and also has the small model property. To show that the implication and unrestricted implication coincide, observe first that unrestricted implication entails finite implication. Conversely, there exists a finite set of inference rules that is sound and complete for both implication and unrestricted implication (see Section 2.2.3). As a result, if $\Sigma \models \varphi$ then φ can be proven from Σ using the rules by the completeness of the inference system for implication, and hence, $\Sigma \models_{\mathsf{unr}} \varphi$ by the soundness of the inference system for unrestricted implication. □

When CFDs and CINDs are taken together, however, unrestricted implication and implication are distinct. Indeed, it is known that the equivalence of unrestricted implication and implication for a class of logical sentences implies the decidability of their decision problem [Dreben and Goldfarb, 1979]. More specifically, while unrestricted implication is r.e. (recursively enumerable), implication is co-r.e. From this and Corollary 2.24 it follows that unrestricted implication and implication cannot possibly coincide for CFDs and CINDs put together. Along the same lines, from Corollary 2.24 it follows that unrestricted satisfiability and satisfiability are also not equivalent for CFDs and CINDs taken together.

2.2.3 FINITE AXIOMATIZABILITY

Another central issue in dependency theory has been the development of inference rules, for generating symbolic proofs of logical implication (see, e.g., [Abiteboul et al., 1995]). For example, Armstrong's Axioms for FDs can be found in almost every database textbook:

Reflexivity:	If $Y \subseteq X$, then $X \rightarrow Y$
Augmentation:	If $X \rightarrow Y$, then $XZ \rightarrow YZ$
Transitivity:	If $X \rightarrow Y$ and $Y \rightarrow Z$, then $X \rightarrow Z$

where X, Y, and Z range over sets of attributes a relation schema. These inference rules are fundamental to the implication analysis of FDs. Similarly, inference rules have also been developed for INDs.

For CFDs and CINDs, inference rules are also important, because they reveal insight into implication analysis and help us understand how data quality rules interact with each other. In light of this, we extend classical dependency theory by developing inference rules for conditional dependencies, and establishing their finite axiomatizability.

Finite axiomatization. We start with a brief introduction to finite axiomatization. Consider a set $\mathfrak{I}$ of inference rules for a class $\mathcal{C}$ of dependencies. We consider, without loss of generality, rules ρ of the form $\xi_1 \wedge \cdots \wedge \xi_k \rightarrow \phi$, where for each $i \in [1, k]$, ξ_i is either a dependency in $\mathcal{C}$ or a condition, and ϕ is a dependency in $\mathcal{C}$, all specified with variables ranging over sets (or lists) of attributes from a set U of attributes. We refer to ξ_i as an *antecedent* (or *premise*) of ρ, and ϕ as the *consequence* of ρ.

For a set Σ of dependencies in $\mathcal{C}$ and another dependency φ in $\mathcal{C}$, we say that φ is *provable from Σ using $\mathfrak{I}$*, denoted by $\Sigma \vdash_{\mathfrak{I}} \varphi$, if there exists a sequence $\phi_1, \ldots, \phi_n$ of dependencies in $\mathcal{C}$ such that $\varphi = \phi_n$ and moreover, for each $i \in [1, n]$, either

- $\phi_i \in \Sigma$, or
- there exist a rule $\rho = \xi_1 \wedge \cdots \wedge \xi_k \rightarrow \phi$ in $\mathfrak{I}$ and a mapping μ from variables in ρ to sets (or lists) of attributes in U, such that (a) $\phi_i = \mu(\phi)$, and (b) for each $j \in [1, k]$, either $\mu(\xi_j)$ is one of ϕ_l for $1 \leq l < i$, or $\mu(\xi_j)$ is a condition that is satisfied. Here, $\mu(\xi)$ is obtained from ξ by substituting each variable x in ξ with $\mu(x)$.

That is, either ϕ_i is given in Σ, or it is the consequence of a rule ρ in which all the antecedents have been proved from Σ using $\mathfrak{I}$.

For logical implication of dependencies in $\mathcal{C}$, the set $\mathfrak{I}$ of rules is

- *sound* if $\Sigma \vdash_{\mathfrak{I}} \varphi$ implies $\Sigma \models \varphi$;
- *complete* if $\Sigma \models \varphi$ implies $\Sigma \vdash_{\mathfrak{I}} \varphi$.

A finite sound and complete set of inference rules for $\mathcal{C}$ is called a *finite axiomatization* of $\mathcal{C}$. If a finite axiomatization exists for $\mathcal{C}$, $\mathcal{C}$ is said to be finitely *axiomatizable*.

The finite axiomatizability of conditional dependencies. For CFDs and CINDs taken separately, they are finitely axiomatizable (see [Bravo et al., 2007; Fan et al., 2008b] for proofs). However, when

2.2. STATIC ANALYSES OF CONDITIONAL DEPENDENCIES

> **CFD1:** If $A \in X$, then $R(X \to A, t_p)$, where either $t_p[A_X] = t_p[A_Y] =$ "a" for some constant "a" in $\mathsf{dom}(A)$, or both $t_p[A_X]$ and $t_p[A_Y]$ are "_".
>
> **CFD2:** If (1) $R(X \to A_i, t_i)$ such that $t_i[X] = t_j[X]$ for all $i, j \in [1, k]$, (2) $R([A_1, \ldots, A_k] \to B, t_p)$ and moreover, (3) $(t_1[A_1], \ldots, t_k[A_k]) \preceq t_p[A_1, \ldots, A_k]$, then $R(X \to B, t'_p)$, where $t'_p[X] = t_1[X]$ and $t'_p[B] = t_p[B]$.
>
> **CFD3:** If $R([B, X] \to A, t_p)$, $t_p[B] =$ "_", and $t_p[A]$ is a constant, then $R(X \to A, t'_p)$, where $t'_p[X \cup \{A\}] = t_p[X \cup \{A\}]$.
>
> **CFD4:** If (1) $\Sigma \vdash_{\mathfrak{I}_C} R([X, B] \to A, t_i)$ for $i \in [1, k]$, (2) $\mathsf{dom}(B) = \{b_1, \ldots, b_k, b_{k+1}, \ldots, b_m\}$, and $(\Sigma, B = b_l)$ is not consistent except for $l \in [1, k]$, and (3) for $i, j \in [1, k]$, $t_i[X] = t_j[X]$, and $t_i[B] = b_i$, then $\Sigma \vdash_{\mathfrak{I}_C} R([X, B] \to A, t_p)$, where $t_p[B] =$ "_" and $t_p[X] = t_1[X]$.

Figure 2.5: Inference rules $\mathfrak{I}_C$ for CFDs.

CFDs and CINDs are taken together, there exists no finite axiomatization. This is not surprising: traditional FDs and INDs put together are already not finitely axiomatizable (see, e.g., [Abiteboul et al., 1995]).

Theorem 2.26 (a) There exists a finite sound and complete set of inference rules for CFDs. (b) There exists a finite sound and complete set of inference rules for CINDs. (c) CFDs and CINDs taken together are not finitely axiomatizable. □

An inference system for CFDs. As an example, we present a finite axiomatization for CFDs, denoted by $\mathfrak{I}_C$ and shown in Figure 2.5. We refer the interested reader to [Bravo et al., 2007] for an inference system for CINDs, which consists of eight inference rules.

The inference system $\mathfrak{I}_C$ is analogous to Armstrong's Axioms for FDs. Given a finite set $\Sigma \cup \{\varphi\}$ of CFDs, we use $\Sigma \vdash_{\mathfrak{I}_C} \varphi$ to denote that φ is provable from Σ using $\mathfrak{I}_C$. We consider CFDs in normal form.

Example 2.27 Consider a set Σ of CFDs defined on a relation schema R, consisting of four CFDs: $\psi_1 = ([A, B] \to [C], (a, b_1 \parallel c))$, $\psi_2 = ([A, B] \to [C], (a, b_2 \parallel c))$, $\psi_3 = ([C, D] \to [E], (\_, \_ \parallel \_))$ and $\psi_4 = ([B] \to [B], (b_3 \parallel b_2))$, where $\mathsf{dom}(B) = \{b_1, b_2, b_3\}$. Let $\varphi = ([A, D] \to [E], (a, \_ \parallel \_))$, also defined on R. Then $\Sigma \vdash_{\mathfrak{I}_C} \varphi$ can be proved as follows.

(1) $([A, B] \to [C], (a, b_1 \parallel c))$ ψ_1
(2) $([A, B] \to [C], (a, b_2 \parallel c))$ ψ_2
(3) $([A, B] \to [C], (a, \_ \parallel c))$ (1), (2) and **CFD4**; $((\Sigma, B = b_3)$ is not consistent)
(4) $([A] \to [C], (a \parallel c))$ (3) and **CFD3**
(5) $([A, D] \to [A], (a, \_ \parallel a))$ **CFD1**
(6) $([A, D] \to [D], (a, \_ \parallel \_))$ **CFD1**
(7) $([A, D] \to [C], (a, \_ \parallel c))$ (4), (5) and **CFD2**
(8) $([C, D] \to [E], (\_, \_ \parallel \_))$ ψ_3
(9) $([A, D] \to [E], (a, \_ \parallel \_))$ (6), (7), (8) and **CFD2**

We will elaborate shortly on the notion that $(\Sigma, B = b_3)$ is not consistent. □

We next illustrate the inference rules in $\mathfrak{I}_C$. While the rules CFD1 and CFD2 in $\mathfrak{I}_C$ are extensions of Armstrong's Axioms for FDs, CFD3 and CFD4 do not find a counterpart in Armstrong's Axioms.

(1) CFD1 and CFD2 extend Reflexivity and Transitivity of Armstrong's Axioms, respectively. Rule CFD1 is self explanatory (see lines 5 and 6 in Example 2.27).

In contrast, in order to cope with pattern tuples that are not found in FDs, CFD2 employs an order relation $\preceq$, defined as follows. For a pair η_1, η_2 of constants or "_", we say that $\eta_1 \preceq \eta_2$ if either $\eta_1 = \eta_2 = a$ where a is a constant, or $\eta_2 = $ "_". The $\preceq$ relation naturally extends to pattern tuples. For instance, $(a, b) \preceq (\_, b)$.

Intuitively, the use of $\preceq$ in CFD2 assures that $(t_1[A_1], \ldots, t_k[A_k])$ is in the "scope" of $t_p[A_1, \ldots, A_k]$, i.e., the pattern $t_p[A_1, \ldots, A_k]$ is applicable. In Example 2.27, CFD2 can be applied (line 9) because pattern tuple $t_1[C, D] = (c, \_)$ (obtained from lines 6 and 7) and pattern tuple $t_2[C, D] = (\_, \_)$ on the LHS of ψ_3 (line 8) satisfy $t_1[C, D] \preceq t_2[C, D]$.

To see that CFD2 is sound, note that any tuple t that matches a pattern tuple t_p also matches any pattern tuple t'_p if $t_p \preceq t'_p$. More specifically, assume that conditions (1), (2), and (3) of the rule hold. Let Σ consist of $\varphi_i = R(X \to A_i, t_i), \phi = R([A_1, \ldots, A_k] \to B, t_p)$ and $\psi = R(X \to B, t'_p)$, for $i \in [1, k]$. Assume that $\Sigma \vdash_{\mathfrak{I}_C} \psi$ by CFD2. We need to show that for any instance I of R, if $I \models \Sigma$, then $I \models \psi$. Indeed, for any two tuples $s, t \in I$, if $s[X] = t[X] \asymp t'_p[X]$, then from condition (1) and the assumption that $t'_p[X] = t_1[X]$ it follows that $s[X] = t[X] \asymp t_i[X]$ and $s[A_i] = t[A_i] \asymp t_i[A_i]$ for $i \in [1, k]$. By condition (3), we have that $s[A_1, \ldots, A_k] = t[A_1, \ldots, A_k] \asymp t_p[A_1, \ldots, A_k]$. Thus, from condition (2) (i.e., $I \models \phi$) it follows that $s[B] = t[B] \asymp t_p[B] = t'_p[B]$. Hence $I \models \psi$.

(2) CFD3 tells us that for a CFD $\varphi = R([B, X] \to A, t_p)$, if $t_p[B] = $ "_" and $t_p[A]$ is a constant "a", then φ can be simplified by dropping the B attribute from the LHS of the embedded FD. To see this, consider an instance I of R such that $I \models \varphi$, and any tuple t in I. Note that since $t_p[B] = $ "_", if $t[X] \asymp t_p[X]$ then $t[B, X] \asymp t_p[B, X]$ and $t[A]$ has to be "a" regardless of what value $t[B]$ has. Thus φ entails $R(X \to A, t_p)$, and $I \models R(X \to A, t_p)$. This rule is illustrated by line 4 in Example 2.27.

(3) CFD4 deals with attributes of finite domains, which are a non-issue for standard FDs since FDs have no pattern tuples. It targets a set Σ of CFDs. More specifically, to use this rule one needs to determine, given Σ defined on a relation schema R, an attribute B in attr(R) with a finite domain and a constant $b \in $ dom(B), whether there exists an instance I of R such that $I \models \Sigma$ and moreover, there is a tuple t in I such that $t[B] = b$. We say that $(\Sigma, B = b)$ is *consistent* if and only if such an instance I exists. That is, since the values of B have finitely many choices, we need to find out for which $b \in $ dom(B), Σ and $B = b$ make sense when put together. For instance, consider the set $\Sigma = \{\psi_2, \psi_3\}$ given in Example 2.13, and the bool attribute A. Then neither $(\Sigma, A = $ true$)$ nor $(\Sigma, A = $ false$)$ is consistent.

CFD4 says that for an attribute B of a finite domain and for a given set Σ of CFDs, if $\Sigma \vdash_{\mathfrak{I}_C} R([X, B] \to A, t_i)$ when $t_i[B]$ ranges over all $b \in \text{dom}(B)$ such that $(\Sigma, B = b)$ is consistent, then $t_i[B]$ can be "upgraded" to "_". That is, for any instance I, if $I \models \Sigma$, then $I \models R([X, B] \to A, t_p)$, where $t_p[B] = $ "_". Indeed, suppose that $I \models \Sigma$ but $I \not\models R([X, B] \to A, t_p)$. Assume that $t_p[A] = $ "_" (similarly for the case $t_p[A] = a \in \text{dom}(A)$). Then there exist $s, t \in I$ such that $\{s, t\} \models \Sigma, s[X, B] = t[X, B] \asymp t_p[X, B]$ but $s[A] \neq t[A]$. Let $b = s[B]$ (and hence $b = t[B]$). Then $\{s, t\} \not\models R([X, B] \to A, t_i)$, where $t_i[B] = b$. This contradicts the assumption that $\Sigma \vdash_{\mathfrak{I}_C} R([X, B] \to A, t_i)$ for $t_i[B]$ ranging over all such $b \in \text{dom}(B)$ that $(\Sigma, B = b)$ is consistent. Thus $I \models R([X, B] \to A, t_p)$, where $t_p[B] = $ "_".

One might wonder why $\mathfrak{I}_C$ has no rule analogous to the Augmentation rule in Armstrong's Axioms. This is because we assume that all our CFDs are in normal form and therefore, they only have a single attribute in their RHS. As a result, there is no need for augmenting the RHS with attributes. However, if one would lift this assumption then (four) additional rules need to be added to $\mathfrak{I}_C$ that allow to transform any CFD into its normal form and back. These rules are straightforward and do not provide any more insight into the intricacies involved in the implication problem for CFDs.

The proof of the completeness of $\mathfrak{I}_C$ is a nontrivial extension of its counterpart for Armstrong's Axioms for FDs (see, for example, [Abiteboul et al., 1995] for that proof). We first provide an algorithm that computes a so-called *closure set* of a given set Σ of CFDs, and establish a characterization of $\Sigma \models \varphi$ in terms of this closure set. We then show that each step in the algorithm can be performed by applications of the inference rules in $\mathfrak{I}_C$, establishing in this way the completeness of $\mathfrak{I}_C$. We refer the interested reader to [Fan et al., 2008b] for details about the closure sets and the characterization.

We compare the complexity bounds for static analyses of CFDs and CINDs with their traditional counterparts in Table 2.1, in which n denotes the size of input dependencies.

2.2.4 DEPENDENCY PROPAGATION

We next deal with dependency propagation (also known as view dependencies [Abiteboul et al., 1995]), another important issue associated with dependencies.

Propagation analysis. Consider two classes of dependencies $\mathcal{L}_1$ and $\mathcal{L}_2$, referred to as *source dependencies* and *view dependencies*, respectively. Consider a view σ defined on relational sources $\mathcal{R}$, a (finite) set $\Sigma \subseteq \mathcal{L}_1$ of source dependencies defined on $\mathcal{R}$, and a view dependency $\varphi \in \mathcal{L}_2$. We say that φ is *propagated* from Σ via σ, denoted by $\Sigma \models_\sigma \varphi$. if for each instance D of $\mathcal{R}$ such that $D \models \Sigma$, the view $\sigma(D)$ is guaranteed to satisfy the view dependency φ. The *dependency propagation problem* is as follows.

- INPUT: A view σ, a set $\Sigma \subseteq \mathcal{L}_1$ of source dependencies defined on $\mathcal{R}$, and a view dependency $\varphi \in \mathcal{L}_2$.
- QUESTION: Does $\Sigma \models_\sigma \varphi$?

Table 2.1: Complexity and finite axiomatizability of conditional dependencies

Dependencies	Satisfiability	Implication	Finite Axiomatizability
CFDs	NP-complete	coNP-complete	Yes
FDs	$O(1)$	$O(n)$	Yes
CINDs	$O(1)$	EXPTIME-complete	Yes
INDs	$O(1)$	PSPACE-complete	Yes
CFDs + CINDs	undecidable	undecidable	No
FDs + INDs	$O(1)$	undecidable	No
in the absence of finite-domain attributes			
CFDs	$O(n^2)$	$O(n^2)$	Yes
CINDs	$O(1)$	PSPACE-complete	Yes
CFDs + CINDs	undecidable	undecidable	No

Observe that the implication problem is a special case of the dependency propagation problem, when the source dependencies ($\mathcal{L}_1$) and view dependencies ($\mathcal{L}_2$) are expressed in the same language, and when the view is defined in terms of an identity query, i.e., simply the relation atom R defined on a relation schema R.

The need for dependency propagation analysis has long been recognized [Klug, 1980; Klug and Price, 1982]. For conditional dependencies, the propagation analysis is particularly important for data exchange, integration and cleaning. Indeed, dependencies on data sources often only hold *conditionally* on the view, as illustrated by the example below.

Example 2.28 Consider three data sources R_1, R_2, and R_3, containing information about customers in the UK, U.S. and the Netherlands, respectively. To simplify the presentation we assume that these data sources have a uniform schema, for $i \in [1, 3]$:

$$R_i(\text{AC, phn, name, street, city, zip}).$$

A set Σ_0 of FDs is defined on the sources, consisting of the following:

$$\text{fd}_3 : R_1([\text{zip}] \to [\text{street}]), \quad \text{fd}_{3+i} : R_i([\text{AC}] \to [\text{city}]).$$

Define a view σ_0 that integrates data from the sources, in terms of a union $Q_1 \cup Q_2 \cup Q_3$ of conjunctive queries (UCQ), where Q_1 is

SELECT AC, phn, name, street, city, zip, "44" as CC
FROM R_1 .

Define Q_2 and Q_3 by substituting '01' and "31" for "44", R_2 and R_3 for R_1 in Q_1, respectively. The target schema R has all the attributes in the sources and an additional country-code attribute CC (44, 01, 31 for the UK, U.S. and the Netherlands, respectively).

2.2. STATIC ANALYSES OF CONDITIONAL DEPENDENCIES

Now one wants to know whether the source dependencies still hold on the target data (view). The answer is negative: one can expect neither $\Sigma_0 \models_{\sigma_0} \text{fd}_3$ nor $\Sigma_0 \models_{\sigma_0} \text{fd}_{3+i}$. Indeed, fd_3 does not hold on, e.g., the data from the R_2 source since as remarked earlier, in the U.S., zip does not uniquely determine street. Moreover, although fd_{3+i} holds on each individual source R_i, it may not hold on the view because, for example, 20 is an area code in both the UK and Netherlands, for London and Amsterdam, respectively.

In other words, the source FDs are *not always* propagated to the view as FDs.

Not all is lost: the source FDs are indeed propagated to the view, but as CFDs. Indeed, $\Sigma_0 \models_{\sigma_0} \varphi_7$ and $\Sigma_0 \models_{\sigma_0} \varphi_8$ for CFDs φ_7 and φ_8:

$$\varphi_7 : R([\text{CC, zip}] \to [\text{street}], T_7), \qquad \varphi_8 : R([\text{CC, AC}] \to [\text{city}], T_8),$$

where T_7 contains a pattern tuple $(44, \_ \parallel \_)$, i.e., in the UK, zip code uniquely determines street, and T_8 consists of pattern tuple $(\_, \_ \parallel \_)$. In other words, fd_3 holds *conditionally* on the view, and fd_{3+i} holds on the view only after an extra attribute is added.

Furthermore, suppose that the following CFDs are defined on the sources:

$$\text{cfd}_4 : R_1([\text{AC}] \to [\text{city}], (20 \parallel \text{London})),$$
$$\text{cfd}_5 : R_3([\text{AC}] \to [\text{city}], (20 \parallel \text{Amsterdam})),$$

then the following CFDs are propagated to the view:

$$\varphi_9 : R([\text{CC, AC}] \to [\text{city}], (44, 20 \parallel \text{London})),$$
$$\varphi_{10} : R([\text{CC, AC}] \to [\text{city}], (31, 20 \parallel \text{Amsterdam})),$$

which carry patterns of semantically related constants. □

This example tells us that FDs are not closed under propagation: source FDs are propagated to view CFDs rather than FDs. This suggests that we revisit the propagation analysis of FDs, by studying propagation of FDs and CFDs to CFDs. Furthermore, even for FD propagation, some complexity results have to be revised. Indeed, propagation from FDs to FDs has been studied long ago (e.g., [Klug, 1980; Klug and Price, 1982]). It is known that for views expressed in relational algebra, the problem is undecidable [Klug, 1980]. It is also generally believed that for source FDs, view FDs, and views defined as an SPCU query (also known as union of conjunctive queries), the propagation problem is in PTIME (cf. [Abiteboul et al., 1995]). However, it has recently been shown that in the presence of finite-domain attributes, the propagation problem already becomes coNP-complete for source FDs, view FDs, and views defined as an SC query (with selection and Cartesian product operators) [Fan et al., 2008c]; in other words, the PTIME result cited above for FD propagation only holds in the absence of finite-domain attributes.

Propagating FDs and CFDs to FDs and CFDs. We next investigate the dependency propagation problem in the following settings: (a) when the class $\mathcal{L}_1$ of source dependencies consists of FDs, and the class $\mathcal{L}_2$ of view dependencies consists of CFDs; (b) when $\mathcal{L}_1$ and $\mathcal{L}_2$ are both CFDs; and (c) when $\mathcal{L}_1$ and $\mathcal{L}_2$ are both FDs.

2. CONDITIONAL DEPENDENCIES

Table 2.2: Complexity of CFD propagation.

Σ	View language	Complexity bounds	
		Infinite domain only	General setting
Propagation from FDs to CFDs			
FDs	SP	PTIME	PTIME
	SC	PTIME	coNP-complete
	PC	PTIME	PTIME
	SPC	PTIME	coNP-complete
	SPCU	PTIME	coNP-complete
	RA	undecidable	undecidable
Propagation from CFDs to CFDs			
CFDs	S	PTIME	coNP-complete
	P	PTIME	coNP-complete
	C	PTIME	coNP-complete
	SPC	PTIME	coNP-complete
	SPCU	PTIME	coNP-complete
	RA	undecidable	undecidable

We study the problem for views expressed in various fragments of FO queries, also referred to as relational algebra (RA), defined in terms of the selection (S), projection (P), Cartesian product (C), union ($\cup$), set difference ($\setminus$), and renaming (ρ) operators. We use SPC and SPCU to denote CQ and UCQ, respectively. We also study fragments of SPC, denoted by listing the operators supported: S, P, C, SP, SC, and PC (the renaming operator is included in all these subclasses by default without listing it explicitly). For instance, SC denotes the class of queries defined in terms of S, C, and ρ operators. In particular, query Q_1 given in Example 2.28 can be expressed as a C query: $\{(CC: 44)\} \times R_1$.

The result below, taken from [Fan et al., 2008c], shows that the presence of finite-domain attributes also complicates the propagation analysis.

Theorem 2.29 The dependency propagation problem is:

- in PTIME for SPCU views, source CFDs and view CFDs, in the absence of finite-domain attributes;
- in PTIME in the general setting, for source FDs, view CFDs, and for PC and SP views;
- coNP-complete in the general setting, for
  - source FDs, view FDs, and SC views;
  - source CFDs, view CFDs, and views defined with any of a single S, C, or P operator.

2.2. STATIC ANALYSES OF CONDITIONAL DEPENDENCIES 35

Table 2.3: Complexity of FD propagation.

View language	Propagation from FDs to FDs	
	Complexity bounds	
	Infinite domain only	General setting
SP	PTIME [Abiteboul et al., 1995; Klug and Price, 1982]	PTIME
SC	PTIME [Abiteboul et al., 1995; Klug and Price, 1982]	coNP-complete
PC	PTIME [Abiteboul et al., 1995; Klug and Price, 1982]	PTIME
SPCU	PTIME [Abiteboul et al., 1995; Klug and Price, 1982]	coNP-complete
RA	undecidable [Klug, 1980]	undecidable

Here in the general setting attributes may have a finite domain or an infinite domain.

Crux. (1) For SPCU views, source CFDs and view CFDs without finite-domain attributes, there exists a PTIME algorithm for testing propagation by extending the chase technique (see [Abiteboul et al., 1995] for chase, and [Klug and Price, 1982] for extensions of chase).

(2) For PC and SP views in the general setting, one can develop PTIME algorithms for determining propagation from FDs to CFDs, by extending chase to CFDs.

(3) In the general setting, for source FDs, view FDs and SC views, the lower bound is verified by reduction from the 3SAT problem to the complement of the propagation problem, where 3SAT is known to be NP-complete (cf. [Garey and Johnson, 1979]). The upper bound is shown by developing an NP algorithm that, given source FDs Σ, a view FD ψ and an SC view σ, decides whether $\Sigma \not\models_\sigma \psi$. Thus the propagation problem is in coNP. The algorithm extends the chase technique to deal with variables with finite domain attributes, such that all those variables are instantiated with constants from their corresponding finite domains. There are exponential number of such instantiations that need to be checked.

For source CFDs, view CFDs, and views defined with any of S, C or P operator, one can show that the problem is coNP-hard by reduction from the implication problem for CFDs. By Theorem 2.22, in the presence of finite-domain attributes, CFD implication is already coNP-complete, and moreover, the implication problem is a special case of the dependency propagation problem. The problem is shown to be in coNP by providing a coNP decision algorithm, again based on extensions of chase techniques. □

To give a complete account of complexity results, we summarize in Table 2.2 complexity bounds on propagation from FDs to CFDs, and from CFDs to CFDs. Moreover, we present the complexity bounds on propagation from FDs to FDs in Table 2.3, including results from [Abiteboul et al., 1995; Klug, 1980; Klug and Price, 1982].

BIBLIOGRAPHIC NOTES

Conditional functional dependencies were proposed by Bohannon et al. [2007], where the intractability of the satisfiability and implication problems for CFDs was shown. In addition, a sound and complete inference system for CFDs was provided there, which was later simplified to the system $\mathcal{I}_C$ by Fan et al. [2008b]. Furthermore, tractable cases and an approximation algorithm for the satisfiability analysis were given by Fan et al. [2008b].

Conditional inclusion dependencies were proposed by Bravo et al. [2007], in which the complexity of the satisfiability and implication problems for CINDs were established, and a sound and complete inference system for CINDs was provided. The undecidability of these decisions problems for CFDs and CINDs put together was also proved there. A restricted form of CINDs was studied earlier in the context of schema matching [Bohannon et al., 2006], which employs contextual foreign keys, an extension of foreign keys with simple conditions, to derive schema mapping from the outcome of schema matching. The formalization of CINDs and their static analysis were not considered there.

Most dependencies studied for relational databases can be expressed as FO sentences of the following form (cf. [Abiteboul et al., 1995]), simply referred to as *dependencies*:

$$\forall x_1, \ldots, x_m \left(\phi(x_1, \ldots, x_m) \to \exists y_1, \ldots, y_n \ \psi(z_1, \ldots, z_k) \right),$$

where (a) $\{y_1, \ldots, y_n\} = \{z_1, \ldots, z_k\} \setminus \{x_1, \ldots, x_m\}$; (b) ϕ is a conjunction of (at least one) relation atoms of the form $R(w_1, \ldots, w_l)$, where w_i is a variable for each $i \in [1, l]$, and ϕ uses all of the variables in $\{x_1, \ldots, x_m\}$; (c) ψ is a conjunction of either relation atoms or equality atoms $w = w'$, where w, w' are variables, and ψ uses all of the variables in $\{z_1, \ldots, z_k\}$; and (d) no equality atoms in ψ use existentially quantified variables.

Dependencies are often classified as follows.

- *Full dependencies*: universally quantified dependencies.
- *Tuple generating dependencies* (TGDs): dependencies whose right-hand side (RHS) is a relation atom. A TGD says that if a certain pattern of entries appears then another pattern must appear. INDs are a special case of TGDs.
- *Equality generating dependencies* (EGDs): full dependencies in which the RHS is an equality atom. An EGD says that if a certain pattern of entries appears then a certain equality must hold. The best known EGDs are FDs.

These dependencies are defined in terms of relation atoms, variables, and equality, *in the absence of constants*. To capture errors in real-life data one might want to revise these full-fledged constraint languages by incorporating data-value patterns. However, this may not be very practical: the implication problem is already EXPTIME-complete for full dependencies, and is undecidable for TGDs (cf. [Fagin and Vardi, 1984]). To balance the tradeoff between expressive power and complexity, it is often more realistic to consider revisions of fragments of these constraint languages for data quality tools.

2.2. STATIC ANALYSES OF CONDITIONAL DEPENDENCIES

A variety of extensions of classical dependencies have been proposed, mostly for specifying constraint databases [Baudinet et al., 1999; De Bra and Paredaens, 1983; Maher, 1997; Maher and Srivastava, 1996]. Constraints of De Bra and Paredaens [1983], also called conditional functional dependencies, are of the form $(X \to Y) \to (Z \to W)$, where $X \to Y$ and $Z \to W$ are standard FDs. Constrained dependencies of Maher [1997] extend these by allowing $\xi \to (Z \to W)$, where ξ is an arbitrary constraint that is not necessarily an FD. These dependencies cannot express CFDs since $Z \to W$ does not allow constants. More expressive are constraint-generating dependencies (CGDs) proposed by Baudinet et al. [1999] and constrained tuple-generating dependencies (CTGDs) by Maher and Srivastava [1996], both subsuming CFDs. A CGD is of the form $\forall \bar{x}(R_1(\bar{x}) \wedge \cdots \wedge R_k(\bar{x}) \wedge \xi(\bar{x}) \to \xi'(\bar{x}))$, where R_i's are relation atoms, and ξ, ξ' are arbitrary constraints that may carry constants. A CTGD is of the form $\forall \bar{x}(R_1(\bar{x}) \wedge \cdots \wedge R_k(\bar{x}) \wedge \xi \to \exists \bar{y}(R'_1(\bar{x}, \bar{y}) \wedge \cdots \wedge R'_s(\bar{x}, \bar{y}) \wedge \xi'(\bar{x}, \bar{y})))$, subsuming both CINDs and TGDs. The increased expressive power of CGDs and CTGDs comes at the price of higher complexity for reasoning about these dependencies. No previous work has studied these extensions for data cleaning.

Extensions of CFDs were studied by Bravo et al. [2008] and Chen et al. [2009a,b], to increase the expressiveness of CFDs without incurring extra cost in their static analyses.

- Extended CFDs (eCFDs) [Bravo et al., 2008]. An eCFD allows disjunction and negation in the pattern tuples of CFDs. For example, the eCFD $R([\text{city}] \to [\text{AC}], (\text{NYC} \parallel \{212, 718, 646\}))$ states that for tuples t such that $t[\text{city}] = $ NYC, their area codes must come from the *set* $\{212, 718, 646\}$. As another example, $R([\text{city}] \to [\text{AC}], (\overline{\{\text{NYC}, \text{LI}\}} \parallel \_))$ says that all cities in New York State, *except* NYC and Long Island, have a unique area code.

- CFDs with embedded cardinality constraints and synonym rules (CFD ^{c}) [Chen et al., 2009a]. An example CFD ^{c} is $R([\text{country}, \text{zip}] \to [\text{street}], (\text{UK}, \_ \parallel \_), c)$, where c is an integer. It states that for all tuples t such that $t[\text{country}, \text{zip}] \asymp (\text{UK}, \_)$, all tuples that are synonymous to t in country and zip can only have at most c distinct street values.

- Conditional dependencies with built-in predicates [Chen et al., 2009b]. Both CFDs and CINDs are extended by allowing pattern tuples to contain $\neq, <, \leq, >$ and $\geq$. For example, $R([\text{book}] \to [\text{price}], (\_ \parallel > 0))$ says that every book should have a price greater than zero. A similar extension in which pattern tuples can specify ranges in some numeric domain was considered by Golab et al. [2008].

For all these extensions, it has been shown that despite their increased expressive power, their satisfiability and implication analyses have the same complexity as their standard CFD and CIND counterparts, respectively [Bravo et al., 2008; Chen et al., 2009a,b].

Since the introduction of conditional dependencies, several other dependency formalisms have been considered in the context of data quality. Examples are sequential dependencies [Golab et al., 2009], metric dependencies [Koudas et al., 2009], matching dependencies [Fan et al., 2011a], differential dependencies [Song and Chen, 2011] and currency dependencies [Fan et al., 2012b], among others. We will study matching dependencies and currency dependencies in more detail in Chapters 4 and 6, respectively. We refer the reader to [Fan and Geerts, 2011] for a survey on more variations of standard FDs.

The story of constraint formalisms studied for data quality would not be complete without mentioning edits [Boskovitz et al., 2003; Fellegi and Holt, 1976]. Edits have been extensively used for decades by census bureaus around the world. They were introduced by Fellegi and Holt [1976] in an attempt to provide a formal foundation for checking the validity of questionnaires and for repairing the data thereof. Simply stated, edits are of the form $e = S_1 \times \cdots \times S_k$, where $S_i \subseteq D_i$ for a finite domain D_i, for each $i \in [1, k]$. A record t corresponds to an element in $D_1 \times \cdots \times D_k$, and is regarded clean relative to the edit e if $t \notin e$. Edits can be viewed as a special case of eCFDs. Indeed, an edit e can be expressed as an eCFD of the form $([A_1, \ldots, A_{k-1}] \to [A_k], (S_1, \ldots, S_{k-1} \parallel \overline{S_k}))$. A logical framework for edits was proposed by Boskovitz et al. [2003]. The focus of that line of work is the localization of errors and the imputation of data, by treating input records individually and separately, without checking inconsistencies between different records.

Besides CFDs and CINDs, non-traditional dependencies studied for data cleaning include denial constraints, which are universally quantified FO sentences of the form

$$\forall \bar{x}_1, \ldots, \forall \bar{x}_k \, \neg\big(R_1(\bar{x}_1) \wedge \cdots \wedge R_k(\bar{x}_k) \wedge \xi(\bar{x}_1, \ldots, \bar{x}_k)\big),$$

where R_i is a relation atom for $i \in [1, k]$ and ξ is a conjunction of built-in predicates such as $=, \neq, <, \leq, >$ and $\geq$. Note that FDs are a special case of denial constraints. While some denial constraints in the literature allow constants, numerical values, and aggregate functions, the implication and consistency problems and finite axiomatizability for these constraints are yet to be settled [Bertossi, 2011; Bertossi et al., 2008]. Denial constraints have been primarily used in consistent query answering (see [Bertossi, 2011] for a survey). As will be seen in Chapter 6, currency constraints are an extension of denial constraints by supporting temporal (currency) orders.

The results on dependency propagation presented here are taken from [Abiteboul et al., 1995; Klug, 1980; Klug and Price, 1982] for FDs and from [Fan et al., 2008c] for CFDs and FDs. In addition, Fan et al. [2008c] developed algorithms for finding so-called propagation covers, i.e., a minimal set of CFDs that is equivalent to the set of all CFDs that are propagated to SPC views. Earlier work on propagation covers considered FDs and projection views, in the absence of finite-domain attributes [Gottlob, 1987]. Another line of research studies the closure problem of dependencies under views. It is to decide whether the set of views $\sigma(D)$ for which $D \models \Sigma$ can be characterized by a set Γ of dependencies in the same dependency language [Fagin, 1982; Ginsburg and Zaiddan, 1982; Hull, 1984]. It is shown by Ginsburg and Zaiddan [1982] that FDs are not closed in this sense. This is also exemplified in this chapter: FDs on the source are often propagated as CFDs on the view, rather than as FDs.

CHAPTER 3
Cleaning Data with Conditional Dependencies

We have seen that conditional dependencies can be used as data quality rules to tell us whether our data are dirty or clean. To make practical use of conditional dependencies in a data quality management system, however, several questions have to be answered. The first question concerns how we can get high-quality conditional dependencies. We have so far assumed that conditional dependencies are already provided, either extracted from business rules or designed by domain experts. In practice, however, business rules are often inadequate, and it may be unrealistic to rely on human experts to design dependencies. Hence, it is necessary to automatically discover conditional dependencies from sample data. The second question asks how we can validate a set of conditional dependencies, either manually designed or automatically discovered. We have seen that we can identify a maximum consistent subset of rules from a given set of CFDs, by using an approximation algorithm (Section 2.2.1), and by recruiting the users to inspect the selected rules if necessary. After the rules are in place, the next question concerns how to efficiently detect errors in our data, i.e., violations of the dependencies, using the rules. Finally, after the errors are identified, how can we automatically correct the errors, again by using the data quality rules?

This chapter answers these questions. We first present algorithms for discovering CFDs (Section 3.1). We then introduce SQL-based error detection methods that are efficient on large data and a large number of dependencies (Section 3.2). Finally, we provide a general algorithm for repairing data based on CFDs and CINDs (Section 3.3).

3.1 DISCOVERING CONDITIONAL DEPENDENCIES

We present two methods to *automatically discover* or *learn* conditional functional dependencies from sample data. The first method, CFDMiner, efficiently discovers constant CFDs, capitalizing on a strong connection between constant CFDs and so-called free and closed itemsets. The second method, CTANE, discovers general (both constant and variable) CFDs, by extending the well-known FD-discovery method TANE [Huhtala et al., 1999].

3.1.1 THE CFD DISCOVERY PROBLEM
Before presenting these methods, we formally state the CFD discovery problem.

3. CLEANING DATA WITH CONDITIONAL DEPENDENCIES

	FN	LN	CC	AC	phn	street	city	zip	salary	status
t_1:	Mike	Clark	44	131	1234567	Mayfield	EDI	EH4 8LE	60k	single
t_2:	Rick	Stark	44	131	3456789	Crichton	EDI	EH4 8LE	96k	married
t_3:	Joe	Brady	01	908	4567890	Main Rd	EDI	NJ 07974	90k	married
t_4:	Mary	Smith	01	908	7966899	Mtn Ave	MH	NJ 07974	50k	single
t_5:	Mary	Luth	01	131	7966899	Mtn Ave	MH	NJ 07974	50k	married
t_6:	Mary	Luth	44	131	3456789	Mayfield	NYC	EH4 1DT	80k	married

Figure 3.1: An employee instance.

Given an instance I of a relation schema R, one might want to simply find all CFDs φ defined over R such that $I \models \varphi$. This may not be such a good idea, however. Indeed:

- trivial and redundant CFDs will be returned, and as a result, the set of discovered CFDs will be too large and contain many uninteresting CFDs; and
- the set returned may contain erroneous CFDs, which are generated from errors and noise in the possibly dirty instance I.

To avoid these, we will consider non-trivial, non-redundant, and k-frequent CFDs only. We next formally define these notions. As usual, we consider CFDs in normal form.

(1) We say that a CFD $\varphi = (X \rightarrow A, t_p)$ is *trivial* if $A \in X$. Such CFDs are obviously uninteresting. Indeed, depending on how $t_p[A_X]$ and $t_p[A_Y]$ relate, φ may be satisfied by all instances, or it is not satisfiable at all, or it requires that all tuples in an instance must have the same A-attribute value. Thus, we exclude trivial CFDs by requiring that $A \notin X$.

(2) A CFD $\varphi = (X \rightarrow A, t_p)$ is said to be *non-redundant* on an instance I if whenever $I \models \varphi$, then $I \not\models (Y \rightarrow A, (t_p[Y] \parallel t_p[A]))$ for any proper subset $Y \subsetneq X$. When φ is a variable CFD (i.e., $t_p[A] = $ "_"), we additionally require that if $I \models \varphi$, then $I \not\models (X \rightarrow A, (t'_p[X] \parallel \_))$ for any $t'_p[X]$ obtained from $t_p[X]$ by replacing a constant with the unnamed variable "_". In other words, in a non-redundant CFD, none of its attributes can be removed, and none of the constants in its LHS pattern can be "upgraded" to "_".

Example 3.1 Consider the instance D_0 shown in Figure 3.1 and a variable CFD $\varphi_4 = ([\text{FN}, \text{LN}] \rightarrow [\text{status}], (\_, \text{Luth} \parallel \_))$. Clearly, φ_4 is non-trivial. However, φ_4 is redundant on D_0. Indeed, its left-hand side can be reduced since $D_0 \models ([\text{LN}] \rightarrow [\text{status}], (\text{Luth} \parallel \_))$. In addition, the constant in the pattern tuple of φ_4, "Luth" can be upgraded to "_", since $D_0 \models ([\text{LN}] \rightarrow [\text{status}], (\_ \parallel \_))$. Here the CFD $([\text{LN}] \rightarrow [\text{status}], (\_ \parallel \_))$ is non-redundant. □

(3) To formalize the notion of k-frequent CFDs, observe that although dirty data may abundantly occur in an instance, it is unlikely that the same dirty data items appear frequently. To reduce the impact of dirty data on the discovered CFDs, we consider frequent CFDs. Let $\varphi = (X \rightarrow A, t_p)$ be a CFD and let $k \geq 1$ be a natural number. We define the *support* of φ in I, denoted by $\text{supp}(\varphi, I)$, to be the set consisting of tuples t in I such that $t[X] \asymp t_p[X]$ and $t[A] \asymp t_p[A]$. We say that a CFD

3.1. DISCOVERING CONDITIONAL DEPENDENCIES 41

φ is *k-frequent* if $|\mathsf{supp}(\varphi, I)| \geq k$. That is, the number of tuples that match the pattern tuple of φ is required to exceed k.

Example 3.2 The variable CFDs φ_1 and φ_3 shown in Figure 2.2 are 3-frequent and 6-frequent, respectively, on the instance D_0. As another example, the constant CFD ([CC, AC, phn] $\rightarrow$ [city], (44, 131, _ || EDI)), derived from φ_2 of Figure 2.2, is 2-frequent. □

Putting these together, we define a *canonical cover* of CFDs on instance I w.r.t. k to be a set Σ of non-trivial, non-redundant, and k-frequent CFDs that hold on I, such that Σ is equivalent to the set of all non-trivial k-frequent CFDs that hold on I. In terms of canonical covers, the *CFD discovery problem* can be stated as follows.

- INPUT: A possibly dirty instance I of R and a support threshold $k \in \mathbb{N}$.
- PROBLEM: It is to find a canonical cover of CFDs on instance I w.r.t. k.

We give methods to discover constant CFDs (Section 3.1.2) and general CFDs (Section 3.1.3).

3.1.2 DISCOVERING CONSTANT CFDs

We are to find a canonical cover of k-frequent constant CFDs on an instance I of R. To this end we first characterize non-redundant k-frequent constant CFDs in terms of free and closed itemsets. We then leverage efficient data mining techniques to discover such itemsets.

Free and closed itemsets. An *itemset* is a pair (X, t_p), where $X \subseteq \mathsf{attr}(R)$ is a set of attributes and t_p is a constant pattern over X. That is, t_p is a pattern tuple without "_". Given an instance I of R, we abuse the notation of supports, and denote by $\mathsf{supp}(X, t_p, I)$ the support of (X, t_p) in I, i.e., the set of tuples in I that match t_p on the X-attributes.

Given (X, t_p) and (Y, s_p), we say that (Y, s_p) is *more general* than (X, t_p), denoted by $(X, t_p) \preceq (Y, s_p)$, if $Y \subseteq X$ and $s_p = t_p[Y]$. Furthermore, we say that (Y, s_p) is *strictly more general* than (X, t_p), denoted by $(X, t_p) \prec (Y, s_p)$, if $Y \subset X$ and $s_p = t_p[Y]$. It is readily verified that if $(X, t_p) \preceq (Y, s_p)$ then $\mathsf{supp}(X, t_p, I) \subseteq \mathsf{supp}(Y, s_p, I)$.

An itemset (X, t_p) is called *closed* in I if there exists no itemset (Y, s_p) such that $(Y, s_p) \prec (X, t_p)$ and $\mathsf{supp}(X, t_p, I) = \mathsf{supp}(Y, s_p, I)$. Intuitively, a closed itemset (X, t_p) cannot be specialized without decreasing its support. For (X, t_p) we denote by $\mathsf{clo}(X, t_p)$ the unique closed itemset that extends (X, t_p) and has the same support as (X, t_p).

Similarly, an itemset (X, t_p) is called *free* in I if there exists no itemset (Y, s_p) such that $(X, t_p) \preceq (Y, s_p)$ and $\mathsf{supp}(X, t_p, I) = \mathsf{supp}(Y, s_p, I)$. Intuitively, a free itemset (X, t_p) cannot be generalized without increasing its support.

For a natural number $k \geq 1$, an itemset (X, t_p) is called *k-frequent* if $|\mathsf{supp}(X, t_p, I)| \geq k$. We refer to [Pasquier et al., 1999] for more details about closed and free itemsets.

Constant CFD discovery algorithm. The following proposition relates k-frequent non-redundant constant CFDs to k-frequent free and closed itemsets. As will be seen shortly, this is the basis of our algorithm for discovering constant CFDs.

Proposition 3.3 *For any instance I of R and any non-trivial, non-redundant, and k-frequent constant CFD $\varphi = (X \to A, (t_p \| a))$, $I \models \varphi$ if and only if*

- *the itemset (X, t_p) is free, k-frequent and $A \notin X$;*
- $\mathsf{clo}(X, t_p) \preceq (A, a)$; *and*
- *there exists no $(Y, s_p) \prec (X, t_p)$ with $\mathsf{clo}(Y, s_p) \preceq (A, a)$.* □

Crux. Suppose that $I \models \varphi$, where $\varphi = (X \to A, (t_p \| a))$ is a non-trivial, non-redundant, and k-frequent constant CFD. We know from the semantics of CFDs that $\mathsf{supp}(X, t_p, I) = \mathsf{supp}(\{X, A\}, (t_p, a), I)$. Hence, $\mathsf{clo}(X, t_p) \preceq (A, a)$. Furthermore, since φ is k-frequent, $|\mathsf{supp}(\{X, A\}, (t_p, a), I)| \geqslant k$ and (X, t_p) is k-frequent. Moreover, since φ is non-redundant, there exists no (strict) subset Y of X such that $\mathsf{supp}(Y, t_p[Y], I) = \mathsf{supp}(\{Y, A\}, (t_p[Y], a), I)$. Hence, (X, t_p) is a k-frequent itemset that is free, and is minimal among all free itemsets $(Y, t_p[Y])$ that satisfy $\mathsf{supp}(Y, t_p[Y], I) = \mathsf{supp}(\{Y, A\}, (t_p[Y], a), I)$. In other words, (X, t_p) is a minimal k-frequent free itemset among all itemsets (Y, s_p) with $\mathsf{clo}(Y, s_p) \preceq (A, a)$. Conversely, a similar argument verifies that given the conditions on (X, t_p) and (A, a) stated in Proposition 3.3, the corresponding CFD is non-trivial, non-redundant, and k-frequent. □

Based on this proposition, we present algorithm CFDMiner as Algorithm 1, which finds a canonical cover of k-frequent constant CFDs. In a nutshell, it first finds all k-frequent free and closed itemsets in the instance I. This can be done by invoking one of many available frequent itemset mining algorithms that discover k-frequent itemsets, from which closed and free itemsets can be derived (see [Bayardo et al., 2004] for an overview of such algorithms); or by combining algorithms that mine closed [Pasquier et al., 1999; Wang et al., 2003; Zaki and Hsiao, 2005] or free frequent itemsets [Calders and Goethals, 2007; Li et al., 2006]. Notably, the GCGrowth algorithm is particularly well suited for our purpose since it *simultaneously* discovers free and closed itemsets (see [Li et al., 2007] for details about GCGrowth). It suffices to observe that the output of GCGrowth is a mapping C2F that associates with each k-frequent closed itemset its set of k-frequent free itemsets (line 1). Proposition 3.3 assures that we can focus on the discovery of constant CFDs of the form $(X \to A, (t_p \| a))$, where $(X, t_p[X])$ is a k-frequent free itemset for which $\mathsf{clo}(X, t_p) \preceq (A, a)$. Algorithm CFDMiner starts from the k-frequent closed itemsets in I, which identify the possible RHS attributes in the CFD; and for each closed itemset (Y, s_p), it then considers the corresponding k-frequent free itemsets (X, t_p) (for which $\mathsf{clo}(X, t_p) = (Y, s_p)$) as candidate LHS attributes of the CFD. The initial candidate RHS attributes for (X, t_p) are taken from (Y, s_p) (lines 4-6). In order to satisfy the minimality condition stated in Proposition 3.3, the algorithm then reduces the candidate RHS attributes for each k-frequent itemset (lines 7-10) such that: (a) if no candidate attributes are left, then the corresponding CFD is redundant; and (b) if candidate attributes are present, then

3.1. DISCOVERING CONDITIONAL DEPENDENCIES 43

Algorithm 1 CFDMiner.

Input: An instance I of R and a natural number $k \geq 1$.
Output: A canonical cover of k-frequent constant CFDs.

1: compute a mapping C2F that associates with each k-frequent closed itemset in I its set of k-frequent free itemsets;
2: **for all** k-frequent closed itemset (Y, s_p) in I **do**
3:    let L be the list of all free itemsets in C2F(Y, s_p);
4:    **for all** $(X, t_p) \in L$ **do**
5:       initialize RHS$(X, t_p) := (Y \setminus X, s_p[Y \setminus X])$;
6:    **end for**
7:    **for all** $(X, t_p) \in L$ **do**
8:       **for all** $(X', t_p[X']) \in L$ such that $X' \subset X$ **do**
9:          RHS$(X, t_p) := $ RHS$(X, t_p) \cap $ RHS$(X', t_p[X'])$;
10:       **end for**
11:       **if** RHS$(X, t_p) \neq \emptyset$ **then**
12:          **return** $(X \rightarrow A, (t_p \parallel a))$ for all $(A, a) \in $ RHS(X, t_p);
13:       **end if**
14:    **end for**
15: **end for**

the corresponding non-redundant CFD is returned as output (line 11-13). The correctness of the algorithm is a direct consequence of Proposition 3.3.

Example 3.4 Consider the instance D_0 of Figure 3.1. Let $k = 2$. An example 2-frequent itemset in D_0 that contains CC, AC, and city is $((CC, AC, city), (44, 131, EDI))$. Then the corresponding 2-frequent closed itemset is $((CC, AC, city, zip), (44, 131, EDI, EH4\ 8LE))$, which has a unique 2-frequent free set (zip, EH4 8LE). Hence $([zip] \rightarrow A, (EH4\ 8LE \parallel a))$ is a 2-frequent CFD with (A, a) as an attribute-constant pair taken from $\{(CC, 44), (AC, 131), (city, EDI)\}$, i.e., the single itemsets present in the closed itemset that are different from (zip, EH4 8LE). This CFD is non-redundant: there is no smaller 2-frequent free set in D_0 whose closed itemset contains any element of the single itemsets $\{(CC, 44), (AC, 131), (city, EDI)\}$. □

Various optimizations can be employed when implementing CFDMiner. For example, hash tables can substantially speedup checking for subsets of particular free itemsets (see line 8 in Algorithm 1). In addition, pruning strategies can be used to avoid the generation of unnecessary free and closed itemsets [Li et al., 2012a]. We refer to [Fan et al., 2011b] for more details regarding the implementation of CFDMiner and its related experimental study.

3.1.3 DISCOVERING GENERAL CFDs

We next present CTANE, a method to compute a canonical cover of k-frequent general (variable and constant) CFDs from a given instance I. This method is a generalization of a well-known algorithm, TANE, for discovering FDs [Huhtala et al., 1999]. Algorithm TANE discovers FDs by traversing a lattice of attribute sets in a bottom-up level-wise way. Along the same lines, CTANE traverses an extended lattice consisting of pairs of attribute sets and patterns, to cope with pattern tuples. Similar to TANE, CTANE scales well with the size of I but is sensitive to the arity (the number of attributes) of I (i.e., its schema).

More specifically, CTANE considers the lattice $(\mathcal{L}, \sqsubseteq)$, where $\mathcal{L}$ consists of all pairs (X, t_p) such that $X \subseteq \text{attr}(R)$ and t_p is a pattern tuple over X, possibly with "_". Moreover, we say that $(X, t_p) \sqsubseteq (Y, s_p)$ if $X \subseteq Y$ and $t_p \preceq s_p[X]$. Here $t_p \preceq s_p[X]$ denotes that for every attribute $X_i \in X$, either $t_p[X_i] = s_p[X_i]$ or $s_p[X_i] =$"_". Given (X, t_p), we denote by (X^c, t_p^c) the restriction of (X, t_p) to the attributes for which t_p is a constant. Given a natural number $k \geq 1$, we define $(\mathcal{L}_k, \sqsubseteq)$ to be the sub-lattice of $(\mathcal{L}, \sqsubseteq)$ in which $\mathcal{L}_k$ consists of pairs (X, t_p) such that the itemset (X^c, t_p^c) is k-frequent. We denote by L_k^ℓ the set of elements (X, t_p) in $\mathcal{L}_k$ such that $|X| = \ell$. We assume that L_k^ℓ is ordered such that (X, t_p) comes before (X, s_p) in the order whenever $s_p \preceq t_p$. Elements in L_k^ℓ are considered in this order to ensure that the most general patterns are considered first.

Algorithm CTANE is shown as Algorithm 2. The algorithm treats each $(X, t_p) \in L_k^\ell$ as a possible LHS of a CFD and associates with each $(X, t_p) \in L_k^\ell$ a set of candidate RHS, denoted by $\mathsf{CandRHS}(X, t_p)$. This set consists of elements (A, c_A), where $A \in \text{attr}(R)$ and c_A is either a constant or "_". The set is used to determine whether $\varphi = ([X \setminus \{A\}] \to A, (t_p[X \setminus \{A\}] \| c_A))$ is a non-redundant k-frequent CFD that holds on I. We refer to [Fan et al., 2011b] for more details about $\mathsf{CandRHS}(X, t_p)$. To understand the general idea underlying CTANE, it suffices to consider the following two properties of $\mathsf{CandRHS}(X, t_p)$:

(P1) if $I \models \varphi$ then φ is non-redundant and k-frequent if and only if for all attributes $B \in X$, $(A, c_A) \in \mathsf{CandRHS}(X \setminus \{B\}, t_p[X \setminus \{B\}])$. In other words, $\mathsf{CandRHS}(X, t_p)$ can be computed during the bottom-up level-wise traversal of the lattice since it can be expressed in terms of $\mathsf{CandRHS}(Y, s_p)$ with $|Y| < |X|$; and

(P2) if $\mathsf{CandRHS}(X, t_p) = \emptyset$ then (X, t_p) does not lead to a non-redundant k-frequent CFD that holds on I, and hence, (X, t_p) can be disregarded.

Given this, CTANE works as follows (see Algorithm 2). We start by initializing the first level of the lattice L_k^1 (line 1). These elements are all considered as candidate RHS for CFDs in which the LHS is the bottom element $\emptyset$ in the lattice (line 2). Then, for $\ell \geq 1$, as long as there are elements in L_k^ℓ, and thus there exist possible LHS of CFDs, CTANE computes corresponding candidate RHS (lines 4–6) as suggested by property (P1). The validity of the CFD $\varphi = ([X \setminus \{A\}] \to A, (t_p[X \setminus \{A\}] \| c_A))$

3.1. DISCOVERING CONDITIONAL DEPENDENCIES

Algorithm 2 CTANE.

Input: An instance I of R, and a natural number $k \geq 1$.
Output: A canonical cover of k-frequent CFDs.

1: $L_k^1 := \{(A, \_) \mid A \in \text{attr}(R)\} \cup \{(A, a) \mid \text{supp}((A, a), I) \geq k, A \in \text{attr}(R)\}$;
2: $\text{CandRHS}(\emptyset) := L_k^1$; $\ell := 1$;
3: **while** $L_k^\ell \neq \emptyset$ **do**
4:    **for all** $(X, t_p) \in L_k^\ell$ **do**
5:       $\text{CandRHS}(X, t_p) := \bigcap_{B \in X} \text{CandRHS}(X \setminus \{B\}, t_p[X \setminus \{B\}])$;
6:    **end for**
7:    **for all** $(X, t_p) \in L_k^\ell, A \in X, (A, c_A) \in \text{CandRHS}(X, t_p)$ **do**
8:       $\varphi := ([X \setminus \{A\}] \to A, (t_p[X \setminus \{A\}] \| c_A))$;
9:       **if** $I \models \varphi$ **then**
10:          output φ;
11:          update $\text{CandRHS}(X, u_p)$ for all u_p such that
                    $u_p[A] = c_A$ and $u_p[X \setminus \{A\}] \preceq t_p[X \setminus \{A\}]$;
12:       **end if**
13:    **end for**
14:    remove all (X, t_p) from L_k^ℓ with $\text{CandRHS}(X, t_p) = \emptyset$;
15:    generate $L_k^{\ell+1}$ from L_k^ℓ and set $\ell := \ell + 1$;
16: **end while**

(line 8), obtained from the current element in the lattice (X, t_p) and candidate RHS (A, c_A) in $\text{CandRHS}(X, t_p)$, is subsequently verified. If $I \models \varphi$ then property (P1) tells us that φ is non-redundant and k-frequent.

Observe, however, that if $I \models \varphi$ then $I \models ([X \setminus \{A\}] \to A, (u_p[X \setminus \{A\}] \| c_A))$ for any $u_p[X \setminus \{A\}] \preceq t_p[X \setminus \{A\}]$. To avoid the generation of such CFDs when considering (X, u_p) at a later stage, recall that elements in L_k^ℓ are ordered such that (X, u_p) comes after (X, t_p). Hence we remove (A, c_A) from $\text{CandRHS}(X, u_p)$. Similarly, we remove all $B \in \text{attr}(R) \setminus X$ from $\text{CandRHS}(X, u_p)$. Indeed, if $I \models (X \to B, (u_p[X] \| c_B))$, where c_B is either a constant or "_", then we also have that $I \models ([X \setminus \{A\}] \to B, (u_p[X \setminus \{A\}] \| c_B))$, and this yields redundant CFDs. These two optimization strategies are performed at line 11 in the algorithm.

When all candidate RHS attributes are in place for elements in L_k^ℓ, CTANE then proceeds by pruning irrelevant elements (line 14) from L_k^ℓ based on property (P2). Finally, the next level $L_k^{\ell+1}$ is generated in a standard way by joining compatible elements from L_k^ℓ; and the elements in $L_k^{\ell+1}$ are subsequently considered (line 15). As remarked earlier, this process proceeds until no further elements in $\mathcal{L}_k$ need to be considered. The correctness of the algorithm follows from property (P1)

3. CLEANING DATA WITH CONDITIONAL DEPENDENCIES

and the fact that CTANE correctly maintains CandRHS (see [Fan et al., 2011b] for a detailed proof of the correctness).

Example 3.5 We show how algorithm CTANE works as follows. Consider the employee instance D_0 given in Figure 3.1. We describe a partial run of CTANE involving only attributes CC, AC, and city. Assume that $k = 3$. In the initialization phase, L_3^1 is computed, which consists of the following elements (represented as tabular):

$$L_3^1 = \left\{ \begin{array}{|c|} \hline \text{CC} \\ \hline \text{--} \\ 44 \\ 01 \\ \hline \end{array} , \begin{array}{|c|} \hline \text{AC} \\ \hline \text{--} \\ 131 \\ \hline \end{array} , \begin{array}{|c|} \hline \text{city} \\ \hline \text{--} \\ \text{EDI} \\ \hline \end{array} \right\}.$$

The elements in L_3^1 constitute CandRHS($\emptyset$). However, since the instance does not satisfy any CFD with empty LHS, we have that CandRHS$(A, c_A) = L_3^1$ for all $(A, c_A) \in L_3^1$. The algorithm thus immediately proceeds with the generation of L_3^2. It is readily verified that

$$L_3^2 = \left\{ \begin{array}{|cc|} \hline \text{CC} & \text{AC} \\ \hline \text{--} & \text{--} \\ 44 & \text{--} \\ 01 & \text{--} \\ \text{--} & 131 \\ 44 & 131 \\ \hline \end{array} , \begin{array}{|cc|} \hline \text{CC} & \text{city} \\ \hline \text{--} & \text{--} \\ 44 & \text{--} \\ 01 & \text{--} \\ \text{--} & \text{EDI} \\ \hline \end{array} , \begin{array}{|cc|} \hline \text{AC} & \text{city} \\ \hline \text{--} & \text{--} \\ 131 & \text{--} \\ \text{--} & \text{EDI} \\ \hline \end{array} \right\}.$$

Again, since no elements are removed from the candidate sets, CandRHS initially consists of L_3^1 for each element in L_3^2. By considering all possible CFDs obtained from L_3^1, one identifies two valid CFDs: $\phi_1 = ([CC] \to [AC], (44 \parallel \_))$ and $\phi_2 = ([CC] \to [AC], (44 \parallel 131))$. As a consequence, (AC, _) and (AC, 131) are removed from CandRHS((CC, AC), (44, _)) and CandRHS((CC, AC), (44, 131)). Furthermore, CTANE removes (city, _) and (city, EDI) from these candidate sets, as optimizations described earlier (recall how CTANE updates candidate sets). After this, L_3^3 is computed. This set consists of the following elements:

$$L_3^2 = \left\{ \begin{array}{|ccc|} \hline \text{CC} & \text{AC} & \text{city} \\ \hline \text{--} & \text{--} & \text{--} \\ 44 & \text{--} & \text{--} \\ 01 & \text{--} & \text{--} \\ \text{--} & 131 & \text{--} \\ \text{--} & \text{--} & \text{EDI} \\ 44 & 131 & \text{--} \\ \hline \end{array} \right\}.$$

We now initialize the candidate sets of elements in L_3^3 by taking the big intersection of candidate sets of elements at level L_3^2. Here, most candidate sets are still equal to L_3^1, except those affected by the updates to the candidate sets in the previous step. For example, CandRHS((CC, AC, city), (44, _, _)) only contains elements involving CC; similarly for CandRHS((CC, AC, city), (44, 131, _)). After considering all possible CFDs obtained from L_3^3, we now identify a valid CFD $\phi_3 = ([AC, city] \to [CC], (\_, \_ \parallel \_))$. As before, this implies that (CC, _) is removed as a candidate from all other pattern tuples in L_3^2, to prevent the generation of redundant CFDs such as ([AC, city] $\to$ [CC], (44, 131 $\parallel$

_)). Since we are only considering three attributes, no further levels in the lattice are considered in this example. We may thus conclude that there are only three non-trivial, non-redundant, 3-frequent CFDs in the canonical cover for D_0 when considering attributes AC, CC and city only. □

To efficiently implement CTANE, care must be taken in the following issues:
- the maintenance of the sets CandRHS;
- the validation of candidate non-redundant k-frequent CFDs;
- the generation of $L_k^{\ell+1}$; and
- the checking of the support of itemsets to determine whether they are k-frequent.

Fan et al. [2011b] adopted a partition-based approach for all four aspects, by revising a similar technique used in TANE [Huhtala et al., 1999]. In a nutshell, given an element (X, t_p), the instance I is partitioned such that any two tuples that agree on their X-attributes and match t_p are in the same partition. Such partitions can be efficiently computed during the bottom-up traversal of the lattice. We refer the interested reader to [Fan et al., 2011b] and [Huhtala et al., 1999] for more details.

3.2 ERROR DETECTION

We next develop techniques to detect violations of CFDs. That is, given an instance I of a relation schema R and a set Σ of CFDs defined on R, we find all the *violating tuples* in I, i.e., the tuples that (perhaps together with other tuples in I) violate some CFD in Σ.

We first present an SQL technique to find violations of a single CFD, and then generalize it to validate multiple CFDs. These methods *only* use SQL queries. Hence, error detection can be readily supported by DBMS without requiring any additional functionality.

3.2.1 CHECKING A SINGLE CFD WITH SQL

To simplify the discussion, in this section we assume that the right-hand side of a CFD consists of a single attribute only. However, we do allow the pattern tableau T_p to contain multiple pattern tuples. The detection methods presented here can be trivially extended to multiple RHS attributes, as will be illustrated by examples later. Given such a CFD $\varphi = (X \to A, T_p)$, the following two SQL queries suffice to find the tuples violating φ:

Q_φ^C SELECT * FROM $R\ t,\ T_p\ t_p$
       WHERE $t[X] \asymp t_p[X]$ AND $t[A] \not\asymp t_p[A]$

Q_φ^V SELECT DISTINCT X FROM $R\ t,\ T_p\ t_p$
       WHERE $t[X] \asymp t_p[X]$ AND $t_p[A] =$ "_"
       GROUP BY X HAVING COUNT(DISTINCT A)> 1,

where for an attribute $B \in (X \cup \{A\})$, $t[B] \asymp t_p[B]$ is a short-hand for the SQL expression ($t[B] = t_p[B]$ OR $t_p[B] =$ "_"), while $t[B] \not\asymp t_p[B]$ is for ($t[B] \neq t_p[B]$ AND $t_p[B] \neq$ "_").

3. CLEANING DATA WITH CONDITIONAL DEPENDENCIES

$Q_{\varphi_2}^C$ SELECT * FROM employee t, T_2 t_p
       WHERE $t[\text{CC}] \asymp t_p[\text{CC}]$ AND $t[\text{AC}] \asymp t_p[\text{AC}]$ AND $t[\text{phn}] \asymp t_p[\text{phn}]$ AND
       ($t[\text{street}] \not\asymp t_p[\text{street}]$ OR $t[\text{city}] \not\asymp t_p[\text{city}]$ OR $t[\text{zip}] \not\asymp t_p[\text{zip}]$)

$Q_{\varphi_2}^V$ SELECT DISTINCT CC, AC, phn FROM employee t, T_2 t_p
       WHERE $t[\text{CC}] \asymp t_p[\text{CC}]$ AND $t[\text{AC}] \asymp t_p[\text{AC}]$ AND $t[\text{phn}] \asymp t_p[\text{phn}]$ AND
       ($t_p[\text{street}] = $ "_" OR $t_p[\text{city}] = $ "_" OR $t_p[\text{zip}] = $ "_")
       GROUP BY CC, AC, phn HAVING COUNT(DISTINCT street, city, zip) > 1

Figure 3.2: SQL queries for checking CFD φ_2 of Figure 2.2.

More specifically, the detection is conducted by a two-step process, in which each step of the process is carried out by a query, illustrated as follows.

(1) Query Q_φ^C detects *single-tuple* violations, i.e., those tuples t in I that match some pattern tuple $t_p \in T_p$ on the X attributes, but t does not match t_p in A since the *constant* value $t_p[A]$ is different from $t[A]$. That is, Q_φ^C finds violating tuples based on differences between the constants in the tuples and patterns in T_p.

(2) On the other hand, query Q_φ^V finds *multi-tuple* violations, i.e., tuples t in I for which there exists a tuple t' in I such that $t[X] = t'[X]$ and moreover, both t and t' match a pattern t_p on the X attributes, and $t_p[A]$ is a variable, but $t[A] \neq t'[A]$. Query Q_φ^V uses the GROUP BY clause to group tuples with the same value on X, and it counts the number of their distinct A attribute values. If there exist more than one value, then there exists a violation. Note that Q_φ^V returns only the X attributes of violating tuples, to make the output more concise, but the complete tuples can be easily obtained using a join.

Example 3.6 We illustrate how the SQL technique can be easily extended to handle CFDs with an RHS consisting of multiple attributes. Recall the CFD φ_2 given in Figure 2.2, where RHS(φ_2) has three attributes. The SQL queries $Q_{\varphi_2}^C$ and $Q_{\varphi_2}^V$ shown in Figure 3.2 check violations of φ_2. Consider an employee instance D_1 that consists of the first three tuples t_1, t_2, and t_3 given in Figure 3.1. Executing these queries on D_1, it identifies and returns violating tuples t_3 (due to $Q_{\varphi_2}^C$), and t_1 and t_2 (due to $Q_{\varphi_2}^V$).   □

A salient feature of the SQL translation is that the pattern tableau T_p is treated as an ordinary *data table*. Therefore, each query is bounded by the size of the embedded FD $X \to A$ in the CFD, and is *independent* of the (possibly large) tableau T_p.

3.2.2 VALIDATING MULTIPLE CFDS

We next generalize the detection method for a single CFD to deal with multiple CFDs. Clearly, a naive way to validate a set Σ of CFDs is to use one query pair for each CFD φ in Σ. This approach, however, requires $2 \times |\Sigma|$ passes of the database instance at hand.

3.2. ERROR DETECTION 49

$\varphi_4 = ([\text{CC}, \text{AC}, \text{phn}] \to [\text{street}, \text{city}, \text{zip}], T_4)$, where T_4 is

CC	AC	phn	street	city	zip
_	_	_	_	_	_
44	131	_	_	EDI	_
01	908	_	_	MH	_
_	_	@	@	_	@

Figure 3.3: Merging CFDs φ_2 and φ_3.

We present an alternative approach that only requires two passes. The key idea is to generate a *single* query pair to check all the constrains in Σ at once. The proposed solution works in two phases. In its first phase, a linear scan of all the pattern tableaux of the CFDs in Σ is performed, and all those tableaux are *merged* into a single tableau, denoted by T_Σ. Intuitively, tableau T_Σ captures the constraints expressed by all the tableaux of the CFDs in Σ. Then in its second phase, a query pair is generated to find all those tuples that violate some CFDs in Σ, hereby generalizing the single CFD validation method.

Merging multiple CFDs. Consider a set Σ of CFDs which we assume, without loss of generality, contains just two CFDs φ and φ' on R, where $\varphi = (X \to A, T)$ and $\varphi' = (X' \to A', T')$. For now, assume that neither A nor A' is in $X \cup X'$, an assumption that will be removed later. There are two main challenges to the generation of the merged tableau T_Σ. The first challenge is that tableaux T and T' may not be *union-compatible*, i.e., $X \neq X'$ or $A \neq A'$. We thus need to extend tableau T (resp. T') with all the attributes in $(X' \cup \{A'\}) \setminus (X \cup \{A\})$ (resp. $(X \cup \{A\}) \setminus (X' \cup \{A'\})$ for T'). This can be done as follows: for each attribute B in $(X' \cup \{A'\}) \setminus (X \cup \{A\})$ and each tuple t_p in the original tableau T, we set the value of $t_p[B]$ to be a *special symbol* denoted by "@". Intuitively, the symbol "@"; denotes a *don't care* value. After this extension, the resulted tableaux are union-compatible. The final tableau T_Σ is defined to be the union of these tableaux. For example, Figure 3.3 shows how the CFDs φ_2 and φ_3 of Figure 2.2 can be made union-compatible.

To cope with "@", we need to revise the notion of CFD satisfaction. Let $Z = X \cup X'$ and $W = \{A, A'\}$. Consider a tuple $t_p[Z, W]$ in the tableau T_Σ that includes "@". We use $Z_{t_p}^{free}$ and $W_{t_p}^{free}$ to denote the "@"-free subset of Z and W attributes of t_p, respectively, i.e., it has no "@" symbol. A relation I of R *satisfies* the CFD φ_Σ whose tableau is T_Σ, denoted by $I \models \varphi_\Sigma$, if for *each pair* of tuples $t_1, t_2 \in I$, and for *each* tuple t_p in the pattern tableau T_Σ of φ_Σ, if $t_1[Z_{t_p}^{free}] = t_2[Z_{t_p}^{free}] \asymp t_p[Z_{t_p}^{free}]$ then $t_1[W_{t_p}^{free}] = t_2[W_{t_p}^{free}] \asymp t_p[W_{t_p}^{free}]$.

The second challenge is introduced by the need for different treatments of left-hand side and right-hand side attributes of CFDs. To illustrate this, recall the detection of violations of a single CFD φ using SQL. When writing the detection SQL queries, we assume implicit knowledge about whether an attribute is part of LHS(φ) or RHS(φ). After the merging of pattern tableaux, however, an attribute that appears in the left-hand side of one component CFD might appear in the right-hand

3. CLEANING DATA WITH CONDITIONAL DEPENDENCIES

id	CC	AC	phn	city
1	–	–	–	@
2	44	131	–	@
3	01	908	–	@
4	@	@	@	–

(a) Tableau T_Σ^Z

id	street	city	zip	AC
1	–	–	–	@
2	–	EDI	–	@
3	–	MH	–	@
4	@	@	@	–

(b) Tableau T_Σ^W

Figure 3.4: T_Σ for CFDs φ_3 and φ_5.

side of another component CFD. We thus need to distinguish the two sets of tuples and treat each set separately.

This can be done as follows: we split the tableau T of each CFD $\varphi = (X \to A, T)$ into two parts, namely, T^X and T^A, one tableau for X and one for A. Then the tableau T_Σ^Z (and similarly T_Σ^W) is generated by making all the T^X tableaux in Σ union-compatible (similarly for the T^A tableaux). Note that an attribute can appear in both T_Σ^Z and T_Σ^W. This removes the assumption that RHS attributes A and A' do not appear in $X \cup X'$ given earlier. To be able to restore pattern tuples from T_Σ^Z and T_Σ^W, we create a distinct *tuple id* $t_p[\text{id}]$ for each pattern tuple t_p, and associate it with the corresponding tuples in T_Σ^Z and T_Σ^W. The original pattern tuples can then be obtained by a join on the id attribute.

For example, consider the CFD φ_2 shown in Figure 2.2 and $\varphi_5 = ([\text{city}] \to [\text{AC}], T_5)$, where T_5 consists of a single tuple $(\_ \parallel \_)$. Figure 3.4 shows their merged T_Σ^Z and T_Σ^W tableaux. Note that attributes city and AC appear in both tableaux.

Query generation. Consider the merged tableaux T_Σ^Z and T_Σ^W from a set Σ of CFDs over a relation schema R. Then on any instance I of R, the following two SQL queries can be used to detect tuples in I that violate φ:

Q_Σ^C SELECT * FROM $R\ t,\ T_\Sigma^Z\ t_p^Z,\ T_\Sigma^W\ t_p^W$
 WHERE $t_p^Z[\text{id}] = t_p^W[\text{id}]$ AND $t[Z] \asymp t_p^Z[Z]$ AND $t[W] \not\asymp t_p^W[W]$

Q_Σ^V SELECT DISTINCT Z FROM Macro t^M
 GROUP BY Z HAVING COUNT(DISTINCT W)> 1,

where Macro is:

 SELECT (CASE $t_p^Z[B_i]$ WHEN "@" THEN "@" ELSE $t[B_i]$ END) AS B_i $\cdots$
  (CASE $t_p^W[C_j]$ WHEN "@" THEN "@" ELSE $t[C_j]$ END) AS C_j $\cdots$
 FROM $R\ t,\ T_\Sigma^Z\ t_p^Z,\ T_\Sigma^W\ t_p^W$
 WHERE $t_p^Z[\text{id}] = t_p^W[\text{id}]$ AND $t[Z] \asymp t_p^Z[Z]$ AND $(t_p^W[C_1] = \text{"}\_\text{"}$ OR $\cdots$ OR $t_p^W[C_n] = \text{"}\_\text{"})$.

CC	AC	phn	city	street	city'	zip	AC'
@	@	@	EDI	@	@	@	131
@	@	@	NYC	@	@	@	908
@	@	@	MH	@	@	@	908
@	@	@	NYC	@	@	@	131

Figure 3.5: Macro relation instance.

Here for each attribute $B_i \in Z$, $t[B_i] \asymp t_p[B_i]$ has to take "@" into account; it is now a short-hand for $(t[B_i] = t_p[B_i]$ OR $t_p[B_i] =$ "_" OR $t_p[B_i] =$ "@"). Similarly, for each $C_j \in W$, $t[C_j] \not\asymp t_p[C_j]$ stands for $(t[C_j] \neq t_p[C_j]$ AND $t_p[C_j] \neq$ "_" AND $t_p[C_j] \neq$ "@"). Note that query Q_Σ^C is similar in spirit to the query Q_φ^C that checks inconsistencies between the constants in the instance and the constants in the pattern tableau, for a single CFD. The only difference is that now the query deals with the presence of the "@" symbol in the tableau.

Query Q_Σ^V is more intricate than the query Q_φ^V for a single CFD. Indeed, the attributes used in GROUP BY have to be adjusted for each pattern tuple. In other words, for each pattern tuple we have to ensure that the right set of attributes is used to detect multi-tuple violations. This is achieved by leveraging the relation Macro. Intuitively, Macro inspects each tuple in the tableau, and uses it as a *mask* over the tuples of the instance. If the pattern tuple indicates a *don't care* value @ for an attribute, then all the (possibly different) attribute values in the relation tuples are masked and replaced by an "@" in Macro. Note that this relation has the same sort as T_Σ^Z and T_Σ^W (we rename attributes that appear in both tableaux so as not to appear twice), and it is essentially the join on the Z attributes of relation I with T', where T' is the result of the join on tuple id $t_p[\text{id}]$ of T_Σ^Z and T_Σ^W. The value of each attribute, for each tuple t^M in Macro, is determined by the CASE clause, which is supported by popular DBMS like DB2, Oracle, and MySQL. Indeed, for each attribute $B \in Z$, $t^M[B]$ is set to be "@" if $t_p^Z[B]$ is "@", and it is $t[B]$ otherwise; similarly for each $C \in W$ and $t^M[C]$. Note that relation I is not joined on the W attributes with the tableaux. Thus, $t^M[C]$ is set to be $t[C]$ if for some tuple t with $t[Z] \asymp t_p^Z[Z]$, there is an attribute C with $t_p^W[C]$ being a constant and $t[C] \neq t_p^W[C]$ (i.e., t violates the merged tableau). This creates no problems since this violating tuple is already detected by Q_Σ^C.

Example 3.7 Figure 3.5 shows the result of joining the fourth tuple of tableaux T_Σ^Z and T_Σ^W in Figure 3.4 with the employee relation of Figure 3.1. Note that the query masks the attributes values of CC, AC and phn. This masking allows the subsequent GROUP BY over X to essentially consider, for each tuple, only those Z attributes that have no *don't care* values. Note that although $Z = \{$CC, AC, phn, city$\}$, the GROUP BY by query Q_Σ^V is actually performed over attribute city only. The query returns the NYC tuples, which violate φ_5. Also observe that AC is renamed to distinguish its occurrences in the RHS and LHS of CFDs. □

In this way we *automatically* generate a *single pair* of SQL queries to validate a *set* Σ of multiple CFDs. The queries are guaranteed to be bounded by the size of the embedded FDs in Σ, *independent* of both the size of the tableaux in Σ and the number of CFDs in Σ. Furthermore, to validate a set Σ of CFDs, only two passes of the database are required.

Along the same lines, one can validate a set Γ of CINDs by automatically generating a pair of SQL queries, independent of the size and cardinality of Γ (see [Chen et al., 2009b]).

Incremental detection methods have also been developed [Fan et al., 2008b], to efficiently identify changes to violating tuples in response to changes to the data.

3.3 DATA REPAIRING

After we find violating tuples in a dirty instance D by using a set Σ of conditional dependencies, we want to *fix* the errors and make D consistent. That is, we want to *minimally edit* the data in D such that it satisfies the dependencies in Σ. In other words, we want to find a *repair* of D, i.e., an instance Repair(D) that satisfies Σ and is as close to the original D as possible. This is the data cleaning approach that U.S. national statistical agencies, among others, have been practicing for decades [Fellegi and Holt, 1976; Winkler, 2004]. Nevertheless, manually editing the data is a daunting task, unrealistic when D is large. This highlights the need for automated methods to repair D. Automated repairing alone, however, may only suggest candidate repairs. We often need the users or better still, domain experts, to inspect the candidate repairs and provide feedback, which is incorporated into the repairing process. This is particularly important when repairing critical data.

Putting these together, a data repairing framework is depicted in Figure 3.6, which integrates automated repairing and user interaction. It consists of three modules. (1) The repairing module takes as input a dirty instance D and a set Σ of dependencies. It automatically finds a candidate repair Repair(D). (2) The incremental repairing module takes updates ΔD to D as additional input, and finds changes ΔRepair to Repair(D) in response to ΔD, such that Repair($D \oplus \Delta D$) = Repair(D) $\oplus$ ΔRepair, where $D \oplus \Delta D$ denotes the instance obtained from updating D with ΔD; similarly for Repair(D) $\oplus$ ΔRepair. (3) The repairs generated by these modules are sent to the sampling module, which generates a sample of the repairs and lets the user inspect it. The user may opt to suggest changes to the dependencies and to the sample repairs. The repairing or incremental repairing module is invoked again based on the user feedback, to improve the quality of repairs. The process may continue until the user is satisfied with the sample repair generated by the system.

In this section we focus on automated repairing methods underlying the framework, based on CFDs and CINDs. Cong et al. [2007] discuss incremental repairing methods and sampling strategies. In Chapter 7 we will revise the framework to find "certain fixes" to critical data and to provide guarantees on the quality of repairs.

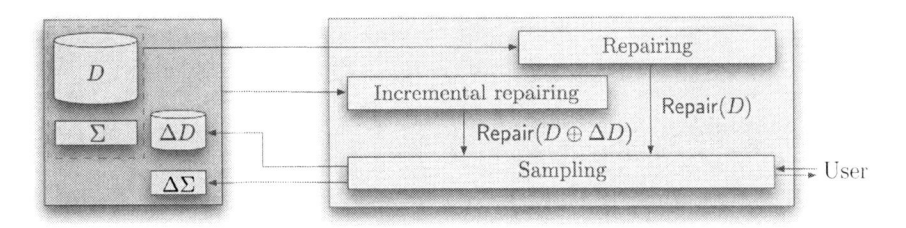

Figure 3.6: An interactive framework for data repairing.

3.3.1 THE DATA REPAIRING PROBLEM

We begin with a formal statement for the *data repairing problem*, first formulated by Arenas et al. [1999]. Consider a relational schema $\mathcal{R}$, a database instance D of $\mathcal{R}$ and a set Σ of CFDs and CINDs defined on $\mathcal{R}$. To keep track of tuples during a repairing process, we assume a temporary unique tuple id for each tuple t. For a repair D' of D, we use t^D and $t^{D'}$ to denote the tuple t in D and D', respectively, carrying the same id. In other words, $t^{D'}$ is an updated version of t^D, where $t^{D'}$ and t^D may differ in some attribute values.

We want to repair D by means of a small number of edits. To measure the difference between D and its repair D', it is a common practice to use a cost function, denoted by cost(). In general, a cost function returns a value cost(D, D') in some ordered domain $(\mathbb{D}, \leq)$. Intuitively, cost(D, D') $\leq$ cost(D, D'') implies that D' is closer to D than D''.

Definition 3.8 A *repair of D relative to Σ and* cost() is an instance D' of $\mathcal{R}$ such that $D' \models \Sigma$ and cost(D, D') is minimum among all instance D'' of $\mathcal{R}$ such that $D'' \models \Sigma$. □

The *data repairing problem* can now be stated as follows.
- INPUT: An instance D of $\mathcal{R}$, a set Σ of CFDs and CINDs on $\mathcal{R}$, and a function cost().
- PROBLEM: Compute a repair of D relative to Σ and cost().

Observe the following. (1) The conditional dependencies and cost function do not necessarily determine a unique repair. Indeed, in most cases multiple repairs may exist, as will be seen in an example shortly. (2) The semantics of repairs depends on the choice of the cost function and repairing models. A variety of cost functions have been studied for consistent query answering for different repairing models defined in terms of tuple deletions, or tuple deletions and insertions, or value modifications (see [Bertossi, 2011] for a survey).

Example 3.9 Consider the employee instance D_0 shown in Figure 3.1, and the CFDs φ_1, φ_2 and φ_3 given in Figure 2.2. The following tuples violate some of these CFDs: for φ_1, tuples t_1 and t_2; for φ_2, tuples t_2, t_3 and t_6; and for φ_3, tuples t_1, t_2, t_3, t_4 and t_6. Suppose that we consider repairs obtained by a minimal number of tuple deletions. A natural choice of cost function in this context is given by $\text{cost}_{del}(I, I') = |I \setminus I'|$. For $\text{cost}_{del}()$, the ordered domain $(\mathbb{D}, \leq)$ is simply $(\mathbb{N}, \leq)$. Then a

54   3. CLEANING DATA WITH CONDITIONAL DEPENDENCIES

repair Repair(D_0) of D_0 relative to $\{\varphi_1, \varphi_2, \varphi_3\}$ and $\text{cost}_{del}()$ can be obtained by deleting t_1, t_3, and t_6 form D_0. This repair is not unique. Indeed, another repair can be obtained by deleting t_3, t_6, and t_2 instead of t_1.   □

It is readily verified that for CFDs and CINDs a repair can always be obtained by deleting tuples. However, the deletion of tuples may cause unnecessary loss of information.

Example 3.10   Consider D_0 and φ_1, φ_2, and φ_3 as described in Example 3.9. Suppose that cost() now measures the number of changes to attribute values in the tuples of D_0. Then here a repair of D_0 can be obtained by the following value modifications: change t_2[street] from Crichton to Mayfield, t_3[city] from EDI to MH, t_6[city] from NYC to EDI, and finally, change t_6[zip] from EH4 1DT to EH4 8LE. One can verify that these modifications eliminate all the violations of the given CFDs. Intuitively, this repair is preferable to the repair given in the previous example as it retains more information of the original instance D_0.   □

We use a cost function based on attribute value modifications, as suggested by Example 3.10. We consider a slightly more general setting in which each tuple t in an instance carries a weight $w(t, A)$ for each attribute A. This weight may reflect the confidence of the accuracy placed by the user in the attribute $t[A]$. Furthermore, we assume the presence of a function $\text{dis}(v, v')$ that measures the distance between two values v and v' taken from the same domain. Intuitively, the smaller $\text{dis}(v, v')$ is, the greater the similarity is between v and v'. To make this more concrete, we consider the Damerau-Levenshtein (DL) metric, but any other distance function can be used instead. The DL-metric is defined as the minimum number of single-character insertions, deletions and substitutions required to transform v to v', and has been shown useful in data cleaning [Galhardas et al., 2001]. The weights on attributes and the DL-metric are then combined as follows:

$$\text{cost}_v(v, v') = w(t, A) \cdot \text{dis}(v, v') / \max(|v|, |v'|).$$

Obviously, the more accurate the original $t[A]$ value v is and the more distant the new value v' is from v, the higher the cost of this change is. We use $\text{dis}(v, v')/\max(|v|, |v'|)$ to measure the similarity of v and v' and to ensure that longer strings with 1-character difference are closer than shorter strings with 1-character difference. We extend $\text{cost}_v()$ to tuples as

$$\text{cost}_t(t^D, t^{D'}) = \sum_{A \in \text{attr}(R)} \text{cost}(t^D[A], t^{D'}[A]),$$

where D and D' are instances of $\mathcal{R}$. Finally, we define the cost of repairing D with D' as:

$$\text{cost}(D, D') = \sum_{t \in D} \text{cost}_t(t^D, t^{D'}).$$

We use this cost function in the remainder of this section.

Unfortunately, it is NP-complete to find a repair with this cost function, even when only a fixed set of FDs or a fixed set of INDs is considered, and when the schema is predefined and fixed [Bohannon et al., 2005]. Consequently, any efficient automated method for data repairing is necessarily heuristic.

Theorem 3.11 Given an instance D of $\mathcal{R}$, a set Σ of CFDs and CINDs, the cost function cost() given above, and a natural number $k \geq 0$, it is NP-complete to decide whether there exists an instance D' such that $D' \models \Sigma$ and $\text{cost}(D, D') \leq k$. This problem is already NP-hard when Σ is a fixed set of FDs or a fixed set of INDs over a fixed schema $\mathcal{R}$.

Crux. An NP algorithm can be developed to check whether there exists an instance D' such that $D' \models \Sigma$ and $\text{cost}(D, D') \leq k$. Indeed, given D one can simply guess an instance D' and verify, in PTIME, whether it satisfies the desired conditions.

One can verify that the problem is NP-hard by reduction from the vertex cover problem, for FDs, and from the 3-dimensional matching problem, for INDs. The vertex cover problem and the 3-dimensional matching problem are known to be NP-complete (cf. [Garey and Johnson, 1979]). The reductions use a fixed schema and a fixed set of FDs or INDs. Hence, the data complexity of the data cleaning problem with value modification is NP-complete (see [Abiteboul et al., 1995; Vardi, 1982] or Chapter 6 for data complexity). □

3.3.2 REPAIRING VIOLATIONS OF CFDs AND CINDs

We next present a heuristic repairing algorithm for CFD and CINDs, denoted by GenRepair and outlined as Algorithm 3. It is a combination of the repairing algorithm for FDs and INDs [Bohannon et al., 2005] and the algorithm for CFDs [Cong et al., 2007]. In a nutshell, GenRepair takes as input a dirty instance D and a set Σ of CFDs and CINDs. It returns an instance D' such that $D' \models \Sigma$. Due to the heuristic nature of GenRepair, D' may not have the minimum cost, but the algorithm makes effort to avoid excessive modifications to D.

The algorithm works as follows. Initially, D' is set to be the dirty input instance D (line 1), and a set of unresolved tuples, denoted by Unresolved, is identified (line 2). More specifically, Unresolved collects all tuples in the current instance that need to be modified in order to satisfy Σ. These unresolved tuples are found by using SQL queries similar to those for detecting errors described in Section 3.2. Note that as long as Unresolved is nonempty, modifications to the instances will have to be made (the while loop lines 3–10). What tuples to modify and how to modify the tuples are decided by a procedure called PickNext (line 4). The procedure takes as input the current instance D', Unresolved and Σ, and it returns a set Δ of modifications to resolve some of the violations of Σ in one step.

As we will see shortly, modifications come in two forms: (a) value modifications (into a constant or null); and (b) identification of tuple-attribute pairs that should be equalized by grouping them together. After the modifications are made (line 5), D' is a normal database instance but carries some additional information about which tuple-attributes pairs should be equalized. Then, Unresolved is updated (line 6) by incrementally detecting unresolved tuples [Fan et al., 2008b]. This process continues until no further tuples need to be resolved.

3. CLEANING DATA WITH CONDITIONAL DEPENDENCIES

Algorithm 3 GenRepair.

Input: An instance D of $\mathcal{R}$, and a set Σ of CFDs and CINDs.
Output: An instance D' of $\mathcal{R}$ such that $D' \models \Sigma$.

1: $D' := D$;
2: initialize Unresolved sets from D' for the CFDs and CINDs in Σ;
3: **while** Unresolved $\neq \emptyset$ **do**
4:     $\Delta := \mathsf{PickNext}(D', \mathsf{Unresolved}, \Sigma, \mathsf{cost})$;
5:     update D' with Δ;
6:     update Unresolved;
7:     **if** Unresolved $= \emptyset$ **then**
8:        $(D', \mathsf{Unresolved}) := \mathsf{Impute}(D', \Delta)$;
9:     **end if**
10: **end while**
11: **return** D'.

At this point, a procedure $\mathsf{Impute}(D', \Delta)$ is called (lines 7–9) to enforce the identification of those tuple-attributes pairs as specified by Δ. In a nutshell, this procedure picks a value for each such group of pairs that need to be equalized, guided by the cost() function; it assigns the value to the group *if* no new unresolved tuples are introduced by the modification. If all identifications are enforced, $\mathsf{Impute}(D', \Delta)$ returns an instance D' such that $D' \models \Sigma$, and sets Unresolved to the empty set. The clean instance D' is then returned (line 11). If, however, some identification creates new unresolved tuples, then the procedure returns an updated instance D' (not necessarily satisfying Σ) and updates Unresolved accordingly. The process, starting from line 4, is then repeated on the updated D'.

Care is taken to minimize cost(D, D') by procedures PickNext and Impute. Procedure PickNext greedily selects the "best" modifications Δ to the current instance D', i.e., modifications that resolve some violations of Σ while incurring the smallest changes based on the metric cost(). To do this, it performs a 1-step lookahead to guide the repairing process through the search space of all possible instances that can be generated from D. Similarly, procedure Impute greedily selects the "best" value for each group of attribute values that need to be equalized, i.e., a value that introduces the least number of new unresolved tuples and at the same time, incurs the least cost based on the metric cost().

In the rest of the section, we describe how modifications Δ can be generated to eliminate unresolved (violating) tuples of Σ and in addition, how to guarantee that the repairing algorithm terminates. We will also give an example of how Impute selects values. We refer the reader to

[Bohannon et al., 2005] and [Cong et al., 2007] for more details about procedures Picknext and Impute and about other implementation issues of GenRepair.

Equivalence classes. Consider an instance I of a relation schema R. We classify tuple attributes in I into a set $\mathcal{E}$ of equivalence classes. Each equivalence class consists of pairs of the form (t^I, A), where t^I is a tuple in I and A is an attribute in t^I. An equivalence class, denoted by $\text{eq}(t^I, A)$, is associated with each tuple-attribute pair (t^I, A), for each tuple t^I in I and each attribute A in t^I. As will be seen shortly, when we eliminate unresolved tuples, we merge two equivalence classes $\text{eq}(t_1^I, A_1)$ and $\text{eq}(t_2^I, A_2)$ into one class if $t_1^I[A_1]$ and $t_2^I[A_2]$ have to be equalized in order to satisfy Σ. In other words, an equivalence class collects those tuple-attribute pairs that should be identified, and later on, all the pairs in the class will be assigned a *unique value*, denoted by $\text{targ}(E)$. *Modifications* Δ to I are defined on $\mathcal{E}$ by grouping tuples into classes and by assigning $\text{targ}(E)$, rather than on individual $t^I[A]$.

The motivation behind the use of $\mathcal{E}$ is to separate the decision of which attribute values need to be equivalent from the decision of exactly what value should be assigned to the eventually-produced equivalent class. Delaying value assignment allows poor local decisions to be improved. For example, consider a name that is sometimes spelled correctly and sometimes incorrectly. If the correct spelling is more frequent and/or has higher weight, then the accumulation of versions of the name in an equivalence class over time will allow the correct spelling to be chosen as the value of the class. Further, the equivalence class abstraction allows the users to check or modify a repair. The classes help expose the structure of data relationships, and if the users want to override a value chosen by the repairing algorithm, it can be accomplished on the *whole equivalence class in one step*.

For each equivalence class E, the value $\text{targ}(E)$ can be one of "_", a constant c, and null. Here, "_" indicates that $\text{targ}(E)$ is yet to be decided by assigning a value, null means that $\text{targ}(E)$ is fixed but uncertain due to conflicts, and c means that $\text{targ}(E)$ is fixed to be constant c. When $\mathcal{E}$ is in place, modifications are now implicitly defined by I and $\mathcal{E}$ together. Indeed, an instance $I' = \text{Upd}(I, \mathcal{E})$ can be obtained from I by replacing each $t^I \in I$ by a tuple $t^{I'} \in I'$ such that for all attributes $A \in \text{attr}(R)$, $t^{I'}[A] = t^I[A]$ if $\text{targ}(E_A) = \_$, and $t^{I'}[A] = \text{targ}(E_A)$ otherwise. Here, E_A denotes the equivalence class $\text{eq}(t, A)$. In other words, I' and I agree on all tuple-attribute pairs for which the target value is not yet fixed, and I' takes the target values for those pairs whose target value is already determined.

Unresolved tuples. To see how unresolved tuples are eliminated, we now revise the notion of $D' \models \varphi$ (Chapter 2) by incorporating equivalence classes, when φ is a CFD or a CIND.

CFDs. Let I be an instance of schema R, let $\mathcal{E}$ be the current set of equivalence classes, and let $\varphi = R(X \to A, t_p)$ be a CFD. Let $I' = \text{Upd}(I, \mathcal{E})$, obtained by applying the modifications specified by $\mathcal{E}$ to I. Given I and $\mathcal{E}$ we revise the semantics of CFDs as follows.

- When φ is a constant CFD. We say that a tuple t^I is *resolved relative to φ and $\mathcal{E}$* if $t^{I'} \models \varphi$ in I'. That is, the standard notion of satisfaction applies to the updated $t^{I'}$.

58   3. CLEANING DATA WITH CONDITIONAL DEPENDENCIES

- When φ is a variable CFD. We say that tuples s^I and t^I are *resolved relative to φ and $\mathcal{E}$* in I' if whenever $s^{I'}[X] = t^{I'}[X] \asymp t_p[X]$ then also $\text{eq}(s^{I'}, A) = \text{eq}(t^{I'}, A)$. That is, although $s^{I'}[A]$ and $t^{I'}[A]$ may still have distinct values in I', their eventual equality is already determined by $\mathcal{E}$ and thus they will eventually satisfy φ.

CINDs. Let $D = (I_1, I_2)$ be an instance of schemas (R_1, R_2), $\mathcal{E}^D$ be the current set of equivalence classes, and let $\phi = (R_1[X; X_p] \subseteq R_2[Y; Y_p], t_p)$ be a CIND. Let $D' = (I'_1, I'_2) = \text{Upd}(D, \mathcal{E}^D)$, obtained by applying modifications specified by $\mathcal{E}^D$ to D.

Given D and $\mathcal{E}^D$, we say that a tuple t^{I_1} is *resolved relative to ϕ and $\mathcal{E}^D$* in I'_1 if whenever $t^{I'_1}_1[X_p] = t_p[X_p]$, then there exists some tuple $s^{I'_2}_2$ such that $s^{I'_2}_2[Y_p] = t_p[Y_p]$ and furthermore, for each pair of corresponding attributes $X_i \in X$ and $Y_i \in Y$, $\text{eq}(t^{I'_1}_1, X_i) = \text{eq}(s^{I'_2}_2, Y_i)$. That is, while $t^{I'_1}_1$ and $s^{I'_2}_2$ may disagree on some of the corresponding attributes in X and Y, the equivalence classes $\text{eq}(t^{I'_1}_1, X_i)$ and $\text{eq}(s^{I'_2}_2, Y_i)$ are merged into one in $\mathcal{E}^D$, and hence, $t^{I'_1}_1(X)$ and $s^{I'_2}_2(Y)$ will eventually be equalized and will satisfy ϕ.

Let Σ be a set of CFDs and CINDs, and $\mathcal{E}^D$ be the current set of equivalence classes. An instance D' of (R_1, R_2) is *resolved relative to Σ and $\mathcal{E}^D$* if all (pairs of) tuples in D' are resolved for all dependencies in Σ. When $\mathcal{E}^D$ is clear from the context we say that D' is resolved for Σ. We use $\text{unres}(I, \mathcal{E}^I, \varphi)$ to denote the set of all tuples in I that are *unresolved* for φ, i.e., all those tuples that violate φ, for each $\varphi \in \Sigma$.

Termination. The definition of resolved instances indicates how equivalence classes should be modified in order to eliminate unresolved tuples. Care has to be taken here, however, when resolving conflicts by modifications. Indeed, allowing arbitrary changes to $\mathcal{E}$ may lead to cyclic modifications and non-termination of the repairing process.

Example 3.12 Consider the employee instance D_0 shown in Figure 3.1 and CFDs $\phi_1 = ([AC] \to [city], (131 \parallel \text{EDI}))$ and $\phi_2 = ([zip] \to [city], (\text{NJ } 07974 \parallel \text{MH}))$ on D_0. Initially, $\mathcal{E}^{D_0}$ contains equivalence classes $\{(t, A)\}$, one for each tuple $t \in D_0$ and attribute A in the employee schema. No modifications have been made and thus $\text{targ}(E) = \_$ for all $E \in \mathcal{E}^{D_0}$.

Consider tuple $t_5 \in D_0$. This tuple is unresolved for ϕ_1 but can be resolved by changing $t_5[city]$ from MH to EDI. That is, we update $\mathcal{E}^{D_0}$ by changing $\text{targ}(E)$ from $\_$ to the constant EDI, where $E = \text{eq}(t_5, city)$. Let D'_0 be the resulting instance and $\mathcal{E}^{D'_0}$ be the updated set of equivalence classes. Denote by $E^{D'_0}$ the class in $\mathcal{E}^{D'_0}$ corresponding to E. This change, however, introduces a new violation. Indeed, $t_5^{D'_0}$ is now unresolved for ϕ_2. To resolve this conflict, one might change $\text{targ}(E^{D'_0})$ from EDI back to MH. However, this brings us back to the original $\mathcal{E}^{D_0}$ and we are back from where we started.

Observe that there is a modification around this, e.g., changing $t_5^{D'_0}[zip]$ to some zip code distinct from NJ 07974 will yield a resolved tuple.   □

3.3. DATA REPAIRING

We avoid cyclic modifications as follows. Consider two instances, D and D', where D' is obtained from D by modifications specified by equivalence classes. We use $\mathcal{E}^D$ and $\mathcal{E}^{D'}$ to denote sets of equivalence classes in D and D', respectively. Note that by leveraging the tuple identifiers in the instances, we can easily relate equivalence classes in $\mathcal{E}^D$ to classes in $\mathcal{E}^{D'}$. We use $E^{D'} \in \mathcal{E}^{D'}$ to denote the equivalence class corresponding to $E^D \in \mathcal{E}^D$. We say that $\mathcal{E}^D$ is *more general than* $\mathcal{E}^{D'}$, denoted by $\mathcal{E}^D \preceq \mathcal{E}^{D'}$, if the following conditions hold:

1. for all $E^D \in \mathcal{E}^D$ there exists a class $E^{D'} \in \mathcal{E}^{D'}$ such that $E^D \subseteq E^{D'}$;
2. if $\mathrm{target}(E^D)$ is a constant, then either $\mathrm{target}(E^{D'}) = \mathrm{target}(E^D)$ or $\mathrm{target}(E^{D'})$ is null; and
3. if $\mathrm{target}(E^D)$ is null then $\mathrm{target}(E^{D'}) = $ null.

It is readily verified that $\preceq$ defines a partial order on sets of equivalence classes. We say that $\mathcal{E}^D$ is *strictly more general than* $\mathcal{E}^{D'}$, denoted by $\mathcal{E}^D \prec \mathcal{E}^{D'}$ if $\mathcal{E}^D \preceq \mathcal{E}^{D'}$ but $\mathcal{E}^D \neq \mathcal{E}^{D'}$. In this case, we also say that $\mathcal{E}^{D'}$ is *strictly more specific* than $\mathcal{E}^D$.

To guarantee non-cyclic modifications and thus a terminating repairing process, we require that whenever $\mathcal{E}^D$ is changed to $\mathcal{E}^{D'}$, it is necessary that $\mathcal{E}^D \prec \mathcal{E}^{D'}$. That is, each modification will move to a strictly more specific set of equivalence classes: by merging two classes with target values "_", instantiating the target value "_" of a class with a constant, or by resolving conflicts with null. Note that if $\mathrm{target}(E^D)$ is a constant, $\mathrm{target}(E^{D'})$ may not be a distinct constant. One can show that there is an upper bound on possible sets of equivalence classes. We can thus conclude that any sequence of modifications will terminate.

Given $\mathcal{E}$ we next describe how $\mathcal{E}'$ is derived, for resolving CFDs and CINDs.

Eliminating unresolved tuples for CFDs. Consider an instance I_0 of a relation schema R and a CFD $\varphi = R(X \to A, t_p)$. Suppose that $\mathcal{E}^I$ is the current set of equivalence classes that we have got so far, and $I = \mathrm{Upd}(I_0, \mathcal{E}^I)$, i.e., I is obtained from I_0 by applying modifications specified in $\mathcal{E}^I$. Assume that $\mathrm{unres}(I, \mathcal{E}^I, \varphi)$ is non-empty, i.e., there are tuples in I that need to be resolved. Consider a set $S^I \subseteq \mathrm{unres}(I, \mathcal{E}^I, \varphi)$. We eliminate unresolved tuples in S^I by changing $\mathcal{E}^I$ to $\mathcal{E}^{I'}$, and thus obtain $I' = \mathrm{Upd}(I, \mathcal{E}^{I'})$ such that $S^{I'} \not\subseteq \mathrm{unres}(I', \mathcal{E}^{I'}, \varphi)$.

To do this, we distinguish two cases of φ: when φ is a constant CFD and when φ is a variable CFD. Assume first that φ is a constant CFD. Let $E^I_{X_i} = \mathrm{eq}(t^I, X_i)$ for $X_i \in X$ and let $E^I_A = \mathrm{eq}(t^I, A)$. Consider the following cases for $S = \{t^I\} \subseteq \mathrm{unres}(I, \mathcal{E}^I, \varphi)$.

(1) If $\mathrm{targ}(E^I_A) = \_$, we set $\mathrm{targ}(E^{I'}_A) := t_p[A]$ to satisfy the constant pattern of φ.

(2) If $\mathrm{targ}(E^I_A)$ is a constant, then we cannot enforce $t_p[A]$ as in case (1). Indeed, this would violate condition 2 for extending equivalence classes given above. Instead, we modify t^I such that the LHS of φ is not satisfied and thus φ vacuously holds, as follows.

  - If for all $X_i \in X$, $\mathrm{targ}(E^I_{X_i})$ is already determined, then we change $\mathrm{targ}(E^{I'}_{X_i}) := $ null, where X_i is such that $w(t^I, X_i)$ has the smallest weight. By the semantics of CFDs in the presence of null values given in Section 2.1.1, $t^{I'}$ is resolved.
  - Otherwise, we change $\mathrm{targ}(E^{I'}_{X_i})$ to a constant that is distinct from $t_p[X_i]$ and such that the change incurs a minimal increase in the cost based on $\mathrm{cost}()$.

60 3. CLEANING DATA WITH CONDITIONAL DEPENDENCIES

(3) If $\text{targ}(E_A^I)$ is null, we resolve tuple t^I by letting $\text{targ}(E_{X_i}^{I'}) := $ null for some attribute X_i in the LHS of φ, in the same way as in case (2) above.

When φ is a variable CFD, let S be the set of all tuples in $\text{unres}(I, \mathcal{E}^I, \varphi)$ that all agree on their X-attributes. Let s^I and t^I be tuples in S, which violate φ. Let $E_{X_i}^I = \text{eq}(t^I, X_i)$ for $X_i \in X$, and $E_A^I = \text{eq}(t^I, A)$. Similarly, let $F_{X_i}^I = \text{eq}(s^I, X_i)$ for $X_i \in X$, and $F_A^I = \text{eq}(s^I, A)$. We resolve the inconsistencies between s^I and t^I as follows.

(1) If neither $\text{targ}(E_A^I)$ nor $\text{targ}(F_A^I)$ is null, and at least one of them is "_", then we can merge E_A^I and F_A^I into *a single equivalence class* $E_A^{I'}$ in $\mathcal{E}^{I'}$. Moreover,

- if both $\text{targ}(E_A^I)$ and $\text{targ}(F_A^I)$ are "_", we will set the target value of $E_A^{I'}$ to a constant c *later on*, where c is selected such that it incurs a minimal cost; and
- if one of the target values of $\text{targ}(E_A^I)$ and $\text{targ}(F_A^I)$ is already determined to be a constant c, we let the target value of $E_A^{I'}$ take the same constant c.

(2) If $\text{targ}(E_A^I)$ and $\text{targ}(F_A^I)$ are distinct constants c and c', respectively, then the violation cannot be resolved by changing the values of the RHS attributes. In this case, we modify some LHS attribute of t^I, along the same lines as case (2) for constant CFDs.

(3) If $\text{targ}(E_A^I) = $ null or $\text{targ}(F_A^I)$ is null, then by the semantics of CFDs in the presence of null (Section 2.1.1), s^I and t^I are not in $\text{unres}(I, \mathcal{E}^I, \varphi)$, and nothing needs to be done.

Clearly, these steps reduce the number of tuples that are part of unresolved pairs in S. We process all pairs in S as described above and update S accordingly, until no further unresolved tuples remain in S. The set $\mathcal{E}^{I'}$ is obtained from $\mathcal{E}^I$ in this way.

The following proposition can be readily verified (see [Cong et al., 2007] for a proof).

Proposition 3.13 *Consider an instance I_0 of R and a CFD φ. Let $\mathcal{E}^I$ be the current set of equivalence classes, and $I = \text{Upd}(I_0, \mathcal{E}^I)$. Let $S \subseteq \text{unres}(I, \mathcal{E}^I, \varphi)$ and let $\mathcal{E}^{I'}$ be the extension of $\mathcal{E}^I$ by resolving tuples in S as described above, and $I' = \text{Upd}(I, \mathcal{E}^{I'})$. Then (1) $\mathcal{E}^I \prec \mathcal{E}^{I'}$ and (2) all tuples in S are eliminated from $\text{unres}(I', \mathcal{E}^{I'}, \varphi)$.* □

That is, in the instance $I' = \text{Upd}(I, \mathcal{E}^{I'})$, the tuples in S are no longer unresolved for the CFD φ and furthermore, $\mathcal{E}^{I'}$ is strictly more specific than $\mathcal{E}^I$. In light of this, repair processes composed of sequences of repair operations as above will terminate.

Example 3.14 We now revisit Example 3.10. In Figure 3.7, we show the instance D_0 together with a set of equivalence classes, each represented by a colored rectangle. Here, a yellow rectangle indicates that the target value is yet to be determined, whereas the green ones have a fixed target value. We reorder the tuples in the figure for ease of exposition. Let $\mathcal{E}$ be the initial set of equivalence classes when no modifications are made, i.e., all target values are "_". Consider the variable CFD $\varphi_1 = ([\text{CC}, \text{zip}] \to [\text{street}], (44, \_ \parallel \_))$, and tuples t_1 and t_2 in D_0 that are unresolved relative to φ_1.

3.3. DATA REPAIRING 61

	FN	LN	CC	AC	phn	street	city	zip	salary	status
t_1:	Mike	Clark	44	131	1234567	Mayfield	EDI	EH4 8LE	60k	single
t_2:	Rick	Stark	44	131	3456789	Crichton	EDI	EH4 8LE	96k	married
t_6:	Mary	Luth	44	131	3456789	Mayfield	EDI	EH4 1DT	80k	married
t_3:	Joe	Brady	01	908	4567890	Main Rd	MH	NJ 07974	90k	married
t_4:	Mary	Smith	01	908	7966899	Mtn Ave	MH	NJ 07974	50k	single
t_5:	Mary	Luth	01	131	7966899	Mtn Ave	MH	NJ 07974	50k	married

Figure 3.7: A resolved employee instance.

Since eq(t_1, street) = {(t_1, street)} and eq(t_2, street) = {(t_2, street)}, both with _ as the target value, we can simply merge these two classes into a single one, {(t_1, street), (t_2, street)}. Let $\mathcal{E}_1$ be the set of equivalence classes obtained from $\mathcal{E}$ after the merge. Figure 3.7 reflects this change by the yellow rectangle covering the equivalence classes eq(t_1, street) and eq(t_2, street). Let $D_0^1 = \mathsf{Upd}(D_0, \mathcal{E}_1)$.

Consider next the constant CFD ([CC, AC, phn] → [city], (44, 131, _ || EDI)), and tuple $t_6^{D_0^1}$ that is unresolved for this CFD. Then the target value of eq($t_6^{D_0^1}$, city) is updated from _ to EDI, to satisfy the CFD. Let $\mathcal{E}_2$ be obtained from $\mathcal{E}_1$ by incorporating the change. In Figure 3.7 this is shown by the green rectangle with target value EDI. Let $D_0^2 = \mathsf{Upd}(D_0^1, \mathcal{E}_2)$.

Now consider the variable CFD ([CC, AC, phn] → [street], (44, 131, _ || _)) and unresolved tuples $t_2^{D_0^2}$ and $t_6^{D_0^2}$. To resolve these, we can merge equivalence classes eq(t_2, street) = {(t_1, street), (t_2, street)} and eq(t_6, street) = {(t_6, street)}. Since the target values of these classes are undetermined (i.e., _), there is no conflict here. Let $\mathcal{E}_3$ be obtained from $\mathcal{E}_2$ after the merge. Figure 3.7 shows a yellow rectangle that covers the values of attribute street in t_1, t_2, and t_6, still with an undetermined target value. Let $D_0^3 = \mathsf{Upd}(D_0^2, \mathcal{E}_3)$.

Consider the constant CFD ([CC, AC, phn] → [street], (01, 908, _ || MH)) and an unresolved tuple $t_3^{D_0^2}$ for this CFD. Tuple $t_3^{D_0^2}$ is resolved by updating the target value of eq($t_3^{D_0^3}$, city) from _ to MH. Let $\mathcal{E}_4$ be obtained from $\mathcal{E}_3$ by incorporating the change. In Figure 3.7 this is shown by the green rectangle with target value MH. Let $D_0^4 = \mathsf{Upd}(D_0, \mathcal{E}_4)$.

Next consider the variable CFD ([CC, AC, phn] → [zip], (44, 131, _ || _)). We now have unresolved tuples $t_2^{D_0^4}$ and $t_6^{D_0^4}$ for this CFD. As before, we merge eq($t_2^{D_0^4}$, zip) and eq($t_6^{D_0^4}$, zip) into a single equivalence class with a yet to be determined target value (i.e., _). Let $\mathcal{E}_5$ be obtained from $\mathcal{E}_4$ by incorporating the change and let $D_0^5 = \mathsf{Upd}(D_0^4, \mathcal{E}_5)$.

Finally, consider the variable CFD ([CC, AC] → [city], (_, _ || _)). We have unresolved tuples $t_1^{D_0^5}$, $t_2^{D_0^5}$ and $t_6^{D_0^5}$ for this CFD, as well as $t_3^{D_0^5}$ and $t_4^{D_0^5}$. As before, we merge their equivalence classes and as a result, obtain two classes {($t_1^{D_0^5}$, city), ($t_2^{D_0^5}$, city), ($t_6^{D_0^5}$, city)} and {($t_3^{D_0^5}$, city), ($t_4^{D_0^5}$, city)}. In contrast to the previous cases, while the target values of eq($t_1^{D_0^5}$, city) and eq($t_2^{D_0^5}$, city) are undetermined, the target value of eq($t_6^{D_0^5}$, city) is EDI. As a consequence, the target value of

3. CLEANING DATA WITH CONDITIONAL DEPENDENCIES

	FN	LN	type	number
s_1:	Joe	Brady	Master Card	111111111
s_2:	Mary	Smiths	Visa	222222222

Figure 3.8: A creditcard instance C_0.

$\{(t_1^{D_0^5}, \text{city}), (t_2^{D_0^5}, \text{city}), (t_6^{D_0^5}, \text{city})\}$ is set to EDI. Similarly for $\{(t_3^{D_0^5}, \text{city}), (t_4^{D_0^5}, \text{city})\}$ that inherits the target value MH from eq$(t_3^{D_0^5}, \text{city})$. Let $\mathcal{E}_6$ be obtained from $\mathcal{E}_5$ by incorporating the change and let $D_0^6 = \text{Upd}(D_0^5, \mathcal{E}_6)$. It is readily verified that D_0^6 is resolved relative to $\{\varphi_1, \varphi_2, \varphi_3\}$ and $\mathcal{E}_6$. Figure 3.7 shows D_0^6 together with $\mathcal{E}_6$. Note that many equivalence classes still have an undetermined target value at this stage. We will describe in Example 3.17 how target values are selected for the remaining classes.

Along the same lines, one can resolve the violating tuples described in Example 3.12, and find that no cyclic modifications will be encountered. □

Eliminating unresolved tuples for CINDs. We now consider how to eliminate tuples that are unresolved for CINDs. Let $D_0 = (I_1^0, I_2^0)$ be an instance of schemas (R_1, R_2), $\mathcal{E}^D$ be the current set of equivalence classes, and $\phi = (R_1[X; X_p] \subseteq R_2[Y; Y_p], t_p)$ be a CIND. Let $D = (I_1, I_2) = \text{Upd}(D_0, \mathcal{E}^D)$, and $S = \{t^D\} \subseteq \text{unres}(D, \mathcal{E}^D, \Sigma)$. We resolve t^D by extending $\mathcal{E}^D$ to $\mathcal{E}^{D'}$, and thus get $D' = \text{Upd}(D, \mathcal{E}^{D'})$, as follows.

- Suppose that there exists a tuple $s^D \in I_2$ such that for each pair of corresponding attributes $X_i \in X$ and $Y_i \in Y$, we can merge $E_{X_i}^D$ with $E_{Y_i}^D$ and in addition, we set $\text{targ}(E_{Y_i}^{D'})$ to be $t_p[Y_i]$ for all $Y_i \in Y_p$ such that (a) no conflicts are introduced by the merge (as described in case (2) for constant CFDs above), and (b) the cost of the merge is below a predefined threshold. Then $\mathcal{E}^{D'}$ is obtained from $\mathcal{E}^D$ by performing these modifications. Here, $E_{X_i}^D = \text{eq}(t^D, X_i)$ for $X_i \in X \cup X_p$, and $E_{Y_i}^D = \text{eq}(s^D, Y_i)$ for $Y_i \in Y \cup Y_p$. The cost of the merging is measured by $\text{cost}(D, D')$.

- If no such tuple s^D exists, or it is too costly to make these modifications, we add a *new* tuple $s^{D'}$ to I_2 such that (a) for each pair of corresponding attributes $X_i \in X$ and $Y_i \in Y$, $s^{D'}[Y_i] := t^D[X_i]$ and $(s^{D'}, Y_i)$ is added to eq(t^D, X_i); (b) $s^{D'}[Y_p] := t_p[Y_p]$, and for each $Y_i \in Y_p$, we create the equivalence class $\{(s^{D'}, Y_i)\}$ with $\text{targ}(E_{Y_i}^{D'}) = t_p[Y_i]$; and moreover, (c) for any other attribute B of $s^{D'}$, $s^{D'}[B] := \text{null}$ and we create an equivalence class $\{(s^{D'}, B)\}$ with $\text{targ}(E_B^{D'}) = \text{null}$.

The set $\mathcal{E}^{D'}$ is obtained from $\mathcal{E}^D$ in this way.

Example 3.15 Consider the creditcard instance C_0 shown in Figure 3.8 and CIND $\phi = ((\text{employee}(\text{FN}, \text{LN}; \text{CC}) \subseteq \text{creditcard}(\text{FN}, \text{LN}; \text{nil})), t_p)$ with $t_p = (01 \parallel)$. This CIND requires each U.S. employee to have a credit card. Consider the employee instance D_0 given in Figure 3.1. Then

3.3. DATA REPAIRING

there are three unresolved tuples for the CIND ϕ: tuples t_3, t_4, and t_5 in D_0. Let $\mathcal{E}_e$ denote the set of equivalence classes for D_0 computed in Example 3.14. Let $\mathcal{E}_c$ be the set of initial equivalence classes for C_0 in which no target values are set yet (i.e., "_"). These are indicated by yellow rectangles in Figure 3.8.

To resolve t_3, one can pick s_1 from C_0, merge the equivalence classes eq(t_3, FN) and eq(s_1, FN) into one, and also merge eq(t_3, LN) and eq(s_1, LN). Both resulting classes have an undetermined target value. This is illustrated in Figure 3.9 by the yellow rectangles across the two instances. The reason that s_1 is selected is because if we were to assign the target values, Joe and Brady, for these classes, respectively, the changes would incur a small cost by the metric cost(). The target values will be set at a later stage, however.

To resolve t_4, one could pick s_2 as the corresponding tuple in C_0. That is, eq(t_4, FN) and eq(s_2, FN) are merged and the target value is yet to be determined. Similarly, eq(t_4, LN) and eq(s_2, LN) are merged as shown in Figure 3.9. The selection of s_2 is based on the following: there are target values, Mary and Smith, respectively, that would incur a cost of changes below a predefined threshold. Indeed, Smith and Smiths only differ in one character and hence, the cost incurred would not increase substantially based on cost().

In contrast, to match t_5 with any of tuples s_1 and s_2 in C_0 would incur a large cost above the threshold. In this case, it is better to insert a new tuple $s_3 = $ (Mary, Luth, null, null) to C_0, and merge eq(t_5, FN) and eq(s_3, FN) into a single equivalence class, which takes "_" as its target value; similarly for the LN attribute. Here, eq(s_3, type) = {(s_3, type)} and eq(s_3, number) = {(s_3, number)}, both with the target value set to null.

These changes to $\mathcal{E}_c$ ensure that the instances obtained are resolved for the CIND ϕ. □

Similar to the CFD case, an unresolved tuple for a CIND can be eliminated and a more specific set of equivalence classes is computed, as stated below.

Proposition 3.16 *Consider an instance $D_0 = (I_1, I_2)$ of schemas $\mathcal{R} = (R_1, R_2)$ and a CIND ϕ defined on $\mathcal{R}$. Let $\mathcal{E}^D$ be a set of equivalence classes for D_0, and $D = \mathsf{Upd}(D_0, \mathcal{E}^D)$. Let $S = \{t^D\} \subseteq \mathsf{unres}(D, \mathcal{E}^D, \phi)$, $\mathcal{E}^{D'}$ be the extension of $\mathcal{E}^D$ by resolving t^D as described above, and $D' = \mathsf{Upd}(D, \mathcal{E}^{D'})$. Then (1) $\mathcal{E}^D \prec \mathcal{E}^{D'}$ and (2) $t^{D'} \notin \mathsf{unres}(D', \mathcal{E}^{D'}, \phi)$.* □

Turning a resolved instance into a repair. Given an instance D_0 of schema $\mathcal{R}$ and a set Σ of CFDs and CINDs defined on $\mathcal{R}$, we know how to obtain a set of equivalence classes $\mathcal{E}^D$ such that $D = \mathsf{Upd}(D_0, \mathcal{E}^D)$ is resolved relative to Σ and $\mathcal{E}^D$. As shown in Examples 3.14 and 3.15, equivalence classes in $\mathcal{E}^D$ may have undetermined target values at this stage. As remarked earlier, algorithm GenRepair invokes a procedure Impute to select target values as soon as a resolved instance is obtained. This is illustrated by the following example.

Example 3.17 Consider the resolved instances shown in Figures 3.7 and 3.9. Only four equivalence classes (shown in green) have a fixed target value so far. At this point, procedure Impute inspects each

64 3. CLEANING DATA WITH CONDITIONAL DEPENDENCIES

	FN	LN	CC
t_1:	Mike	Clark	44
t_2:	Rick	Stark	44
t_6:	Mary	Luth	44

	FN	LN	type	number
s_1:	Joe	Brady	Master Card	111111111
s_2:	Mary	Smiths	Visa	222222222
s_3:	Mary	Luth	null	null

	FN	LN	CC
t_3:	Joe	Brady	01
t_4:	Mary	Smith	01
t_5:	Mary	Luth	01

Figure 3.9: A resolved (employee, creditcard) instance.

equivalence class with undetermined target value, and selects the "best" target value as explained earlier. For each equivalence class, the target value is taken from the class itself to preserve the information of the original data, unless it is necessary to use null. As an example, consider three equivalence classes: $E_1 = \{(t_1, \text{street}), (t_2, \text{street}), (t_6, \text{street})\}$, $E_2 = \{(t_2, \text{zip}), (t_6, \text{zip})\}$ and $E_3 = \{(t_4, \text{LN}), (s_2, \text{LN})\}$. For E_1, the best target value is Mayfield since (i) it introduces no new unresolved tuples and (ii) it only requires $t_2[\text{street}]$ to be changed and hence incurs a small cost. For E_2 one can pick either EH4 1DT or EH4 8LE. Finally, for E_3 both Smith and Smiths are possible target values. Assuming that $w(t_4, \text{LN})$ has a higher confidence than $w(s_2, \text{LN})$, then Smith will be selected as it incurs the least increase in the cost. In either case, a database is obtained that satisfies the dependencies $\varphi_1, \varphi_2, \varphi_3$ and ϕ. □

Properties of algorithm GenRepair. Observe the following.

(1) From Propositions 3.13 and 3.16 it follows that GenRepair terminates and returns a clean instance that satisfies the given set Σ of CFDs and CINDs. Indeed, in each step of the algorithm at least one unresolved tuple is eliminated and a strictly more specific set of equivalence classes is generated, which specifies the required modifications. Furthermore, in case new unresolved tuples are created during this process by Impute, GenRepair returns a new resolved instance, taking the values given by Impute into account. For CINDs, in particular, each newly created tuple is constructed using constants from the original database. Hence, there is a bound on the number of possible distinct instances generated by GenRepair. Taken together, these show that GenRepair always terminates. Further, since the algorithm keeps eliminating unresolved tuples until no more such tuples are left, and since undetermined target values are eventually set, it necessarily returns a clean instance.

(2) From the operations for resolving CFD and CIND violations given above, we can see that each step of algorithm GenRepair makes a change that incurs a minimum cost, by a one-step lookahead. In other words, each change is "locally optimal" based on the metric cost().

BIBLIOGRAPHIC NOTES

Discovery. The discovery problem for FDs has been studied extensively for database design, data archiving, OLAP, and data mining [Calders et al., 2003; Flach and Savnik, 1999; Huhtala et al., 1999; Ilyas et al., 2004; King and Legendre, 2003; Lopes et al., 2000; Mannila and Räihä, 1987, 1992; Novelli and Cicchetti, 2001; Wyss et al., 2001]. It was first investigated by Mannila and Räihä [1987], who showed that the problem is inherently exponential in the size of the schema. One of the best-known methods for FD discovery is TANE [Huhtala et al., 1999], on which CTANE is built. The algorithms of Lopes et al. [2000], Novelli and Cicchetti [2001], Calders et al. [2003] and King and Legendre [2003] follow a similar level-wise approach. As remarked earlier, TANE and CTANE are rather sensitive to the schema size.

An alternative FD discovery method, referred to as FastFD, explores the connection between FD discovery and the problem of finding minimal covers of hypergraphs, and employs a depth-first strategy to search minimal covers [Wyss et al., 2001]. This algorithm scales better than TANE when the schema is large, but is more sensitive to the size of sample data. Fan et al. [2011b] proposed an algorithm that extends FastFD to discover CFDs. An alternative bottom-up approach based on techniques for learning general logical descriptions in a hypotheses space was proposed by Flach and Savnik [1999]. As shown by Huhtala et al. [1999], TANE outperforms the algorithm of Flach and Savnik [1999]. An overview of various FD discovery methods can be found in [Liu et al., 2012].

Algorithm CFDMiner for constant CFDs and algorithm CTANE for general CFDs are taken from [Fan et al., 2011b]. Constant CFD discovery is closely related to (non-redundant) association rule mining [Agrawal and Srikant, 1994; Zaki, 2004]. More precisely, constant CFDs coincide with association rules that have 100% confidence and have a single attribute in their consequent. Non-redundant association rules, however, do not precisely correspond to non-redundant constant CFDs. Indeed, non-redundancy is only defined for association rules with the same support. In contrast, testing for non-redundant CFDs requires the comparison of constant CFDs with possibly different supports. The connection between constant CFDs and closed and free itemsets has been further explored by Medina and Nourine [2009]. In addition, Li et al. [2012a] provided additional pruning methods for CFDMiner.

Variations of the general CFD discovery methods have been proposed with measures different from support and confidence [Chiang and Miller, 2008; Yeh and Puri, Paper 8, 2010, 2010; Yeh et al., 2011]. An algorithm for discovering CFDs was developed by Chiang and Miller [2008], which aims to find both traditional FDs and CFDs, the same as what CTANE does. Several quality measures for discovered CFDs were also proposed there, including support (see Section 3.1), conviction and χ^2-test. The minimality of discovered CFDs, however, was not fully addressed by Chiang and Miller [2008]. Aqel et al. [2012] modified CTANE such that the number of discovered CFDs is reduced. In that work, the inference rules $\mathfrak{I}_C$, presented in Chapter 2, are used to avoid the discovery of implied CFDs. It should be mentioned that the notion of frequent CFDs used here is quite different from the notion of approximate FDs [Huhtala et al., 1999]. An approximate FD φ on a relation I is an FD that "almost" holds on I, i.e., there exists a subset $I' \subseteq I$ such that $I' \models \varphi$ and the error $|I \setminus I'|/|I|$ is less than a predefined bound. It is thus not necessary that $I \models \varphi$, in contrast to frequent FDs. A CFD discovery method on XML data was presented by Vo et al. [2011].

Although the discovery of INDs has received considerable attention, to our knowledge, no efficient method for discovering CINDs has been devised. We refer to [Liu et al., 2012] for a survey of existing IND discovering algorithms. A more general approach, encompassing the discovery of both CFDs and CINDs, was proposed by Goethals et al. [2008, 2010]. In that work, association rules of the form $Q_1 \Rightarrow Q_2$ are generated, where Q_1, Q_2 are simple conjunctive queries and Q_2 is contained in Q_1. Since CFDs and CINDs can be viewed as such association rules, the algorithm of Goethals et al. [2008, 2010] may be used to mine general CFDs and CINDs. However, this approach does not take into account non-redundancy.

A related, but different, discovery problem was considered by Cormode et al. [2009] and by Golab et al. [2008, 2011]. They proposed algorithms to compute a close-to-optimal tableau for a CFD when the embedded FD is given. The closeness of the discovered tableau to the optimal tableau is controlled by two parameters, namely, the support and the confidence. In view of the intractability of this problem [Golab et al., 2008], they provided a greedy approximation algorithm and an efficient heuristic method to discover optimal tableaux.

Detection. The SQL-based detection method for CFD violations presented in this chapter is taken from [Fan et al., 2008b]. That paper also developed SQL-based incremental methods for checking CFDs in response to changes to the database. In the incremental setting, given a set ΔI of insertions and deletions to the instance I, the detection methods attempt to solely access those tuples in I that are "affected" by updates ΔI, i.e., the tuples that either become violations of the CFDs, or were violations in I but are no longer violations after updates ΔI are inflicted to I. When adopting the traditional complexity measure in terms of the input size (the size of entire I and the size of CFDs), these methods have the same worst-case performance as the batch detection methods that identify violations in the updated database starting from scratch (see Section 3.2). Nevertheless, their expected performance is likely to be smaller since the operations are confined to the "affected area", i.e., those tuples affected by ΔI, which tend to be small when the updates ΔI are small, as commonly found in practice. This has been experimentally verified by Fan et al. [2008b].

The detection methods of Fan et al. [2008b] have been extended in two directions: Bravo et al. [2008] and Chen et al. [2009b] generalized these methods to accommodate extended CFDs, namely, eCFDs and CFDs with built-in predicates, respectively. Fan et al. [2010a, 2012d] studied batch and incremental detection methods for CFDs when an instance I is distributed, i.e., when I is partitioned either horizontally or vertically, and is distributed to different sites. The challenge in the distributed setting is to minimize the amount of tuples that need to be communicated between the different sites in order to detect violations of the CFDs. It has been shown that it is NP-complete to decide whether all violations of a set of CFDs in a distributed database can be detected when the amount of data shipped between different sites is bounded by a given constant [Fan et al., 2010a]. Similarly, the incremental error detection problem with minimum data shipment is also NP-complete [Fan et al., 2012d]. In another direction, error detection methods for CINDs, even in the presence of built-in predicates, have been reported by Chen et al. [2009b].

Repairing. Three approaches have been put forward for handling inconsistent data: data repairing, consistent query answering, and finding condensed representations of all repairs. The first two methods were formally introduced by Arenas et al. [1999], and the third one was studied by Arenas et al. [2003a], Greco et al. [2003a], and Wijsen [2005]. Most work on these topics has focused on traditional FDs, INDs, full dependencies, and denial constraints. The prior work typically did not consider dependencies with pattern tuples, and adopted tuple deletions and/or insertions for repairing rather than value modifications. We refer the reader to [Bertossi, 2011] for a survey on different repair models and dependencies studied in that context. We remark that consistent query answering is quite different from data repairing. Indeed, the former is to find an answer to a query in every possible repair, while the latter asks for a single "best" repair that is independent of any queries users may ask.

The repairing method (GenRepair) presented in Section 3.3 is a combination of the repairing algorithm for FDs and INDs [Bohannon et al., 2005] and the algorithm for CFDs [Cong et al., 2007]. Bohannon et al. [2005] introduced the notion of equivalence classes to avoid cyclic modifications, established the intractability of the repairing problem for FDs and INDs (Theorem 3.11), and developed a variety of greedy methods for procedure PickNext. Cong et al. [2007] extended these methods to handle CFDs. In addition, they also considered the *incremental data repairing problem*, to efficiently find changes to generated repairs in response to database updates defined as a sequence of tuple deletions and insertions. It was shown there that the incremental repairing problem is also intractable. A statistical sampling method to improve the accuracy of the generated repairs was also given by Cong et al. [2007]. It proposed to interact with the users by providing a sample of the generated repair for the users to inspect and edit. When sufficient corrections to the sample repair are given by the user, the accuracy rate of the repairs are guaranteed to be above a predefined bound with a high confidence. This is achieved by a stratified sampling method and by leveraging Chernoff bounds (see e.g., [Alon and Spencer, 1992] for details about probabilistic methods). As remarked earlier, all algorithms developed in this line of work are heuristic.

Approximation algorithms for data repairing have been studied for FDs and CFDs by Kolahi and Lakshmanan [2010, 2009], using a cost function simpler than cost() given in this chapter. A Minimum Description Length (MDL) approach was proposed by Chiang and Miller [2011], to repair *both* data and constraints (FDs). Conditions on FDs were imposed by Ginsburg and Spanier [1985] to ensure that a partially clean instance can be completed, i.e., extended to be a "full" clean instance. No algorithms for completing instances were provided, however. An FD repairing method was presented by Greco and Molinaro [2008], which resolves FD violations using a method similar to GenRepair. It returns a repair as a v-table, i.e., an instance that contains labeled variables (see Chapter 6 for v-tables). A valuation of these variables generates a normal instance that satisfies the FDs. In contrast to GenRepair, no algorithm was provided there for finding good valuations. Argumentation-based CFD repairing methods were studied by Santos et al. [2010] and Galhardas et al. [2011].

We have seen that repairs are not necessarily unique. To cope with this, Beskales et al. [2010] studied a sample of possible repairs for FDs. In Chapter 7 we will present an alternative method that finds a unique repair and certain fixes whenever possible [Fan et al., 2012c]. In that chapter, we will also introduce methods to improve the accuracy and confidence of the generated repairs by integrating data repairing and record matching.

The repairing framework shown in Figure 3.6 leverages user feedback, similar to the work of Chen et al. [2010], Raman and Hellerstein [2001], Yakout et al. [2010b, 2011], and Galhardas et al. [2000]. AJAX [Galhardas et al., 2000] is based on a declarative language for writing data cleaning programs, in SQL enriched with a set of specific primitives. It allows the users to interact with a running data cleaning program to handle exceptions and to inspect intermediate results. Potter's Wheel [Raman and Hellerstein, 2001] supports interactive data transformations, based on iterative user feedback on example data. USHER [Chen et al., 2010] repairs data by asking users online about erroneous values, identified by a probabilistic method. In the Guided Data Repair (GDR) framework [Yakout et al., 2010a,b, 2011], a CFD-based repairing facility is offered to solicit user feedback on updates for improving consistency. Semandaq [Fan et al., 2008a] is a system based on the algorithms given in this chapter. CerFix [Fan et al., 2011d] is a prototype system for finding unique repairs, based on the methods to be presented in Chapter 7.

Automated repairing methods have been extensively studied for census data [Herzog et al., 2009; Winkler, 2004]. Algorithms for categorical data have been proposed by Fellegi and Holt [1976], Garfinkel et al. [1986] and Winkler [1997]. As remarked earlier, edits are used to specify the consistency of data and to localize errors (see Bibliographic Notes in Chapter 2 for the definition of edits). Once errors are localized, a data imputation process repairs those errors. We refer to [Herzog et al., 2009] for an overview of different imputation methods. Logical approaches to census data repairing were proposed by Bruni and Sassano [2001] and Boskovitz et al. [2003], and disjunctive logic programming methods were used to clean census data by Franconi et al. [2001]. These methods, however, repair a single record at a time and assume no interaction between the records. Furthermore, the size of census data is typically smaller than the size of data residing in many real-life databases.

Algorithm GenRepair repairs database instances, i.e., collections of tuples. An alternative method is to fix individual tuples at the point of entry, known as *data monitoring*, to correct tuples before they are used [Sauter et al., 2007]. This will be studied in Chapter 7.

Finally, a related question concerns repair checking, which is to decide whether a *given* instance is a repair of an input instance. Complexity results for this problem were established by Afrati and Kolaitis [2009] for various notions of repairs and integrity constraints. Their decision algorithms, however, do not necessarily lead to repairing algorithms.

CHAPTER 4

Data Deduplication

Data deduplication is the problem of identifying tuples from one or more relations that refer to the same real-world entity. It is also known as record matching, record linkage, entity resolution, instance identification, duplicate detection, duplicate identification, merge-purge, database hardening, name matching, coreference resolution, identity uncertainty, and object identification. It is a longstanding issue that has been studied for decades, and is perhaps the most extensively studied data quality problem. The need for investigating data deduplication cannot be overstated: it is important in data quality management, data integration, fraud detection, Web search quality, MDM, CRM and ERP, among other things.

In this chapter, we first give an overview of data deduplication techniques (Section 4.1). We then focus on a dependency-based approach, which, as will be seen in Chapter 7, allows us to capture the interaction between data deduplication and other aspects of data quality in a uniform logical framework. We introduce a new form of dependency, referred to as matching dependencies, for data deduplication (Section 4.2). In contrast to (conditional) dependencies we have seen earlier, matching dependencies are dynamic constraints: they tell us what data have to be updated as a consequence of record matching. We also study how to reason about matching dependencies (Section 4.3). To capitalize on matching dependencies in data deduplication, we present a form of matching keys, and outline an algorithm for deducing matching keys from matching dependencies (Section 4.4). In addition, we present an alternative way to enforce matching dependencies for *data repairing*, by giving an operational semantics of matching dependencies (Section 4.5).

4.1 DATA DEDUPLICATION: AN OVERVIEW

The data deduplication problem can be stated as follows. Consider an instance (I_1, I_2) of a pair (R_1, R_2) of relation schemas, and lists Y_{R_1} and Y_{R_2} of attributes in R_1 and R_2, respectively. Given data sources I_1 and I_2, *data deduplication* is to identify all tuples $t_1 \in I_1$ and $t_2 \in I_2$ such that $t_1[Y_{R_1}]$ and $t_2[Y_{R_2}]$ refer to the same real-world entity.

Challenges. One might think that data deduplication would be straightforward: one could first compute the projections $I_1[Y_{R_1}]$ and $I_2[Y_{R_2}]$ of I_1 and I_2 on Y_{R_1} and Y_{R_2}, respectively, and then join $I_1[Y_{R_1}]$ and $I_2[Y_{R_2}]$ on their key attributes. However, matching records in real life is far more intriguing. (1) The same object may be represented differently in different data sources. Indeed, $I_1[Y_{R_1}]$ and $I_2[Y_{R_2}]$ may have *different schemas* that do not share a uniform key. (2) Even when $t_1[Y_{R_1}]$ and $t_2[Y_{R_2}]$ have the same type and refer to the same entity, one may still find that $t_1[Y_{R_1}] \neq t_2[Y_{R_2}]$ due to errors in the data. For instance, a person's name may be represented as "Mark Clifford" or

4. DATA DEDUPLICATION

	c#	FN	LN	addr	tel	email	gender	type
t_1:	111	Mark	Maier	10 Oak St., MH, NJ 07974	908-2345768	mc@gm.com	M	master
t_2:	222	Dave	Smith	620 Elm St., MH, NJ 07976	908-8955664	ds@hm.com	M	visa

(a) Example credit relation I_c

	c#	FN	LN	post	phn	email	item	price
t_3:	111	Marx	Maier	10 Oak St., MH, NJ 07974	908	mc	iPad	169
t_4:	111	Marx	Maier	NJ	908-2345768	mc	book	19
t_5:	111	M.	Maire	10 Oak St., MH, NJ 07974	2345768	mc@gm.com	PSP	269
t_6:	111	M.	Maire	NJ	908-2345768	mc@gm.com	CD	14

(b) Example billing relation I_b

Figure 4.1: Example credit and billing relations.

"Clifford, Mark" in various data sources, and it may even appear as "Marx Clifford" (with an error). Comparing erroneous attributes may lead to false matches or miss true matches.

Example 4.1 Consider two data sources specified by the following relation schemas:

$$\text{credit}(c\#, FN, LN, addr, tel, email, gender, type),$$
$$\text{billing}(c\#, FN, LN, post, phn, email, item, price).$$

Here a credit tuple specifies a credit card (with number c# and type) issued to a card holder who is identified by FN (first name), LN (last name), addr (address), tel (phone), email, and gender. A billing tuple indicates that the price of a purchased item is paid by a credit card of number c#, used by a person specified with name (FN, LN), postal address (post), phone (phn), and email. An example instance (I_c, I_b) of (credit, billing) is shown in Figure 4.1.

For credit card fraud detection, one needs to check whether for all tuples $t \in I_c$ and $t' \in I_b$, if $t[c\#] = t'[c\#]$ then $t[Y_c]$ and $t'[Y_b]$ refer to the same person, where Y_c and Y_b are:

$$Y_c = [FN, LN, addr, tel], \qquad Y_b = [FN, LN, post, phn].$$

That is, we have to determine whether the card holder (identified by $t[Y_c]$) and the card user ($t'[Y_b]$) are the same person. If $t[c\#] = t'[c\#]$ but $t[Y_c]$ and $t'[Y_b]$ do not match, then the chances are that a payment card fraud has been committed.

However, due to errors in the data sources it is not easy to decide whether $t[Y_c]$ and $t'[Y_b]$ match. In the instance of Figure 4.1, for example, the billing tuples t_3–t_6 and the credit tuple t_1 actually refer to the same card holder. However, *no match* can be found if we simply check whether the attributes of $t_3[Y_b]$–$t_6[Y_b]$ and $t_1[Y_c]$ are pairwise identical. □

Another challenge arises from the cost of the data deduplication process. Suppose that billing relation I_b consists of n tuples, and that credit relation I_c has m tuples. Then matching their records

---
Algorithm 4 An algorithm for data deduplication.

Input: Data sources I_1 and I_2.
Output: Classes M and U for matches and non-matches, respectively.

1: *Data preparation*: transform data from various sources into a uniform format by resolving structural heterogeneity;
2: *Search space reduction*: find a new search space $D \subseteq I_1 \times I_2$ to conduct data deduplication;
3: *Comparison function selection*: decide functions and rules for computing the distance between tuples in D;
4: *Match decision*: classify pairs of D into one of the two sets M and U;
5: *Verification*: check the effectiveness of the method, and go back to step 2 if necessary.

---

by comparing each pair $t \in I_c$ and $t' \in I_b$ leads to a time complexity of $O(mn)$, which is often prohibitively expensive when m and n are large.

Data deduplication techniques. A variety of approaches have been proposed for data deduplication: probabilistic (e.g., [Fellegi and Sunter, 1969; Jaro, 1989; Winkler, 2002; Yancey, 2007]), learning-based [Cohen and Richman, 2002; Sarawagi and Bhamidipaty, 2002; Verykios et al., 2002], distance-based [Guha et al., 2004], and rule-based [Ananthakrishna et al., 2002; Hernández and Stolfo, 1995; Lim et al., 1996]. We refer to [Elmagarmid et al., 2007; Herzog et al., 2009; Naumann and Herschel, 2010] for recent surveys.

Given data sources I_1 and I_2 and lists Y_{R_1} and Y_{R_2} of attributes in I_1 and I_2, respectively, these techniques for data deduplication classify each pair $t_1 \in I_1$ and $t_2 \in I_2$ of tuples into one of the two classes M and U defined as follows:

- $(t_1, t_2) \in M$ if the pair is a *match*, i.e., $t_1[Y_1]$ and $t_2[Y_2]$ represent the same entity, and
- $(t_1, t_2) \in U$ if the pair is a *non-match*, i.e., $t_1[Y_1]$ and $t_2[Y_2]$ refer to different entities.

These approaches typically take the steps shown in Algorithm 4 (see [Herzog et al., 2009] for details). These steps are illustrated as follows.

Data preparation may consist of the following steps: (a) schema matching, to associate elements or attributes from different schemas that are semantically related (see, for example, [Rahm and Bernstein, 2001] for a survey); (b) data transformation, to convert data, one field at a time, so that the data fields conform to their corresponding types and satisfy their domain constraints; and (c) data standardization, to convert the information represented in certain fields to a specific content format; for instance, one can standardize the representation of customer names to resolve the difference between "Mark Clifford" and "Clifford, Mark", by adopting a uniform convention.

Search space reduction is often conducted by using blocking or windowing strategies. We defer its discussion to Section 4.4.

Comparison functions are typically defined in terms of similarity predicates to handle typographical errors in data fields. A number of similarity metrics have been proposed, such as edit distance, n-grams, bi-grams, q-grams, Jaro distance, Hamming distance, Smith-Waterman distance, and soundex code. We refer the interested reader to [Elmagarmid et al., 2007; Herzog et al., 2009] for comprehensive surveys on similarity metrics.

To decide whether a pair of tuples in D should be assigned to the class M or U, one can utilize the deduplication approaches mentioned above. In the rest of the chapter we will present one of the techniques, namely, a dependency-based strategy.

After the deduplication process, one often wants to check whether the process accurately identifies matches and non-matches, possibly by involving domain experts to inspect sample matches. If not, the process may reiterate with adjusted thresholds and parameters.

The output of a data deduplication process may be a single file, in which tuples that refer to the same entity are merged into a unique record. This requires *data fusion*, to resolve conflicts, and combine and fuse duplicate representations of the same entity into a single representation (see, for example, [Bleiholder and Naumann, 2008] for a survey).

Criteria. To evaluate the effectiveness of a deduplication method, one needs to consider the efficiency and accuracy of the method. The efficiency is often assessed by the scalability of the method with, for example, the size of the data sets. The accuracy of the method refers to the quality of matches identified, assessed by the degree of false assignments of pairs to M and U, referred to as *false matches* (false positives) and *false non-matches* (false negatives), respectively. It can be measured by the following: (1) *precision*, the ratio of *true matches* (true positives) correctly found by the method to all the duplicates found, and (2) *recall*, the ratio of true matches correctly found to all the duplicates in the data sets. One could also use *F-measure*, defined by F-measure = 2 ·(precision · recall)/(precision + recall).

4.2 MATCHING DEPENDENCIES

We next present a dependency-based approach to detecting duplicates. It aims to improve the accuracy and efficiency of data deduplication in a uniform framework, by matching records and reducing search space based on the semantics of the data.

Matching rules: An overview. From Example 4.1 and Algorithm 4, we can see that to match tuples from unreliable sources, we cannot simply check whether the attribute values of a pair of tuples are pairwise identical. Instead, we have to decide *what attributes to compare* and *how to compare these attributes*. To this end it is often necessary to hinge on the semantics of the data. Indeed, domain knowledge about the data may tell us what attributes to compare. Moreover, by analyzing the semantics of the data we can deduce alternative attributes to inspect such that when matching

4.2. MATCHING DEPENDENCIES 73

cannot be done by comparing attributes that contain errors, we may still find matches by using other more reliable attributes.

Example 4.2 Consider again the credit and billing relations given in Example 4.1. Domain knowledge about the data suggests that we only need to compare LN, FN and address (addr, post) when matching $t[Y_c]$ and $t'[Y_b]$ (see, for example, [Hernández and Stolfo, 1995]): if a credit tuple t and a billing tuple t' have the same address and the same last name, and moreover, if their first names are similar (although they may not be identical), then the two tuples refer to the same person. That is, LN, FN and address, together with two equality operators and a similarity predicate $\approx_d$, make a "key" for matching $t[Y_c]$ and $t'[Y_b]$:

φ_1: If t[LN, addr] = t'[LN, post] and if t'[FN] and t'[FN] are *similar w.r.t.* $\approx_d$, then $t[Y_c]$ and $t'[Y_b]$ are a match. We also refer to φ_1 as matching key rck$_1$.

Such a *matching key* tells us what attributes to compare and how to compare them in order to match $t[Y_c]$ and $t'[Y_b]$. By comparing only the attributes in rck$_1$ we can now match t_1 and t_3, although their FN, tel, and email attributes are not pairwise identical.

A closer examination of the semantics of the data further suggests the following: for any credit tuple t and billing tuple t',

φ_2: if t[tel] = t'[phn], then we can identify t[addr] and t'[post], i.e., these attributes should be updated by taking the same value in any uniform representation of the address.

φ_3: if t[email] = t'[email], then we can identify t[LN, FN] and t'[LN, FN], i.e., they should be equalized via updates.

None of these makes a key for matching $t[Y_c]$ and $t'[Y_b]$, i.e., we cannot match entire $t[Y_c]$ and $t'[Y_b]$ by just comparing their email or phone attributes. Nevertheless, from these and the matching key rck$_1$ given above, we can deduce the following new matching keys:

rck$_2$: LN, FN and phone, to be compared with =, $\approx_d$, = operators, respectively;
rck$_3$: address and email, both to be compared via equality =; and
rck$_4$: phone and email, to be compared via =.

These *deduced keys* have added value: while we cannot match t_1 and t_4–t_6 by using the initial matching key rck$_1$, we can match these tuples based on the deduced keys. Indeed, using key rck$_4$, we can now match t_1 and t_6 in Figure 4.1: they have the same phone and the same email, and can thus be identified, although their name and address attributes are *radically different*. That is, although there are errors in their name and address attributes, we are still able to match the records by inspecting their email and phone attributes. Similarly we can match t_1 and t_4 using rck$_2$, and match t_1 and t_5 using rck$_3$. □

This example highlights the need for a new form of dependency to specify the semantics of data in unreliable relations, and for effective techniques to deduce matching keys for data deduplication. One can draw an analogy of this to our familiar notion of functional dependencies (FDs). Indeed,

4. DATA DEDUPLICATION

to identify a tuple in a relation we use candidate keys. To find the keys we first specify a set of FDs, and then infer keys by the *implication analysis* of the FDs [Abiteboul et al., 1995]. For all the reasons that we need FDs and their reasoning techniques for identifying tuples in a clean relation, it is also important to develop (a) dependencies to specify the semantics of data in relations that may contain errors, and (b) effective techniques to derive matching keys from these dependencies.

Matching dependencies. We have seen that we need dependencies to specify how to match records based on the semantics of data. But what dependencies should we use? One might be tempted to use FDs in record matching. Unfortunately, FDs are developed for designing schema of clean data. In contrast, for record matching we have to accommodate errors in the data and different representations in different data sources. In this context we need a form of dependency quite *different* from its traditional counterparts, and a reasoning mechanism more *intriguing* than the standard notion of implication analysis.

To this end we introduce a class of dependencies, referred to as matching dependencies (MDs), for record matching. Consider two relation schemas R_1 and R_2, with attributes, attr(R_1) and attr(R_2), respectively. We say that attributes $A \in$ attr(R_1) and $B \in$ attr(R_2) are *compatible* if they have the same domain, i.e., dom(A) and dom(B) are identical. For lists X_1 and X_2 of attributes, we say that X_1 and X_2 are *pairwise compatible* if $X_1 = [A_1, \ldots, A_k]$, $X_2 = [B_1, \ldots, B_k]$ for some $k \geq 1$, and A_i and B_i are compatible for all $i \in [1, k]$.

To cope with errors in data sources, we define MDs in terms of similarity predicates, a departure from our familiar FDs. For each domain dom(A), we assume a binary similarity relation $\approx_A \subseteq$ dom(A) $\times$ dom(A). Note that if attributes A and B are compatible, then $\approx_A$ and $\approx_B$ are identical. When it is clear from the context, we simply write $\approx_A$ as $\approx$. We write $x \approx y$ if (x, y) is in $\approx$, and refer to $\approx$ as a *similarity predicate*. The predicate can be defined in terms of any similarity metric used in record matching, e.g., q-grams, Jaro distance or edit distance [Elmagarmid et al., 2007], with an accuracy parameter set by domain experts.

We assume that each $\approx$ is symmetric, i.e., if $x \approx y$ then $y \approx x$, and that it subsumes equality, i.e., if $x = y$ then $x \approx y$.

For lists $X_1 = [A_1, \ldots, A_k]$ and $X_2 = [B_1, \ldots, B_k]$ of pairwise compatible attributes, we use $X_1 \approx X_2$ to denote $A_1 \approx_1 B_1 \wedge \cdots \wedge A_k \approx_k B_k$, where $\approx_i$ is the similarity predicate defined on dom(A_i) = dom(B_i).

Using similarity predicates, we define matching dependencies as follows.

Definition 4.3 A *matching dependency* (MD) φ for (R_1, R_2) is syntactically defined as:

$$R_1[X_1] \approx R_2[X_2] \rightarrow R_1[Y_1] \rightleftharpoons R_2[Y_2],$$

where X_1 and X_2 are pairwise compatible lists of attributes in R_1 and R_2, respectively; similarly for Y_1 and Y_2; and $\rightleftharpoons$ is called the *matching operator*.

We refer to $R_1[X_1] \approx R_2[X_2]$ and $R_1[Y_1] \rightleftharpoons R_2[Y_2]$ as the LHS and the RHS of φ, denoted by LHS(φ) and RHS(φ), respectively. □

Intuitively, the MD φ states that for each R_1 tuple t_1 and each R_2 tuple t_2, if the attribute values in $t_1[X_1]$ are pairwise similar to the attribute values in $t_2[X_2]$, then $t_1[Y_1]$ and $t_2[Y_2]$ refer to the same real-world entity and hence, their attribute values should be made pairwise identical. This is indicated by the matching operator $\rightleftharpoons$: $t_1[Y_1] \rightleftharpoons t_2[Y_2]$ means that $t_1[Y_1]$ and $t_2[Y_2]$ have to be identified via updates, i.e., we update $t_1[Y_1]$ and $t_2[Y_2]$ such that they take identical values.

Example 4.4 The matching rules given in Example 4.2 can be expressed as MDs, as follows:

- φ_1: credit[LN] = billing[LN] $\wedge$ credit[addr] = billing[post] $\wedge$ credit[FN] $\approx_d$ billing[FN]
  $\rightarrow$ credit[Y_c] $\rightleftharpoons$ billing[Y_b],

- φ_2: credit[tel] = billing[phn] $\rightarrow$ credit[addr] $\rightleftharpoons$ billing[post],

- φ_3: credit[email] = billing[email] $\rightarrow$ credit[FN, LN] $\rightleftharpoons$ billing[FN, LN].

Here, φ_1 states that for any credit tuple t and billing tuple t', if t and t' have the same last name and the same address, and if their first names are similar w.r.t. $\approx_d$ (but may not necessarily be identical), then $t[Y_c]$ and $t'[Y_b]$ should be identified. Similarly, if t and t' have the same phone number then we should identify their addresses (φ_2), and if t and t' have the same email then their names should be identified (φ_3). Note that while name, address, and phone are part of Y_b and Y_c, email is *not*. More specifically, the LHS attributes of an MD is neither necessarily contained in nor disjoint from the attributes Y_b and Y_c. □

A denotational semantics. The matching operator $\rightleftharpoons$ indicates that MDs have a dynamic semantics. Below we first present a denotational semantics for MDs, following the work of Fan et al. [2011a], for deriving matching keys. Following Bertossi et al. [2011], we will give a different operational semantics in Section 4.5, for repairing data based on MDs.

Recall that an FD $R(X \rightarrow Y)$ simply assures that for all tuples t_1 and t_2 in a single instance I of schema R, if $t_1[X] = t_2[X]$ then $t_1[Y] = t_2[Y]$. In contrast, to characterize the dynamic semantics of an MD $\varphi = R_1[X_1] \approx R_2[X_2] \rightarrow R_1[Y_1] \rightleftharpoons R_2[Y_2]$, we need two instances $D = (I_1, I_2)$ and $D' = (I'_1, I'_2)$ of schema (R_1, R_2), denoting the data before and after the matching operation is conducted, respectively. To keep track of tuples during a matching process, we assume a temporary unique tuple id for each tuple t. We write $D \sqsubseteq D'$ if for each tuple t in D there exists a tuple in D' such that they have the same tuple id. We use t^D and $t^{D'}$ to denote the tuple t in D and D', respectively, as in Section 3.3.1.

We next give the denotational semantics of MDs.

Definition 4.5 Consider a pair (D, D') of instances of (R_1, R_2), where $D \sqsubseteq D'$. We say that (D, D') *satisfies* the MD $\varphi = R_1[X_1] \approx R_2[X_2] \rightarrow R_1[Y_1] \rightleftharpoons R_2[Y_2]$, denoted by $(D, D') \models \varphi$, if

76 4. DATA DEDUPLICATION

[Figure 4.2 depiction:]

	tel	addr
t_1:	908-2345768	10 Oak Street, MH, NJ 07974
	Equal ↕	↕
	phn	post
t_4:	908-2345768	NJ

$D_c = (I_c, I_b)$

MD φ_2 identifies $t_1[\text{addr}]$ & $t_4[\text{post}]$ ⟶

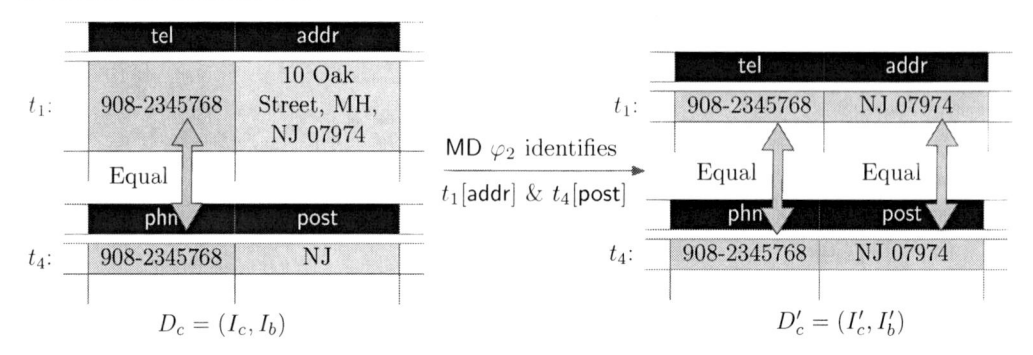

	tel	addr
t_1:	908-2345768	NJ 07974
	Equal ↕	Equal ↕
	phn	post
t_4:	908-2345768	NJ 07974

$D'_c = (I'_c, I'_b)$

Figure 4.2: Enforcing MDs.

for every R_1 tuple t_1 and every R_2 tuple t_2 in D that match the LHS of φ, i.e., $t_1^D[X_1] \approx t_2^D[X_2]$, the following two conditions hold in the instance D':

- $t_1^{D'}[Y_1] = t_2^{D'}[Y_2]$, i.e., the values of the RHS attributes of φ in t_1 and t_2 have been identified in D'; and
- $t_1^{D'}[X_1] \approx t_2^{D'}[X_2]$, i.e., t_1 and t_2 in D' also match the LHS of φ. □

Intuitively, φ is *enforced* as a *matching rule*: whenever t_1 and t_2 in an instance D match the LHS of φ, $t_1[Y_1]$ and $t_2[Y_2]$ ought to be made equal. The outcome of the enforcement is reflected in the other instance D'. That is, some values $\bar{v}$ are to be found such that $t_1^{D'}[Y_1] = t_2^{D'}[Y_2] = \bar{v}$ in D', although we do not explicitly specify what the values $\bar{v}$ are.

Example 4.6 Consider the MD φ_2 of Example 4.4 and the instance $D_c = (I_c, I_b)$ of Figure 4.1, in which $t_1^{D_c}$ and $t_4^{D_c}$ match the LHS of φ_2. As depicted in Figure 4.2, the enforcement of φ_2 yields another instance $D'_c = (I'_c, I'_b)$ in which $t_1^{D'_c}[\text{addr}] = t_4^{D'_c}[\text{post}]$, while $t_1^{D_c}[\text{addr}]$ and $t_4^{D_c}[\text{post}]$ are *different* in D_c.

Note that the operator $\rightleftharpoons$ only requires that $t_1^{D'_c}[\text{addr}]$ and $t_4^{D'_c}[\text{post}]$ are identified, but it does not specify how these values are updated. That is, in any D'_c such that $D_c \sqsubseteq D'_c$, φ_2 is considered enforced on D'_c, i.e., $(D_c, D'_c) \models \varphi_2$, as long as (a) $t_1^{D'_c}[\text{addr}] = t_4^{D'_c}[\text{post}]$ and $t_1^{D'_c}[\text{tel}] = t_4^{D'_c}[\text{phn}]$, and (b) similarly, $t_1^{D'_c}[\text{addr}] = t_6^{D'_c}[\text{post}]$ and $t_1^{D'_c}[\text{tel}] = t_6^{D'_c}[\text{phn}]$.

It should be clarified that we use updates just to give the semantics of MDs. In the matching process D may *not* be updated, i.e., there is *no* destructive impact on D. □

For a set Σ of MDs defined on a relational schema $\mathcal{R}$, and instances D and D' of $\mathcal{R}$, we say that (D, D') *satisfies* Σ, denoted by $(D, D') \models \Sigma$, if $(D, D') \models \varphi$ for all $\varphi \in \Sigma$.

Matching dependencies versus functional dependencies. MDs are quite *different* from traditional dependencies such as FDs.

4.2. MATCHING DEPENDENCIES

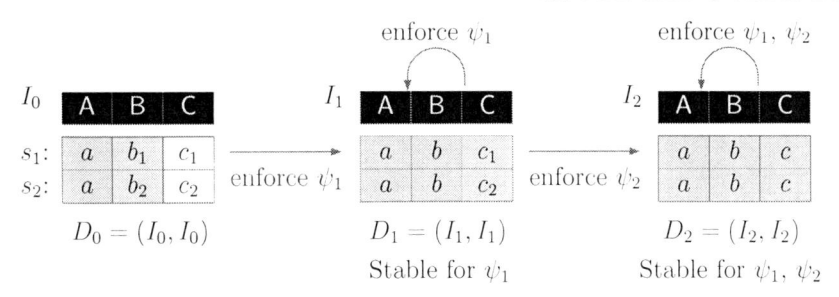

	I_0	A	B	C		I_1	A	B	C		I_2	A	B	C
s_1:		a	b_1	c_1			a	b	c_1			a	b	c
s_2:		a	b_2	c_2			a	b	c_2			a	b	c

$D_0 = (I_0, I_0)$ $\quad$ enforce ψ_1 $\quad$ $D_1 = (I_1, I_1)$ $\quad$ enforce ψ_2 $\quad$ $D_2 = (I_2, I_2)$

Stable for ψ_1 $\quad\quad$ Stable for ψ_1, ψ_2

enforce ψ_1 $\quad\quad\quad\quad\quad$ enforce ψ_1, ψ_2

Figure 4.3: The dynamic semantics of MDs.

- MDs adopt a "dynamic" semantics to accommodate errors and different representations of the data: if $t_1^D[X_1] \approx t_2^D[X_2]$ in the instance D, then $t_1^{D'}[Y_1]$ and $t_2^{D'}[Y_2]$ are updated and made equal in *another instance* D'. Here, D' results from the updates to D, while $t_1^D[Y_1]$ and $t_2^D[Y_2]$ may be *radically different* in the original instance D.

  In contrast, FDs have a "static" semantics: if certain attributes are equal in D, then some other attributes must be equal in *the same* instance D.

- MDs are defined in terms of *similarity predicates* and the matching operator $\rightleftharpoons$, whereas FDs are defined with equality only.

- MDs are defined across two relations with *possibly different* schemas, while FDs are defined on a single relation.

Example 4.7 Consider two FDs defined on schema $R(A, B, C)$:

$$\text{fd}_1 : [A] \rightarrow [B], \quad\quad \text{fd}_2 : [B] \rightarrow [C].$$

Consider the instances I_0 and I_1 of R shown in Figure 4.3, in which $b_1 \neq b_2$ and $c_1 \neq c_2$. Observe that tuples s_1 and s_2 in I_0 violate the FD fd_1, since $s_1^{I_0}[A] = s_2^{I_0}[A]$ but $s_1^{I_0}[B] \neq s_2^{I_0}[B]$; similarly, $s_1^{I_1}$ and $s_2^{I_1}$ in I_1 violate fd_2.

In contrast, consider two MDs defined on (R, R):

$$\psi_1 : R[A] = R[A] \rightarrow R[B] \rightleftharpoons R[B], \quad\quad \psi_2 : R[B] = R[B] \rightarrow R[C] \rightleftharpoons R[C],$$

where ψ_1 states that for any instance $D = (I, I')$ of (R, R) and any pair of tuples (s_1, s_2) in (I, I'), if $s_1^D[A] = s_2^D[A]$, then $s_1[B]$ and $s_2[B]$ should be identified; similarly for ψ_2.

Let $D_0 = (I_0, I_0)$ and $D_1 = (I_1, I_1)$. Then $(D_0, D_1) \models \psi_1$. While $s_1^{D_0}[A] = s_2^{D_0}[A]$ and $s_1^{D_0}[B] \neq s_2^{D_0}[B]$ in I_0, s_1 and s_2 are *not* treated as a violation of ψ_1. Instead, some value b is found such that $s_1^{D_0}[B]$ and $s_2^{D_0}[B]$ are changed to b in D_1. This yields instance D_1, in which $s_1^{D_1}[B] = s_2^{D_1}[B]$. This is how MDs accommodate errors in unreliable data sources.

Also note that $(D_0, D_1) \models \psi_2$ since $s_1^{D_0}[B] \neq s_2^{D_0}[B]$ in I_0; in other words, $s_1^{D_0}$ and $s_2^{D_0}$ do not match the LHS of ψ_2 in D_0, and hence, the RHS of ψ_2 is not enforced. On the other hand, ψ_2

78 4. DATA DEDUPLICATION

should be enforced on D_1 since $s_1^{D_1}[B] = s_2^{D_1}[B]$ but $s_1^{D_1}[C] \neq s_2^{D_1}[C]$. Enforcing ψ_2 on D_1 yields another instance D_2, in which $s_1^{D_2}[C] = s_2^{D_2}[C]$. □

4.3 REASONING ABOUT MATCHING DEPENDENCIES

As shown in Example 4.2, for data deduplication we want to deduce matching keys from matching rules (i.e., MDs). In this section we study how to deduce MDs from a set of given MDs, by presenting a generic mechanism to reason about MDs. In the next section we will show that matching keys are a special case of MDs, and hence can be deduced from MDs.

The deduction mechanism for MDs is, however, a departure from our familiar terrain of the implication analysis of traditional dependencies such as FDs. Indeed, in contrast to FDs, MDs have a dynamic semantics and moreover, are defined in terms of domain-specific similarity predicates. These introduce new challenges to the analysis of MDs.

The limitations of implication analysis. Recall the notion of implication for traditional dependencies: given a set Γ of dependencies and another dependency ϕ, Γ *implies* ϕ if for any database D that satisfies Γ, D also satisfies ϕ. For an example of our familiar FDs, if Γ consists of $X \to Y$ and $Y \to Z$, then it implies $X \to Z$ (the transitivity). However, this notion of implication is no longer applicable to MDs on unreliable data, as illustrated below.

Example 4.8 Let Σ_0 be the set $\{\psi_1, \psi_2\}$ of MDs, and Γ_0 be the set $\{\text{fd}_1, \text{fd}_2\}$ of FDs, both given in Example 4.7. Consider the following additional MD and FD:

$$\text{MD } \psi_3 : R[A] = R[A] \to R[C] \rightleftharpoons R[C],$$
$$\text{FD fd}_3 : [A] \to [C].$$

Then Γ_0 implies fd_3. However, Σ_0 *does not* imply ψ_3, although intuitively, ψ_3 is indeed a logical consequence of Σ_0. To see this, consider D_0 and D_1 that are defined in terms of I_0 and I_1 given in Figure 4.3. Observe the following.

(1) $(D_0, D_1) \models \Sigma_0$ but $(D_0, D_1) \not\models \psi_3$. Indeed, $(D_0, D_1) \models \psi_1$ and $(D_0, D_1) \models \psi_2$. However, $(D_0, D_1) \not\models \psi_3$: while $s_1^{D_0}[A] = s_2^{D_0}[A]$, $s_1^{D_1}[C] \neq s_2^{D_1}[C]$. This tells us that Σ_0 does *not* imply ψ_3 if the traditional notion of implication is adopted for MDs.

(2) In contrast, neither I_0 nor I_1 contradicts the implication of FD fd_3 from Γ_0. Indeed, $I_0 \not\models \text{fd}_3$: $s_1^{I_0}[A] = s_2^{I_0}[A]$ but $s_1^{I_0}[C] \neq s_2^{I_0}[C]$. That is, $s_1^{I_0}$ and $s_2^{I_0}$ violate fd_3. However, $I_0 \not\models \Gamma_0$ either, since $I_0 \not\models \text{fd}_1$: $s_1^{I_0}[A] = s_2^{I_0}[A]$ but $s_1^{I_0}[B] \neq s_2^{I_0}[B]$. Thus, the conventional implication of FDs remains valid on I_0. Similarly, I_1 satisfies neither fd_2 in Γ_0 nor fd_3. □

4.3. REASONING ABOUT MATCHING DEPENDENCIES 79

Deduction. This example suggests that we develop a new deduction mechanism for MDs. To capture the dynamic semantics of MDs in the deduction analysis, we need the following.

Definition 4.9 For a set Σ of MDs defined on a relational schema $\mathcal{R}$, an instance D of $\mathcal{R}$ is called *stable* if $(D, D) \models \Sigma$. □

Intuitively, a stable instance D is an ultimate outcome of enforcing Σ: each and every rule in Σ is enforced until no more updates have to be conducted.

Example 4.10 As illustrated in Figure 4.3, D_2 is a stable instance for the set Σ_0 of MDs given in Example 4.8. It is an outcome of enforcing MDs in Σ_0 as matching rules: when ψ_1 is enforced on D_0, it yields another instance (e.g., D_1) in which $s_1^{D_1}[B] = s_2^{D_1}[B]$. When ψ_2 is further enforced on D_1, it leads to an instance D_2 in which $s_1^{D_2}[C] = s_2^{D_2}[C]$. Now $(D_2, D_2) \models \Sigma_0$, i.e., no further changes are necessary for enforcing the MDs in Σ_0. □

We are now ready to formalize the notion of deductions.

Definition 4.11 For a set Σ of MDs and another MD φ defined on a relational schema $\mathcal{R}$, φ is said to be *deduced* from Σ, denoted by $\Sigma \models_d \varphi$, if for any instance D of $\mathcal{R}$, and *for each* stable instance D' of $\mathcal{R}$ for Σ, if $(D, D') \models \Sigma$ then $(D, D') \models \varphi$. □

Intuitively, a stable instance D' is a "fixpoint" reached by enforcing the rules of Σ on D. There are *possibly many* such stable instances, depending on how D is updated, such as what values are changed and in which order the update operations are conducted. The deduction analysis inspects *all* such stable instances for Σ.

The notion of deductions is generic: no matter how MDs are interpreted, if Σ is enforced, then so must be φ. That is, φ is a *logical consequence* of the given MDs in Σ.

Example 4.12 For Σ_0 and ψ_3 given in Example 4.8, one can verify that $\Sigma_0 \models_d \psi_3$. In particular, for the instance D_0 and the stable instance D_2 of Example 4.10, one can see that $(D_0, D_2) \models \Sigma_0$ and $(D_0, D_2) \models \psi_3$. □

Inference system. The *deduction problem* for MDs is to decide, given a set Σ of MDs and another MD φ defined on a relational schema $\mathcal{R}$, whether $\Sigma \models_d \varphi$.

Along the same lines as Armstrong's Axioms for the implication analysis of FDs, one may want to develop an inference system for the deduction analysis of MDs. A new challenge encountered here involves similarity predicates in MDs, which are often domain-specific. To this end, we assume only *generic axioms* for each similarity predicate $\approx$: it is symmetric and it subsumes equality. Nevertheless, except equality $=$, $\approx$ is *not* assumed transitive, i.e., from $x \approx y$ and $y \approx z$ it does *not* necessarily follow that $x \approx z$. As usual, the equality relation $=$ is reflexive (i.e., $x = x$), symmetric, and transitive (i.e., if $x = y$ and $y = z$ then $x = z$). In addition, we adopt the following axiom: if $x \approx y$ and $y = z$, then $x \approx z$.

We also consider *dense* predicate $\approx$: for any number k and value v, there exist values $v_1, \ldots, v_k$ such that $v \approx v_i$ for $i \in [1, k]$, and $v_i \not\approx v_j$ for all $i, j \in [1, k]$ and $i \neq j$. That is, there are unboundedly many distinct values that are within a certain distance of v w.r.t. $\approx$, but these values are not similar to each other.

With these assumptions, MDs are finitely axiomatizable and, moreover, their deduction analysis can be conducted in PTIME [Fan et al., 2011a].

Theorem 4.13 (1) There exists a finite set of inference rules that is sound and complete for the deduction analysis of MDs. (2) There exists an algorithm that, given as input a set Σ of MDs and another MD φ defined on a relational schema $\mathcal{R}$, determines whether or not $\Sigma \models_d \varphi$ in $O(n^2 + h^3)$ time, where n is the size of the input Σ and φ, and h is the total number of distinct attributes appearing in Σ or φ.

Crux. An inference system consisting of nine rules is provided by Fan et al. [2011a], and is shown sound and complete for the deduction analysis of MDs. An algorithm for deciding MD deduction is also given there, with the complexity bound claimed above. □

4.4 RELATIVE KEYS FOR RECORD MATCHING

Recall that our ultimate goal is to settle the *data deduplication problem*:

- INPUT: An instance (I_1, I_2) of (R_1, R_2), and lists Y_1 and Y_2 of attributes in R_1 and R_2, respectively.
- QUESTION: For each pair of tuples $t_1 \in I_1$ and $t_2 \in I_2$, does $t_1[Y_{R_1}] \rightleftharpoons t_2[Y_{R_2}]$?

To decide whether $t_1[Y_{R_1}]$ and $t_2[Y_{R_2}]$ are a match, i.e., they refer to the same entity, we want to find a minimal number of attributes to compare. To do this, we identify a special case of MDs as matching keys, such that $t_1[Y_{R_1}]$ and $t_2[Y_{R_2}]$ are a match as long as the values of their attributes in a matching key are pairwise similar. We show that such keys can effectively improve both the accuracy and efficiency of data deduplication. Moreover, they can be automatically deduced from available matching dependencies.

Relative candidate keys. We first define a notion of relative keys, along the same lines as superkeys for relations (see, e.g., [Abiteboul et al., 1995] for superkeys).

Definition 4.14 A *key κ relative to* attributes (Y_{R_1}, Y_{R_2}) of (R_1, R_2) is an MD in which the RHS is fixed to be (Y_{R_1}, Y_{R_2}), i.e., an MD of the form

$$R_1[X_1] \approx R_2[X_2] \rightarrow R_1[Y_{R_1}] \rightleftharpoons R_2[Y_{R_2}].$$

We simply write κ as a set of triples:

$$\big((A_1, B_1, \approx_1), \ldots, (A_k, B_k, \approx_k)\big),$$

when $X_1 = [A_1, \ldots, A_k]$ and $X_2 = [B_1, \ldots, B_k]$, and when R_1, R_2 and (Y_{R_1}, Y_{R_2}) are clear from the context. □

Intuitively, κ assures that for any tuples (t_1, t_2) of (R_1, R_2), to identify $t_1[Y_{R_1}]$ and $t_2[Y_{R_2}]$ one only needs to check whether for all $j \in [1, k]$, $t_1[A_j]$ and $t_2[B_j]$ satisfy the similarity predicate $\approx_j$. This is analogous to a superkey: to identify two tuples in a relation it suffices to inspect only their attributes in the key. Observe that there are possibly multiple superkeys for a relation; similarly for relative keys.

Along the same lines as candidate keys studied for schema design, we next define a notion of relative candidate keys as "minimal" relative keys.

Definition 4.15 A *relative candidate key* (RCK) for (Y_{R_1}, Y_{R_2}) is a key κ relative to (Y_{R_1}, Y_{R_2}) such that no proper subset of κ is a key relative to (Y_{R_1}, Y_{R_2}). □

Intuitively, to identify $t_1[Y_{R_1}]$ and $t_2[Y_{R_2}]$, an RCK specifies a *minimal* set of attributes to inspect, and tells us *how* to compare these attributes via similarity predicates.

Example 4.16 Candidate keys relative to the lists (Y_c, Y_b) given in Example 4.1 include:

rck_1: $\big((\text{LN, LN, =}), (\text{addr, post, =}), (\text{FN, FN}, \approx_d)\big)$,
rck_2: $\big((\text{LN, LN, =}), (\text{tel, phn, =}), (\text{FN, FN}, \approx_d)\big)$,
rck_3: $\big((\text{email, email, =}), (\text{addr, post, =})\big)$,
rck_4: $\big((\text{email, email, =}), (\text{tel, phn, =})\big)$.

Here, rck_4 states that for any credit tuple t and billing tuple t', if $t[\text{email, tel}] = t'[\text{email, phn}]$, then $t[Y_c]$ and $t'[Y_b]$ are a match; similarly for rck_1, rck_2 and rck_3. Note that email is not part of Y_b or Y_c, i.e., RCKs may contain attributes that are *outside* of those to be identified. □

One can draw an analogy of RCKs to our familiar notion of candidate keys for relations: both notions attempt to provide an invariant connection between tuples and the real-world entities they represent. However, there are *sharp differences* between the two notions. First, RCKs bring domain-specific *similarity* predicates into play. Second, RCKs are defined *across possibly different relations*; in contrast, keys are defined on a single relation. Third, RCKs have a *dynamic semantics* and aim to identify tuples in *unreliable* data, a departure from the classical dependency theory.

Naturally, RCKs provide matching keys: they tell us what attributes to compare and how to compare them. As observed by Jaro [1989], to match tuples of arity n, there are 2^n possible comparison configurations. Thus it is unrealistic to enumerate all matching keys exhaustively and then manually select "the best keys" among possibly exponentially many candidates. In contrast, as will be seen shortly, RCKs can be automatically deduced from MDs *at the schema level and at compile time*. In addition, RCKs reduce the cost of inspecting a single pair of tuples by minimizing the number of attributes to compare.

Better still, RCKs improve match quality. Indeed, deduced RCKs *add value*: as we have seen in Example 4.2, while tuples t_4–t_6 and t_1 cannot be matched by the given key, they are identified by the deduced RCKs. The added value of deduced rules has long been recognized in census data cleaning: deriving implicit rules from explicit ones is a routine practice of the U.S. Census Bureau [Fellegi and Holt, 1976; Winkler, 2004]. To improve the match quality, one can use multiple RCKs such that if an error in a tuple occurs in an attribute of one RCK, the tuple may still find its match using other RCKs with more reliable attribute values.

Reducing search space. When conducting data deduplication on (I_1, I_2), we want to reduce the search space to $D \subseteq I_1 \times I_2$ and better still, reduce the quadratic-time complexity. This is often carried out by using blocking or windowing.

Blocking. Blocking is an extension of hash join, which partitions large relations into "buckets" such that any pair of records that share the same join attribute values will be assigned to the same bucket. As a result, we only need to compute joins locally on those records within each bucket. Along the same lines, blocking is to partition tuples of I_1 and I_2 into mutually disjoint blocks, such that no matches exist across different blocks. In other words, we only need to compare those tuples that are within the same block.

Blocking is typically implemented by choosing a blocking key, e.g., a set of highly discriminating attributes, such that tuples sharing the same blocking key are grouped into the same block. Let $m = |I_1|$ and $n = |I_2|$. Then based on blocking the complexity of deduplication may reduce from $O(mn)$ to $O(m + n + mn/b)$, where b is the number of blocks.

Obviously, the match quality is highly dependent on *the choice of blocking keys*. Indeed, while blocking improves the efficiency of data deduplication, it comes at a price of an increased number of false non-matches when t_1 and t_2 are a match but they do not agree on the blocking key, if the blocking key is not properly chosen. To this end, one can find high-quality blocking keys by selecting and combining attributes from RCKs. The accuracy can be further improved by repeating the deduplication process multiple times, each time using a different blocking key derived from RCKs.

Windowing. An alternative way to cope with large relations is by first sorting tuples using a key, and then comparing the tuples using sliding windows [Hernández and Stolfo, 1995]. More specifically, one can first pick a sorting key and sort tuples in I_1 and I_2 based on the same key in the same order. Two windows of a fixed size w are then moved down the lists, one tuple at a time. Each new tuple that enters a window is compared with the w tuples in the other window to find a match, and the tuple on the top of the window slides out of it. This reduces the number of comparisons from $O(mn)$ to $O((m + n)w)$, where w is a constant. Taking the sorting cost into account, the time complexity of deduplication based on windowing is down to $O(m \log m + n \log n + (m + n)w)$.

Like blocking, the match quality of data deduplication via sliding windows depends on the choice of sorting keys. Here we can again create sorting keys by selecting and combining attributes from various RCKs, and conduct multiple independent runs of the deduplication process to improve the accuracy, each run based on a different sorting key.

Deducing relative candidate keys. We have seen that RCKs are useful in improving the accuracy and efficiency of data deduplication. But how can we find high-quality RCKs? We next show that RCKs can be automatically deduced from available MDs. In addition, algorithms are already in place for automatically discovering MDs from data (e.g., [Song and Chen, 2011, 2009]), along the same lines as CFD discovery (Section 3.1).

We study *the problem for computing RCKs* : given a set Σ of MDs, a pair of lists (Y_{R_1}, Y_{R_2}) of pairwise compatible attributes, and a natural number m, it is to compute a set Γ of m high-quality RCKs relative to (Y_{R_1}, Y_{R_2}), deduced from Σ.

This problem is nontrivial. One question concerns what metrics we should use to select RCKs. Another question is how to find m high-quality RCKs based the metric. One might be tempted to first compute all RCKs from Σ, sort these keys based on the metric, and then select the top m keys. This is, however, beyond reach in practice: it is known that for a single relation, there are possibly exponentially many traditional candidate keys [Lucchesi and Osborn, 1978]. For RCKs, unfortunately, the exponential-time complexity remains intact.

Below we first present a model to assess the quality of RCKs. Based on the model, we then outline an efficient algorithm to deduce m RCKs from Σ. As verified by the experimental study of Fan et al. [2011a], even when Σ does not contain many MDs, the algorithm is still able to find a reasonable number of RCKs. In addition, in practice it is rare to find exponentially many RCKs; indeed, the algorithm often finds the set of *all* quality RCKs when m is not very large.

Quality model. To find the set Γ, we select RCKs based on the following criteria.

- The *diversity* of RCKs in Γ. We do not want RCKs containing attributes $(R_1[A], R_2[B])$ that appear frequently in RCKs that are already in Γ. In other words, we want Γ to include diverse attributes so that if errors appear in some attributes, matches can still be found by comparing other attributes in the RCKs of Γ. To do this we maintain a counter $ct(R_1[A], R_2[B])$ for each pair, and increase it by 1 whenever an RCK with the pair is added to Γ.

- Statistics. We consider the accuracy of each attribute pair $acc(R_1[A], R_2[B])$, i.e., the confidence placed by the user in the attributes, and the average lengths $lt(R_1[A], R_2[B])$ of the values of each attribute pair. Intuitively, the longer $lt(R_1[A], R_2[B])$ is, the more likely errors occur in the attributes; and the greater $acc(R_1[A], R_2[B])$ is, the more reliable $(R_1[A], R_2[B])$ are.

Putting these together, we define the *cost* of including $(R_1[A], R_2[B])$ in an RCK as:

$$\text{cost}(R_1[A], R_2[B]) = w_1 \cdot ct(R_1[A], R_2[B]) + w_2 \cdot lt(R_1[A], R_2[B]) + w_3/acc(R_1[A], R_2[B]),$$

where w_1, w_2, w_3 are weights associated with these factors. The cost of an RCK (or MD) is defined to be the sum of the costs of all of its attribute pairs. Our algorithm selects RCKs with attributes of low cost or, equivalently, high quality.

4. DATA DEDUPLICATION

Algorithm. We next outline an algorithm for deducing RCKs, referred to as findRCKs (see [Fan et al., 2011a] for details). Given Σ, (Y_{R_1}, Y_{R_2}) and m as input, the algorithm returns a set Γ of at most m RCKs relative to (Y_{R_1}, Y_{R_2}) that are deduced from Σ. The algorithm selects RCKs defined with low-cost attribute pairs. The set Γ contains m RCKs if there exist at least m RCKs, and otherwise it consists of all RCKs deduced from Σ. The algorithm is in $O(m(l+n)^3)$ time, where l is the length $|Y_{R_1}|$ ($|Y_{R_2}|$) of Y_{R_1} (Y_{R_2}), and n is the size of Σ. In practice, m is often a *predefined* constant, and the algorithm is in *cubic-time*.

Assume that $Y_{R_1} = [A'_1, \ldots, A'_{|Y_{R_1}|}]$ and $Y_{R_2} = [B'_1, \ldots, B'_{|Y_{R_1}|}]$. Then a default relative key is $\kappa_0 = ((A'_1, B'_1, =), \ldots, (A'_{|Y_{R_1}|}, B'_{|Y_{R_1}|}, =))$. To simplify the discussion, we include κ_0 in Γ initially, and deduce such RCKs $((A_1, B_1, \approx_1), \ldots, (A_k, B_k, \approx_k))$ that for each $i \in [1, k]$, $R_1[A_i] \approx_i R_2[B_i]$ appears in either κ_0 or in an MDs of Σ. Such attributes are identified as sensible to compare by domain experts or by learning from sample data.

To determine whether Γ includes all RCKs that can be deduced from Σ, algorithm findRCKs leverages a notion of *completeness*, first studied by Lucchesi and Osborn [1978] for traditional candidate keys. To present this notion we need the following.

Consider an RCK κ and an MD ϕ. We define apply(κ, ϕ) to be the relative key κ' obtained by (1) removing all $(E, F, \approx)$ from κ if $(E, F, \rightleftharpoons)$ appears in RHS(ϕ), and (2) adding all $(A, B, \approx)$ in LHS(ϕ) to κ.

Example 4.17 Recall the RCK rck$_1$ from Example 4.16 and the MD φ_2 from Example 4.4:

rck$_1$: $((\text{LN}, \text{LN}, =), (\text{addr}, \text{post}, =), (\text{FN}, \text{FN}, \approx_d))$,

φ_2: credit[tel] = billing[phn] $\rightarrow$ credit[addr] $\rightleftharpoons$ billing[post].

Then apply(rck$_1$, φ_2) = $((\text{LN}, \text{LN}, =), (\text{FN}, \text{FN}, \approx_d), (\text{tel}, \text{phn}, =))$. □

We are now ready to define the notion of completeness. A nonempty set Γ of RCKs is said to be *complete w.r.t.* Σ if for each RCK κ in Γ and each MD ϕ in Σ, there exists a RCK κ_1 in Γ such that $\kappa_1 \subseteq$ apply(κ, ϕ).

Intuitively, Γ is complete if all those RCKs that can be deduced by possible applications of MDs in Σ are covered by "smaller" RCKs that are already in the set Γ. The notion of completeness allows us to check whether Γ consists of all the RCKs deduced from Σ, or in other words, whether Γ needs to be further expanded. Indeed, this is justified by the following proposition (see [Fan et al., 2011a] for a detailed proof).

Proposition 4.18 *Let Σ be a set of MDs, and Γ be a set of RCKs defined on the same schema. Then Γ consists of all RCKs deduced from Σ if and only if Γ is complete w.r.t. Σ.*

Crux. First assume that Γ consists of all RCKs that can be deduced from Σ. Then for any RCK $\kappa \in \Gamma$ and each MD $\phi \in \Sigma$, $\kappa_1 =$ apply(κ, ϕ) is a relative candidate key.

4.4. RELATIVE KEYS FOR RECORD MATCHING

Conversely, assume that Γ is complete w.r.t. Σ. Then one can show that for any RCK κ such that $\Sigma \models_d \kappa$, κ can be deduced by repeated uses of the apply operator on RCKs in Γ and MDs in Σ. This suffices. For if it holds, then κ must be in Γ since Γ is complete. □

Based on this proposition, we now present Algorithm findRCKs.

(1) *Initialization.* The algorithm uses a counter c to keep track of the number of RCKs in Γ, initially set to 0. It collects all pairs $(R_1[A], R_2[B])$ that are in either (Y_{R_1}, Y_{R_2}) or some MD of Σ. The counter $\mathrm{ct}(R_1[A], R_2[B])$ is set to 0. It uses a set variable Γ' to store relative keys that need to be processed, initially consisting of the default relative key κ_0 only.

(2) *Expanding Γ.* After these initialization steps, findRCKs repeatedly checks whether Γ is complete w.r.t. Σ. If so, it terminates, and otherwise it expands Γ. More specifically, for each unprocessed $\kappa \in \Gamma'$ and $\phi \in \Sigma$, it inspects the condition for the completeness. If Γ is not complete, it adds an RCK κ' to both Γ and Γ', where κ' is an RCK obtained from $\zeta = \mathrm{apply}(\kappa, \phi)$. To do this, it inspects each $(R_1[A], R_2[B], \approx)$ in ζ, and *removes* it from ζ as long as $\Sigma \models_d \zeta \setminus \{(R_1[A], R_2[B], \approx)\}$. The deduction is checked by invoking the algorithm mentioned in Theorem 4.13 for the deduction analysis of MDs, since relative keys are a special case of MDs. The process repeats until no more attributes can be removed from ζ, and yields κ'. After κ' is added to Γ, the algorithm increases the counter c by 1.

(3) *Termination.* The process proceeds until either Γ contains m RCKs (excluding the default key κ_0, which may not be a RCK), or it cannot be further expanded, i.e., either Γ is complete w.r.t. Σ or Γ' is empty when there exist no more than m RCKs. In the latter case, Γ already *includes all* the RCKs that can be deduced from Σ, by Proposition 4.18.

The algorithm takes the following steps to deduce RCKs defined with attributes of low costs. (1) It sorts MDs in Σ and relative keys in Γ' based on their costs, and applies low-cost MDs and keys first. (2) Moreover, it *dynamically adjusts* the costs after each RCK κ' is added, by increasing $\mathrm{ct}(R_1[A], R_2[B])$ for each $(R_1[A], R_2[B])$ that remains in κ'. It re-sorts MDs in Σ and keys in Γ' based on the updated costs. (3) Furthermore, when computing κ' from ζ, it retains attributes pairs with low costs in the RCKs and removes those of high costs. To do this, it first sorts $(R_1[A], R_2[B], \approx)$ in ζ based on $\mathrm{cost}(R_1[A], R_2[B])$. It then processes each $(R_1[A], R_2[B], \approx)$ in *descending* order, starting with the *most costly* one, such that the high-cost attributes are removed from ζ whenever possible.

Example 4.19 Consider the set Σ_c consisting of three MDs $\varphi_1, \varphi_2, \varphi_3$ given in Example 4.4, and the attribute lists (Y_c, Y_b) given in Example 4.1. Given Σ_c, $m = 6$ and (Y_c, Y_b), and fixing $w_1 = 1$ and $w_2 = w_3 = 0$, algorithm findRCKs returns a set Γ consisting of RCKs $\mathrm{rck}_1, \mathrm{rck}_2, \mathrm{rck}_3$, and rck_4 presented in Example 4.16. Observe that Γ contains four RCKs although $m = 6$, since when the counter $c \geq 4$, Γ is complete w.r.t. Σ_c and no new RCKs can be added to Γ. The algorithm starts with a set Γ' consisting of only the default relative key:

rck$_0$: ((FN, FN, =), (LN, LN, =), (addr, post, =), (tel, phn, =), (gender, gender, =)).

Nevertheless, rck$_0$ is not returned, since it is not an RCK. □

4.5 MATCHING DEPENDENCIES FOR DATA REPAIRING

We have studied MDs for data deduplication. The denotational semantics of MDs given in Section 4.3 aims to deduce RCKs as logical consequences of a given set of matching rules. As we have seen earlier, the RCKs may serve as matching keys to identify matches, as well as blocking keys and sorting keys to speed up data deduplication.

Matching dependencies can also be used as data quality rules for data repairing. To do this we present an operational semantics of MDs proposed by Bertossi et al. [2011].

An operational semantics. The denotational semantics given in Definition 4.5 states that when enforcing an MD $\varphi = R_1[X_1] \approx R_2[X_2] \to R_1[Y_1] \rightleftharpoons R_2[Y_2]$ on a pair (t_1, t_2) of tuples, $t_1[Y_1]$ and $t_2[Y_2]$ should be identified via updates, but it does not specify what values should be assigned to $t_1[Y_1]$ and $t_2[Y_2]$. In contrast, the operational semantics assumes an explicit binary *matching function* $m_A : \text{dom}(A) \times \text{dom}(A) \to \text{dom}(A)$ associated with each domain A, such that the value $m_A(a_1, a_2)$ is used to replace two values $a_1, a_2 \in \text{dom}(A)$ whenever a_1 and a_2 need to be identified. Such a matching function is assumed to be

- *idempotent*: $m_A(a, a) = a$;
- *commutative*: $m_A(a_1, a_2) = m_A(a_2, a_1)$; and
- *associative*: $m_A(a_1, m_A(a_2, a_3)) = m_A(m_A(a_1, a_2), a_3)$.

Intuitively, matching functions tell us what values to pick when we need to update $t_1[Y_1]$ and $t_2[Y_2]$ and make them equal.

Based on matching functions, a chase-like procedure is developed by Bertossi et al. [2011] to repair data (see [Abiteboul et al., 1995; Greco and Spezzano, 2012] for details about chase). It aims to obtain a clean instance from a dirty instance D by enforcing MDs. Consider two instances D, D' of schemas (R_1, R_2) with tuples having the same set of tuple identifiers, a pair of tuples (t_1, t_2) of (R_1, R_2), a set Σ of MDs, and an MD $\varphi = R_1[X_1] \approx R_2[X_2] \to R_1[A_1] \rightleftharpoons R_2[A_2]$ in Σ, where $\text{dom}(A_1) = \text{dom}(A_2) = \text{dom}(A)$. The rule for enforcing φ is given as follows.

Definition 4.20 Instance D' is an immediate result of enforcing φ on (t_1, t_2) in instance D, denoted by $(D, D')_{[t_1, t_2]} \models_o \varphi$, if

1. $t_1^D[X_1] \approx t_2^D[X_2]$ but $t_1^D[A_1] \neq t_2^D[A_2]$;
2. $t_1^{D'}[A_1] = t_2^{D'}[A_2] = m_A(t_1^D[A_1], t_2^D[A_2])$; and
3. D and D' agree on every other tuple and attribute value.

4.5. MATCHING DEPENDENCIES FOR DATA REPAIRING   87

In contrast to Definition 4.5, here we specify explicitly that $t_1^{D'}[A_1]$ and $t_2^{D'}[A_2]$ should take the value given by the matching function. Moreover, $t_1^{D'}[X_1'] \approx t_2^{D'}[X_2']$, corresponding to $R_1[X_1'] \approx R_2[X_2']$ in the LHS of some $\phi \in \Sigma$, is no longer required, as opposed to Definition 4.5. That is, the update does not have to preserve the similarity $t_1^{D}[X_1'] \approx t_2^{D}[X_2']$ in D'. Furthermore, only $t_1^{D}[A_1]$ and $t_2^{D}[A_2]$ are allowed to be updated when φ is applied.

We use a chase-like procedure to repair a dirty instance D_0. It starts from D_0 and enforces the MDs in Σ step by step, until we reach a stable instance. Intuitively, the stable instance is a clean instance of D_0, to which no more MDs of Σ can be applied. Each step of the chase procedure is conducted by applying an MD in Σ, as described in Definition 4.20.

Definition 4.21   For an instance D_0 and a set Σ of MDs, a *chasing sequence* of D_0 by Σ is a sequence of instances $D_1, \ldots, D_l, \ldots$, such that for each $i \geq 1$, $(D_{i-1}, D_i)_{[t_1^{i-1}, t_2^{i-1}]} \models_o \varphi_i$ for some $\varphi_i \in \Sigma$ and for some tuples $t_1^{i-1}, t_2^{i-1} \in D_{i-1}$.

A chasing sequence $D_1, \ldots, D_k$ is *terminal* if it is finite and, moreover, D_k is stable. The instance D_k is called a *repair of D_0 by Σ*.

The example below, also taken from [Bertossi et al., 2011], illustrates how MDs are used to repair data.

Example 4.22   Consider a set Σ of MDs consisting of $R[A] \approx R[A] \to R[B] \rightleftharpoons R[B]$ and $R[B] \approx R[B] \to R[C] \rightleftharpoons R[C]$. An instance D_0 of R is shown in Figure 4.4, in which $a_1 \approx a_2$ and $b_2 \approx b_3$. Two repairs D_2 and D_3' of D_0 by Σ are also given in Figure 4.4, obtained by enforcing MDs of Σ in different orders. Here for ease of exposition, we use $\langle a_1, \ldots, a_l \rangle$ to denote $m_A(a_1, m_A(a_2, m_A(\ldots, a_l)))$, which is well-defined by the associativity of m_A.

Properties of the chase. We next study the properties of the chase procedure, which employs MDs as data quality rules.

Termination. The first question concerns whether the chase procedure always terminates and yields a repair by MDs. The answer is affirmative.

Theorem 4.23   For any set Σ of MDs and instance D_0, each chasing sequence of D_0 by Σ is finite and is an initial subsequence of a terminal chasing sequence, such that the terminal sequence leads to a repair of D_0 by Σ in a polynomial number of steps in the size of D_0.

Crux. This is verified by defining a strict partial order $\sqsubset$ on instances such that (a) for any chasing sequence $D_1, \ldots, D_l, \ldots$ of D_0, $D_{i-1} \sqsubset D_i$; (b) there exists an upper bound $D_{\max}$ for the

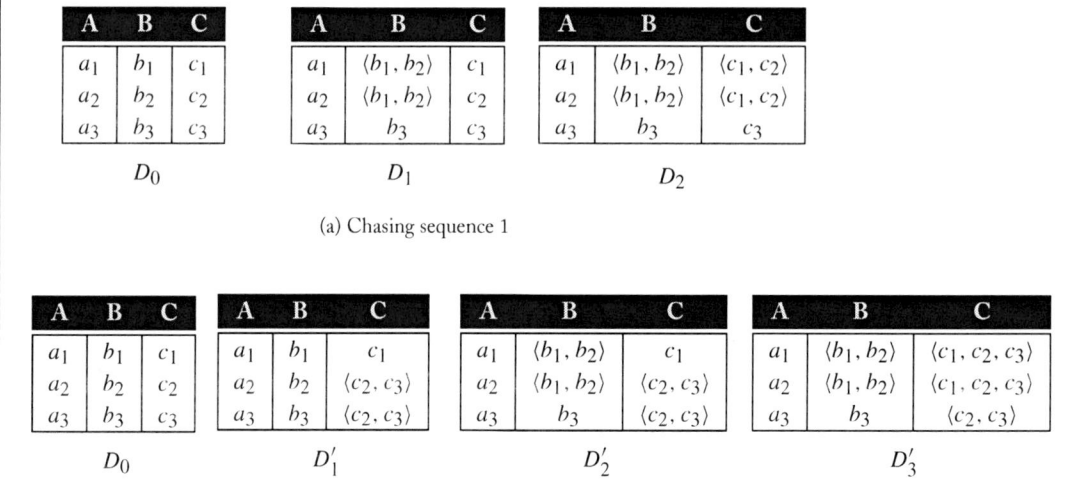

88   4. DATA DEDUPLICATION

A	B	C
a_1	b_1	c_1
a_2	b_2	c_2
a_3	b_3	c_3

D_0

A	B	C
a_1	$\langle b_1, b_2 \rangle$	c_1
a_2	$\langle b_1, b_2 \rangle$	c_2
a_3	b_3	c_3

D_1

A	B	C
a_1	$\langle b_1, b_2 \rangle$	$\langle c_1, c_2 \rangle$
a_2	$\langle b_1, b_2 \rangle$	$\langle c_1, c_2 \rangle$
a_3	b_3	c_3

D_2

(a) Chasing sequence 1

A	B	C
a_1	b_1	c_1
a_2	b_2	c_2
a_3	b_3	c_3

D_0

A	B	C
a_1	b_1	c_1
a_2	b_2	$\langle c_2, c_3 \rangle$
a_3	b_3	$\langle c_2, c_3 \rangle$

D'_1

A	B	C
a_1	$\langle b_1, b_2 \rangle$	c_1
a_2	$\langle b_1, b_2 \rangle$	$\langle c_2, c_3 \rangle$
a_3	b_3	$\langle c_2, c_3 \rangle$

D'_2

A	B	C
a_1	$\langle b_1, b_2 \rangle$	$\langle c_1, c_2, c_3 \rangle$
a_2	$\langle b_1, b_2 \rangle$	$\langle c_1, c_2, c_3 \rangle$
a_3	b_3	$\langle c_2, c_3 \rangle$

D'_3

(b) Chasing sequence 2

Figure 4.4: Example Σ repairs of D_0.

sequence and, moreover, (c) $D_{\max}$ can be reached in polynomial number of applications of MDs (see [Bertossi et al., 2012b] for details of the proof). □

The Church-Rosser property. Another important question concerns whether the results of different terminal chasing sequences coincide, or in other words, whether these terminal sequences lead to the same unique repair, no matter in what order the MDs in Σ are applied. This is known as the *Church-Rosser property* (see, for example, [Abiteboul et al., 1995]). Unfortunately, the chase procedure described in Definitions 4.20 and 4.21 *do not* have the Church-Rosser property. Indeed, as shown in Example 4.22, both D_2 and D'_3 are repairs of D_0 by Σ, but they are different. In general, for a set Σ of MDs and an instance D_0, there exist (finitely) many repairs of D_0 by Σ, produced by different orders of applications of MDs on D_0 and by enforcing MDs on different tuples in D_0. Some sufficient conditions were identified by Bertossi et al. [2011] to assure a single clean instance.

Observe that when a terminal chasing sequence D_0 by Σ yields a repair D_k of D_0, we may not have that $(D_0, D_k) \models_d \Sigma$. Indeed, in Example 4.22, $(D_0, D_2) \not\models_d \Sigma$, since $\langle b_1, b_2 \rangle \approx b_3$ may not hold. Similarly, $(D_0, D'_3) \not\models_d \Sigma$. This is because Definition 4.20 does not require similarity preservation when applying MDs, and hence, some of the similarities that existed in D_0 could have been broken by iteratively enforcing the MDs to produce D_k. Nevertheless, each repair D_k of D_0 by Σ is stable and retains the values that are not affected by MDs.

Minimal instance. The chase procedure makes only necessary changes required by MDs. That is, it incurs minimal changes to obtain a repair. In particular, if D_0 is already stable, then D_0 is the unique repair of D_0 by Σ, i.e., no updates are incurred to D_0 to enforce Σ.

To further explore the semantics of enforcing MDs for data repairing, we present the notion of information ordering studied by Bertossi et al. [2011]. For values $a, a' \in \text{dom}(A)$, we say that a' *semantically dominates* a if $m_A(a, a') = a'$, denoted by $a \preceq_A a'$. When we identify $t_1[A]$ and $t_2[A]$ by an MD, we take $m_A(t_1[A], t_2[A])$ as the new value, which semantically dominates both $t_1[A]$ and $t_2[A]$. For a tuple t in D_1 and D_2, we write $t^{D_1} \preceq t^{D_2}$ if $t^{D_1}[A] \preceq_A t^{D_2}[A]$ for every attribute A of t. We write $D_1 \sqsubseteq_o D_2$ if for every tuple t in D_1, there exists a tuple in D_2 with the same tuple id and moreover, $t^{D_1} \preceq t^{D_2}$. One can readily show that $\sqsubseteq_o$ is a partial order.

One can see that in any chasing sequence $D_1, \ldots, D_k$ of D_0 by Σ, $D_{i-1} \sqsubseteq_o D_i$ for each $i \in [1, k]$. Moreover, $D_0 \sqsubseteq_o D_k$, i.e., each repair D_k of D_0 semantically dominates D_0.

Nevertheless, D_k is not at a minimal distance to D_0 w.r.t. $\sqsubseteq_o$. Indeed, in Example 4.22, both D_2 and D_3' are repairs of D_0, while $D_2 \sqsubseteq_o D_3'$ but $D_3' \not\sqsubseteq_o D_2$; hence D_3' is not at a minimal distance to D_0 w.r.t. $\sqsubseteq_o$.

BIBLIOGRAPHIC NOTES

A variety of methods have been developed for data deduplication [Ananthakrishna et al., 2002; Arasu et al., 2008, 2009; Chaudhuri et al., 2007a,b; Fellegi and Sunter, 1969; Galhardas et al., 2001; Guha et al., 2004; Hernández and Stolfo, 1998, 1995; Jaro, 1989; Lim et al., 1996; Naumann et al., 2006; Sarawagi and Bhamidipaty, 2002; Verykios et al., 2002; Weis et al., 2008; Whang and Garcia-Molina, 2010; Whang et al., 2009; Winkler, 2004, 2006, 2002]. There have also been a number of record matching tools. e.g., Febrl [Christen, 2008], TAILOR [Elfeky et al., 2002], WHIRL [Cohen, 2000], BigMatch [Yancey, 2007], Swoosh [Benjelloun et al., 2009]. We refer to [Bleiholder and Naumann, 2008; Elmagarmid et al., 2007; Herzog et al., 2009; Naumann and Herschel, 2010] for recent surveys.

The matching dependencies presented in this chapter were introduced by Fan [2008] and Fan et al. [2011a]. The record matching framework and deduction algorithms were provided there, along with a sound and complete inference system for MDs. The operational semantics of MDs in terms of matching functions was proposed by Bertossi et al. [2011]. This issue has also been explored in [Bertossi et al., 2012a; Gardezi and Bertossi, 2012a,b; Gardezi et al., 2012], which, among other things, did not use matching functions but adopted a minimal number of changes instead. Its connections to consistent query answering were also explored there. The integration of data repairing and record matching via MDs was studied by Fan et al. [2011e], which will be detailed in Chapter 7.

Declarative methods for record matching have been studied [Ananthakrishna et al., 2002; Arasu et al., 2008, 2009; Chaudhuri et al., 2007b; Hernández and Stolfo, 1998, 1995; Lim et al., 1996; Shen et al., 2005; Singla and Domingos, 2005; Weis et al., 2008]. In particular, a class of matching rules was introduced by Hernández and Stolfo [1998, 1995], which can be expressed as relative candidate keys presented in this chapter. Extensions to this rule-based approach were proposed by Ananthakrishna et al. [2002] and Arasu et al. [2008], by supporting dimensional hierarchies and constant transformations to identify domain-specific abbreviations and conventions. It has been shown that matching rules and matching keys play an important role in industry-scale credit checking [Weis et al., 2008]. The need for dependencies for record matching was also highlighted in [Chaudhuri et al., 2007b; Shen et al., 2005]. The AJAX system [Galhardas et al., 2000, 2001] also advocates matching transformations specified in a declarative language. A class of constant keys was studied by Lim et al. [1996], to match records in a single relation.

Recursive algorithms were developed by Arasu et al. [2009], to compute matches based on domain-specific hard and soft constraints. i.e., constraints that have to be enforced and those that are likely to hold, respectively. They used Dedupalog, a variation of Datalog, to write the constraints as rules. The matching process attempts to satisfy all the hard constraints, by minimizing the number of violations to the soft constraints. Dedupalog is used for identifying groups of tuples that could be merged, but the actual merging is deferred to a post-processing step. Probabilistic record matching based on declarative Markov Logic constraints was proposed by Singla and Domingos [2005]. Declarative methods have also been studied in the context of the Semantic Web [Saïs et al., 2007]. However, that line of work does not consider automated reasoning methods that are important, as is shown in this Chapter, in deducing minimal matching keys.

There are other approaches to deciding what attributes to compare in data deduplication [Jaro, 1989; Weis and Naumann, 2005; Winkler, 2002]. A heuristic method was proposed by Weis and Naumann [2005] to identify relevant elements in XML documents, by means of their structural similarity such as navigational paths. Probabilistic methods were studied by Jaro [1989] and Winkler [2002], using an expectation maximization (EM) algorithm. In this monograph we focus on relational data and non-probabilistic methods only.

For the same reasons that the automated discovery of conditional dependencies is important, as described in Chapter 3, methods are also needed for automatically discovering matching dependencies or minimal matching keys. In Chapter 3, we discussed a variety of methods for discovering CFDs and FDs. A specialized method for finding traditional keys, defined on a single relation and in terms of equality, can be found in, e.g., [Sismanis et al., 2006]. Like FDs [Mannila and Räihä, 1987], exponentially many keys may need to be considered [Lucchesi and Osborn, 1978]. To extend these methods to MDs one has to decide what attributes across different schemas relate to each other and what similarity predicates should be used to compare them. Schema matching techniques (see, e.g., [Aumueller et al., 2005; Rahm and Bernstein, 2001]) are likely to play an important role in this context. Preliminary work on the discovery of MDs was presented by Song and Chen [2011, 2009].

There have been extensions of FDs by supporting similarity predicates [Belohlávek and Vychodil, 2006; Koudas et al., 2009]. There has also be been work on schema design for uncertain relations by extending FDs [Das Sarma et al., 2009]. Like traditional FDs, these extensions are defined on a single relation and have a static semantics. They are quite different from MDs that are defined across possibly different relations and have a dynamic semantics. An extension of FDs over two relations but without similarity predicates was proposed by Wang [2007], which also has a static semantics.

Dynamic semantics of constraints have been developed for database evolution [Vianu, 1987] and for XML updates [Cautis et al., 2009]. These constraints aim to express an invariant connection between the old value and the new value of a data element when the data are updated. They differ from MDs in that these constraints are *restrictions* on how given updates should be carried out. In contrast, MDs specify how data elements should be identified for record matching. In other words, MDs are to determine what (implicit) updates are necessary for identifying records. Furthermore, similarity predicates are not supported by the dynamic constraints studied by Vianu [1987] and Cautis et al. [2009].

CHAPTER 5

Information Completeness

When we query a database, we naturally expect that the database has complete information to answer our query. As we have seen in Section 1.2.4, if the database does not have complete information, its answer to our query may be inaccurate or even incorrect. Unfortunately, real-life databases are often incomplete, from which both tuples and attribute values may be missing. This raises two questions: How can we determine whether our database has complete information to answer our query? If the information in our database is incomplete for our tasks at hand, what additional data should be included in our database to meet our requests? The classical Closed World Assumption (CWA) and Open World Assumption (OWA) fall short of providing us with a practical model to answer these questions.

This chapter gives an overview of recent efforts to answer these questions. We introduce a model of relative information completeness, to rectify the limitations of the CWA and the OWA. We begin with an introduction to relative completeness, focusing on missing tuples (Section 5.1), and study the two questions in this model (Section 5.2). We then extend the model to capture both missing tuples and missing values. To this end, we first review traditional representation systems for querying incomplete information (Section 5.3), and then extend our model for relative information completeness by allowing missing values (Section 5.4). Finally, we provide the complexity bounds of answering these questions for various query languages (Section 5.5). It should be remarked that the study of relative information completeness has not reached maturity: our understanding of its issues is still rather rudimentary. In particular, effective algorithms and metrics are yet to be developed, to assess the completeness of information in our database for answering our queries.

5.1 RELATIVE INFORMATION COMPLETENESS

Database texts typically tell us that the world is closed: all the real-world entities of our interest are assumed already to be represented by tuples residing in our database, although the values of some fields in those tuples may be missing. This is known as the Closed World Assumption (CWA). After all, this is the basis of negation in our queries: a fact is viewed as false unless it can be proven from explicitly stated facts in our database.

Unfortunately, real-life databases are often not closed-world. For instance, when medical data are concerned, "pieces of information perceived as being needed for clinical decisions were missing from 13.6% to 81% of the time" [Miller Jr. et al., 2005]. Indeed, a database may only be a proper subset of the set of tuples that represent real-world entities. In other words, not only attribute values but also tuples are often missing from our database. This is known as the Open World Assumption (OWA).

Neither the CWA nor the OWA is very helpful when we query a real-life database. On one hand, the CWA is too strong to hold in the real world. On the other hand, the OWA is too weak, under which one can often expect few sensible queries to find complete answers.

Not all is lost. Below we first show that in the real world, a database is neither entirely closed-world nor entirely open-world. More specifically, it is often "partially closed" (Section 5.1.1). To model partially closed databases, we introduce a notion of relative information completeness (Section 5.1.2). Furthermore, we show that information completeness and data consistency can actually be modeled in a uniform logical framework (Section 5.1.3).

5.1.1 PARTIALLY CLOSED DATABASES

An enterprise nowadays typically maintains *master data* (*a.k.a. reference data*), a single repository of high-quality data that provides various applications with a synchronized, consistent view of the core business entities of the enterprise (see, for example, [Dreibelbis et al., 2007; Loshin, 2009; Radcliffe and White, 2008], for master data management mdm). The master data contain complete information about the enterprise in certain categories, e.g., employees, departments, projects, and equipment.

Master data can be regarded as a closed-world database for the core business entities of the enterprise. Meanwhile a number of other databases may be in use in the enterprise for, e.g., sales, project control and customer support. On one hand, the information in these databases may not be complete, e.g., some sale transaction records may be missing. On the other hand, certain parts of the databases are *constrained by* the master data, e.g., employees and projects. In other words, these databases are neither entirely closed-world nor entirely open-world. As illustrated by the example below, one can often find complete answer to queries in such a partially closed database.

Example 5.1 Consider a company that maintains DCust(cid, name, AC, phn), a master data relation consisting of all its domestic customers, in which a tuple (c, n, a, p) specifies the id c, name n, area code a, and phone number p of a customer. In addition, the company also has databases (a) Cust(cid, name, CC, AC, phn) of all customers of the company, domestic (with country code CC = 01) or international; and (b) Supt(eid, dept, cid), indicating that employee eid in dept supports customer cid. Neither Cust nor Supt is part of the master data. Nevertheless, Cust and Supt are constrained by DCust when domestic customers are concerned: they cannot include domestic customers whose information is not recorded in the master relation. In other words, the Cust and Supt relations are partially closed.

Consider a query Q_1 posed on Supt to find all the customers in NJ with AC = 908 who are supported by the employee with eid = e_0. The query may *not* get a complete answer since some tuples may be missing from Supt. However, if Q_1 returns all NJ customers with AC = 908 found in the master relation DCust, then we can safely conclude that query Q_1 can find a complete answer from Supt. That is, Supt contains complete information about those customers needed for answering query Q_1. Hence there is no need to add more tuples to Supt in order to answer query Q_1.

Now consider a query Q_2 to find *all* customers, either domestic or international, who are supported by the employee e_0. Note that the international customers of Cust are not constrained by the master data; in other words, the company may not maintain a complete list of its customers. As a result, we are not able to tell whether any Supt tuples in connection with e_0 are missing. Worse still, we do not know what tuples and even how many tuples should be added to Supt such that the answer to Q_2 in Supt is complete.

The situation is not as bad as it seems. If we know that [eid] → [dept, cid] is a functional dependency (FD) on Supt, then we can also conclude that the answer to Q_2 in Supt is complete as long as it is nonempty. More generally, suppose that there is a constraint which asserts that an employee supports at most k customers. Then if the answer to Q_2 in Supt returns k customers, we know that the seemingly incomplete relation Supt is actually complete for query Q_2. That is, adding more tuples to Supt does not change the answer to Q_2 in Supt. Even when Q_2 returns k' tuples, where $k' < k$, we know that we need to add at most $k - k'$ tuples to Supt to make it complete for Q_2. □

This example tells us that we may find a complete answer to our query in a partially closed database. It also gives rise to the following questions. Given a query Q posed on a database D that is partially constrained by master data D_m, can we find complete information from D to answer Q? Does there exist a database D at all that is partially constrained by D_m and has the complete information to answer Q (i.e., adding tuples to D will not change the answer to Q in D)? These questions are not only of theoretical interest, but are also important in practice. Indeed, the ability to answer these questions not only helps us determine whether a query can find a complete answer from a database, but also provides a guidance for what data should be collected in order to answer a query.

5.1.2 A MODEL FOR RELATIVE INFORMATION COMPLETENESS

We next present a model to characterize partially closed databases.

Databases and master data. A database is specified by a relational schema $\mathcal{R} = (R_1, \ldots, R_n)$. We say that an instance $D = (I_1, \ldots, I_n)$ of $\mathcal{R}$ is *contained in* another instance $D' = (I'_1, \ldots, I'_n)$ of $\mathcal{R}$, denoted by $D \subseteq D'$, if $I_j \subseteq I'_j$ for all $j \in [1, n]$. If $D \subseteq D'$ then we also say that D' is an *extension* of D.

Master data are in a closed-world database D_m, specified by a relational schema $\mathcal{R}_m$. As remarked earlier, an enterprise typically maintains master data that are assumed consistent and complete about certain information of the enterprise. We do not impose any restriction on the relational schemas $\mathcal{R}$ and $\mathcal{R}_m$.

Containment constraints. To specify relationships between data in the databases and master data, we use a class of constraints (dependencies). Let $\mathcal{L}_C$ be a query language.

A *containment constraint* (CC) ϕ_v in $\mathcal{L}_C$ is of the form $q_v(\mathcal{R}) \subseteq p(\mathcal{R}_m)$, where q_v is a query in $\mathcal{L}_C$ defined over schema $\mathcal{R}$, and p is a projection query over schema $\mathcal{R}_m$. That is, p is a query of the form $\exists \bar{x}\ R_i^m(\bar{x}, \bar{y})$ for some relation R_i^m in $\mathcal{R}_m$.

An instance D of $\mathcal{R}$ and master data instance D_m of $\mathcal{R}_m$ *satisfy* ϕ_v, denoted by $(D, D_m) \models \phi_v$, if $q_v(D) \subseteq p(D_m)$. We say that D and D_m *satisfy* a set V of CCs, denoted by $(D, D_m) \models V$, if for each $\phi_v \in V$, $(D, D_m) \models \phi_v$.

Intuitively, ϕ_v assures that D_m is an "upper bound" of the information extracted by $q_v(D)$. In other words, the CWA is asserted for D_m that constrains the part of data in D identified by $q_v(D)$. That is, while this part of D can be extended, the expansion cannot go beyond the information already in D_m. On the other hand, the OWA is assumed for the part of D that is not constrained by ϕ_v.

We simply write $q_v(\mathcal{R}) \subseteq p(\mathcal{R}_m)$ as $q_v \subseteq p$ when $\mathcal{R}$ and $\mathcal{R}_m$ are clear from the context. We write $q_v \subseteq p$ as $q_v \subseteq \emptyset$ if p is a projection on an empty master relation.

Example 5.2 Recall Cust, Supt, and DCust from Example 5.1. We can write a CC $\phi_0 = q(\text{Cust}, \text{Supt}) \subseteq p(\text{DCust})$ in the language of conjunctive queries, where

$$q(c_{id}) = \exists n, c, a, p, e, d\ (\text{Cust}(c_{id}, n, c, a, p) \wedge \text{Supt}(e, d, c_{id}) \wedge c = 01),$$
$$p(c_{id}) = \exists n, a, p\ \text{DCust}(c_{id}, n, a, p),$$

asserting that all domestic customers are constrained by master relation DCust.

Another CC ϕ_1 in the language of conjunctive queries is $q \subseteq \emptyset$, where

$$q(e) = \exists c_1, d_1, \ldots, c_{k+1}, d_{k+1} \Big(\bigwedge_{i \in [1, k+1]} \text{Supt}(e, d_i, c_i) \wedge \bigwedge_{i, j \in [1, k+1], i \neq j} (c_i \neq c_j) \Big).$$

It asserts that each employee supports at most k customers. □

We are now ready to define partially closed databases, which are characterized in terms of master data D_m and a set V of containment constraints.

Definition 5.3 A database D is called *partially closed* w.r.t. (D_m, V) if $(D, D_m) \models V$, for master data D_m and a set V of containment constraints. The set of *partially closed extensions* of D is defined as $\text{Ext}(D, D_m, V) = \{D' \mid D \subset D', (D', D_m) \models V\}$. We write $\text{Ext}(D, D_m, V)$ simply as $\text{Ext}(D)$ when D_m and V are clear from the context. □

As a special case of CCs, observe that a CC $q_v(\mathcal{R}) \subseteq p(\mathcal{R}_m)$ is an *inclusion dependency* (IND) when q_v is also a projection query. In the sequel we simply refer to such CCs as INDs.

5.1. RELATIVE INFORMATION COMPLETENESS

Relative completeness. We now formalize the notion of relative information completeness. Let $\mathcal{L}_Q$ be a query language, which is not necessarily the same as $\mathcal{L}_C$.

Definition 5.4 For a query Q in $\mathcal{L}_Q$, and a partially closed database D w.r.t. master data D_m and a set V of CCs, we say that D is *complete for query Q relative to* (D_m, V) if for all instances D' of $\mathcal{R}$, if $D \subseteq D'$ and $(D', D_m) \models V$, then $Q(D) = Q(D')$. □

That is, D is relative complete for Q if (a) D is partially closed w.r.t. (D_m, V), and (b) for *all* partially closed extensions D' of D, $Q(D) = Q(D')$. In other words, no matter how D is expanded by including new tuples, as long as the extension does not violate V, the answer to Q remains unchanged. Intuitively, D has complete information for answering Q. The notion is *relative to* the master data D_m and CCs in V: the extensions of D should not violate the CCs in V, i.e., $(D', D_m) \models V$. That is, the CWA for D_m is observed.

We also use the following notations.

- For D_m, V, and Q, *the set of complete databases* for Q w.r.t. (D_m, V), denoted by $\text{RCQ}(Q, D_m, V)$, is the set of all complete databases for Q relative to (D_m, V).

- When $\text{RCQ}(Q, D_m, V)$ is nonempty, Q is called a *relatively complete query w.r.t.* (D_m, V). Intuitively, Q is relatively complete if it is possible to find a database D such that the answer to Q in D is complete, and $(D, D_m) \models V$.

Example 5.5 As described in Example 5.1, the relations Cust and Supt are complete for query Q_1 w.r.t. DCust and CC ϕ_0 of Example 5.2, provided that the query result contains all domestic customers in DCust. In this case, the database consisting of the Cust and Supt relations is in $\text{RCQ}(Q_1, \text{DCust}, \phi_0)$, and hence, Q_1 is relatively complete w.r.t. (DCust, ϕ_0).

When the CC ϕ_1 of Example 5.2 is in place for $k = 1$, Supt is complete for query Q_2 of Example 5.1 w.r.t. $(\emptyset, \phi_1)$, as long as the query result is nonempty. Hence, in this case, Q_2 is complete w.r.t. $(\emptyset, \phi_1)$. □

Query languages. Depending on the applications, the user may choose any languages to express containment constraints and queries, such as CQ, UCQ, $\exists\text{FO}^+$, FO, and FP given in Section 1.4. They may opt to use the same language or different languages for $\mathcal{L}_C$ and $\mathcal{L}_Q$.

The completeness of information in our database is also relative to what query language we use to express our queries. To illustrate this, let us consider the following example.

Example 5.6 Consider a master relation $\text{Manage}_m(\text{eid}_1, \text{eid}_2)$, in which a tuple indicates that employee eid_2 directly reports to eid_1. Our database has a relation $\text{Manage}(\text{eid}_1, \text{eid}_2)$, in which a tuple indicates that eid_2 reports to eid_1, directly or indirectly. It is not part of master data, but contains all the tuples in Manage_m.

We want to pose a query on Manage, to find all the people above e_0 in the management hierarchy, i.e., the set S of all the people to whom e_0 reports, directly or indirectly. We write the query in two languages: one is Q_3 in Datalog (denoted by FP), which finds S by computing the transitive closure of $\text{Manage}_m(\text{eid}_1, \text{eid}_2)$ embedded in Manage; the other is Q'_3 expressed as a conjunctive query (CQ), which scans the Manage relation and includes e in S for each tuple (e, e_0) in the relation.

Observe that the Manage relation is complete for Q_3 relative to Manage_m. In contrast, it is not complete for Q'_3 if Manage does not contain the transitive closure of Manage_m. In the latter case, the seemingly complete Manage relation turns out to be "incomplete".

Nevertheless, Q'_3 is relatively complete *w.r.t.* Manage_m: one can make the Manage relation complete for Q_3 by including the transitive closure of Manage_m. □

5.1.3 RELATIVE COMPLETENESS AND DATA CONSISTENCY

To answer a query using a database D, one naturally wants the information in D to be both complete and consistent. Recall from Chapter 2 that to characterize data consistency, we use constraints such as conditional dependencies. That is, a set Σ of dependencies is imposed on a database D such that errors in D are detected as violations of one or more dependencies in Σ. In light of this, one might be tempted to extend the notion of partially closed databases by incorporating conditional dependencies.

Constraints for data consistency. The good news is that there is no need to overburden the notion with conditional dependencies. Indeed, conditional functional dependencies (CFDs) and conditional inclusion dependencies (CINDs) are expressible as simple containment constraints. As a result, we can assure that only consistent and partially closed databases are considered, by enforcing containment constraints. That is, in a uniform framework we can deal with both relative information completeness and data consistency.

Proposition 5.7 *(a) CFDs can be expressed as containment constraints (CCs) in CQ. (b) CINDs can be expressed as CCs in FO. In both cases only an empty master data relation is required.*

To see this, observe the following.

CFDs. A CFD can be written as

$$\varphi_{cfd} = \forall \bar{x}_1, \bar{x}_2, \bar{y}_1, \bar{y}_2, \bar{z}_1, \bar{z}_2 \, \big(R(\bar{x}_1, \bar{z}_1, \bar{y}_1) \wedge R(\bar{x}_2, \bar{z}_2, \bar{y}_2) \wedge \phi(\bar{x}_1) \wedge \phi(\bar{x}_2) \wedge \bar{x}_1 = \bar{x}_2 \\ \to \bar{y}_1 = \bar{y}_2 \wedge \psi(\bar{y}_1) \wedge \psi(\bar{y}_2)\big),$$

where R is a relation atom, and $\phi(\bar{x})$ is a conjunction of the form $x_{i_1} = c_1 \wedge \cdots \wedge x_{i_k} = c_k$; here $\{x_{i_j} \mid j \in [1, k]\}$ is a subset of $\bar{x}$, and c_j is a constant. The expression $\psi(\bar{y})$ is defined similarly.

The CFD φ_{cfd} is equivalent to two sets of CCs in CQ. For each pair (y_1, y_2) of variables in $(\bar{y}_1, \bar{y}_2)$, the first set contains $q(\bar{x}_1, \bar{z}_1, \bar{y}_1, \bar{x}_2, \bar{z}_2, \bar{y}_2) \subseteq \emptyset$, where q is

$$R(\bar{x}_1, \bar{z}_1, \bar{y}_1) \wedge R(\bar{x}_2, \bar{z}_2, \bar{y}_2) \wedge \phi(\bar{x}_1) \wedge \phi(\bar{x}_2) \wedge \bar{x}_1 = \bar{x}_2 \wedge y_1 \neq y_2.$$

This CC assures that the CFD is not violated by two distinct tuples.

The second set contains a CC of the form $q'(\bar{x}, \bar{z}, \bar{y}) \subseteq \emptyset$ for each variable y in $\bar{y}_1$ (resp. $\bar{y}_2$) such that $y = c$ is in $\psi_1(\bar{y}_1)$ (resp. $\psi_2(\bar{y}_2)$), where q' is

$$R(\bar{x}, \bar{z}, \bar{y}) \wedge \phi(\bar{x}) \wedge y \neq c.$$

These CCs ensure that φ_{cfd} is not violated by a single tuple that does not observe the constant patterns.

It is easy to verify that for any database D, D satisfies φ_{cfd} if and only if D and D_m satisfy these two sets of CCs, where $D_m = \emptyset$.

CINDs. Observe that a CIND can be expressed as:

$$\varphi_{cind} = \forall \bar{x}, \bar{y}_1, \bar{z}_1 \left(R_1(\bar{x}, \bar{y}_1, \bar{z}_1) \wedge \phi(\bar{y}_1) \to \exists \bar{y}_2, \bar{z}_2 \left(R_2(\bar{x}, \bar{y}_2, \bar{z}_2) \wedge \psi(\bar{y}_2) \right) \right).$$

Then we can define a single CC $q(\bar{x}, \bar{y}_1, \bar{z}_1) \subseteq \emptyset$ in FO, where q is

$$R_1(\bar{x}, \bar{y}_1, \bar{z}_1) \wedge \phi(\bar{y}_1) \wedge \forall \bar{y}_2, \bar{z}_2 \left(\neg R_2(\bar{x}, \bar{y}_2, \bar{z}_2) \vee \neg \psi(\bar{y}_2) \right).$$

Then for any database D, D satisfies φ_{cind} if and only if D and D_m satisfy this CC, for $D_m = \emptyset$.

Dependencies posed on databases. A database D may carry other dependencies to specify the semantics of its data. These dependencies are posed on D regardless of master data D_m. Nevertheless, dependencies on D that are commonly found in practice can also be expressed as CCs, which are defined on (D, D_m). In particular, the class of denial constraints that we have seen in Chapter 2 are expressible as CCs. Better still, these dependencies often help us decide relative completeness and make our database complete.

Example 5.8 Recall query Q_2 from Example 5.1 and CC ϕ_1 from Example 5.2, both defined over schema Supt. The query is to find all customers supported by the employee e_0, i.e., all Supt tuples t with $t[\text{eid}] = e_0$, and can be expressed in CQ. The CC ensures that no employee supports more than k customers. Consider an instance I_1 of Supt such that $Q_2(I_1)$ returns k distinct tuples. Then adding any new tuple to I_1 violates ϕ_1 if the new tuple is in connection with e_0, and it does not change the answer to Q_2 in I_1 otherwise. That is, there already exist k "witnesses" for the completeness of Q_2 for I_1 relative to $(\emptyset, \phi_1)$, which "block" further additions of tuples in connection with e_0. Thus by simply checking the cardinality of $Q_2(I_1)$, we can determine whether I_1 is in RCQ($Q_2, \emptyset, \{\phi_1\}$).

As another example, recall from Example 5.1 the FD [eid] $\to$ [dept, cid] defined on Supt. As FDs are a special case of CFDs, we can actually express the FD as a single CC in CQ, denoted by φ_{fd}, using an empty master relation. Consider an instance I_2 of Supt in which there exists no tuple t such that $t[\text{eid}] = e_0$. Then I_2 is not complete for Q_2 relative to $(\emptyset, \varphi_{fd})$, since $Q_2(I_2) = \emptyset$. Nevertheless, the FD tells us that it suffices to add a single tuple t with $t[\text{eid}] = e_0$ to I_2 that leads to a nonempty answer to Q_2 in the updated I_2. In other words, a single tuple insertion makes I_2 complete for Q_2.

□

5.2 DETERMINING RELATIVE COMPLETENESS

Having defined the notion of $\text{RCQ}(Q, D_m, V)$, we are now ready to formalize and study the two questions raised in Section 5.1.1.

Decision problems. One is the *relatively complete database problem* for $\mathcal{L}_Q$ and $\mathcal{L}_C$, denoted by $\text{RCDP}(\mathcal{L}_Q, \mathcal{L}_C)$ and stated as follows.

- INPUT: A query $Q \in \mathcal{L}_Q$, master data D_m, a set V of CCs in $\mathcal{L}_C$, and a partially closed database D w.r.t. (D_m, V).
- QUESTION: Is D in $\text{RCQ}(Q, D_m, V)$, i.e., is D complete for Q relative to (D_m, V)?

The other problem is the *relatively complete query problem* for $\mathcal{L}_Q$ and $\mathcal{L}_C$, denoted by $\text{RCQP}(\mathcal{L}_Q, \mathcal{L}_C)$ and stated as follows:

- INPUT: A query $Q \in \mathcal{L}_Q$, master data D_m, and a set V of CCs in $\mathcal{L}_C$.
- QUESTION: Is $\text{RCQ}(Q, D_m, V)$ nonempty? That is, does there exist a database that is complete for Q relative to (D_m, V)?

Intuitively, RCDP is to decide whether a particular database has complete information to answer a user query, and RCQP is to decide whether there exists a database at all that is relatively complete for a given query with respect to available master data.

Assessing information completeness. Before we establish the complexity of these problems, we first demonstrate how decision procedures for RCDP and RCQP can help us assess the quality of our data and the quality of query answers. We illustrate this by using the application described in Example 5.1, which is a simplified instance of Customer Relationship Management (CRM), a typical usage scenario of mdm [Loshin, 2009]. We should remark that relative completeness may also find applications in Enterprise Resource Planning (ERP), Supply Chain Management (SCM), and in traditional application domains studied [Grahne, 1991; Imieliński and Lipski Jr, 1984; Levy, 1996; Motro, 1989].

Consider (a) a master relation I_m of the schema DCust, which maintains a complete list of domestic customers of a company, and (b) a database D consisting of two relations Cust and Supt that contain information about customers of the company (domestic or international) and about employees of the company for customer support, respectively (see Example 5.1). Consider a set V consisting of the CC ϕ_0 given in Example 5.2, assuring that I_m imposes an upper bound on domestic customers in the relations Cust and Supt.

(1) Assessing the completeness of the data in a database. Let us first consider a query Q_0 posed on the database D, which is to find all the customers of the company based in NJ with AC = 908. In the absence of master data, one cannot decide whether $Q_0(D)$ returns the complete list of customers we want to find. Indeed, as observed by Loshin [2009], it is typical to find information missing from a transitional database in an enterprise; hence, one could only assume the OWA for D, and there is not much we can do about it. In contrast, provided the availability of the master data I_m, we can

5.2. DETERMINING RELATIVE COMPLETENESS

determine whether D has complete information to answer Q_0. More specifically, we can invoke a static analysis procedure for RCDP and decide whether D is in RCQ(Q_0, I_m, V). If the procedure returns an affirmative answer, we know that we can trust the query answer $Q_0(D)$.

(2) Guidance for what data should be collected in a database. Suppose that the decision procedure for RCDP returns a negative answer, i.e., D is not complete for Q_0. The next question is whether D can be expanded at all to be complete for Q_0. To this end we capitalize on a decision procedure for RCQP, to determine whether RCQ(Q_0, I_m, V) is empty, i.e., whether there exists a complete database for Q_0 relative to the master data available. If the procedure tells us that there indeed exists a database complete for Q_0 relative to (I_m, V), we can make D complete for Q_0 by including, e.g., the information about domestic customers that is in I_m but is missing from D.

(3) A guideline for how master data should be expanded. Now consider a query Q'_0 to find all the customers of the company, domestic or international. In this case the RCDP analysis shows that D is not complete for Q'_0 in the presence of I_m. Worse still, the RCQP analysis tells us that there exists *no* database complete for Q_0 relative to the current master data I_m. This suggests that to find a complete answer for Q'_0, we need to expand *the master data*. As pointed out by Loshin [2009], a practical challenge for mdm is to identify what data should be maintained as master data. The study of RCQP provides a guidance on when to expand master data and on what master data to maintain such that one can find complete answer for a workload of queries commonly used in practice.

Similar RCDP and RCQP analyses can be carried out for queries Q_1 and Q_2 of Example 5.1, to decide whether the database is complete for these queries and if not, whether we have to expand the database or the master data. We remark that the traditional OWA does not allow these analyses, in the absence of master data.

Complexity bounds. We next provide combined complexity of RCDP($\mathcal{L}_Q, \mathcal{L}_C$) and RCQP($\mathcal{L}_Q, \mathcal{L}_C$), when $\mathcal{L}_C$ and $\mathcal{L}_Q$ range over various languages given in Section 1.4. We focus on the combined complexity [Vardi, 1982] of these problems (see Section 6.3 for discussions about combined complexity). We refer the interested reader to [Fan and Geerts, 2010b] for proofs of the results to be presented in this section.

RCDP($\mathcal{L}_Q, \mathcal{L}_C$). The complexity of RCDP($\mathcal{L}_Q, \mathcal{L}_C$) is highly dependent on what languages $\mathcal{L}_C$ and $\mathcal{L}_Q$ we use to express containment constraints and queries, respectively. We begin with some negative results: when either $\mathcal{L}_Q$ or $\mathcal{L}_C$ is FO or FP, it is infeasible to determine whether a database D is relatively complete for a query Q w.r.t. (D_m, V). Worse still, if $\mathcal{L}_Q$ is FO or FP the undecidability remains intact even when master data D_m and the set V of CCs are predefined and fixed.

Theorem 5.9 RCDP($\mathcal{L}_Q, \mathcal{L}_C$) is undecidable when:
1. $\mathcal{L}_Q$ is FO and $\mathcal{L}_C$ is CQ;
2. $\mathcal{L}_C$ is FO and $\mathcal{L}_Q$ is CQ;
3. $\mathcal{L}_Q$ is FP and $\mathcal{L}_C$ is CQ; or

4. $\mathcal{L}_C$ is FP and $\mathcal{L}_Q$ consists of a fixed query in FP.

If $\mathcal{L}_Q$ is FO or FP, the problem remains undecidable for fixed master data and fixed containment constraints.

Crux. (1) When $\mathcal{L}_Q$ or $\mathcal{L}_C$ is FO, the undecidability of RCDP($\mathcal{L}_Q, \mathcal{L}_C$) is proven by reduction from the satisfiability problem for FO queries, which is known to be undecidable (cf. [Abiteboul et al., 1995]). In the reduction the master data D_m and the set V of CCs are both fixed: D_m is an empty relation, and V is an empty set.

(2) When $\mathcal{L}_Q$ or $\mathcal{L}_C$ is FP, it is verified by reduction from the emptiness problem for deterministic finite 2-head automata (2-head DFA), which is undecidable [Spielmann, 2000]. A 2-head DFA is a quintuple $\mathcal{A} = (Q, \Sigma, \Delta, q_0, q_{acc})$, with a finite set Q of states, an input alphabet $\Sigma = \{0, 1\}$, an initial state q_0, an accepting state q_{acc}, and a transition function $\Delta : Q \times \Sigma_\epsilon \times \Sigma_\epsilon \to Q \times \{0, +1\} \times \{0, +1\}$, where $\Sigma_\epsilon = \Sigma \cup \{\epsilon\}$. A configuration of $\mathcal{A}$ is a triple $(q, w_1, w_2) \in Q \times \Sigma^* \times \Sigma^*$, representing that $\mathcal{A}$ is in state q, and the first and second heads of $\mathcal{A}$ are positioned on the first symbol of w_1 and w_2, respectively. On an input string $w \in \Sigma^*$, $\mathcal{A}$ starts from the initial configuration (q_0, w, w); the successor configuration is defined as usual. The 2-head DFA $\mathcal{A}$ accepts w if it can reach a configuration (q_{acc}, w_1, w_2) from the initial configuration for w. The emptiness problem for 2-head DFA's is to determine, given a 2-head DFA $\mathcal{A}$, whether the language accepted by $\mathcal{A}$ is empty. In our reduction we use a fixed master relation D_m and a fixed set V of CCs when $\mathcal{L}_Q$ is FP. □

We next consider RCDP($\mathcal{L}_C, \mathcal{L}_Q$) when $\mathcal{L}_C$ and $\mathcal{L}_Q$ are one of CQ, UCQ, and ∃FO⁺. The good news is that the absence of negation and recursion in our queries makes our lives easier: RCDP($\mathcal{L}_Q, \mathcal{L}_C$) is in the polynomial hierarchy for these query languages. The complexity bounds are rather robust: the problem is Π_2^p-complete when $\mathcal{L}_Q$ and $\mathcal{L}_C$ are ∃FO⁺, and it remains Π_2^p-complete when $\mathcal{L}_Q$ is CQ and $\mathcal{L}_C$ is the class of INDs.

Theorem 5.10 RCDP($\mathcal{L}_Q, \mathcal{L}_C$) is Π_2^p-complete when:
1. $\mathcal{L}_C$ is the class of INDs and $\mathcal{L}_Q$ is CQ, UCQ or ∃FO⁺;
2. $\mathcal{L}_Q$ and $\mathcal{L}_C$ are CQ;
3. $\mathcal{L}_Q$ and $\mathcal{L}_C$ are UCQ; or
4. $\mathcal{L}_Q$ and $\mathcal{L}_C$ are ∃FO⁺.

Crux. It suffices to show (1) and (2) below.

(1) RCDP($\mathcal{L}_Q, \mathcal{L}_C$) is Π_2^p-hard when $\mathcal{L}_C$ is the class of INDs and $\mathcal{L}_Q$ is CQ. The Π_2^p lower bound is verified by reduction from the complement of the ∃*∀*3DNF problem, which is Σ_2^p-complete [Stockmeyer, 1976]. The reduction uses a fixed set of CCs and a fixed D_m.

(2) RCDP($\mathcal{L}_Q, \mathcal{L}_C$) is in Π_2^p when $\mathcal{L}_C$ and $\mathcal{L}_Q$ are both ∃FO⁺. This is shown by providing an

algorithm that checks whether a database D is *not* complete for a given Q w.r.t. (D_m, V), by using a non-deterministic PTIME Turing machine with an NP oracle. Since the algorithm is in Σ_2^p, the problem for deciding whether $D \in \mathsf{RCQ}(Q, D_m, V)$ is hence in Π_2^p. □

In practice, master data D_m and containment constraints V are often predefined and fixed, and only databases and user queries vary. One might be tempted to think that fixing D_m and V would lower the complexity. Unfortunately, the lower bound of Theorem 5.10 remains unchanged when D_m and V are fixed, even when V is a fixed set of INDs.

Corollary 5.11 $\mathsf{RCDP}(\mathcal{L}_Q, \mathcal{L}_C)$ *remains* Π_2^p-*complete when master data* D_m *and the set* V *of containment constraints are fixed, for the combinations of* $\mathcal{L}_C$ *and* $\mathcal{L}_Q$ *considered in Theorem 5.10.*

Crux. The results follow from the proof of Theorem 5.10. The upper bound of Theorem 5.10 carries over to fixed D_m and V. For the lower bound, the proof for Theorem 5.10 shows that the problem is Π_2^p-hard when V is a fixed set of INDs, and when D_m is fixed. □

$\mathsf{RCQP}(\mathcal{L}_Q, \mathcal{L}_C)$. We next study $\mathsf{RCQP}(\mathcal{L}_Q, \mathcal{L}_C)$. Recall from Theorem 5.9 that it is undecidable to decide whether a database is in $\mathsf{RCQ}(Q, D_m, V)$ when either $\mathcal{L}_Q$ or $\mathcal{L}_C$ is FO or FP. It is no better for $\mathsf{RCQP}(\mathcal{L}_Q, \mathcal{L}_C)$: in these settings $\mathsf{RCQP}(\mathcal{L}_Q, \mathcal{L}_C)$ is also undecidable. Moreover, the undecidability is rather robust: the problem is already beyond reach in practice when master data and containment constraints are fixed, if $\mathcal{L}_Q$ is FO or FP.

Theorem 5.12 $\mathsf{RCQP}(\mathcal{L}_Q, \mathcal{L}_C)$ *is undecidable when:*

1. $\mathcal{L}_Q$ *is FO and* $\mathcal{L}_C$ *is CQ;*
2. $\mathcal{L}_C$ *is FO and* $\mathcal{L}_Q$ *is CQ;*
3. $\mathcal{L}_Q$ *is FP and* $\mathcal{L}_C$ *is CQ; or*
4. $\mathcal{L}_C$ *is FP and* $\mathcal{L}_Q$ *is CQ.*

When $\mathcal{L}_Q$ *is FO or FP, it remains undecidable for fixed master data and fixed containment constraints.*

Crux. (1,2) When either $\mathcal{L}_Q$ or $\mathcal{L}_C$ is FO, the proofs are by reduction from the satisfiability problem for FO queries.

(3) When $\mathcal{L}_Q$ is FP, the proof is by reduction from the satisfiability problem for FP in the presence of FDs. That is, given an FP query p and a set Θ of FDs, it is to decide whether there exists an instance D such that $D \models \Theta$ and $p(D) \neq \emptyset$. The undecidability of this problem was claimed by Levy et al. [1993]. The undecidability remains to hold if Θ is assumed to be fixed [Fan and Geerts, 2010a].

(4) When $\mathcal{L}_C$ is FP, the proof is by reduction from the emptiness problem for 2-head DFA. Given a 2-head DFA $\mathcal{A}$, we construct a database schema $\mathcal{R}$ consisting of several relations, which intend to encode a string, positions in the string, a successor relation, transitions of $\mathcal{A}$, and the transitive

closure of the transitions. We define a set V of CCs using FP queries, to help us assure that instances of $\mathcal{R}$ encode a valid run of $\mathcal{A}$. We also define a CQ query to inspect whether a run is valid and whether there is a valid run of $\mathcal{A}$ that accepts a string. Fixed master data D_m is used. Using these, we show that $\mathcal{A}$ accepts some strings (i.e., the language accepted by $\mathcal{A}$ is nonempty) if and only if $\text{RCQ}(Q, D_m, V)$ is nonempty.

The proofs only use fixed (D_m, V) if $\mathcal{L}_Q$ is FO or FP. □

For CQ, UCQ, and $\exists\text{FO}^+$, we have seen from Theorem 5.10 that the absence of negation and recursion in $\mathcal{L}_Q$ and $\mathcal{L}_C$ simplifies the analysis of $\text{RCDP}(\mathcal{L}_Q, \mathcal{L}_C)$. This is also the case for $\text{RCQP}(\mathcal{L}_Q, \mathcal{L}_C)$. In contrast to Theorem 5.10, however, the complexity bound for $\text{RCQP}(\mathcal{L}_Q, \mathcal{L}_C)$ when $\mathcal{L}_C$ is $\exists\text{FO}^+$ is no longer the same as its counterpart when $\mathcal{L}_C$ is the class of INDs. In addition, when $\mathcal{L}_Q$ and $\mathcal{L}_C$ are CQ, $\text{RCQP}(\mathcal{L}_Q, \mathcal{L}_C)$ becomes NEXPTIME-complete, and hence the analysis is harder than its $\text{RCDP}(\mathcal{L}_Q, \mathcal{L}_C)$ counterpart. On the other hand, when $\mathcal{L}_C$ is the class of INDs, the complexity is down to coNP-complete, better than its Π_2^p-complete counterpart for $\text{RCDP}(\mathcal{L}_Q, \mathcal{L}_C)$.

Theorem 5.13 $\text{RCQP}(\mathcal{L}_Q, \mathcal{L}_C)$ is:

1. coNP-complete when $\mathcal{L}_C$ is the class of INDs and $\mathcal{L}_Q$ is CQ, UCQ or $\exists\text{FO}^+$; and
2. NEXPTIME-complete when:

    (a) $\mathcal{L}_Q$ and $\mathcal{L}_C$ are CQ;
    (b) $\mathcal{L}_Q$ and $\mathcal{L}_C$ are UCQ; or
    (c) $\mathcal{L}_Q$ and $\mathcal{L}_C$ are $\exists\text{FO}^+$.

Crux. (1) *Lower bounds.* The coNP lower bound is verified by reduction from 3SAT to the complement of $\text{RCQP}(\text{CQ}, \text{INDs})$. The reduction uses fixed master data and CCs only.

When $\mathcal{L}_C$ and $\mathcal{L}_Q$ are CQ, we verify the NEXPTIME lower bound by reduction from the tiling problem for $2^n \times 2^n$ squares, which is NEXPTIME-complete (see, e.g., [Dantsin and Voronkov, 1997]). Given an instance of the tiling problem, we construct a database schema $\mathcal{R}$ consisting of relations $R_1, \ldots, R_n$ such that R_i encodes a $2^i \times 2^i$ square of tiles for $i \in [1, n]$. We define master data D_m and a set V of CCs in CQ to assure the vertical and horizontal compatibility of the tiling. Finally we define a CQ query Q such that $\text{RCQ}(Q, D_m, V)$ is nonempty if and only if there exists a valid tiling of the given instance.

(2) *Upper bounds.* We show the upper bounds by giving constructive proofs. We develop sufficient and necessary conditions for $\text{RCQ}(Q, D_m, V)$ to be nonempty.

Given master data D_m, a set V of INDs and a query Q in $\exists\text{FO}^+$, we show that it suffices to check whether for any set Δ of tuples, either $(\Delta, D_m) \not\models V$ or certain syntactic conditions on Q and V hold. Better still, it suffices to inspect "bounded" Δ: its size is no larger than that of Q, and its active domain is determined by D_m, Q and V. Based on this, an NP algorithm is developed to check whether $\text{RCQ}(Q, D_m, V)$ is *empty*.

When $\mathcal{L}_Q$ and $\mathcal{L}_C$ are $\exists FO^+$, we prove a small model property: given D_m, a query Q in $\exists FO^+$ and a set V of CCs in $\exists FO^+$, $RCQ(Q, D_m, V)$ is nonempty if and only if there exists a partially closed database D such that: (a) the size of D is bounded by an exponential in the sizes of Q, V and D_m; (b) for any partial extension $D' = D \cup \Delta$ of D, either $Q(D') = Q(D)$ or $(D', D_m) \not\models V$; and furthermore; and (c) it suffices to inspect increments Δ that are bounded as described above. The small model property is established by leveraging the monotonicity of $\exists FO^+$ queries. Based on this property, an NEXPTIME algorithm can be readily developed for checking whether $RCQ(Q, D_m, V)$ is nonempty. □

As remarked earlier, master data D_m and containment constraints V are often predefined and fixed in practice. Recall from Corollary 5.11 that fixing D_m and V has no impact on the complexity of $RCDP(\mathcal{L}_Q, \mathcal{L}_C)$. In contrast, fixed D_m and V do make our lives easier here, to some extent. (a) When $\mathcal{L}_Q$ and $\mathcal{L}_C$ are CQ, UCQ or $\exists FO^+$, $RCQP(\mathcal{L}_Q, \mathcal{L}_C)$ becomes Σ_3^p-complete, down from NEXPTIME-complete. (b) On the other hand, when $\mathcal{L}_Q$ is CQ and $\mathcal{L}_C$ is the class of INDs, the problem remains coNP-complete. (c) Fixed D_m and V do not help when either $\mathcal{L}_Q$ or $\mathcal{L}_C$ is FO or FP, as we have seen in Theorem 5.12.

Corollary 5.14 *When master data and CCs are fixed, $RCQP(\mathcal{L}_Q, \mathcal{L}_C)$ is:*

1. *coNP-complete if $\mathcal{L}_C$ is the class of INDs and $\mathcal{L}_Q$ is CQ, UCQ, or $\exists FO^+$; and*
2. *Σ_3^p-complete if $\mathcal{L}_Q$ and $\mathcal{L}_C$ are CQ, UCQ, or $\exists FO^+$.*

Crux. It suffices to show the following.

(1) $RCQP(\mathcal{L}_Q, \mathcal{L}_C)$ is coNP-hard when $\mathcal{L}_Q$ is CQ and $\mathcal{L}_C$ is the class of INDs. This follows from the proof for the coNP lower bound of Theorem 5.13 (1), in which only fixed master data D_m and a set V of fixed INDs are used. Its coNP upper bound carries over here.

(2) We show that $RCQP(\mathcal{L}_Q, \mathcal{L}_C)$ is Σ_3^p-hard when $\mathcal{L}_Q$ and $\mathcal{L}_C$ are CQ, by reduction from the $\exists^*\forall^*\exists^*3CNF$ problem, which is known to be Σ_3^p-complete [Stockmeyer, 1976].

Recall the proof for $RCQP(\exists FO^+, \exists FO^+)$ given for Theorem 5.13 (2). When V and D_m are fixed, it suffices to inspect "small models" D of a polynomial size. Based on this, we develop an algorithm to check whether $RCQ(Q, D_m, V)$ is nonempty. The algorithm uses a non-deterministic PTIME Turing machine with a Π_2^p oracle to inspect whether the conditions given in the proof of Theorem 5.13 (2) hold. □

Summary. We summarize the complexity bounds for $RCDP(\mathcal{L}_Q, \mathcal{L}_C)$ and $RCQP(\mathcal{L}_Q, \mathcal{L}_C)$ in Tables 5.1 and 5.2, respectively, where fixed($\mathcal{L}$) indicates a set of fixed queries in $\mathcal{L}$. When master data and containment constraints are fixed, we only show complexity bounds that differ from their counterparts in the general settings.

We can see that $RCDP(\mathcal{L}_Q, \mathcal{L}_C)$ and $RCQP(\mathcal{L}_Q, \mathcal{L}_C)$ are nontrivial: they are intractable in all the cases considered. To cope with these, it is necessary to identify special yet practical cases

Table 5.1: Complexity of RCDP($\mathcal{L}_Q, \mathcal{L}_C$)

RCDP($\mathcal{L}_Q, \mathcal{L}_C$)	Complexity
(FO, CQ), (CQ, FO), (FP, CQ), (fixed(FP), FP)	undecidable
(CQ, INDs), ($\exists$FO$^+$, INDs), (CQ, CQ), (UCQ, UCQ), ($\exists$FO$^+$, $\exists$FO$^+$)	Π_2^p-complete

Table 5.2: Complexity of RCQP($\mathcal{L}_Q, \mathcal{L}_C$)

RCQP($\mathcal{L}_Q, \mathcal{L}_C$)	Complexity
(FO, CQ), (CQ, FO) (FP, CQ), (CQ, FP)	undecidable
(CQ, INDs), ($\exists$FO$^+$, INDs)	coNP-complete
(CQ, CQ), (UCQ, UCQ), ($\exists$FO$^+$, $\exists$FO$^+$)	NEXPTIME-complete
When D_m and V are fixed	
(CQ, CQ), (UCQ, UCQ), ($\exists$FO$^+$, $\exists$FO$^+$)	Σ_3^p-complete

that are tractable, and to develop efficient heuristic algorithms for the analyses of RCDP and RCQP. Nevertheless, such algorithms remain to be studied.

5.3 REPRESENTATION SYSTEMS FOR POSSIBLE WORLDS

We have so far considered information completeness in the setting where tuples may be missing, but all the values of the existing tuples are in place. In practice, however, *both tuples* and *values* are commonly found missing from a database. In the rest of the chapter, we reconsider RCDP and RCQP when both values and tuples may be missing. To do this, we first review traditional representation systems for databases with missing values.

Conditional tables. To specify databases with missing values, we adopt *conditional tables* (or *c-tables*) that are specified in terms of variables and local conditions [Abiteboul et al., 1995; Grahne, 1991; Imieliński and Lipski Jr, 1984; van der Meyden, 1998]. To define *c*-tables, for each relation schema R_i and each attribute A in R_i, we assume a countably infinite set var(A) of distinct *variables* such that var(A) $\cap$ dom(A) = $\emptyset$, and var(A) $\cap$ var(B) = $\emptyset$ for any attribute B distinct from A.

A *c-table* of R_i is a pair (T, ξ), where (a) T is a tableau in which for each tuple t and each attribute A in R_i, $t[A]$ is either a constant in dom(A) or a variable in var(A); and (b) ξ is a mapping that associates a condition $\xi(t)$ with each tuple t in T. The condition $\xi(t)$ is built up from atoms

5.3. REPRESENTATION SYSTEMS FOR POSSIBLE WORLDS

	name	street	city	zip	YoB	cond
t_1:	John	3 Elm	EDI	EH8 9AB	2000	true
t_2:	x	y	EDI	EH8 9AB	z	$(x \neq \text{John})$
t_3:	Mary	5 Mayfield	w	u	2000	$(w \neq \text{EDI})$

Figure 5.1: A c-table of Patient.

$x = y$, $x \neq y$, $x = c$, $x \neq c$, by closing under conjunction $\wedge$, where x, y are variables and c is a constant. Conditions $\xi(t)$ that are always true (i.e., tautologies) are denoted by true, or simply omitted. A c-table corresponds to a standard database instance if all its conditions are tautologies. In this setting standard databases are also referred to as *ground instances*. We write (T, ξ) simply as T when ξ is clear from the context.

Example 5.15 Consider an incomplete database of UK patients, specified by the schema Patient(name, street, city, zip, YoB), from which values are missing. It is represented by the c-table T_1 shown in Figure 5.1. In T_1, tuple t_1 has no missing values and has a tautological condition (true); tuple t_2 has missing values t_2[name], t_2[street] and t_2[YoB] denoted by variables, and the condition t_2[cond] tells us that t_2[name] is not John; similarly for t_3. □

Two special cases of c-tables are commonly used in practice.

1. Codd tables [Codd, 1975]: These are c-tables in which only a single variable may be present and no conditions are allowed. They syntactically resemble pattern tableaux used in CFDs, where the unnamed variable "_" corresponds to the single variable. However, as will be seen shortly, Codd tables have an entirely different semantics.

2. v-tables [Grahne, 1991; Imieliński and Lipski Jr, 1984]: These are c-tables in which multiple variables may be present but tuples do not carry any conditions.

To define the semantics of c-tables (and thus also for Codd tables and v-tables) we need the notion of valuation. A *valuation* μ of (T, ξ) is a mapping such that for each tuple t in T and each attribute A in R, $\mu(t[A])$ is a constant in dom(A) if $t[A]$ is a variable, and $\mu(t[A]) = t[A]$ if $t[A]$ is a constant. Let $\mu(t)$ denote the tuple of R obtained by substituting $\mu(x)$ for each occurrence of x in t. Then we define

$$\mu(T) = \{\mu(t) \mid t \in T \text{ and } \xi(\mu(t)) \text{ evaluates to true}\}.$$

That is, $\mu(T)$ is a ground instance *without* variables or conditions. In the *possible world* semantics of c-tables one associates with (T, ξ) a set of (possible) ground instances, referred to as *the set of instances represented by* (T, ξ), as follows.

$$\text{Mod}(T) = \{\mu(T) \mid \mu \text{ is a valuation of } (T, \xi)\}.$$

The concept of c-table naturally extends to database instances. A c-*instance* $\mathcal{T}$ of $\mathcal{R}$ is of the form $(T_1, \ldots, T_n)$, where for each $i \in [1, n]$, T_i is a c-table of R_i. A *valuation* μ of $\mathcal{T}$ is of the form $(\mu_1, \ldots, \mu_n)$, where μ_i is a valuation of T_i. We use $\mu(\mathcal{T})$ to denote the ground instance $(\mu_1(T_1), \ldots, \mu_n(T_n))$ of $\mathcal{R}$, and define $\mathsf{Mod}(\mathcal{T})$ as above.

Given a c-instance, one naturally wants to know whether it indeed represents a set of database instances, i.e., its conditions make sense and are satisfiable. This gives rise to the *consistency problem* for c-instances, stated as follows.

- INPUT: A c-instance $\mathcal{T}$.
- QUESTION: Is $\mathsf{Mod}(\mathcal{T})$ nonempty?

Whereas any Codd table or v-table is consistent, i.e., it always has a possible world, this no longer holds for c-tables. Indeed, it is easy to come up with a c-table (T, ξ) such that $\mathsf{Mod}(T) = \emptyset$. Worse still, the consistency problem is intractable [Abiteboul et al., 1991].

Proposition 5.16 *The consistency problem for c-tables is NP-complete.*

Representation systems. Let $\mathcal{M}$ be a class of models for incomplete databases such that with each $M \in \mathcal{M}$ one can associate a set of possible worlds (i.e., ground instances), denoted by $\mathsf{Mod}(M)$. For example, $\mathcal{M}$ can be taken as the class of c-tables, Codd tables or v-tables, among others. Given such a class of models $\mathcal{M}$, a natural question concerns how to query them. Let $\mathcal{L}_Q$ be a query language. Clearly, one would like to be able to represent the result of a query in $\mathcal{L}_Q$ inside the same class $\mathcal{M}$. That is, for each $M \in \mathcal{M}$ and query $Q \in \mathcal{L}_Q$, there should exist a computable element $\overline{Q}(M)$ in $\mathcal{M}$ such that

$$\mathsf{Mod}(\overline{Q}(M)) = Q(\mathsf{Mod}(M)),$$

where $Q(\mathsf{Mod}(M)) = \{Q(D) \mid D \in \mathsf{Mod}(M)\}$. If this condition holds then $\mathcal{M}$ is said to form a *strong representation system* for $\mathcal{L}_Q$. It is known that c-tables are a good class of models when $\mathcal{L}_Q$ is either FO (i.e., relational algebra) or FP (i.e., Datalog; see [Abiteboul et al., 1995; Grahne, 1991; Imieliński and Lipski Jr, 1984] for a proof).

Theorem 5.17 *When $\mathcal{L}_Q$ is FO or FP, c-tables form a strong representation system for $\mathcal{L}_Q$.*

In contrast, Codd tables and v-tables do not form a strong representation system for FO [Imieliński and Lipski Jr, 1984]. Nonetheless, Codd and v-tables suffice to represent certain answers to queries. As before, let $\mathcal{M}$ be a class of models for incomplete databases. For a model $M \in \mathcal{M}$ and query $Q \in \mathcal{L}_Q$, the *certain answer* to Q in M is defined as

$$\bigcap_{D \in \mathsf{Mod}(M)} Q(D).$$

We say that $\mathcal{M}$ forms a *weak representation system* for $\mathcal{L}_Q$ if for each query $Q \in \mathcal{L}_Q$, there exists a computable element $\overline{Q}(M)$ in $\mathcal{M}$ such that for all queries $Q' \in \mathcal{L}_Q$:

$$\bigcap_{D \in \mathsf{Mod}(\overline{Q}(M))} Q'(D) = \bigcap_{D' \in Q(\mathsf{Mod}(M))} Q'(D').$$

Note that if $\mathcal{M}$ forms a weak representation system for $\mathcal{L}_Q$ then, in particular,

$$\bigcap_{D \in \mathsf{Mod}(\overline{Q}(M))} D = \bigcap_{D' \in \mathsf{Mod}(M)} Q(D'),$$

i.e., the certain answer to Q in M can already be found in $\overline{Q}(M)$.

It is known that Codd tables and v-tables form a weak representation system for certain fragments of FO (recall the class of SP queries from Section 2.2.4; see [Grahne, 1991; Imieliński and Lipski Jr, 1984] for proofs).

Theorem 5.18 Codd tables form a weak representation system for SP queries, and v-tables form a weak representation system for $\exists FO^+$ queries.

5.4 CAPTURING MISSING TUPLES AND MISSING VALUES

We now reinvestigate the relative completeness of databases from which both tuples and values may be missing. We represent such an "incomplete" database as a c-instance $\mathcal{T}$. As before, consider master data D_m and a set V of containment constraints.

As a first step, we extend Definition 5.3 from ground instances to c-instances. More specifically, a *partially closed c-instance* $\mathcal{T}$ w.r.t. (D_m, V) represents a set of partially closed ground instances, denoted by $\mathsf{Mod}(\mathcal{T}, D_m, V)$ and defined as follows:

$$\mathsf{Mod}(\mathcal{T}, D_m, V) = \{\mu(\mathcal{T}) \mid \mu \text{ is a valuation and } (\mu(\mathcal{T}), D_m) \models V\}.$$

We write $\mathsf{Mod}(\mathcal{T}, D_m, V)$ as $\mathsf{Mod}(\mathcal{T})$ when D_m and V are clear from the context.

In the sequel we consider only c-instances $\mathcal{T}$ for which $\mathsf{Mod}(\mathcal{T})$ is nonempty. We will see shortly that it is decidable to determine whether $\mathsf{Mod}(\mathcal{T})$ is nonempty.

We study three notions of completeness for c-instances, including but not limited to the semantics suggested by the notions of strong and weak representation systems.

Definition 5.19 Relative to (D_m, V), a partially closed c-instance $\mathcal{T}$ is said to be:

- *strongly complete for a query Q* if *for all* ground instances $D \in \mathsf{Mod}(\mathcal{T})$ and *for all* extensions $D' \in \mathsf{Ext}(D)$, $Q(D) = Q(D')$;

- *weakly complete for Q* if either for all $D \in \mathsf{Mod}(\mathcal{T})$, $\mathsf{Ext}(D) = \emptyset$, or

$$\bigcap_{D \in \mathsf{Mod}(\mathcal{T})} Q(D) = \bigcap_{D \in \mathsf{Mod}(\mathcal{T}), D' \in \mathsf{Ext}(D)} Q(D');$$

- *completable for Q* if there exists a ground instance $D \in \mathsf{Mod}(\mathcal{T})$ such that for all extensions $D' \in \mathsf{Ext}(D)$, $Q(D) = Q(D')$.

Intuitively, (a) $\mathcal{T}$ is strongly complete if no matter how missing values in $\mathcal{T}$ are filled in, it yields a ground instance that is relatively complete for Q as specified by Definition 5.4; (b) $\mathcal{T}$ is weakly complete if the certain answer to Q over all partially closed extensions of $\mathcal{T}$ can already be found in $\mathcal{T}$; and (c) $\mathcal{T}$ is completable if there exists a way to instantiate missing values in $\mathcal{T}$ that produces a ground instance relatively complete for Q.

Observe the following. (a) If $\mathcal{T}$ is strongly complete, then it is both weakly complete and completable. (b) A ground instance is strongly complete and completable for a query Q if and only if it is relatively complete for Q, i.e., the notion of relative completeness for ground instances coincide with both strong completeness and the notion of completable. However, a ground instance may be weakly complete but not relatively complete.

Example 5.20 Consider the c-table T_1 shown in Figure 5.1, and a master relation I_m that is specified by the schema Patient$_m$(name, street, zip, YoB) and maintains a complete set of those patients living in EDI and born after 1990. We specify a set V of CCs such that for each year y in the range [1991, 2012], V includes the CC q_y(Patient) $\subseteq I_m$, where $q_y(n, s, z, d)$ is query Patient$(n, s, c, z, y) \wedge c = $ EDI. These CCs assure that I_m is an upper bound on the information about patients who live in EDI and were born after 1990. We also include in the set V those CCs for the functional dependency [zip] $\rightarrow$ [city, street], which states that in the UK, the zip code determines the city and street. We have seen that FDs can be represented by CCs (Section 5.1.3). Consider the following queries posed on T_1.

(1) Query Q_4 is to find the streets of those patients who live in EDI with zip = "EH8 9AB" and were born in 2000. Then T_1 is strongly complete for Q_4 relative to (I_m, V). Indeed, by the FD ϕ encoded as CCs in V, we have that for any valuation μ of T_1, $Q_4(\mu(T_1))$ returns a single tuple (street = "3 Elm"), and furthermore, the answer to Q_4 does not change for any partially closed extension in Ext$(\mu(T_1))$.

(2) Query Q_5 is to find the names of patients in Edinburgh who were born in 2000. Suppose that t_m^1 and t_m^2 are the only patients in I_m born in 2000, where $t_m^1 = $ (John, 3 Elm, EH8 9AB, 2000) and $t_m^2 = $ (Bob, 3 Elm, EH8 9AB, 2000). Then relative to (I_m, V), T_1 is completable for Q_5, since there exists a valuation μ of T_1 such that $\mu(T_1)$ is complete. For instance, this happens for $\mu(x) = $ Bob and $\mu(z) = $ 2000. The c-instance T_1 is also weakly complete, since the certain answer (name = John) can already be found from Mod(T_1). However, T_1 is not strongly complete for Q_5. Indeed, consider $\mu'(T_1)$ with $\mu'(x) = $ John and $\mu'(z) = $ 2000, and $\mu(T_1)$ defined as before. Then clearly, $\mu'(T_1) \subseteq \mu(T_1)$ and moreover, $Q_5(\mu'(T_1))$ only returns John whereas $Q_5(\mu(T_1))$ returns both John and Bob. □

5.5 THE COMPLEXITY OF FUNDAMENTAL PROBLEMS

In the rest of the chapter, we first study some basic problems in connection with partially closed c-instances, and then revisit RCDP and RCQP for c-instances.

Reasoning about partially closed c-instances. The first problem, referred to as the *consistency problem* for partially closed c-instances, is a generalization of the consistency problem for c-instances described in Section 5.3. It is stated as follows.

- INPUT: A c-instance $\mathcal{T}$, master data D_m, and a set V of CCs in CQ.
- QUESTION: Is $\text{Mod}(\mathcal{T}, D_m, V)$ nonempty?

It asks whether the c-instance $\mathcal{T}$ has conflicts with the CCs and master data.

The second problem, referred to as *the extensibility problem*, is stated as follows.

- INPUT: A ground instance D, master data D_m, and a set V of CCs in CQ.
- QUESTION: Is $\text{Ext}(D, D_m, V)$ nonempty?

That is, can a ground instance D be extended at all without violating the CCs?

The analyses of these problems are needed for determining relative completeness for partially closed c-instances. No matter how important they are, the result below tells us that these problems are nontrivial, although decidable. In particular, it shows that CCs and master data complicate the consistency analysis of c-tables. Indeed, the problem is Σ_2^p-complete in contrast to NP-complete in the absence of such constraints (Proposition 5.16).

Proposition 5.21 *The consistency problem for partially closed c-instances and the extensibility problem are both Σ_2^p-complete. The complexity bounds remain unchanged even in the absence of local conditions in c-instances.*

Crux. The lower bounds are verified by reduction from the $\forall^*\exists^*$3CNF problem to the complement of these problems. The reductions do not use local conditions in the c-instances. For the upper bounds, Σ_2^p algorithms are developed for deciding these problems. □

RCDP and RCQP revisited. We next revisit RCDP and RCQP for c-instances. Refining the notion $\text{RCQ}(Q, D_m, V)$ (see Section 5.1.2), for a query Q, we use $\text{RCQ}^s(Q, D_m, V)$, $\text{RCQ}^w(Q, D_m, V)$, and $\text{RCQ}^c(Q, D_m, V)$ to denote the set of all strongly complete, weakly complete, and completable c-instances of $\mathcal{R}$ w.r.t. (D_m, V), respectively.

We want to find out the increased complexity introduced by c-instances to RCDP and RCQP. To discern the essential from the noise, we simply consider the case when $\mathcal{L}_C$ is CQ and hence, do not include $\mathcal{L}_C$ as a parameter of these decisions problems.

For RCDP, we study the *relatively complete database problem in the strong model* for $\mathcal{L}_Q$, denoted by $\text{RCDP}^s(\mathcal{L}_Q)$ and stated as follows.

- INPUT: A query $Q \in \mathcal{L}_Q$, master data D_m, a set V of CCs in CQ, and a partially closed c-instance $\mathcal{T}$ w.r.t. (D_m, V).

- QUESTION: Is $\mathcal{T}$ in RCQ^s(Q, D_m, V), i.e., is $\mathcal{T}$ strongly complete for Q relative to (D_m, V)?

Similarly, RCDP^w and RCDP^c are defined in the weak and completable models, respectively.

For RCQP, we consider the *relatively complete query problem in the strong model* for $\mathcal{L}_Q$, denoted by RCQP^s($\mathcal{L}_Q$) and stated as follows.

- INPUT: A query $Q \in \mathcal{L}_Q$, master data D_m, and a set V of CCs in CQ.
- QUESTION: Is RCQ^s(Q, D_m, V) nonempty? That is, does there exist a partially closed c-instance that is strongly complete for Q relative to (D_m, V)?

Similarly, RCQP^w and RCQP^c are defined in the weak and completable models, respectively.

Complexity bounds. We next provide the combined complexity bounds of RCDP($\mathcal{L}_Q$) and RCQP($\mathcal{L}_Q$), when $\mathcal{L}_Q$ ranges over the various languages given in Section 1.4. and for the three notions of completeness (strong, weak, and completable) defined earlier. We refer the interested reader to [Fan and Geerts, 2010a] for proofs of the results given in this section.

Strong model. We have seen that for ground instances, RCDP($\mathcal{L}_Q, \mathcal{L}_C$) is undecidable when $\mathcal{L}_Q$ is FO or FP and $\mathcal{L}_C$ is CQ (Theorem 5.9). Since ground instances are c-instances themselves, these undecidability results carry over. Indeed, for ground instances, strong completeness coincides with relative completeness (Section 5.4). When $\mathcal{L}_Q$ is CQ, UCQ, or $\exists$FO$^+$, the result below tells us that missing values do not complicate the analysis of RCDP.

Theorem 5.22 *For c-instances, RCDP^s($\mathcal{L}_Q$) is:*
1. *undecidable when $\mathcal{L}_Q$ is either FO or FP; and*
2. *Π_2^p-complete when $\mathcal{L}_Q$ is CQ, UCQ or $\exists$FO$^+$.*

The complexity bounds remain unchanged when master data D_m and the set V of CCs are fixed.

Crux. As mentioned above, the undecidability of Theorem 5.9 carries over to c-instances, since ground instances are c-instances themselves, and relative and strong completeness coincide for ground instances. Similarly, the Π_2^p-lower bound of Corollary 5.11 carries over as well. The upper bound is shown by generalizing the Π_2^p algorithm for ground instances given in the proof of Theorem 5.10 to c-instances, retaining the same complexity. □

When it comes to RCQP^s($\mathcal{L}_Q$), one does not have to worry about missing values either. In other words, missing values do not make our lives harder. Indeed, RCQP^s($\mathcal{L}_Q$) for c-instances and its counterpart for ground instances (Theorems 5.12 and 5.13) coincide.

Corollary 5.23 *For c-instances, RCQP^s($\mathcal{L}_Q$) is:*
1. *undecidable when $\mathcal{L}_Q$ is FO or FP; and*
2. *NEXPTIME-complete when $\mathcal{L}_Q$ is CQ, UCQ, or $\exists$FO$^+$.*

5.5. THE COMPLEXITY OF FUNDAMENTAL PROBLEMS

Crux. One can readily verify the following: in the strong model, for any query Q, master data D_m and any set V of CCs, there exists a c-instance $\mathcal{T}$ such that $\mathcal{T} \in \text{RCQ}^s(Q, D_m, V)$ if and only if there exists a ground instance D such that $D \in \text{RCQ}^s(Q, D_m, V)$. Since strong and relative completeness coincide for ground instances, it suffices to consider ground instances. From this and Theorems 5.12 and 5.13, Corollary 5.23 immediately follows. □

Weak model. Compared to their counterparts in the strong model, the complexity results in the weak model are more diverse. On one hand, the certain answer semantics simplifies the analysis of RCDP and RCQP when $\mathcal{L}_Q$ is FP, since both problems become decidable, in contrast to their undecidability in the strong model. On the other hand, when $\mathcal{L}_Q$ is CQ, UCQ, or $\exists$FO$^+$, RCDP becomes Π_3^p-complete as opposed to Π_2^p.

Theorem 5.24 For c-instances and for ground instances, RCDP$^w(\mathcal{L}_Q)$ is:

1. undecidable when $\mathcal{L}_Q$ is FO;
2. coNEXPTIME-complete when $\mathcal{L}_Q$ is FP; and
3. Π_3^p-complete when $\mathcal{L}_Q$ is CQ, UCQ, or $\exists$FO$^+$.

The complexity bounds remain unchanged when D_m and V are fixed.

Crux. It suffices to show the following.

(1) RCDP$^w(\mathcal{L}_Q)$ is undecidable when $\mathcal{L}_Q$ is FO for ground instances. This is proven by reduction from the satisfiability problem for FO queries. In the reduction master data and CCs are fixed: they are both empty.

(2) RCDP$^w(\mathcal{L}_Q)$ is coNEXPTIME-hard when $\mathcal{L}_Q$ is FP for ground instances, and is in coNEXPTIME for c-instances. We show that for ground instances, RCDP^w(FP) is coNEXPTIME-hard by reduction from the succinct-taut problem, which is coNEXPTIME-complete (cf. [Papadimitriou, 1994]). An instance of the succinct-taut problem is defined by a Boolean circuit C consisting of a finite set of gates $\{g_i = (a_i, j, k) \mid 1 \leq i \leq M\}$, where $a_i \in \{\wedge, \vee, \neg, \text{in}\}$ is the type of the gate, g_j and g_j for $j, k < i$ are the inputs of the gate (unless g_i is an in-gate when $j = k = 0$, and unless g_i is a $\neg$-gate when $j = k$). Suppose that C has n input gates, then C defines the Boolean function $f_C : \{0, 1\}^n \to \{0, 1\}$, where $f_C(\bar{w}) = 1$ if and only if C evaluates to true on input string $\bar{w}$. The succinct-taut problem is to decide whether for all $\bar{w} \in \{0, 1\}^n$, $f_C(\bar{w}) = 1$, or in other words, whether C is a tautology. Given an instance of the latter problem, we define relational schemas $\mathcal{R}$ and $\mathcal{R}_m$, a ground instance D of $\mathcal{R}$, a fixed set V of CCs, fixed master data D_m of $\mathcal{R}_m$, and an FP query Q. We show that C is a tautology if and only if D is weakly complete for Q relative to (D_m, V).

For the upper bound, we show that RCDP^w(FP) is in coNEXPTIME by providing an NEXPTIME algorithm that decides the complement problem. That is, given a c-instance $\mathcal{T}$, master data D_m, a set V of CCs and an FP query Q, the algorithm returns "yes" if $\mathcal{T}$ is not weakly complete for Q relative to (D_m, V), and "no" otherwise.

(3) RCDP($\mathcal{L}_Q$) is Π_3^p-hard when $\mathcal{L}_Q$ is CQ for ground instances, and is in Π_3^p for c-instances when $\mathcal{L}_Q$ is $\exists$FO$^+$. We show that the complement problem is Σ_3^p-hard by reduction from the $\exists^*\forall^*\exists^*$3CNF problem. The reduction only uses ground instances and fixed V and D_m. The upper bound is shown by providing a Σ_3^p algorithm that decides whether a given c-instances $\mathcal{T}$ is not weakly complete for a given $\exists$FO$^+$ query Q relative to (D_m, V). □

Recall that in the strong model, RCQP for c-instances is equivalent to RCQP for ground instances, as observed in the proof of Corollary 5.23. However, the example below tells us that it is no longer the case in the weak completeness model.

Example 5.25 Consider an FO query Q defined on a pair of relations: $Q(I_1, I_2) = \{(a)\}$ if $I_1 \subseteq I_2$, and $Q(I_1, I_2) = \{(b)\}$ otherwise, where a and b are distinct. For empty master relation D_m and an empty set V of CCs, no ground instances are in RCQ(Q, D_m, V) since $Q(I_1, I_2) \neq \emptyset$ for all (I_1, I_2) while $\bigcap_{\mathcal{I}' \in \text{Ext}(I_1, I_2)} Q(\mathcal{I}') = \emptyset$. In contrast, there exists a c-instance $\mathcal{T} = (T_1, T_2)$ in RCQ(Q, D_m, V), where T_1 and T_2 are singleton c-tables without conditions, each having a tuple with variables only. Indeed, $Q(\mathcal{T}) = \bigcap_{(I_1, I_2) \in \text{Mod}(\mathcal{T})} Q(I_1, I_2) = \emptyset = \bigcap_{(I_1, I_2) \in \text{Mod}(\mathcal{T}), (I_1', I_2') \in \text{Ext}(I_1, I_2)} Q(I_1', I_2')$. □

This tells us that from the undecidability of RCQP(FO) for ground instances (Theorems 5.12) we cannot conclude the undecidability for c-instances. For c-instances, the decidability of RCQP^w(FO) remains open. Below we establish the undecidability of this problem for ground instances only. In contrast to Theorem 5.23. RCQP($\mathcal{L}_Q$) becomes trivially decidable when $\mathcal{L}_Q$ is FP, CQ, UCQ or $\exists$FO$^+$, for c-instances and for ground instances.

Theorem 5.26 RCQP^w($\mathcal{L}_Q$) is:

- undecidable for ground instances if $\mathcal{L}_Q$ is FO; and
- decidable in $O(1)$-time for c-instances and for ground instances when $\mathcal{L}_Q$ is FP, CQ, UCQ, or $\exists$FO$^+$.

The complexity bounds remain unchanged when D_m and V are fixed.

Crux. (1) The undecidability of RCQP^w(FO) is also shown by reduction from the satisfiability problem for FO queries. The reduction uses empty D_m and an empty set V.

(2) We show that RCQ^w(Q, D_m, V) is always nonempty, by providing an algorithm to construct a ground instance $D_0 \in$ RCQ^w(Q, D_m, V). The construction starts from the empty instance, and it adds tuples, one at a time, as long as the CCs are not violated. The added tuples take values from a domain defined in terms of constants appearing in the input (i.e., Q, D_m, and V) and a finite set of new values. The correctness of the construction follows from the monotonicity of queries in FP and

a small model property, which allows us to consider partially closed extensions that extend D_0 by including a single tuple. □

Completable model. In the completable model, missing values complicate the analyses of RCDP and RCQP. In contrast to Theorem 5.22 in the strong model, $\text{RCDP}^c(\text{CQ})$ for completable c-instances is Σ_3^p-complete rather than Π_2^p. Furthermore, $\text{RCDP}^c(\text{FP})$ remains undecidable, as opposed to its counterpart in the weak model (Theorem 5.24).

Theorem 5.27 For c-instances and ground instances, $\text{RCDP}^c(\mathcal{L}_Q)$ is:
- undecidable when $\mathcal{L}_Q$ is FO or FP; and
- Σ_3^p-complete when $\mathcal{L}_Q$ is CQ, UCQ, or $\exists\text{FO}^+$.

The complexity is unchanged when D_m and V are fixed.

Crux. (1) Similar to its counterpart in the strong model, the undecidability results follow from Theorem 5.9, as a ground instance is relative complete if and only if it is completable.

(2) We show that $\text{RCDP}^c(\text{CQ})$ is Σ_3^p-hard by reduction from the $\exists^*\forall^*\exists^*$3CNF-problem. The upper bound is established by providing a Σ_3^p algorithm for testing whether c-instances are completable when $\mathcal{L}_Q$ is $\exists\text{FO}^+$. □

In contrast to Theorem 5.24 in the weak model, $\text{RCQP}(\mathcal{L}_Q)$ is no longer trivial for completable c-instances when $\mathcal{L}_Q$ is FP. However, RCQP for relatively completable c-instances coincides with RCQP for ground instances. For the latter, the complexity results are already established by Theorem 5.23. From these the corollary below follows.

Corollary 5.28 For c-instances and ground instances, $\text{RCQP}^c(\mathcal{L}_Q)$ is:
- undecidable when $\mathcal{L}_Q$ is FO or FP; and
- NEXPTIME-complete when $\mathcal{L}_Q$ is CQ, UCQ, or $\exists\text{FO}^+$.

The complexity is unchanged when D_m and V are fixed.

Crux. One can readily show the following equivalence: there exists a completable c-instance $\mathcal{T}$ in $\text{RCQ}^c(Q, D_m, V)$ if and only if there exists a ground instance D in $\text{RCQ}^c(Q, D_m, V)$. Since ground instances are relative complete if and only if they are completable, the results follow immediately from Theorems 5.12 and 5.13. □

Summary. We summarize the complexity bounds for $\text{RCDP}(\mathcal{L}_Q)$ and $\text{RCQP}(\mathcal{L}_Q)$ in Table 5.3, for c-instances in the three models of relative completeness. The question mark indicates that in the weak model, the decidability and complexity of $\text{RCQP}^w(\text{FO})$ are unknown for c-instances. The results tell us that similar to the case of only ground instances, RCDP and RCQP are both beyond reach in practice, and hence, heuristic approaches need to be devised. To develop heuristic algorithms one may need to use representation systems for partially complete databases which, however, are not yet in place.

Table 5.3: Complexity of RCDP($\mathcal{L}_Q$) and RCQP($\mathcal{L}_Q$) for c-instances in the strong, weak and completable models

$\mathcal{L}_Q$	RCDP($\mathcal{L}_Q$)	RCQP($\mathcal{L}_Q$)
Strong Model		
FO, FP	undecidable	undecidable
CQ, UCQ, ∃FO⁺	Π_2^p-complete	NEXPTIME-complete
Weak Model		
FO	undecidable	? (undecidable for ground instances)
FP	coNEXPTIME-complete	$O(1)$
CQ, UCQ, ∃FO⁺	Π_3^p-complete	$O(1)$
Completable Model		
FO, FP	undecidable	undecidable
CQ, UCQ, ∃FO⁺	Σ_3^p-complete	NEXPTIME-complete

BIBLIOGRAPHIC NOTES

The model and results for relative information completeness presented in this chapter are taken from [Fan and Geerts, 2010b], when only missing tuples are considered, and from [Fan and Geerts, 2010a], when both missing tuples and missing values are taken into account. In addition to RCDP and RCQP, Fan and Geerts [2010a] studied the complexity analysis of: (1) the *minimality problem* that asks whether a given c-instance $\mathcal{T}$ is a *minimal* instance that is complete for Q relative to (D_m, V), i.e., whether removing any tuple from $\mathcal{T}$ makes $\mathcal{T}$ incomplete; and (2) the *boundedness problem* that is to determine the existence of a complete c-instances of a bounded size. These problems have quite different complexities in different models (strong, weak, completable) and for different query languages. A revision of RCDP was studied by Geerts and Marnette [2010] for data exchange.

Several other approaches have been proposed to represent or query databases with missing tuples. Vardi [1986] defined a complete and consistent extension of an incomplete database D to be a database D_c such that $D \subseteq \pi_L(D_c)$ and $D_c \models \Sigma$, where π is the projection operator, L is a list of attributes in D, and Σ is a set of integrity constraints. Complexity bounds for computing the set of complete and consistent extensions of D w.r.t. Σ were established there. A notion of *open null* was introduced by Gottlob and Zicari [1988] to model locally controlled open-world databases: parts of a database D, values or tuples, can be marked with open null and are assumed open-world, while the rest is closed-world. Relational operators were extended there to tables with open null. In contrast, partially closed databases are partially constrained by master data D_m and consistency specifications, both via containment constraints.

Partially complete databases D have also been studied by Motro [1989], who assumed a virtual database D_c with "complete information," and assumed that part of D is known as a view of D_c. The *query answer completeness problem* was investigated there, which is to determine whether a query posed on D_c can be answered by an equivalent query on D. In this setting, the problem can be

5.5. THE COMPLEXITY OF FUNDAMENTAL PROBLEMS

reduced to *query answering using views*. Along the same lines, Levy [1996] reduced the query answer completeness problem to the independence problem for deciding the *independence* of queries from updates [Blakeley et al., 1989; Elkan, 1990; Levy and Sagiv, 1993], assuming that D contains some CQ views of D_c. Complexity results in that context were provided by Razniewski and Nutt [2011]. As opposed to the work of Levy [1996] and Motro [1989], the model given in this chapter assumes neither a database D_c with complete information nor that an incomplete database D contains views of D_c. Instead, we leverage master data D_m as an "upper bound" of certain information in D.

We next address in turn the relationship between relative completeness and answering queries using view, and its connection to the independence problem. There has been a large body of work on answering queries using views (e.g., [Abiteboul and Duschka, 1998; Calvanese et al., 2007; Li, 2003; Segoufin and Vianu, 2005]), to determine certain answers [Abiteboul and Duschka, 1998], compute complete answers from views with limited access patterns [Deutsch et al., 2007; Li, 2003], or decide whether views determine queries [Segoufin and Vianu, 2005] or are lossless [Calvanese et al., 2007]. However, a relatively complete database D cannot always be modeled as view of a database with complete information. Indeed, D is only *partially* constrained by master data D_m, while D_m itself may not contain the complete information that D intends to represent.

The independence problem (e.g., [Blakeley et al., 1989; Elkan, 1990; Levy and Sagiv, 1993]) resembles, but is different from, the decision problems considered in this chapter. Indeed, the former is to determine whether a query Q is independent of updates generated by another query Q^u, such that *for all* databases D, $Q(D) = Q(D \oplus \Delta)$, where Δ denotes updates generated by Q^u, and $D \oplus \Delta$ is the database obtained by updating D with Δ. In contrast, relatively complete queries Q are such that *there exists* a database D that is complete for Q relative to master data D_m and containment constraints V, where D and D_m satisfy V. That is, we want to decide (a) whether for a query Q *there exists* a relatively complete database D and (b) whether a given D that satisfies V together with D_m is a witness for Q to be relatively complete. The problems studied by [Levy, 1996] and Motro [1989] are thus quite different from RCDP and RCQP. Furthermore, no missing values are considered in those papers.

Models for missing values have been extensively studied, particularly in the context of representation systems (see [Abiteboul et al., 1995; van der Meyden, 1998] for surveys and more recently, [Olteanu et al., 2008]). In this chapter we adopt c-tables [Grahne, 1991; Imieliński and Lipski Jr, 1984] to represent databases with missing values. The weak model for relative completeness is based on the certain answer semantics [Imieliński and Lipski Jr, 1984], and the strong model has a resemblance to strong representation systems. In contrast, completable c-instances do not find a counterpart in the work by Grahne [1991] and the work of Imieliński and Lipski Jr [1984]. The consistency issues for c-instances are similar to the problems studied by Abiteboul et al. [1991], but are in the presence of master data and containment constraints and hence, are more involved (see Propositions 5.16 and 5.21). There has also been work on modeling negative information via logic programming (see [van der Meyden, 1998] for a survey), which considers neither partially complete databases nor the decision problems studied in this chapter.

5. INFORMATION COMPLETENESS

There has also been an extensive body of work on the certain answer semantics used in weak representation systems and in the notion of weakly complete databases. Indeed, this semantics forms the basis of consistent query answering (e.g., [Arenas et al., 2003b; Cali et al., 2003; Chomicki, 2007]) to find certain answers to a query in all repairs of a database. Master data D_m are not considered in that setting, and most containment constraints are *not* expressible as integrity constraints studied for repairs. Finally, Denecker et al. [2010] studied how to compute possible and certain answers in a database instance that is partially complete. In that work, a database D is considered partially complete if it satisfies local conditions that are specified by means of queries. Intractability results and approximation methods for query answering were developed there, based on three-valued logic.

CHAPTER 6

Data Currency

Data in real-life databases become obsolete rapidly. One often finds that multiple values of the same entity reside in a database. While all of these values were once correct, many of them may have become stale and hence inaccurate. Worse still, the values often do not carry reliable timestamps. With this comes the need for studying data currency. There are three fundamental problems in connection with data currency: How to identify the current value of an entity in a database in the absence of reliable timestamps. How can we answer queries posed on a possibly stale database by using current values? To answer a query with current values, do we need to import data from other sources and if so, what to copy?

This chapter presents recent advances in the study of data currency. We first give an overview of data currency issues and their challenges (Section 6.1). We then introduce a simple data currency model (Section 6.2). We identify fundamental problems associated with data currency and provide their complexity (Section 6.3). After these, we further enrich the data currency model by supporting copy functions, to import current data from other data sources (Section 6.3). Finally, we study central technical problems associated with copy functions, and establish their complexity (Section 6.4). The study of data currency is still preliminary. Among other things, effective methods for evaluating the currency of data in our databases and for identifying current values of entities are not yet in place.

6.1 DATA CURRENCY: AN OVERVIEW

The quality of data in a real-life database quickly degenerates over time. As remarked earlier, it is estimated that "2% of records in a customer file become obsolete in one month" [Eckerson, 2002]. That is, in a database of customer records, within two years about 50% of all the records may be obsolete. In light of this, we often find that multiple values of the same entity reside in a database, which were *once correct*, i.e., they were true values of the entity at some time. However, many of them have become *obsolete* and *inaccurate*. As an example from daily life, when one moves to a new address, a bank may keep her old address, and worse still, send credit card bills to the old address for quite some time (see, e.g., [Knowledge Integrity, 2003] for more examples). Stale data are one of the central problems to data quality. It is known that dirty data cost U.S. companies 600 billion USD each year [Eckerson, 2002], and stale data account for a large part of the losses.

These motivate us to study the *currency of data*, which aims to identify the current values of entities in a database, and to answer queries using the most current values only.

The question of data currency would be trivial if all data values carried valid timestamps. In practice, however, one often finds that timestamps are unavailable or imprecise [Zhang et al., 2010].

120   6. DATA CURRENCY

	FN	LN	address	salary	status
s_1:	Mary	Smith	2 Small St.	50k	single
s_2:	Mary	Dupont	10 Elm Av.	50k	married
s_3:	Mary	Dupont	6 Main St.	80k	married
s_4:	Bob	Luth	8 Cowan St.	80k	married
s_5:	Robert	Luth	8 Drum St.	55k	married

(a) An employee relation I_{emp}

	dname	mgrFN	mgrLN	mgrAddr	budget
t_1:	R&D	Mary	Smith	2 Small St.	6500k
t_2:	R&D	Mary	Smith	2 Small St.	7000k
t_3:	R&D	Mary	Dupont	6 Main St.	6000k
t_4:	R&D	Ed	Luth	8 Cowan St.	6000k

(b) A department relation I_{dept}

Figure 6.1: A company database.

Moreover, data values are often imported from other sources [Berti-Equille et al., 2009; Dong et al., 2010, 2009a], which may not support a uniform scheme of timestamps. These make it challenging to identify the current values.

The situation is serious, but not hopeless. It is often possible to deduce currency orders of data values from the semantics of the data. Moreover, data copied from other sources inherit currency orders from those sources. Taken together, these may provide sufficient current values of the entities to answer certain queries, as illustrated below.

Example 6.1   Consider two relations, I_{emp} and I_{dept} shown, in Figure 6.1. An employee tuple specifies an employee with name, address, salary, and marital status. A department tuple specifies the name, manager and budget of a department. Records in these relations may be stale, and do not carry timestamps. By data deduplication, we know that tuples s_1, s_2, and s_3 refer to the same employee Mary, but s_4 and s_5 represent a person distinct from Mary. Consider the following queries on these relations, including those given in Section 1.2.5.

(1) Query Q_1 is to find Mary's current salary. No timestamps are available for us to tell which of 50k or 80k is more current. However, we may know that the salary of each employee in the company is monotonically increasing, as commonly found in the real world. This yields currency orders $s_1 \prec_{\text{salary}} s_3$ and $s_2 \prec_{\text{salary}} s_3$, indicating that $s_3[\text{salary}]$ is more current than both $s_1[\text{salary}]$ and $s_2[\text{salary}]$. Hence, the answer to Q_1 is 80k.

(2) Query Q_2 is to find Mary's current last name. We can no longer answer Q_2 as above. Nonetheless, we may know the following: (a) the marital status can only change from single to married and from married to divorced; but not from married to single; and (b) employee tuples with the most current

marital status also contain the most current last name. Therefore, $s_1 \prec_{LN} s_2$ and $s_1 \prec_{LN} s_3$, and the answer to Q_2 is Dupont.

(3) Query Q_3 is to find Mary's current address. We may know that employee tuples with the most current status or salary also contain the most current address. Putting this and (1) above together, we know that the answer to Q_3 is "6 Main St."

(4) Finally, query Q_4 is to find the current budget of department R&D. Again no timestamps are available for us to evaluate the query. However, we may know the following: (a) department tuples t_1 and t_2 have copied their mgrAddr values from employee tuple s_1[address]; similarly, t_3 has copied from s_3, and t_4 from s_4; and (b) department tuples with the most current address also have the most current budget. Taken together, these tell us that $t_1 \prec_{budget} t_3$ and $t_2 \prec_{budget} t_3$. Although we do not know which budget in t_3 or t_4 is more current, in both cases the budget is 6000K, and hence it is the answer to Q_4. □

In the rest of the chapter we aim to answer the following questions. How should we specify currency orders on data values in the absence of timestamps? When currency orders are only partly available, can we decide whether an attribute value is more up-to-date than another? How can we answer a query with only current data in a database? To answer a query, do we need to import current data from another source, and if so, what to copy? How can we incorporate copy relationships into the model? The ability to answer these questions may provide guidance for practitioners to decide, e.g., whether the answer to a query is corrupted by stale data, or what copy functions are needed, among other things.

6.2 A DATA CURRENCY MODEL

We begin with a simple model for specifying data currency, in terms of partial currency orders and simple currency constraints. We then study consistent completions of currency orders and show how queries can be answered using current instances derived from these completions. In Section 6.4 we will enrich the model by supporting copy functions.

Data with partial currency orders. A relation schema can be naturally specified as $R = (EID, A_1, \ldots, A_n)$, where EID denotes entity id that identifies tuples pertaining to the same entity, as introduced by Codd [1979]. Such EID values can be obtained using data deduplication techniques we have seen in Chapter 4. A finite instance I of R is referred to as a *normal instance of R*, to distinguish from temporal instances to be introduced shortly.

To determine the current values of an entity, we need currency orders defined on those tuples pertaining to the entity. To do this we extend normal instances of R as follows.

A *temporal instance* I_t of R is given as $(I, \prec_{A_1}, \ldots, \prec_{A_n})$, where each $\prec_{A_i}$ is a strict partial order defined on I such that for tuples t_1 and t_2 in I, $t_1 \prec_{A_i} t_2$ implies $t_1[EID] = t_2[EID]$. Intuitively, if $t_1 \prec_{A_i} t_2$, then t_1 and t_2 refer to *the same entity*, and t_2 contains a *more current* A_i-value for that entity than t_1. In other words, t_2 is more current than t_1 *in attribute A_i*. In contrast to normal instances, I_t carries partial currency orders.

We call $\prec_{A_i}$ the *currency order for attribute A_i*. Recall that a strict partial order is irreflexive and transitive, and therefore, asymmetric. It should be noted that a currency order $\prec_{A_i}$ is possibly empty, when no currency information is known for A_i.

We assume that the currency orders in I_t are partially known or unknown at all (when $\prec_{A_i}$ is empty). To answer queries with current values, we have to consider various completions of the partial currency orders in a temporal instance. More specifically, a *completion* of $I_t = (I, \prec_{A_1}, \ldots, \prec_{A_n})$ is a temporal instance $I_t^c = (I, \prec_{A_1}^c, \ldots, \prec_{A_n}^c)$ of R, such that for each $i \in [1, n]$, (1) $\prec_{A_i} \subseteq \prec_{A_i}^c$, and (2) for all tuples $t_1, t_2 \in I$, t_1 and t_2 are comparable under $\prec_{A_i}^c$ if and only if $t_1[\text{EID}] = t_2[\text{EID}]$. The latter condition implies that $\prec_{A_i}^c$ induces a *total order* on tuples that refer to the same entity, while tuples representing distinct entities are not comparable under $\prec_{A_i}^c$. We call $\prec_{A_i}^c$ a *completed currency order*.

Currency constraints. We use a class of denial constraints we have seen in Chapter 2 to specify additional currency information derived from the semantics of data, which enriches $\prec_{A_i}$. A *currency constraint* φ for R is a universally quantified FO sentence of the form:

$$\forall t_1, \ldots, t_k : R \left(\bigwedge_{j \in [1,k]} (t_1[\text{EID}] = t_j[\text{EID}]) \wedge \psi \to t_u \prec_{A_i} t_v \right),$$

where $u, v \in [1, k]$, each t_j is a tuple variable denoting a tuple of R, and ψ is a conjunction of predicates of the one of the following forms: (1) $t_j \prec_{A_l} t_h$, i.e., t_h is more current than t_j in attribute A_l; (2) $t_j[A_l] = t_h[A_l]$ (resp. $t_j[A_l] \neq t_h[A_l]$), i.e., $t_j[A_l]$ and $t_h[A_l]$ are identical (resp. distinct) values; (3) $t_j[A_l] = c$ (resp. $t_j[A_l] \neq c$), where c is a constant; and (4) possibly other built-in predicates defined on particular domains.

Currency constraints are interpreted over completions I_t^c of temporal instances of R. We say that I_t^c satisfies φ, denoted by $I_t^c \models \varphi$, if for all tuples $t_1, \ldots, t_k$ in I that have the same EID value, if these tuples satisfy the predicates in ψ following the standard semantics of first-order logic, then $t_u \prec_{A_i}^c t_v$. Observe that the use of EID in φ enforces that φ is imposed on tuples that refer to *the same entity*. We say that I_t^c satisfies a set Σ of currency constraints, denoted by $I_t^c \models \Sigma$, if $I_t^c \models \varphi$ for all $\varphi \in \Sigma$.

Example 6.2 Recall relations employee and department given in Figure 6.1. Currency constraints defined on these relations include the following:

$\varphi_1: \forall s, t : \text{emp}\big((s[\text{EID}] = t[\text{EID}] \wedge s[\text{salary}] > t[\text{salary}]) \to t \prec_{\text{salary}} s\big)$
$\varphi_2: \forall s, t : \text{emp}\big((s[\text{EID}] = t[\text{EID}] \wedge s[\text{status}] = \text{"married"} \wedge t[\text{status}] = \text{"single"}) \to t \prec_{\text{LN}} s\big)$
$\varphi_3: \forall s, t : \text{emp}\big((s[\text{EID}] = t[\text{EID}] \wedge t \prec_{\text{salary}} s) \to t \prec_{\text{address}} s\big)$
$\varphi_4: \forall s, t : \text{dept}\big((s[\text{EID}] = t[\text{EID}] \wedge t \prec_{\text{mgrAddr}} s) \to t \prec_{\text{budget}} s\big)$.

Here, φ_1 states that when employee tuples s and t refer to the same employee, if $s[\text{salary}] > t[\text{salary}]$,

6.2. A DATA CURRENCY MODEL   123

then s is more current than t in attribute salary. Note that ">" denotes the built-in predicate "greater-than" in the numeric domain of salary, whereas $\prec_{\text{salary}}$ is the currency order for salary. Constraint φ_2 asserts that if $s[\text{status}]$ is married and $t[\text{status}]$ is single, then s is more current than t in LN. Constraint φ_3 states that if s is more current than t in salary, then s is also more current than t in address; similarly for φ_4. □

Recall that denial constraints have been used to improve data consistency (Chapter 2). These constraints also suffices to express currency semantics commonly found in practice. Along the same lines as Proposition 5.7, one can show that currency constraints can be expressed as containment constraints in CQ. In light of this, we can deal with data currency, data consistency, and relative information completeness in a uniform logical framework.

Consistent completions of temporal orders. We specify data currency in terms of temporal instances and currency constraints. Consider a relational schema $\mathcal{R} = (R_1, \ldots, R_s)$, and a normal instance $D = (I_1, \ldots, I_s)$ of $\mathcal{R}$.

Definition 6.3   A *specification* $\mathbf{S}$ of data currency consists of the following, for each $i \in [1, s]$:
  (1) a collection of temporal instances $I_{(t,i)} = (I_i, \prec_{A_1^i}, \ldots, \prec_{A_{n_i}^i})$ of schema R_i; and
  (2) a set Σ_i of currency constraints imposed on each $I_{(t,i)}$. □

Intuitively, it specifies data values and entities (by the normal instance I_i embedded in each $I_{(t,i)}$), partial currency orders known for entities in each relation (by $\prec_{A_j^i}$), and additional currency information derived from the semantics of the data (by Σ_i).

We are naturally interested in such completions $I_{(t,i)}^c$ of $I_{(t,i)}$ that satisfy Σ_i. That is, $I_{(t,i)}^c$ should observe the currency constraints imposed on $I_{(t,i)}$. As will be seen shortly, we will define current instances of an entity and answer queries with current instances based on such completions. This notion of completions is defined as follows.

Definition 6.4   A *consistent completion* D^c of a specification $\mathbf{S}$ consists of a temporal instance $I_{(t,i)}^c$ of R_i for each $i \in [1, s]$ such that:
  (1) $I_{(t,i)}^c$ is a completion of $I_{(t,i)}$; and
  (2) $I_{(t,i)}^c \models \Sigma_i$.

We use $\text{Mod}(\mathbf{S})$ to denote the set of all consistent completions of $\mathbf{S}$. We say that $\mathbf{S}$ is *consistent* if $\text{Mod}(\mathbf{S}) \neq \emptyset$, i.e., there exists at least one consistent completion of $\mathbf{S}$. □

That is, if $I_{(t,i)} = (I_i, \prec_{A_1}, \ldots, \prec_{A_n})$ is part of $\mathbf{S}$ and $I_{(t,i)}^c = (I_i, \prec_{A_1}^c, \ldots, \prec_{A_n}^c)$ is its consistent completion, then each $\prec_{A_j}^c$ extends $\prec_{A_j}$ to a total order on all tuples *pertaining to the same entity*, and the completed orders satisfy the currency constraints Σ_i.

Example 6.5   Consider a specification $\mathbf{S}_0$ consisting of the instances I_{emp} and I_{dept} of Figure 6.1, and the currency constraints φ_1–φ_4 given in Example 6.2. Assume that no currency orders are known for I_{emp} and I_{dept} initially, i.e., all the partial currency orders in $\mathbf{S}_0$ are empty. A consistent completion D_0^c of $\mathbf{S}_0$ defines:

- $s_1 \prec_A s_2 \prec_A s_3$ when A ranges over FN, LN, address, salary, and status for employee tuples; and

- $t_1 \prec_B t_2 \prec_B t_4 \prec_B t_3$ when B ranges over mgrFN, mgrLN, mgrAddr, and budget for department tuples (here we assume that dname is the EID attribute of Dept).

One can verify that D_0^c satisfies the currency constraints and hence, $D_0^c \in \text{Mod}(\mathbf{S}_0)$. Here, we assume that s_4 and s_5 refer to distinct entities. Note that no currency order is defined between any of s_1, s_2, s_3 and any of s_4, s_5, since they represent different entities. □

Current instances. We next define the current tuple of an entity in a database, i.e., a tuple that is composed of the most current value in the database for each attribute of the entity. To do this, in a temporal instance $I_t = (I, \prec_{A_1}, \ldots, \prec_{A_n})$ of R, let $E = \{t[\text{EID}] \mid t \in D\}$, and for each entity $e \in E$, let $I_e = \{t \in I \mid t[\text{EID}] = e\}$. That is, E contains all the EID values in I, and I_e is the set of tuples pertaining to the entity with EID $= e$.

Definition 6.6 In a consistent completion I_t^c of I_t, for each attribute A of R, the *current A-value* for entity $e \in E$ is $t[A]$, where t is the greatest (i.e., most current) tuple in the totally ordered set $(I_e, \prec_A^c)$. The *current tuple* for entity $e \in E$, denoted by $\text{LST}(e, I_t^c)$, is tuple t_e such that for each attribute A of R, $t_e[A]$ is the current A-value for entity e.

We use $\text{LST}(I_t^c)$ to denote $\{\text{LST}(e, I_t^c) \mid e \in E\}$, referred to as the *current instance* of I_t^c. For each $D^c \in \text{Mod}(\mathbf{S})$, we define $\text{LST}(D^c) = (\text{LST}(I_{(t,1)}^c), \ldots, \text{LST}(I_{(t,s)}^c))$, referred to as *the current instance* of D^c. □

Intuitively, one can construct from I_t^c the current tuple $\text{LST}(e, I_t^c)$ for each entity e w.r.t. completed orders $\prec_A^c$. It is a tuple that contains the entity's most current A-value for each attribute A. Here LST stands for "last" since $\text{LST}(e, I_t^c)$ is formed by collecting the last values in totally ordered sets in I_t^c. This yields the *current instance* $\text{LST}(I_t^c)$ of I_t^c consisting of only the current tuples of the entities in I, from which currency orders are removed. Observe that $\text{LST}(I_t^c)$ is a *normal instance* of R, carrying no currency orders; so is $\text{LST}(D^c)$, the current instance of D^c, which does not carry currency orders.

Example 6.7 Recall the completion D_0^c of $\mathbf{S}_0$ from Example 6.5. We have that $\text{LST}(D_0^c)$ = $(\text{LST}(I_{\text{emp}}), \text{LST}(I_{\text{dept}}))$, where $\text{LST}(I_{\text{emp}}) = \{s_3, s_4, s_5\}$, and $\text{LST}(I_{\text{dept}}) = \{t_3\}$. Note that $\text{LST}(I_{\text{emp}})$ and $\text{LST}(I_{\text{dept}})$ are normal instances; and so is $\text{LST}(D_0^c)$.

Now suppose that s_4 and s_5 refer to the same person, and extend D_0^c by adding $s_4 \prec_A s_5$ and $s_5 \prec_B s_4$, where A ranges over FN, LN, address and status while B is salary. Then the current tuple of this person is (Robert, Luth, 8 Drum St, 80K, married), in which the first four attributes are taken from s_5 while its salary attribute is taken from s_4. □

Certain current answers. Consider a query Q posed on a normal instance D of $\mathcal{R}$, where Q does not refer to currency orders. Let **S** be a specification of data currency for D, which augments D with (possibly empty) partial currency orders available, along with currency constraints. As remarked earlier, we want to evaluate Q with only the current values of the entities represented by tuples in D. To do this, we evaluate Q on the current instance of D^c without worrying about currency orders, where D^c is a consistent completion of **S**. We are interested in certain current answers to Q in D, i.e., those tuples that are in the answers to Q in the current instances of *all possible* consistent completions of **S**. More specifically, certain current answers to a query are defined as follows.

Definition 6.8 We say that a tuple t is a *certain current answer* to Q w.r.t. **S** if
$$t \in \bigcap_{D^c \in \mathrm{Mod}(\mathbf{S})} Q(\mathrm{LST}(D^c)).$$
□

That is, tuple t is guaranteed to belong to the answer computed from the current instances of all possible consistent completions of **S**, no matter how the partial currency orders in **S** are completed, as long as the currency constraints of **S** are satisfied.

Example 6.9 Recall queries Q_1, Q_2, and Q_3 from Example 6.1, and the specification $\mathbf{S}_0$ from Example 6.5. One can verify that the answers to these queries described in Example 6.1 are certain current answers *w.r.t.* $\mathbf{S}_0$, i.e., these answers remain unchanged in $\mathrm{LST}(D^c)$ for all possible consistent completions $D^c \in \mathrm{Mod}(\mathbf{S}_0)$. □

6.3 REASONING ABOUT DATA CURRENCY

Having developed the data currency model, we are now ready to investigate fundamental problems for data currency. We study problems for determining whether a specification makes sense, whether some currency order is certain among all possible consistent completions of a specification, and whether a tuple is a certain current query answer. We encourage the reader to consult [Fan et al., 2012b] for proofs of the result of this section.

Complexity of queries. We establish the data complexity and combined complexity of these problems. Before we present the complexity results, we first review these notions of complexity introduced by Vardi [1982] (see, e.g., [Abiteboul et al., 1995] for details):

- *combined complexity*: the complexity of evaluating *variable queries* on *variable databases*, when both the queries and the databases are taken as input; and

- *data complexity*: the complexity of evaluating *a fixed query* on *variable databases*, when only the databases are taken as input.

When it comes to our problems for reasoning about data currency, for data complexity we fix currency constraints (and queries when certain current query answering is considered), and study the complexity when varying size of data sources (temporal instances). For combined complexity we also allow currency constraints and queries to vary.

The consistency of specifications. The first problem is to decide whether a given specification **S** makes sense, i.e., whether there exists a consistent completion of **S**. This problem is referred to as the *consistency problem for specifications* and is denoted by CPS.

- INPUT: A specification **S** of data currency.
- QUESTION: Is Mod(**S**) nonempty?

This problem is nontrivial: it is Σ_2^p-complete, and remains intractable even when currency constraints are fixed (data complexity).

Theorem 6.10 For CPS:
- the combined complexity is Σ_2^p-complete; and
- the data complexity is NP-complete.

Crux. (1) *Lower bounds*. For the combined complexity, we show that CPS is Σ_2^p-hard by reduction from the ∃*∀*3DNF problem, which is Σ_2^p-complete [Stockmeyer, 1976].

For the data complexity, we show that CPS is NP-hard by reduction from the betweenness problem, which is NP-complete (cf. [Garey and Johnson, 1979]). Given two sets E and $F = \{(e_i, e_j, e_k) \mid e_i, e_j, e_k \in E\}$, the betweenness problem is to decide whether there exists a bijection $\pi : E \to \{1, \ldots, |E|\}$ such that for each $(e_i, e_j, e_k) \in E$, either $\pi(e_i) < \pi(e_j) < \pi(e_k)$ or $\pi(e_k) < \pi(e_j) < \pi(e_i)$.

(2) *Upper bounds*. We provide an algorithm that, given a specification **S**, guesses a completion D^c of total orders for entities in **S**, and then checks whether $D^c \in \text{Mod}(\mathbf{S})$. The algorithm is in Σ_2^p, and when the input currency constraints are fixed, it is in NP. □

Certain currency orders and instances. The next two questions ask whether some currency order is entailed by the partial currency orders and currency constraints given in a specification **S**, i.e., whether a given currency order is contained in all consistent completions of **S**. More specifically, given two temporal instances $I_{(t,1)} = (I, \prec_{A_1}, \ldots, \prec_{A_n})$ and $I_{(t,2)} = (I, \prec'_{A_1}, \ldots, \prec'_{A_n})$ of the same schema R, we say that $I_{(t,1)}$ is *contained in* $I_{(t,2)}$, denoted by $I_{(t,1)} \sqsubseteq I_{(t,2)}$, if $\prec_{A_j} \subseteq \prec'_{A_j}$ for all $j \in [1, n]$.

Consider a specification **S** in which $I_t = (I, \prec_{A_1}, \ldots, \prec_{A_n})$ is a temporal instance of schema R. A *currency order* for I_t is a temporal instance $O_t = (I, \prec'_{A_1}, \ldots, \prec'_{A_n})$ of R. Observe that O_t does not necessarily contain I_t.

One of the problems is the *certain ordering problem*, denoted by COP.

6.3. REASONING ABOUT DATA CURRENCY 127

- INPUT: A consistent specification **S** of data currency in which I_t is a temporal instance of relation schema R, and a currency order O_t of R.
- QUESTION: Is it the case that $O_t \subseteq I_t^c$ for all $D^c \in \text{Mod}(\mathbf{S})$? Here I_t^c denotes the completion of I_t in D^c.

Example 6.11 Consider the specification $\mathbf{S}_0$ given in Example 6.5. We want to know whether $s_1 \prec_{\text{salary}} s_3$ is assured by every completion $D^c \in \text{Mod}(\mathbf{S}_0)$. To this end we construct a currency order $O_t = (I_{\text{emp}}, \prec_{\text{FN}}, \prec_{\text{LN}}, \prec_{\text{address}}, \prec_{\text{salary}}, \prec_{\text{status}})$, in which $s_1 \prec_{\text{salary}} s_3$ is in $\prec_{\text{salary}}$, but the partial orders for all other attributes are empty. One can verify that O_t is indeed a certain currency order, as assured by currency constraint φ_1.

As another example, one can define a currency order O_t' to check whether $t_3 \prec_{\text{mgrFN}} t_4$ is entailed by all $D^c \in \text{Mod}(\mathbf{S}_0)$. One can readily verify that it is not the case. Indeed, there exists a $D_1^c \in \text{Mod}(\mathbf{S}_0)$, such that $t_4 \prec_{\text{mgrFN}} t_3$ is given in D_1^c. □

The other question asks whether certain currency orders and currency constraints in a specification **S** of data currency have sufficient information to determine a "certain current instance." Given **S**, we want to know whether every consistent completion of **S** yields the same current instance. We say that a specification **S** of data currency is *deterministic for current instances* if for all consistent completions $D_1^c, D_2^c \in \text{Mod}(\mathbf{S})$, $\text{LST}(D_1^c) = \text{LST}(D_2^c)$. This definition naturally carries over to a particular relation schema R: a specification **S** is said to be *deterministic for current R instances* if for all consistent completions $D_1^c, D_2^c \in \text{Mod}(\mathbf{S})$, the instance of R in $\text{LST}(D_1^c)$ is equal to the instance of R in $\text{LST}(D_2^c)$.

This problem, referred to as the *deterministic current instance problem* and denoted by DCIP, is stated as follows.

- INPUT: A consistent specification **S** and a relation schema R defined in **S**.
- QUESTION: Is **S** deterministic for current R instances?

Example 6.12 The specification $\mathbf{S}_0$ given in Example 6.5 is deterministic for current employee instances. Indeed, for all $D^c \in \text{Mod}(\mathbf{S}_0)$, if I_{emp}^c is a consistent completion of I_{emp}, then $\text{LST}(I_{\text{emp}}^c) = \{s_3, s_4, s_5\}$. □

Unfortunately, both COP and DCIP are nontrivial.

Theorem 6.13 For both COP and DCIP:
- the combined complexity is Π_2^p-complete; and
- the data complexity is coNP-complete.

Crux. (1) *Lower bounds.* For the combined complexity, one can verify that COP and DCIP are Π_2^p-hard by reduction from the complement of the ∃*∀*3DNF problem. As mentioned earlier, the latter problem is known to be Σ_2^p-complete [Stockmeyer, 1976].

For the data complexity, COP and DCIP are shown to be coNP-hard by reduction from the complement of the 3SAT problem. As we have seen earlier, 3SAT is NP-complete.

(2) *Upper bounds.* Decision algorithms can be developed for COP and DCIP that are in Π_2^p (combined complexity) and in coNP (data complexity). □

Certain current query answering. Given a query Q in a query language $\mathcal{L}_Q$, we want to know whether a tuple t is in $Q(\text{LST}(D^c))$ for all $D^c \in \text{Mod}(\mathbf{S})$. This is referred to as the *certain current query answering problem*, and is denoted by $\text{CCQA}(\mathcal{L}_Q)$.

- INPUT: A consistent specification $\mathbf{S}$, a tuple t and a query $Q \in \mathcal{L}_Q$.
- QUESTION: Is t a certain current answer to Q w.r.t. $\mathbf{S}$?

We study $\text{CCQA}(\mathcal{L}_Q)$ when $\mathcal{L}_Q$ ranges over CQ, UCQ, ∃FO⁺, and FO (see Section 1.4 for these query languages). While different query languages have no impact on the data complexity of $\text{CCQA}(\mathcal{L}_Q)$, the result below tells us that for different $\mathcal{L}_Q$, $\text{CCQA}(\mathcal{L}_Q)$ may have different combined complexity. More specifically, (1) disjunctions in UCQ and ∃FO⁺ do not incur extra complexity to CCQA (indeed, CCQA has the same complexity for CQ as for UCQ and ∃FO⁺), but (2) the presence of negation in FO complicates the analysis.

Theorem 6.14 The combined complexity of $\text{CCQA}(\mathcal{L}_Q)$ is:
- Π_2^p-complete when $\mathcal{L}_Q$ is CQ, UCQ, or ∃FO⁺; and
- PSPACE-complete when $\mathcal{L}_Q$ is FO.

The data complexity is coNP-complete when $\mathcal{L}_Q \in \{\text{CQ, UCQ, ∃FO}^+, \text{FO}\}$.

Crux. (1) *Lower bounds.* For the combined complexity, it suffices to show the following: (a) $\text{CCQA}(\mathcal{L}_Q)$ is Π_2^p-hard when $\mathcal{L}_Q$ is CQ, by reduction from the ∀*∃*3CNF problem, which is known to be Π_2^p-complete [Stockmeyer, 1976]; and (b) $\text{CCQA}(\mathcal{L}_Q)$ is PSPACE-hard when $\mathcal{L}_Q$ is FO, by reduction from Q3SAT, which is PSPACE-complete (cf. [Papadimitriou, 1994]). These reductions do not use any currency constraints.

For the data complexity, $\text{CCQA}(\mathcal{L}_Q)$ is shown to be coNP-hard when $\mathcal{L}_Q$ is CQ, Q is fixed and currency constraints are absent, by reduction from the complement of 3SAT.

(2) *Upper bounds.* There exists a decision algorithm for $\text{CCQA}(\mathcal{L}_Q)$ that is in Π_2^p for ∃FO⁺ and in PSPACE for FO (combined complexity). It is in coNP for all these query languages when the queries and currency constraints are fixed (data complexity). □

Special cases. The results above tell us that CPS, COP, DCIP, and $\text{CCQA}(\mathcal{L}_Q)$ are beyond reach in practice. These motivate us to look for special tractable cases. One practical case is when reliable timestamps are provided for part of the data, but currency constraints are absent. This indeed simplifies the analysis of CPS, COP, and DCIP.

Theorem 6.15 In the absence of currency constraints, CPS, COP, and DCIP are in PTIME.
Crux. A PTIME decision algorithm can be developed for each of these problems. □

For CCQA($\mathcal{L}_Q$), however, dropping currency constraints does not make our lives easier.

Corollary 6.16 *In the absence of currency constraints, CCQA($\mathcal{L}_Q$) remains:*
- *coNP-hard (data complexity) and Π_2^p-hard (combined complexity) even for CQ; and*
- *PSPACE-hard (combined complexity) for FO.*

Crux. These lower bounds follow from the proof of the lower bounds of Theorem 6.14, which do not use currency constraints. □

We next consider simpler queries for CCQA. Theorem 6.14 shows that the complexity of CCQA for CQ is rather robust: adding disjunctions does not increase the complexity. We next investigate the impact of removing Cartesian product from CQ on the complexity of CCQA. We consider SP queries, which support projection and selection only (recall SP from Section 2.2.4). For instance, queries $Q_1 - Q_4$ of Example 6.1 are SP queries.

Unfortunately, the following result tells us that in the presence of currency constraints, CCQA is no easier for identity queries than for $\exists FO^+$ (see Section 2.2.4 for identity queries).

Corollary 6.17 *For SP queries, CCQA is coNP-complete (data complexity) and Π_2^p-complete (combined complexity) in the presence of currency constraints, even for identity queries.*

Crux. The upper bounds follow from Theorem 6.14. The lower bounds can be verified by reduction from the complement of CPS, which is NP-complete (data complexity) and Σ_2^p-complete (combined complexity) by Theorem 6.10. □

However, in the absence of currency constraints, CCQA(SP) becomes tractable. That is, SP and the absence of currency constraints taken together simplify the analysis of CCQA.

Proposition 6.18 *For SP queries, CCQA is in PTIME in the absence of currency constraints.*
Crux. A PTIME decision algorithm can be readily developed for CCQA($\mathcal{L}_Q$) in the absence of currency constraints, when $\mathcal{L}_Q$ is SP. □

We summarize the main complexity results of this section in Tables 6.1 and 6.2.

Table 6.1: Complexity of reasoning about data currency (CPS, COP, DCIP)

	CPS	COP	DCIP
Data complexity	NP-complete	coNP-complete	coNP-complete
Combined complexity	Σ_2^p-complete	Π_2^p-complete	Π_2^p-complete
Special case	In the absence of currency constraints		
Combined and data complexity	PTIME	PTIME	PTIME

Table 6.2: Complexity of CCQA($\mathcal{L}_Q$)

CCQA($\mathcal{L}_Q$)	Combined complexity	Data complexity
CQ, UCQ, $\exists$FO$^+$	Π_2^p-complete	coNP-complete
FO	PSPACE-complete	coNP-complete
Special case	SP queries in the absence of currency constraints	
CQ, UCQ, $\exists$FO$^+$, FO	PTIME	PTIME

6.4 INCORPORATING COPY FUNCTIONS

We have seen a simple model for specifying data currency in Section 6.2. As observed by Berti-Equille et al. [2009] and Dong et al. [2010, 2009a], it is common in the real world to copy or import values from one data source to another, along with the currency orders on the data values. This is typically carried out by using copy functions. In light of this, below we extend our basic data currency model by supporting copy functions.

When copy relationships are taken into account, it is natural to ask what values should be copied from one data source to another in order to answer a query. To characterize this intuition we introduce a notion of currency preservation. In the next section we will study fundamental problems associated with currency preserving copy functions.

6.4.1 THE DATA CURRENCY MODEL REVISITED

We first augment our data currency model by incorporating copy functions.

Copy functions. Consider two temporal instances $I_{(t,1)} = (I_1, \prec_{A_1}, \ldots, \prec_{A_p})$ and $I_{(t,2)} = (I_2, \prec_{B_1}, \ldots, \prec_{B_q})$ of (possibly distinct) relation schemas R_1 and R_2, respectively.

Definition 6.19 A *copy function* ρ of signature $R_1[\vec{A}] \Leftarrow R_2[\vec{B}]$ is a partial mapping from I_1 to I_2, where $\vec{A} = (A_1, \ldots, A_\ell)$ and $\vec{B} = (B_1, \ldots, B_\ell)$ denote attributes in R_1 and R_2, respectively. Here, ρ is required to satisfy *the copying condition*: for each tuple t in I_1, if $\rho(t) = s$, then $t[A_i] = s[B_i]$ for all $i \in [1, \ell]$.

6.4. INCORPORATING COPY FUNCTIONS

We say that ρ is $\prec$-*compatible* if for all $t_1, t_2 \in I_1$, for each $i \in [1, \ell]$, if $\rho(t_1) = s_1, \rho(t_2) = s_2$, $t_1[\text{EID}] = t_2[\text{EID}]$, and $s_1[\text{EID}] = s_2[\text{EID}]$, then $s_1 \prec_{B_i} s_2$ implies $t_1 \prec_{A_i} t_2$. □

Intuitively, $\rho(t) = s$ indicates that the values of the $\vec{A}$ attributes of t have been imported from the $\vec{B}$ attributes of tuple s in I_2. Here, $\vec{A}$ specifies a list of *correlated attributes* that should be copied together. The $\prec$-*compatibility* requires that copy functions preserve the currency orders in the original source, i.e., when attribute values are imported from I_2 to I_1, the currency orders on the corresponding tuples in $I_{(t,2)}$ are inherited by $I_{(t,1)}$.

Example 6.20 On the relations I_{emp} and I_{dept} of Figure 6.1, a copy function ρ of signature department[mgrAddr] $\Leftarrow$ employee[address] is depicted in Figure 6.1 by arrows. It is defined by $\rho(t_1) = s_1$, $\rho(t_2) = s_1$, $\rho(t_3) = s_3$, and $\rho(t_4) = s_4$. That is, the mgrAddr values of t_1 and t_2 have both been imported from $s_1[\text{address}]$, while $t_3[\text{mgrAddr}]$ and $t_4[\text{mgrAddr}]$ are copied from $s_3[\text{address}]$ and $s_4[\text{address}]$, respectively. It satisfies the copying condition: $t_1[\text{mgrAddr}] = t_2[\text{mgrAddr}] = s_1[\text{address}]$, $t_3[\text{mgrAddr}] = s_3[\text{address}]$, and $t_4[\text{mgrAddr}] = s_4[\text{address}]$.

Assume that $\prec_A$ is $\emptyset$ for all attributes A in I_{emp} or I_{dept}. Then ρ is $\prec$-compatible w.r.t. the temporal instances of I_{emp} and I_{dept}. By contrast, assume that partial currency orders $s_1 \prec_{\text{address}} s_3$ on I_{emp} and $t_3 \prec_{\text{mgrAddr}} t_1$ on I_{dept} are given. Then ρ is not $\prec$-compatible: since s_1 and s_3 pertain to the same person Mary, and t_1 and t_3 refer to the same department R&D, $s_1 \prec_{\text{address}} s_3$ should carry over to $t_1 \prec_{\text{mgrAddr}} t_3$, as $\rho(t_1) = s_1$ and $\rho(t_3) = s_3$. But then $t_3 \prec_{\text{mgrAddr}} t_1$ and $t_1 \prec_{\text{mgrAddr}} t_3$, a contradiction! □

The currency model revised. We now revise the data currency model given in Section 6.2 by extending Definitions 6.3 and 6.4 with copy functions. We should remark that Definitions 6.6 and 6.8 remain unchanged in the presence of copy functions.

Definition 6.21 A *specification* **S** of data currency consists of (1) a collection of temporal instances $I_{(t,i)}$, (2) a set Σ_i of currency constraints on each $I_{(t,i)}$, and (3) a (possibly empty) copy function $\rho_{(i,j)}$ that imports data from $I_{(t,i)}$ to $I_{(t,j)}$ for all $i, j \in [1, s]$. □

The revised notion of specifications for data currency extends Definition 6.3 by specifying data that have been copied from one source to another (by $\rho_{(i,j)}$).

Definition 6.22 A *consistent completion* D^c of a specification **S** consists of a temporal instance $I^c_{(t,i)}$ of R_i for all $i \in [1, s]$ such that (1) $I^c_{(t,i)}$ is a completion of $I_{(t,i)}$, (2) $I^c_{(t,i)} \models \Sigma_i$, and (3) $\rho_{(i,j)}$ is $\prec$-compatible w.r.t. the completed currency orders in $I^c_{(t,i)}$ and $I^c_{(t,j)}$. □

Compared to Definition 6.4, each $I^c_{(t,i)}$ is now additionally required to satisfy the constraints imposed by copy functions. Observe that the copying condition and $\prec$-compatibility impose constraints on consistent completions. This is particularly evident when a data source imports data from multiple sources, and when two data sources copy from each other, directly or indirectly. In addition, these constraints interact with currency constraints.

Example 6.23 Consider the specification $\mathbf{S}'_0$ that extends $\mathbf{S}_0$ given in Example 6.5 by including the copy function ρ given in Example 6.20. Then D^c_0 of Example 6.5 is still a consistent completion of $\mathbf{S}'_0$ since it satisfies the constraints imposed by ρ. Moreover, one can verify that the answer to Q_4 given in Example 6.1 is the certain current answer $w.r.t.$ $\mathbf{S}'_0$.

As another example, suppose that there is a copy function ρ_1 that imports budget attribute values of t_1 and t_3 from the budget attributes of s'_1 and s'_3 in another source I_1, respectively, where $s'_1 = t_1$ and $s'_3 = t_3$, but in I_1, $s'_3 \prec_{\text{budget}} s'_1$. Then there exists no consistent completion in this setting. Indeed, all completed currency orders of $\prec_{\text{budget}}$ in I_{dept} have to satisfy the currency constraints φ_1, φ_3 and φ_4, which enforce $t_1 \prec_{\text{budget}} t_3$, but ρ_1 is not $\prec$-compatible with this currency order. This demonstrates the interaction between currency constraints and the currency constraints imposed by copy functions. □

The impact of copy functions on decision problems. One might think that copy functions would complicate the analyses of CPS, COP, DCIP, and CCQA($\mathcal{L}_Q$). The good news is that copy functions *do not* increase the complexity of these problems: when copy functions are present, CPS, COP, DCIP, and CCQA($\mathcal{L}_Q$) have the same complexity bounds given in Theorem 6.10, 6.13, 6.14, 6.15, Corollaries 6.16 and 6.17, and Proposition 6.18.

Corollary 6.24 *In the presence of copy functions, CPS, COP, DCIP, and CCQA($\mathcal{L}_Q$) have the same complexity as their counterparts without copy functions.*

Crux. The lower bounds of Theorem 6.10, 6.13, 6.14, 6.15, Corollaries 6.16 and 6.17, and Proposition 6.18 carry over to the setting when copy functions are present. Moreover, their upper-bound proofs can be readily extended to accommodate the presence of copy functions, and verify that the upper bounds remain intact in this setting. □

In the sequel, we consider specifications of data currency with copy functions.

6.4.2 CURRENCY PRESERVING COPY FUNCTIONS

Copy functions tell us what data values in a relation are imported from other data sources. Naturally, we want to leverage the imported values to improve the quality of query answers. This gives rise to the following questions: Do the copy functions import sufficient current values for answering a query Q? If not, can we extend the copy functions such that Q can be answered with more up-to-date data? If so, how to do it? To answer these questions we first introduce a notion of currency-preserving copy functions.

To simplify the discussion, we consider a specification $\mathbf{S}$ of data currency consisting of two data sources, i.e., two collections of temporal instances $D = (I_1, \ldots, I_p)$ and $D' = (I'_1, \ldots, I'_q)$,

6.4. INCORPORATING COPY FUNCTIONS   133

with (1) a set Σ_i (resp. Σ'_j) of currency constraints on I_i for each $i \in [1, p]$ (resp. I'_j for $j \in [1, q]$), and (2) a collection $\overline{\rho}$ of copy functions $\rho_{(j,i)}$ that import data from I'_j to I_i, for $i \in [1, p]$ and $j \in [1, q]$, i.e., all the functions of $\overline{\rho}$ import data from D' to D.

Extensions. To formalize currency preservation, we need the following notions. Assume that $I_i = (I, \prec_{A_1}, \ldots, \prec_{A_n})$ and $I'_j = (I', \prec_{B_1}, \ldots, \prec_{B_m})$ are temporal instances of schemas $R_i = (\text{EID}, A_1, \ldots, A_n)$ and $R'_j = (\text{EID}, B_1, \ldots, B_m)$, respectively, where $n \leq m$.

Definition 6.25 An *extension* of I_i is a temporal instance $I_i^e = (I^e, \prec^e_{A_1}, \ldots, \prec^e_{A_n})$ of R_i such that (1) $I \subseteq I^e$, (2) $\prec_{A_h} \subseteq \prec^e_{A_h}$ for all $h \in [1, n]$, and (3) $\pi_{\text{EID}}(I^e) = \pi_{\text{EID}}(I)$. □

Intuitively, I_i^e extends I_i by adding new tuples for those entities that are already in I_i. It does not introduce new entities. Note that I_i^e is not necessarily a completion.

Definition 6.26 Consider two copy functions: $\rho_{(j,i)}$ imports tuples from I'_j to I_i, and $\rho^e_{(j,i)}$ from I'_j to I_i^e, both of signature $R_i[\vec{A}] \Leftarrow R'_j[\vec{B}]$, where $\vec{A} = (A_1, \ldots, A_n)$ and $\vec{B}$ is a sequence of n attributes in R'_j. We say that $\rho^e_{(j,i)}$ *extends* $\rho_{(j,i)}$ if:
1. I_i^e is an extension of I_i;
2. for each tuple t in I_i, if $\rho_{(j,i)}(t)$ is defined, then so is $\rho^e_{(j,i)}(t)$ and $\rho^e_{(j,i)}(t) = \rho_{(j,i)}(t)$; and
3. for each tuple t in $I_i^e \setminus I_i$, there exists a tuple s in I'_j such that $\rho^e_{(j,i)}(t) = s$.

We refer to I_i^e as the *extension of I_i by $\rho^e_{(j,i)}$*. □

Observe that I_i^e is not allowed to expand arbitrarily because (a) each new tuple t in I_i^e is copied from an existing tuple s in I'_j, and (b) no new entity is introduced. Furthermore, only those copy functions that cover all attributes but EID of R_i can be extended. This assures that all the attributes of a new tuple are in place.

Putting these together, we define extensions of a collection of copy functions.

Definition 6.27 An *extension* $\overline{\rho}^e$ of $\overline{\rho}$ is a collection of copy functions $\rho^e_{(j,i)}$ such that $\overline{\rho}^e \neq \overline{\rho}$ and moreover, for all $i \in [1, p]$ and $j \in [1, q]$, $\rho^e_{(j,i)}$ is an extension of $\rho_{(j,i)}$. We denote the set of all extensions of $\overline{\rho}$ as $\text{Ext}(\overline{\rho})$.

For each $\overline{\rho}^e$ in $\text{Ext}(\overline{\rho})$, we define the *extension of* $\mathbf{S}$ *by* $\overline{\rho}^e$, denoted by $\mathbf{S}^e$, to be the specification consisting of: (1) the same source $D' = (I'_1, \ldots, I'_q)$ as in $\mathbf{S}$; (2) the same currency constraints as in $\mathbf{S}$, but in addition; (3) the copy functions $\overline{\rho}^e$; and (4) the other data source $D^e = (I_1^e, \ldots, I_p^e)$ extended by including imported values, where I_i^e is the union of all extensions of I_i, one for each $\rho^e_{(j,i)}$, for all $j \in [1, q]$. □

Currency preservation. We are now ready to define currency preservation. Consider a collection $\overline{\rho}$ of copy functions in a specification $\mathbf{S}$.

Definition 6.28 We say that $\overline{\rho}$ is *currency preserving* for a query Q w.r.t. specification $\mathbf{S}$ if (1) $\text{Mod}(\mathbf{S}) \neq \emptyset$, and moreover, (2) for all $\overline{\rho}^e \in \text{Ext}(\overline{\rho})$ such that $\text{Mod}(\mathbf{S}^e) \neq \emptyset$,

134 6. DATA CURRENCY

	FN	LN	address	salary	status
s'_1:	Mary	Dupont	6 Main St	60k	married
s'_2:	Mary	Dupont	6 Main St	80k	married
s'_3:	Mary	Smith	2 Small St	80k	divorced

Figure 6.2: A Manager relation I_{mgr}.

$$\bigcap_{D^c \in \mathsf{Mod}(\mathbf{S})} Q(\mathsf{LST}(D^c)) = \bigcap_{D^c_e \in \mathsf{Mod}(\mathbf{S}^e)} Q(\mathsf{LST}(D^c_e)). \qquad \square$$

Intuitively, $\overline{\rho}$ is currency preserving if (1) $\overline{\rho}$ is meaningful, i.e., $\mathsf{Mod}(\mathbf{S}) \neq \emptyset$, and (2) for each extension $\overline{\rho}^e$ of $\overline{\rho}$ that makes sense, the certain current answers to Q are not improved by $\overline{\rho}^e$, i.e., no matter what additional tuples are imported for those entities in D, the certain current answers to Q remain unchanged. In other words, $\overline{\rho}$ has already imported all current values needed for computing certain current answers to Q.

Example 6.29 As shown in Figure 6.2, the instance I_{mgr} of schema manager collects manager records. Consider a specification $\mathbf{S}_1$ consisting of the following: (a) the temporal instances I_{mgr} of Figure 6.2 and I_{emp} of Figure 6.1, in which partial currency orders are empty for all the attributes; and (b) the currency constraints φ_1–φ_3 given in Example 6.2, plus another currency constraint φ_5 given as follows:

$$\forall s, t : \mathsf{mgr}\,\big((s[\mathsf{EID}] = t[\mathsf{EID}] \wedge s[\mathsf{status}] = \text{``divorced''} \wedge t[\mathsf{status}] = \text{``married''}) \rightarrow t \prec_{\mathsf{LN}} s\big),$$

which states that if $s[\mathsf{status}]$ is divorced and if $t[\mathsf{status}]$ is married, then s is more current than t in LN; and (c) a copy function ρ with signature $\mathsf{employee}[\vec{A}] \Leftarrow \mathsf{manager}[\vec{A}]$, where $\vec{A}$ is (FN, LN, address, salary, status), such that $\rho(s_3) = s'_2$, i.e., s_3 in the relation I_{emp} is copied from s'_2 of the relation I_{mgr}. Obviously, $\mathbf{S}_1$ is consistent.

Recall query Q_2 from Example 6.1, which is to find Mary's current last name. For Q_2, ρ is not currency preserving. Indeed, there is an extension ρ_1 of ρ by copying s'_3 to I_{emp}. In all consistent completions of the extension I^e_{emp} of I_{emp} by ρ_1, the answer to Q_2 is Smith. However, the answer to Q_2 in all consistent completions of I_{emp} is Dupont (see Examples 6.1 and 6.9 for details). This tells us that we may be able to improve the answer to Q_2 by importing more current values from the I_{mgr} data source.

By contrast, ρ_1 is currency preserving for Q_2. Indeed, copying more tuples from I_{mgr} (i.e., tuple s'_1) to I_{emp} does not change the answer to Q_2 in I^e_{emp}. $\qquad \square$

6.5 DETERMINING CURRENCY PRESERVATION

There are several fundamental problems associated with currency preservation. We next present these problems and establish their combined complexity and data complexity. These problems are studied for various query languages $\mathcal{L}_Q$, when $\mathcal{L}_Q$ is CQ, UCQ, $\exists$FO$^+$, or FO.

Checking currency preservation. The first problem is to decide whether the given copy functions have imported all necessary current data for answering a query. It is referred to as the *currency preservation problem*, denoted by CPP($\mathcal{L}_Q$).

- INPUT: A query Q in $\mathcal{L}_Q$, and a consistent specification **S** of data currency with a collection $\overline{\rho}$ of copy functions.
- QUESTION: Is $\overline{\rho}$ currency preserving for Q?

This problem is nontrivial: its combined complexity is Π_3^p-hard when Q is in CQ, and is PSPACE-complete when Q is in FO. One might be tempted to think that fixing currency constraints would make our lives easier. In practice, currency constraints are often predefined and fixed, and only data, copy functions and query vary. Moreover, as shown in Theorem 6.10 for CPS, fixing currency constraints indeed helps there. However, it does not simplify the combined complexity analysis when it comes to CPP. Even when both query and currency constraints are fixed, the problem is Π_2^p-complete (i.e., data complexity).

Theorem 6.30 For CPP($\mathcal{L}_Q$), the combined complexity is:
1. Π_3^p-complete when $\mathcal{L}_Q$ is CQ, UCQ, or $\exists$FO$^+$;
2. PSPACE-complete when $\mathcal{L}_Q$ is FO; and
3. Its data complexity is Π_2^p-complete when $\mathcal{L}_Q \in \{$CQ,UCQ, $\exists$FO$^+$,FO$\}$.

The combined complexity bounds remain unchanged when currency constraints and copy functions are both fixed.

Crux. (1) *Lower bounds*. For the combined complexity, one can verify the following: (a) CPP(CQ) is Π_3^p-hard by reduction from the complement of the $\exists^*\forall^*\exists^*$3CNF problem, which is Σ_3^p-complete [Stockmeyer, 1976]; and (b) CPP(FO) is PSPACE-hard by reduction from the complement of the Q3SAT problem, which is also PSPACE-complete (cf. [Papadimitriou, 1994]). The reductions employ fixed currency constraints and fixed copy functions only.

For the data complexity, it can be verified that CPP($\mathcal{L}_Q$) is Π_2^p-hard when $\mathcal{L}_Q$ is CQ, by reduction from the $\forall^*\exists^*$3CNF problem [Stockmeyer, 1976].

(2) *Upper bounds*. We develop a decision algorithm for CPP that is in Π_3^p for $\exists$FO$^+$, in PSPACE for FO, and is in Π_2^p when queries and currency constraints are fixed. □

Extending copy functions. Consider a consistent specification **S** in which $\overline{\rho}$ is not currency preserving for a query Q. The next problem, referred to as the *existence problem* and denoted by ECP($\mathcal{L}_Q$), is to decide whether $\overline{\rho}$ in **S** can be made currency preserving for Q.

- INPUT: A query Q in $\mathcal{L}_Q$, and a consistent specification **S** with non-currency-preserving copy functions $\bar{\rho}$.
- QUESTION: Does there exist $\bar{\rho}^e$ in $\text{Ext}(\bar{\rho})$ that is currency preserving for Q?

The good news is that we can always extend $\bar{\rho}$ and make it currency preserving for Q. Hence the decision problem ECP is in $O(1)$ time, although it may take much longer time to explicitly construct a currency preserving extension of $\bar{\rho}$.

Proposition 6.31 $\text{ECP}(\mathcal{L}_Q)$ *is decidable in* $O(1)$ *time for both the combined complexity and data complexity, when* $\mathcal{L}_Q$ *is CQ, UCQ, $\exists$FO$^+$, or FO.*

Crux. Consider data sources $D = (I_1, \ldots, I_p)$ and $D' = (I'_1, \ldots, I'_q)$, with a collection $\bar{\rho}$ of copy functions $\rho_{(j,i)}$ that import tuples from I'_j to I_i, for $i \in [1, p]$ and $j \in [1, q]$. We say that an extension $\rho^e_{(j,i)}$ of $\rho_{(j,i)}$ is *maximum* if either (a) no more tuples from I'_j can be copied to I_i, or (b) adding any new tuple from I'_j to I_i makes the modification $\mathbf{S}^e$ of **S** inconsistent, i.e., $\text{Mod}(\mathbf{S}^e) = \emptyset$. In other words, there exists no extension $\rho'_{(j,i)}$ of $\rho^e_{(j,i)}$ such that $\rho'_{(j,i)} \neq \rho^e_{(j,i)}$ and it makes a consistent specification.

One can show the following. (1) For each $\rho_{(j,i)}$, we can find a maximum extension $\rho^e_{(j,i)}$ of $\rho_{(j,i)}$. (2) The extension $\bar{\rho}^e$ of $\bar{\rho}$ is currency preserving, where $\bar{\rho}^e$ is defined in terms of maximum extensions $\rho^e_{(j,i)}$ of $\rho_{(j,i)}$ for all $i \in [1, p]$ and all $j \in [1, q]$. □

Bounded extension. We also want to know whether it suffices to extend $\bar{\rho}$ by copying additional data of a bounded size, and make it currency preserving. This problem, referred to as the *bounded copying problem* and denoted by $\text{BCP}(\mathcal{L}_Q)$, is stated as follows.

- INPUT: **S**, $\bar{\rho}$ and Q as in ECP, and a positive number k.
- QUESTION: Does there exist $\bar{\rho}^e \in \text{Ext}(\bar{\rho})$ such that $\bar{\rho}^e$ is currency preserving for Q and moreover, $|\bar{\rho}^e| \leq k + |\bar{\rho}|$? Here $|\bar{\rho}|$ denotes the number of tuples copied by $\bar{\rho}$.

The analysis of BCP is far more intricate than ECP. Indeed, the result below tells us that even for CQ, BCP is Σ_4^p-hard, and fixing currency constraints and copy functions does not help. When both queries and currency constraints are fixed, BCP is Σ_3^p-complete.

Theorem 6.32 For $\text{BCP}(\mathcal{L}_Q)$, the combined complexity is
1. Σ_4^p-complete when $\mathcal{L}_Q$ is CQ, UCQ or $\exists$FO$^+$, and
2. PSPACE-complete when $\mathcal{L}_Q$ is FO.
3. Its data complexity is Σ_3^p-complete when $\mathcal{L}_Q \in \{\text{CQ, UCQ, }\exists\text{FO}^+\text{, FO}\}$.

The combined complexity bounds remain unchanged when both currency constraints and copy functions are fixed.

Crux. (1) *Lower bounds.* For the combined complexity, one can verify the following: (a) BCP(CQ) is Σ_4^p-hard by reduction from the $\exists^*\forall^*\exists^*\forall^*$3DNF problem, which is Σ_4^p-complete [Stockmeyer,

Table 6.3: Complexity of the problems for determining currency preservation

Complexity	CPP($\mathcal{L}_Q$)	ECP($\mathcal{L}_Q$)	BCP($\mathcal{L}_Q$)
Data	Π_2^p-complete	$O(1)$	Σ_3^p-complete
Combined ($\mathcal{L}_Q$)			
CQ, UCQ, ∃FO⁺	Π_3^p-complete	$O(1)$	Σ_4^p-complete
FO	PSPACE-complete	$O(1)$	PSPACE-complete
Special case	SP queries in the absence of currency constraints		
Combined & data	PTIME	$O(1)$	PTIME

1976]; and (b) BCP(FO) is PSPACE-hard even when k is *fixed*, by reduction from the complement of Q3SAT. In the reductions only fixed currency constraints and fixed copy functions are used.

For the data complexity, we show that BCP(CQ) is Σ_3^p-hard query Q and currency constraints are fixed, by reduction from the ∃*∀*∃*3CNF problem.

(2) *Upper bounds.* There exists a decision algorithm for BCP that is in Σ_4^p when $\mathcal{L}_Q$ is ∃FO⁺, in PSPACE when $\mathcal{L}_Q$ is FO, and is in Σ_3^p when queries and currency constraints are fixed. □

Special cases. Theorems 6.30 and 6.32 show that fixing currency constraints does not make our lives easier when it comes to CPP or BCP. However, when currency constraints are absent, these problems become tractable for SP queries. These are consistent with Theorem 6.14 for CCQA, which is also in PTIME for SP in the absence of currency constraints.

Theorem 6.33 When currency constraints are absent, for SP queries both the combined complexity and the data complexity are in PTIME for CPP and BCP (when the bound k on the size of additional data copied is fixed).

Crux. There exist a PTIME algorithm for CPP(SP), and a PTIME algorithm for BCP(SP), both in the absence of currency constraints. □

The main complexity results of this section are summarized in Table 6.3.

BIBLIOGRAPHIC NOTES

The model and results of this chapter are taken from [Fan et al., 2011c, 2012b].

There has been a host of work in the area of temporal databases on how to define current tuples by means of timestamps (see, e.g., [Chomicki and Toman, 2005; Snodgrass, 1999] for surveys). Indeed, temporal databases often support timestamps for valid time, transaction time, or both. These timestamps are automatically maintained when updates to the underlying database take place. Given timestamps, one then refers to "now" by means of current-time variables [Clifford et al., 1997; Dyreson et al., 2009]. Dynamic and temporal integrity constraints further allow us to restrict the set of legal database evolutions. In practice, however, one often finds that timestamps are unavailable or imprecise [Zhang et al., 2010]. Furthermore, when different data sources are considered, no uniform scheme of timestamps may be present. The currency model presented in this chapter does not assume the availability of timestamps, but yet can easily accommodate them when they are present. To allow even more flexibility, the model considers temporal information at the attribute level, and thus different values within the same tuple may have distinct currency. In contrast, temporal databases typically consider timestamps on entire tuples.

The study of data currency is also related to research on incomplete information when missing data concerns data currency (see [van der Meyden, 1998] for a survey), and to prior work on querying indefinite data [Koubarakis, 1994, 1997; van der Meyden, 1997]. For instance, van der Meyden [1997] studied the evaluation of CQ queries on data that are linearly ordered but when only a partial order is provided. Close to the currency model described in this chapter is the extension of conditional tables (see Chapter 5) to incorporate indefinite temporal information [Koubarakis, 1994]. In that setting, the complexity bounds for FO query evaluation were provided by Koubarakis [1997]. However, Koubarakis [1994, 1997] assumed explicit timestamps. In that line of work, certain or possible query answer semantics is assumed (see Bibliographic Notes of Chapter 5). The *current certain answer* semantics adopted in this Chapter explicitly distinguishes between stale and current tuples. As such, it may be more suitable for dealing with data currency.

The specification of currency constraints by means of denial constraints is motivated by prior work on consistent query answering [Bertossi, 2006, 2011; Chomicki, 2007] (see Bibliographic Notes of Chapter 2 for denial constraints). However, the use of denial constraints in the temporal setting has not yet received much attention. In particular, such constraints were not considered by the work on indefinite databases mentioned earlier. Moreover, denial constraints are not expressible in CQ, the setting adopted by van der Meyden [1997]. Although they might be encoded in the extended conditional tables of Koubarakis [1994, 1997], an exponential blowup is inevitable.

Finally, copy relationships between data sources have recently been studied by Berti-Equille et al. [2009] and Dong et al. [2010, 2009a]. In that line of work the focus has been on the automatic discovery of copying dependencies and functions. In this chapter, we assume that the copy functions are provided. Observe that currency information may assist in the discovery of "good" copy functions, and on the other hand, that discovered copy functions may enrich currency information. However, such interactions remain to be explored. Initial work linking data currency and data deduplication was reported by Li et al. [2012b].

CHAPTER 7

Interactions between Data Quality Issues

Previous research on data quality has typically focused on one of the five issues mentioned earlier: data consistency, data deduplication, data accuracy, information completeness, and data currency, treating them as independent topics. Nevertheless, to assess the quality of data we have to measure all five aspects. Therefore, a data quality management system should logically deal with each and every one of these issues. Furthermore, as we have seen in Section 1.2.6, these issues interact with each other. In light of this, a practical system should necessarily support a functionality to capitalize on the interactions. This calls for a uniform framework for modeling these issues, in which we can explore their interactions.

This chapter demonstrates how the interactions can help us improve data quality, by presenting case studies for data quality management in a rule-based framework. We begin with an approach for computing certain fixes that are guaranteed to be correct (Section 7.1), based on techniques for data deduplication and for improving data consistency. Certain fixes are important in monitoring critical data, among other things, and are interesting in their own right. We then present an approach for data cleaning by unifying data repairing and record matching (Section 7.2), which is more effective than repairing and matching taken as separate processes. As another case study, we introduce a model for conflict resolution based on both data currency and data consistency (Section 7.3). This is important in data integration, to resolve conflicts between values from different sources. Finally, we highlight open research issues in connection with data quality (Section 7.4).

We opt for breadth rather than depth in the presentation. We outline practical frameworks to handle the interactions and present fundamental problems associated with the interactions, but omit algorithms underlying the frameworks. We refer the interested reader to [Fan et al., 2010b, 2011e, 2012a,c] for details of these algorithms.

7.1 FINDING CERTAIN FIXES

We have seen heuristic methods for data repairing in Section 3.3. However, as will be seen in Section 7.1.1, these methods do not guarantee to find correct fixes; worse still, they may introduce new errors when trying to fix errors. While these heuristic methods can be used to repair, e.g., census data and statistical data, they may not work well when repairing *critical data* such as medical records, in which a minor error often has disastrous consequences.

140 7. INTERACTIONS BETWEEN DATA QUALITY ISSUES

	FN	LN	AC	phn	type	str	city	zip	item
t_1:	Bob	Brady	020	079172485	2	501 Elm St.	EDI	EH7 4AH	cd
t_2:	Robert	Brady	131	6884563	1	null	LDN	null	cd
t_3:	Robert	Brady	020	6884563	1	null	null	EH7 4AH	dvd
t_4:	Mary	Burn	029	9978543	1	null	CAD	null	book

(a) Example input tuples t_1, t_2, t_3 and t_4

	FN	LN	AC	Hphn	Mphn	str	city	zip	DoB
s_1:	Robert	Brady	131	6884563	079172485	51 Elm Row	EDI	EH7 4AH	11/11/55
s_2:	Mark	Smith	020	6884563	075568485	20 Baker St.	LDN	NW1 6XE	25/12/67

(b) Example master relation I_m

Figure 7.1: Example input tuples and master relation.

This highlights the quest for effective methods to find *certain fixes* that are guaranteed correct. In response to the need, we introduce a method to find certain fixes by using master data and a form of editing rules, based on a combination of techniques for correcting data inconsistencies and for matching records. We first present a model for certain fixes, in terms of editing rules (Section 7.1.2) and a notion of certain regions (Section 7.1.3). We then present a framework for finding certain fixes (Section 7.1.4). We also identify fundamental problems associated with certain fixes, and provide their complexity bounds (Section 7.1.5).

We investigate certain fixes in *data monitoring* [Chaudhuri et al., 2003; Sauter et al., 2007]: when a tuple t is created (either entered manually or generated by some process), it is to find errors in t and correct the errors. That is, we want to ensure that t is clean before it is used, to prevent errors introduced by adding t. As noted by Sauter et al. [2007], it is far less costly to correct t at the point of data entry than to repair it afterward.

7.1.1 CERTAIN FIXES: AN INTRODUCTION

As remarked earlier, data repairing methods are typically based on data dependencies, from traditional dependencies (e.g., functional and inclusion dependencies) to their extensions (e.g., conditional dependencies). These dependencies help us determine whether data are dirty or not, i.e., whether errors are present in the data. However, they fall short of telling us precisely which attributes in a tuple are erroneous and moreover, how to correct the errors. As a result, these methods do not guarantee that the fixes they generate are 100% correct. To illustrate this, let us consider a revision of the example we have seen in Chapter 1.

7.1. FINDING CERTAIN FIXES   141

Example 7.1 Consider an input tuple t_1 given in Figure 7.1(a). It specifies a supplier in the UK in terms of name (FN, LN), phone number (area code AC and phone phn) and type, address (street str, city, zip code) and items supplied. Here phn is either home phone or mobile phone, indicated by type (1 or 2, respectively). It is known that in the UK, if AC is 020, city should be London (LDN), and when AC is 131, city must be Edinburgh (EDI). Recall from Chapter 2 that these can be expressed as conditional functional dependencies (CFDs). Observe that tuple t_1 is *inconsistent*: t_1[AC] = 020 but t_1[city] = EDI.

The CFDs detect the inconsistency and tell us that either t_1[AC] or t_1[city] is incorrect, or both. However, they do not tell us which of the two attributes is wrong and to what value it should be changed. As a result, those repairing methods based on CFDs have to adopt a heuristic strategy to decide which value to modify.

In the presence of master data, we can do better. Indeed, suppose that tuple s_1 of Figure 7.1(b) indicates corrections to t_1, which tells us that t_1[AC] should be changed to 131. Nevertheless, the prior repairing methods may opt to change t_1[city] to LDN. This does not fix the erroneous t_1[AC] and worse still, messes up the correct attribute t_1[city]. That is, they *introduce new errors* when attempting to fix an existing error. □

To rectify the limitations of repairing methods, we introduce *editing rules* that tell us how to fix errors, i.e., which attributes are wrong and what values they should take. Editing rules extend conditional functional dependencies for data consistency (CFDs in Chapter 2) and matching dependencies for data deduplication (MDs in Chapter 4). They leverage master data and record matching techniques to identify the correct values when generating a fix. As remarked earlier, MDM is being developed by IBM, SAP, Microsoft, and Oracle. In particular, master data have been explored to provide *a data entry solution* in the Service Oriented Architecture (SOA) at IBM [Sauter et al., 2007], for data monitoring.

Example 7.2 A master relation I_m is shown in Figure 7.1(b). Each tuple in I_m specifies a person in the UK in terms of the name (FN, LN), home phone (Hphn), mobile phone (Mphn), address (str, city, zip) and date of birth (DoB). An example editing rule eR_1 is:

- for an input tuple t, if there exists a master tuple s in I_m such that s[zip] = t[zip], then t should be updated by t[AC, str, city] := s[AC, str, city], provided that t[zip] is *validated*, i.e., it is assured correct.

This rule makes *corrections* to attributes t[AC], t[str] and t[city], by taking corresponding values from master tuple s_1. Another editing rule eR_2 is:

- if t[type] = 2 (indicating mobile phone) and if there exists a master tuple s with s[Mphn] = t[phn], then t[FN, LN] := s[FN, LN], as long as t[phn, type] is validated.

This *standardizes* t_1[FN] by changing Bob to Robert.

As another example, consider input tuple t_2 given in Figure 7.1(a), in which attributes t_2[str, zip] are missing, and t_2[AC] and t_2[city] are inconsistent. Consider an editing rule eR_3:

- if $t[\text{type}] = 1$ (indicating home phone) and if there exists a master tuple $s \in I_m$ such that $s[\text{AC}, \text{phn}] = t[\text{AC}, \text{Hphn}]$, then $t[\text{str}, \text{city}, \text{zip}] := s[\text{str}, \text{city}, \text{zip}]$, provided that $t[\text{type}, \text{AC}, \text{phn}]$ is validated.

This helps us fix $t_2[\text{city}]$ and *enrich* $t_2[\text{str}, \text{zip}]$ by taking master data values from s_1. □

7.1.2 EDITING RULES

In the rest of this section we define editing rules and formalize what we mean by "validating" attributes. We first define editing rules for data monitoring. Given a master relation I_m and an input tuple t, we want to fix errors in t using editing rules and master data values in I_m. We specify input tuples t with a relation schema R. The master relation I_m is an instance of a relation schema R_m, often distinct from R. As remarked earlier, I_m can be assumed consistent and complete for core business entities.

Definition 7.3 An *editing rule* (eR) φ on (R, R_m) is a pair $((X, X_m) \to (B, B_m), t_p[X_p])$, where:

- X and X_m are two lists of distinct attributes in schemas R and R_m, respectively, with the same length, i.e., $|X| = |X_m|$;
- B is an attribute such that $B \in \text{attr}(R) \setminus X$, and B_m is an attribute in R_m; and
- t_p is a pattern tuple over a set of distinct attributes X_p in R such that for each $A \in X_p$, $t_p[A]$ is one of _, a or $\bar{a}$. Here a is a constant drawn from the domain of A, and _ is an unnamed variable (wildcard). □

Here, a and $\bar{a}$ indicate Boolean conditions $x = a$ and $x \neq a$ for a value x, respectively, while _ imposes no conditions. More specifically, we say that a tuple t of R *matches* pattern tuple t_p, denoted by $t[X_p] \simeq t_p[X_p]$, if for each attribute $A \in X_p$, (1) $t[A] = a$ if $t_p[A]$ is a, (2) $t[A] \neq a$ if $t_p[A]$ is $\bar{a}$, and (3) $t[A]$ is any value from the domain of A if $t_p[A]$ is _. Note that $\simeq$ extends the match operator $\asymp$ used for CFDs in Chapter 2.

Example 7.4 Consider the supplier schema R and master relation schema R_m shown in Figure 7.1. The rules eR_1, eR_2 and eR_3 described in Example 7.2 can be expressed as the following editing rules φ_1–φ_4 defined on (R, R_m):

φ_1: ((zip, zip) $\to$ (B_1, B_1), t_{p1} = ());
φ_2: ((phn, Mphn) $\to$ (B_2, B_2), t_{p2}[type] = (2));
φ_3: (([AC, phn], [AC, Hphn]) $\to$ (B_3, B_3), t_{p3}[type, AC] = (1, $\overline{0800}$));
φ_4: ((AC, AC) $\to$ (city, city), t_{p4}[AC] = ($\overline{0800}$)).

Here, eR_1 is expressed as three editing rules of the form φ_1, for B_1 ranging over {AC, str, city}. In φ_1, both X and X_m consist of zip, and B and B_m are B_1. Its pattern tuple t_{p1} poses no constraints.

7.1. FINDING CERTAIN FIXES 143

Similarly, eR$_2$ is written as two rules of the form φ_2, in which B_2 is either FN or LN. Pattern tuple t_{p2}[type] = (2) requires that phn is mobile phone. The rule eR$_3$ is written as φ_3 for B_3 ranging over {str, city, zip}, where t_{p3}[type, AC] requires that type = 1 (home phone) yet AC $\neq$ 0800 (toll free, non-geographic). Moreover, φ_4 says that for a tuple t, if t[AC] $\neq$ 0800 and t[AC] is correct, we can update t[city] using the master data. □

We next give the semantics of editing rules.

Definition 7.5 We say that an eR $\varphi = ((X, X_m) \rightarrow (B, B_m), t_p[X_p])$ and a master tuple $t_m \in I_m$ *apply* to an R tuple t, denoted by $t \rightarrow_{(\varphi, t_m)} t'$, if (1) $t[X_p] \asymp t_p[X_p]$, (2) $t[X] = t_m[X_m]$, and (3) $t'[B] = t_m[B_m]$ while t' and t agree on every other attribute; i.e., t' is obtained from t by the update $t[B] := t_m[B_m]$.

We write $t \nrightarrow_{(\varphi, t_m)} t$, i.e., t is unchanged by φ, if $t[X_p] \not\asymp t_p[X_p]$ or $t[X] \neq t_m[X_m]$. □

Intuitively, if $t[X, X_p]$ is assured correct (validated), we can safely *enrich* $t[B]$ with master data $t_m[B_m]$ as long as (1) $t[X] = t_m[X_m]$ and (2) $t[X_p]$ matches the pattern in φ. This yields a new tuple t' such that $t'[B] = t_m[B_m]$ and t'[attr(R) \ {B}] = t[attr(R) \ {B}].

Example 7.6 As shown in Example 7.2, we can correct tuple t_1 by applying eR φ_1 and master tuple s_1 to t_1. As a result, t_1[AC, str] is changed from (020, 501 Elm St.) to (131, 51 Elm Row). Furthermore, we can normalize t_1[FN] by applying φ_2 and s_1 to t_1, such that t_1[FN] is changed from Bob to Robert. Similarly, eR φ_3 and master tuple s_1 can be applied to input tuple t_2, to correct t_2[city] and enrich t_2[str, zip]. □

We now compare eRs with CFDs (Chapter 2) and MDs (Chapter 4). Note that neither CFDs nor MDs are expressible as eRs, and vice versa.

(1) Both eRs and CFDs are defined in terms of pattern tuples. In contrast to eRs, a CFD $\psi = (X \rightarrow Y, t_p)$ is defined on a single relation, where an eR is defined on an input tuple and a master relation. CFDs have a *static* semantics: two tuples t_1 and t_2 either satisfy or violate ψ, but they are not changed. In contrast, an eR φ specifies an action (update): applying φ and a master tuple t_m to t yields a tuple t' obtained by updating t.

(2) MDs also have a dynamic semantics. In their denotational semantics (Section 4.2), for an R_1 tuple t_1 and an R_2 tuple t_2, an MD $\phi = R_1[X_1] \approx R_2[X_2] \rightarrow R_1[Y_1] \rightleftharpoons R_2[Y_2]$ states that $t_1[Y_1]$ and $t_2[Y_2]$ should be identified, but it does not tell us what values $t_1[Y_1]$ and $t_2[Y_2]$ should take. In contrast, eRs explicitly specify what values should be taken: here t_2 must be a master tuple, and $t_1[Y_1]$ is changed to $t_2[Y_2]$. In the operational semantics of MDs (Section 4.5), the new values of $t_1[Y_1]$ and $t_2[Y_2]$ are computed by matching functions. Furthermore, MDs neither carry data patterns nor use master data; and hence, their analysis is far less challenging. Indeed, as shown in Theorem 4.13, the analysis of MDs is in PTIME. As will be seen in Section 7.1.5, however, the analyses are intractable for editing rules.

7.1.3 CERTAIN FIXES AND CERTAIN REGIONS

We next formalize the notion of certain fixes. Consider a master relation I_m of schema R_m, and a set Σ of editing rules defined on (R, R_m). Given a tuple t of R, we want to find a "certain fix" (repair) t' of t by using Σ and I_m. That is, (1) no matter how eRs of Σ and master tuples in I_m are applied, Σ and I_m yield a unique t' by updating t, and (2) all the attributes of t' are *validated*, i.e., ensured correct.

When applying an eR φ and a master tuple t_m to t, we update t with values in t_m. To ensure that the changes make sense, some attributes of t have to be validated. In addition, we are not able to update t if either it does not match the pattern tuple of φ or it cannot find a master tuple t_m in I_m that carries the information needed for correcting t.

Example 7.7 Consider the master relation I_m given in Figure 7.1(a) and the set Σ_0 consisting of $\varphi_1, \varphi_2, \varphi_3$ and φ_4 defined in Example 7.4. Given input tuple t_3 of Figure 7.1(a), both (φ_1, s_1) and (φ_3, s_2) apply to t_3. However, they suggest us to update $t_3[\text{city}]$ with distinct values EDI and LDN. The conflict arises because $t_3[\text{AC}]$ and $t_3[\text{zip}]$ are inconsistent. Hence, to fix t_3, we need to assure that one of $t_3[\text{AC}]$ and $t_3[\text{zip}]$ is correct.

Now consider input tuple t_4 of Figure 7.1(a). We find that no eRs in Σ_0 and master tuples in I_m can be applied to t_4, and hence, we cannot decide the correctness of t_4. This is because Σ_0 and D_m do not cover all the cases of input tuples. □

Regions. The example motivates us to introduce the following notion.

Definition 7.8 A *region* is a pair (Z, T_c), where Z is a list of distinct attributes in R, T_c is a *pattern tableau* consisting of a set of pattern tuples with attributes in Z, and each pattern tuple is defined as its counterparts in eRs. We say that a tuple t is *covered* by (Z, T_c) if there exists $t_c \in T_c$ such that $t[Z] \simeq t_c$. □

Regions will be used as follows. (1) When we fix errors in a tuple t by applying an eR φ, we require that $t[Z]$ is already validated, and that $t[Z]$ contains the antecedent attributes of φ. This assures that the consequence of the application of φ is also validated. As will be seen later, some attribute values of $t[Z]$ are initially required to be assured correct by the users, and based on these, the other attribute values of $t[Z]$ are validated by automated reasoning. (2) Moreover, we require that t is covered by (Z, T_c) such that there exists a master tuple in I_m that can be applied to t with φ. In other words, the tableau T_c specifies what master data are available in I_m to fix our tuples when $t[Z]$ is assured correct. Note that in contrast to T_c, the pattern tuples in eRs are independent of our master relation I_m. As will seen shortly, we will require (Z, T_c) to be "certain" such that it assures that no two eRs in Σ can be applied to t and lead to inconsistent updates. In other words, T_c imposes constraints to prevent the undesirable cases illustrated in Example 7.7.

7.1. FINDING CERTAIN FIXES   145

Taking regions into account, we now revise Definition 7.5.

Definition 7.9 Consider an eR $\varphi = ((X, X_m) \to (B, B_m), t_p[X_p])$, a master tuple t_m and a region (Z, T_c). We say that φ and t_m *apply* to a tuple t w.r.t. (Z, T_c), denoted by $t \to_{((Z,T_c),\varphi,t_m)} t'$, if:

(1) $t \to_{(\varphi,t_m)} t'$;

(2) $X \subseteq Z, X_p \subseteq Z, B \notin Z$; and moreover,

(3) there exists a pattern tuple $t_c \in T_c$ such that $t[Z] \simeq t_c$.

We define the *extended region* of (Z, T_c) by φ, denoted by $ext(Z, T_c, \varphi)$, to be $(Z \cup \{B\}, T'_c)$, where T'_c is obtained from T_c by expanding each $t_c \in T_c$ with $t_c[B] = \_$. □

That is, it is justified to apply φ and t_m to t for those t covered by (Z, T_c) as long as $t[Z]$ is validated. When $t[Z]$ is correct, we do not allow it to be changed by enforcing $B \notin Z$. Moreover, when $t[Z]$ is already validated, $t'[B]$ is also *validated* as a consequence of the application of φ and t_m. Hence B is included in Z, and $t'[B]$ is assured correct when editing rules are in turn applied to t' in the process for fixing t (see below).

Example 7.10 In the setting of Example 7.7, a region defined on R is $(Z_{AH}, T_{AH}) = ((AC, phn, type), \{(\overline{0800}, \_, 1)\})$. Tuple t_3 of Figure 7.1(a) is covered by this region. Hence, if $t_3[AC, phn, type]$ is validated, then (φ_3, s_2) can be applied to t_3, which yields $t_3 \to_{((Z_{AH}, T_{AH}), \varphi_3, s_2)} t'_3$, where $t'_3[str, city, zip] = s_2[str, city, zip]$, and t'_3 and t_3 agree on all the other attributes of R. Here $ext(Z_{AH}, T_{AH}, \varphi_3)$ is (Z', T'), where Z' consists of attributes AC, phn, type, str, city and zip, and T' has a single pattern tuple $t'_c = (\overline{0800}, \_, 1, \_, \_, \_)$. □

Certain fixes. One can draw the analogy of Definition 7.9 to Definition 4.20: both define the immediate result of applying a rule to a tuple. Along the same lines as Definition 4.21, we use a chase-like procedure to correct errors in a tuple t, and define (certain) fixes to t.

Definition 7.11 We say that a tuple t' is a *fix* of t by (Σ, I_m) w.r.t. (Z, T_c), denoted by $t \to^*_{((Z,T_c),\Sigma,I_m)} t'$, if there exists a finite chasing sequence $t_0 = t, t_1, \ldots, t_k = t'$ of tuples of R such that for each $i \in [1, k]$, there exist $\varphi_i \in \Sigma$ and $t_{m_i} \in I_m$ such that:

(1) $t_{i-1} \to_{((Z_{i-1}, T_{i-1}), \varphi_i, t_{m_i})} t_i$; and

(2) for all $\varphi \in \Sigma$ and $t_m \in I_m$, $t' \to_{((Z_k, T_k), \varphi, t_m)} t'$.

where $(Z_0, T_0) = (Z, T_c)$ and $(Z_i, T_i) = ext(Z_{i-1}, T_{i-1}, \varphi_i)$. We refer to Z_k as the set of attributes of t *covered by* (Z, T_c, Σ, I_m). □

That is, (1) each step of the process is justified and (2) t' is a fixpoint and cannot be further updated, i.e., it is "stable" (recall the notion of stable instances from Definition 4.9). Note that

146 7. INTERACTIONS BETWEEN DATA QUALITY ISSUES

$t_{i-1} \to_{((Z_{i-1}, T_{i-1}), \varphi_i, t_{m_i})} t_i$ assures that $t_i[Z] = t_0[Z] = t[Z]$, i.e., $t[Z]$ is assumed correct and hence, remains unchanged in the process.

We are interested in those fixes that are certain, when different chasing sequences lead to the same unique fixes, no matter what eRs and master tuples are used and in what orders they are applied. Certain fixes raise no inconsistencies when fixing an input tuple.

Definition 7.12 We say that an R tuple t has a *unique fix* by (Σ, I_m) w.r.t. (Z, T_c) if there exists a unique t' such that $t \to^*_{((Z, T_c), \Sigma, I_m)} t'$ for *all* finite chasing sequences.

We say that an R tuple t has a *certain fix* by (Σ, I_m) w.r.t. (Z, T_c) if:

(1) t has a unique fix; and

(2) the set of attributes covered by (Z, T_c, Σ, I_m) includes *all* the attributes in R. □

Intuitively, a unique fix t' becomes a certain fix when the set of attributes covered by (Z, T_c, Σ, I_m) includes *all* the attributes in R. We can find a certain fix (repair) for a tuple t of R covered by a region (Z, T_c) if (a) $t[Z]$ is assured correct, (b) there is a unique fix t', and (c) all the remaining values of $t'[\text{attr}(R) \setminus Z]$ are correctly fixed.

Example 7.13 Given the set Σ_0 of eRs of Example 7.7 and the master data I_m of Figure 7.1(b), tuple t_3 of Figure 7.1(a) has a unique fix *w.r.t.* $(Z_{\text{AH}}, T_{\text{AH}})$, which is tuple t'_3 given in Example 7.10. On the other hand, as observed in Example 7.7, if we extend the region by adding zip, denoted by $(Z_{\text{AHZ}}, T_{\text{AHZ}})$, then t_3 no longer has a unique fix by (Σ_0, I_m) *w.r.t.* $(Z_{\text{AHZ}}, T_{\text{AHZ}})$.

As another example, consider a region $(Z_{\text{ZM}}, T_{\text{ZM}})$, where Z_{ZM} = (zip, phn, type), and T_{ZM} has a single tuple (_, _, 2). As shown in Example 7.6, tuple t_1 of Figure 7.1(a) has a unique fix by Σ_0 and I_m *w.r.t.* $(Z_{\text{ZM}}, T_{\text{ZM}})$, by applying (φ_1, s_1) and (φ_2, s_2). It is *not* a certain fix, since the set of attributes covered by $(Z_{\text{ZM}}, T_{\text{ZM}}, \Sigma_0, I_m)$ does not include item. Indeed, the master data I_m of Figure 7.1(b) has no information about item, and hence, does not help here. To find a certain fix, one has to extend Z_{ZM} by adding item. □

Finally, we introduce a notion of certain regions (Z, T_c) such that for any input R tuple t covered by (Z, T_c), as long as $t[Z]$ is validated, then absolute corrections are warranted for those attributes of t in $\text{attr}(R) \setminus Z$. As will be seen shortly, we use certain regions to guide the users to find certain fixes for their input tuples.

Definition 7.14 A region (Z, T_c) is called a *certain region* for (Σ, I_m) if for all tuples t of R that are covered by (Z, T_c), t has a certain fix by (Σ, I_m) w.r.t. (Z, T_c). □

Example 7.15 As shown in Example 7.13, $(Z_{\text{ZM}}, T_{\text{ZM}})$ is not a certain region. One can verify that a certain region for (Σ_0, I_m) is $(Z_{\text{ZMI}}, T_{\text{ZMI}})$, where Z_{ZMI} extends Z_{ZM} by including item, and T_{ZMI}

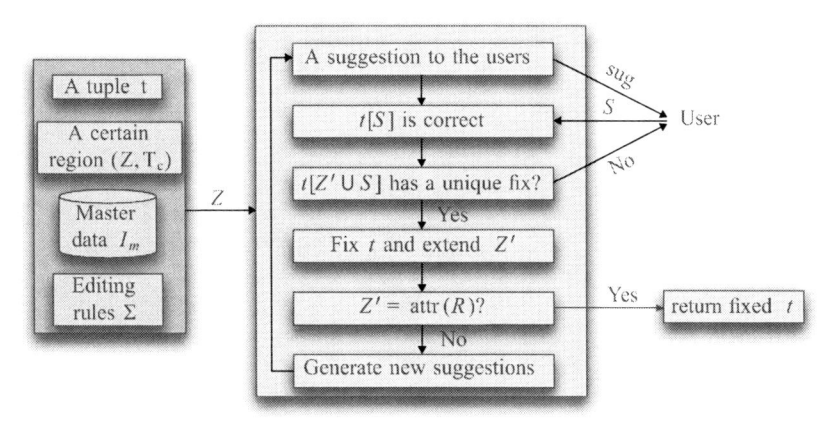

[Figure 7.2: A framework for finding certain fixes.]

consists of patterns of the form $(z, p, 2, \_)$ for (z, p) ranging over $s[\text{zip}, \text{Mphn}]$ for all master tuples s in I_m. For tuples covered by this region, certain fixes are warranted.

There are possibly multiple certain regions. For example, another certain region for (Σ_0, I_m) is (Z_L, T_L), where $Z_L = (\text{FN}, \text{LN}, \text{AC}, \text{phn}, \text{type}, \text{item})$, T_L consists of pattern tuples of the form $(f, l, a, h, 1, \_)$, and (f, l, a, h) is $s[\text{FN}, \text{LN}, \text{AC}, \text{Hphn}]$ for all $s \in I_m$. □

7.1.4 A FRAMEWORK FOR FINDING CERTAIN FIXES

We next outline a framework to find certain fixes for tuples at the point of data entry, based on editing rules and master data, and by interacting with users. As depicted in Figure 7.2, the framework is provided with a master relation I_m of schema R_m and a set Σ of eRs defined on (R, R_m). It takes a tuple t of schema R as input, and finds a certain fix for t.

Given a tuple t, the framework generates and provides the users with suggestions. A *suggestion* is a minimum set Z of attributes such that if $t[Z]$ is validated by the users, a certain fix can be found for t. Here, Z is taken from a certain region (Z, T_c). More specifically, the framework interacts with the users and generates suggestions as follows.

(1) Initialization. Upon receiving t, it first picks a precomputed certain region (Z, T_c), and recommends Z as the first suggestion to the users. If $t[Z]$ is assured correct and if $t[Z]$ matches a pattern tuple in T_c, then a certain fix can be found for t. It also uses a set Z' to keep track of the attributes of t that are already validated, which is initially empty.

(2) Generating correct fixes. In each round of interaction with users, a set sug of attributes is recommended to the users as a suggestion, initially Z. The users get back with a set S of attributes that are asserted correct, where S may *not* necessarily be the same as sug. The framework validates $t[S]$ by checking whether $t[Z' \cup S]$ leads to a unique fix, i.e., whether $t[S]$ can be validated. If $t[S]$ is

invalid, the users are requested to revise the set S of attributes assured correct. If $t[Z' \cup S]$ yields a unique fix, procedure TransFix is invoked to find the fix, which extends Z' by including the newly corrected attributes.

(3) Generating new suggestions. If at this point, the set Z' covers all the attributes of R, then the entire tuple t is validated and the corrected t is returned. Otherwise, it computes a new suggestion from Σ and I_m by invoking a procedure referred to as Suggest. The new suggestion is then recommended to the users in the next round of interaction (step (2)).

This process proceeds until a certain fix is found for t. All the attributes of t are corrected or validated, by using the users' input, the eRs and the master data.

The framework aims to guarantee the following. (a) *The correctness*. Each correcting step is justified by using the eRs and the master data. (b) *Minimizing user efforts*. It requires the users to validate a minimum number of attributes, while automatically deducing other attributes that are entailed correct. (c) *Minimal delays*. It improves the response time by reducing the latency for generating new suggestions at each interactive step.

Note that the users should not necessarily be domain experts, as long as they can assure the correctness of certain attributes of input tuples that are required to match eRs and master tuples. To assure the accuracy in practice, this typically requires different people responsible for data entering to inspect and validate the attributes in the monitoring process.

We now briefly describe the procedures underlying the framework. We refer the interested reader to [Fan et al., 2010b, 2012c] for detailed algorithms.

(1) Finding certain regions. Given a tuple t, we want to find a certain region (Z, T_c) with a minimum set Z of attributes such that t is covered by T_c. The set Z of attributes is recommended to the users as the initial suggestion (step (1)). As will be seen in Section 7.1.5, the problem for finding certain regions is intractable and approximation-hard. Nonetheless, an efficient heuristic algorithm has been provided by Fan et al. [2010b], which is able to derive a set of certain regions from Σ and I_m based on a quality metric. We can thus pick a precomputed region (Z, T_c) with the highest quality. Note that the regions are computed once and are repeatedly used as long as Σ and I_m are unchanged.

(2) Deriving validated attributes. Procedure TransFix takes as input a tuple t, a master relation I_m, a set Σ of eRs, and a set Z' of attributes such that $t[Z']$ has been validated. It finds a unique fix for t, if it exists, by deriving validated attributes from Σ and Z', and extends Z' by including those newly validated attributes (step (2)). While not all of the attributes of t may be validated, the procedure ensures that the attributes updated are correct. A quadratic-time algorithm for TransFix can be found in [Fan et al., 2012c].

(3) Generating suggestions. Given t, I_m, Σ and Z' as for TransFix, procedure Suggest is to find a minimum set S' of attributes such that there exists a certain region $(Z' \cup S', \{t_c\})$, where t_c is a pattern and $t[Z'] \simeq t_c[Z']$. The set S' is recommended to the users as a new suggestion (step (3)).

The problem for finding such a minimum S' is also intractable. Nevertheless, there exists an efficient heuristic algorithm for Suggest (see [Fan et al., 2012c]).

7.1.5 FUNDAMENTAL PROBLEMS FOR CERTAIN FIXES

To give a complete picture of certain fixes, we identify three fundamental problems associated with certain fixes and certain regions, and establish their complexity. Given a set Σ of eRs and a master relation I_m, we want to make sure that they can *correctly* fix *all* errors in those input tuples marked by a region (Z, T_c). For the results below, we give proof sketches but refer the reader to [Fan et al., 2012c] for detailed proofs.

The consistency problem. We say that (Σ, I_m) is *consistent relative to* (Z, T_c) if for each input tuple t of R marked by (Z, T_c), t has a unique fix by (Σ, I_m) w.r.t. (Z, T_c). Intuitively, this says that Σ and I_m do not have conflicts w.r.t. (Z, T_c), as illustrated below.

Example 7.16 There exist (Σ, I_m) and (Z, T_c) that are inconsistent. Indeed, (Σ_0, I_m) described in Example 7.7 is not consistent relative to the region $(Z_{\text{AHZ}}, T_{\text{AHZ}})$ given in Example 7.13, since the eRs in Σ_0 suggest distinct values to update $t_3[\text{city}]$ for the tuple t_3 of Figure 7.1(a), i.e., conflicts arise, as shown in Example 7.7. That is, tuple t_3 does not have a unique fix by (Σ_0, I_m) w.r.t. $(Z_{\text{AHZ}}, T_{\text{AHZ}})$. □

The *consistency problem* for editing rules is stated as follows.

- INPUT: A region (Z, T_c), a set Σ of eRs and a master relation I_m.
- QUESTION: Is (Σ, I_m) consistent relative to (Z, T_c)?

This problem is obviously important, but is nontrivial. We have seen that for dependencies defined with pattern tuples, the presence of attributes with a finite domain makes their static analysis hard. For instance, when it comes to the satisfiability problem for CFDs, the problem is NP-complete if attributes in the CFDs may have a finite domain, but it becomes tractable when all the attributes in the CFDs have an infinite domain (see Theorem 2.14 and Proposition 2.17). In contrast, the consistency problem for editing rules is intractable even when all the attributes involved have an infinite domain. That is, this problem is more intricate than the satisfiability problem for CFDs.

Theorem 7.17 The consistency problem for editing rules is coNP-complete, even when data and master relations have infinite-domain attributes only, and when master data are fixed.

Crux. The upper bound can be verified by providing an NP algorithm to decide whether (Σ, I_m) is *not* consistent relative to (Z, T_c). The lower bound is proved by reduction from 3SAT to its complement. Recall that 3SAT is NP-complete (cf. [Papadimitriou, 1994]). The reduction make use of schemas

7. INTERACTIONS BETWEEN DATA QUALITY ISSUES

with infinite-domain attributes only, when the master data are predefined and fixed (see [Fan et al., 2012c]). □

The certain region problem. Another important problem in connection with certain fixes, referred to as the *certain region problem*, is stated as follows.

- INPUT: (Z, T_c), Σ and I_m as in the consistency problem.
- QUESTION: Is (Z, T_c) a certain region for (Σ, I_m)?

That is, we want to decide whether (Σ, I_m) is able to fix errors in all the attributes of input tuples that are covered by (Z, T_c). This problem is, however, also intractable. The result below can be verified along the same lines as Theorem 7.17.

Theorem 7.18 The certain region problem is coNP-complete, even for input tuples and master relations that have infinite-domain attributes only, and when master data are fixed.

Minimum certain regions. One would naturally want a certain region (Z, T_c) with Z consisting of as few attributes as possible, such that the users only need to assure the correctness of a small number of attributes in input tuples. This suggests us to study the *minimum certain region problem*, stated as follows.

- INPUT: A set Σ of eRs, a master relation I_m, and a positive integer k.
- QUESTION: Does there exist a list Z of attributes such that (a) $|Z| \leq k$ and (b) there is a *non-empty* pattern tableau T_c such that (Z, T_c) is a certain region for (Σ, I_m)?

This problem is also intractable. In addition, it is approximation hard. The result below tells us that unless P = NP, there exists no PTIME algorithm that given Σ and I_m, guarantees to find a certain region (Z, T_c) such that $|Z| \leq c \log n |Z_{\min}|$, where $(Z_{\min}, T_c)$ is a certain region with minimum number of attributes, and n is the input size. This is why we use a heuristic algorithm in step (1) of the framework given in Section 7.1.4.

Theorem 7.19 The minimum certain region problem

1. is NP-complete, and
2. cannot be approximated within $c \log n$ in PTIME for a constant c unless P = NP,

even for input tuples and master relations that have infinite-domain attributes only, and when master data are fixed. Here, n is the size of input eRs Σ and master data I_m.

For approximation we study the optimization version of the minimum certain region problem, which is the minimization problem to compute a certain region (Z, T_c) with a minimum number of attributes in Z. To illustrate the approximation bound, we adopt the notion of L-reductions (see, e.g., [Papadimitriou, 1994]). Let Π_1 and Π_2 be two minimization problems. A L-reduction from Π_1 to Π_2 is a quadruple (f, g, α, β), where f and g are two PTIME computable functions, and α and β are two constants, such that:

- for any instance I_1 of Π_1, $I_2 = f(I_1)$ is an instance of Π_2 such that $\mathsf{OPT}_2(I_2) \leq \alpha \cdot \mathsf{OPT}_1(I_1)$, where OPT_1 (resp. OPT_2) is the objective of an optimal solution to I_1 (resp. I_2); and

- for any solution s_2 to I_2, $s_1 = g(s_2)$ is a solution to I_1 such that $\mathrm{obj}_1(s_1) \leq \beta \cdot \mathrm{obj}_2(s_2)$, where $\mathrm{obj}_1()$ (resp. $\mathrm{obj}_2()$) is a function measuring the objective of a solution to I_1 (resp. I_2).

We say that an algorithm $\mathcal{A}$ for a minimization problem has performance guarantee ϵ ($\epsilon \geq 1$) if for any instance I, $\mathrm{obj}(\mathcal{A}(I)) \leq \epsilon \cdot \mathsf{OPT}(I)$, where ϵ is a constant.

Crux. (1) The lower bound is verified by reduction from the set covering problem, which is known to be NP-complete (cf. [Papadimitriou, 1994]). For the upper bound, an NP decision algorithm can be readily developed to determine minimum certain regions.

(2) The approximation hardness is verified by L-reduction from the set covering problem. It has been shown that the set covering problem cannot be approximated within a factor of $c \log n$ in PTIME for any constant c unless NP = P [Raz and Safra, 1997]. Furthermore, it is known that if (f, g, α, β) is an L-reduction from problems Π_1 to Π_2, and if there is a PTIME algorithm for Π_2 with performance guarantee ϵ, then there exists a PTIME algorithm for Π_1 with performance guarantee $\alpha\beta\epsilon$ (cf. [Papadimitriou, 1994]). □

7.2 UNIFYING DATA REPAIRING AND RECORD MATCHING

Certain fixes aim to clean individual input tuples in data monitoring. A natural question is whether the same framework can be used to clean a database. The answer is, unfortunately, negative: a real-life database I is typically large, and it would be prohibitively expensive if one had to interact with the users when cleaning each individual tuple in I. Furthermore, as we have seen in Chapter 3, we have to process tuples in an equivalence class together when cleaning I, instead of treating them as independent tuples as in data monitoring.

Nevertheless, we can still leverage the interaction between data consistency and deduplication when we clean a relation. Indeed, we can clean the data by integrating data repairing and record matching processes, and by making use of master data. As experimentally verified by Fan et al. [2011e], this method allows us to achieve an accuracy much higher than those approaches that take data repairing and record matching as separate processes.

We outline the data cleaning method in this section. We first illustrate how to clean data based on both CFDs and MDs, using an example (Section 7.2.1). We then give a formal statement of the data cleaning problem and define data cleaning rules deduced from CFDs and MDs (Section 7.2.2). Based on the cleaning rules, we present a rule-based framework for data cleaning (Section 7.2.3). Finally, we identify central problems for data cleaning and establish their complexity, as foundations for further studying data cleaning (Section 7.2.4).

152 7. INTERACTIONS BETWEEN DATA QUALITY ISSUES

	FN	LN	street	city	AC	zip	tel	DoB	gd
s_1:	Mark	Smith	10 Oak St	EDI	131	EH8 9LE	3256778	10/10/1987	M
s_2:	Robert	Brady	5 Wren St	LDN	020	WC1H 9SE	3887644	12/08/1975	M

(a) Master data I_m: An instance of schema **card**

	FN	LN	street	city	AC	post	phn	gd	when	where
t_1:	M.	Smith	10 Oak St	LDN	131	EH8 9LE	9999999	M	9am 28/03	UK
cf	(0.9)	(1.0)	(0.9)	(0.5)	(0.9)	(0.9)	(0.0)	(0.8)	(1.0)	(1.0)
t_2:	Max	Smith	Po Box 25	EDI	131	EH8 9AB	3256778	M	8pm 28/04	India
cf	(0.7)	(1.0)	(0.5)	(0.9)	(0.7)	(0.6)	(0.8)	(0.8)	(1.0)	(1.0)
t_3:	Bob	Brady	5 Wren St	EDI	020	W1H 9SE	3887834	M	6pm 06/06	UK
cf	(0.6)	(1.0)	(0.9)	(0.2)	(0.9)	(0.8)	(0.9)	(0.8)	(1.0)	(1.0)
t_4:	Robert	Brady	null	LDN	020	W1E 7HX	3887644	M	1pm 06/06	US
cf	(0.7)	(1.0)	(0.0)	(0.5)	(0.7)	(0.3)	(0.7)	(0.8)	(1.0)	(1.0)

(b) Database I: An instance of schema **tran**

Figure 7.3: Example master data and database.

7.2.1 INTERACTION OF CFDS AND MDS: AN INTRODUCTION

Most data cleaning systems in the market support record matching, and some systems also provide the functionality of data repairing. These systems treat matching and repairing as separate and independent processes. However, the two processes typically interact with each other: repairing helps us identify matches and matching helps us fix inconsistencies. To illustrate this, let us consider a revision of the example we have seen in Chapter 4.

Example 7.20 Consider two databases, I_m and I, from a UK bank: I_m maintains customer information collected when credit cards are issued, and is treated as *clean master data*; and I consists of transaction records of credit cards in 2012, which may be dirty. The databases I_m and I are specified by the following schemas, respectively:

card(FN, LN, street, city, AC, zip, tel, DoB, gd),
tran(FN, LN, street, city, AC, post, phn, gd, when, where).

A card tuple specifies a UK credit card holder identified by her name (FN, LN), address (street, city, zip code), area code (AC), phone (tel), date of birth (DoB), and gender (gd). A tran tuple is a transaction record of a credit card used at place where and at time when in 2012, by a UK customer who is identified by his name (FN, LN), address (street, city, post code), phone (AC, phn), and gender (gd). Example instances of card and tran relations are shown in Figures 7.3(a) and 7.3(b), which are fractions of master data I_m and transaction relations I, respectively (the cf rows in Figure 7.3(b) will be discussed later).

7.2. UNIFYING DATA REPAIRING AND RECORD MATCHING

We use CFDs φ_1–φ_4 to specify the consistency of the tran data in I, and we employ an MD ψ as a rule for matching tuples across I and master card data I_m:

φ_1: tran([AC] $\rightarrow$ [city], t_{p_1} = (131 $\parallel$ EDI)),
φ_1: tran([AC] $\rightarrow$ [city], t_{p_1} = (020 $\parallel$ LDN)),
φ_3: tran([city, phn] $\rightarrow$ [street, AC, post], t_{p_3} = (_, _ $\parallel$ _, _, _))
φ_4: tran([FN] $\rightarrow$ [FN], t_{p_4} = (Bob $\parallel$ Robert))

ψ: tran[LN, city, street, post] = card[LN, city, street, zip] $\wedge$ tran[FN] $\approx$ card[FN]
$\rightarrow$ tran[FN, phn] $\rightleftharpoons$ card[FN, tel],

where (1) the CFD φ_1 (resp. φ_2) asserts that, for any tran tuple, if its area code is 131 (resp. 020), the city must be EDI (resp. LDN); (2) the CFD φ_3 is a traditional functional dependency (FD), asserting that city and phone number uniquely determine street, area code and postal code; (3) the CFD φ_4 is a data standardization rule: if the first name is Bob, then it should be "normalized" to be Robert; and (4) the MD ψ assures that for any tuple in I and any tuple in I_m, if they have the same last name and address, and moreover, if their first names are *similar*, then their phone and FN attributes can be identified.

Consider tuples t_3 and t_4 in I. The bank suspects that these two tuples refer to the same person. If so, then these transaction records show that the same person made purchases in the UK and in the U.S. at about the same time (counting the 5-h time difference between the two countries). This indicates that a fraud has likely been committed.

Observe that t_3 and t_4 are quite different in their FN, city, street, post and phn attributes. No rule allows us to identify the two tuples directly. Nonetheless, they can indeed be matched by a sequence of *interleaved* match and repair operations as follows:

(a) get a repair t'_3 of t_3 such that t'_3[city] = LDN via CFD φ_2, and t'_3[FN] = Robert by normalization with φ_4;
(b) match t'_3 with master tuple s_2 of I_m, to which ψ can be applied;
(c) as a result of the match operation, get a repair t''_3 of t_3 by correcting t'_3[phn] with the master data s_2[tel];
(d) find a repair t'_4 of t_4 via the FD φ_3: since t''_3 and t_4 agree on their city and phn attributes, φ_3 can be applied. Thus we can enrich t_4[street] and fix t_4[post] by taking corresponding values from t''_3, which have been validated in step (c).

At this point, t''_3 and t'_4 agree on every attribute in connection with personal information. It is now evident that they indeed refer to the same person; hence a fraud.

Observe that the interaction between repairing and matching helps us clean the data: not only repairing helps matching (e.g., from step (a) to (b)), but matching also helps us repair the data (e.g., step (d) is doable only after the match operation in step (b)). □

This example tells us the following. (1) When taken together, record matching and data repairing perform much better than being treated as separate processes. (2) To make practical use

7.2.2 THE DATA CLEANING PROBLEM AND CLEANING RULES

We next formalize the notion of data cleaning by integrating data repairing and record matching. Extending the notion of data repairs we have seen in Section 3.3, data cleaning is defined in terms of both CFDs studied in Chapter 2 and MDs given in Chapter 4. Below we first revise the notion of repairs and state the data cleaning problem. We then define data cleaning rules based on CFDs and MDs by providing an operational semantics.

Repairs revised. Consider a (possibly dirty) relation I of schema R, a master relation I_m of schema R_m, and a set $\Theta = \Sigma \cup \Gamma$, where Σ is a set of CFDs defined on R, and Γ is a set of MDs defined on (R, R_m). Recall the notion of repairs and the quality metric cost() introduced in Section 3.3.1. Now we want to find a "repair" I_r of I such that I_r "satisfies" both the CFDs in Σ and the MDs in Γ (with I_m), and moreover, I_r minimally differs from I in terms of cost(). That is, we further require repairs to satisfy the MDs in Γ. To this end we adopt the same metric cost(), and revise the notion of $(I_r, I_m) \models \Gamma$ as follows.

Recall from Definition 4.5 that MDs have a dynamic semantics: they tell us what data values ought to be updated and made equal when they are enforced. As indicated by Definition 4.21, we update the data by enforcing the MDs of Γ until we reach a fixpoint I_r on which no more MDs can be further applied and incur changes. That is, I_r is a *stable instance* for Γ (recall stable instances from Definition 4.9). In light of this, we define $(I_r, I_m) \models \Gamma$ by focusing on stable instances I_r as follows. It should be remarked that this notion is consistent with Definition 4.5 when only stable instances are considered.

Definition 7.21 A stable instance (I, I_m) of schemas (R, R_m) *satisfies* an MD $\psi = R[X_1] \approx R_m[X_2] \to R[Y_1] \rightleftharpoons R_m[Y_2]$, denoted by $(I, I_m) \models \psi$, if for *all* tuples t in I and *all* tuples s in I_m, if $t[X_1] \approx s[X_2]$, then $t[Y_1] = s[Y_2]$. We say that (I, I_m) *satisfies* a set Γ of MDs, denoted by $(I, I_m) \models \Gamma$, if $(I, I_m) \models \psi$ for all $\psi \in \Gamma$. □

Using this notion, we are now ready to revise repairs as follows.

Definition 7.22 For a relation I of schema R, a master relation I_m of schema R_m, a set Σ of CFDs defined on R, and a set Γ of MDs defined on (R, R_m), a *repair* I_r of I is another instance of R such that (a) $I_r \models \Sigma$, (b) $(I_r, I_m) \models \Gamma$, and (c) cost($I_r, I$) is minimum. □

Intuitively, (a) a repair I_r should be *consistent*, i.e., it satisfies the set Σ of CFDs, (b) no more changes can be made to I_r by enforcing the MDs of Γ, i.e., all possible *matches* have already been found; and (c) I_r is as accurate and close to the original data I as possible. In contrast to the notion of repairs given Section 3.3.1, I_r is required to satisfy the MDs Γ.

7.2. UNIFYING DATA REPAIRING AND RECORD MATCHING

The data cleaning problem. In terms of this notion of repairs, the *data cleaning problem* is stated as follows. Given I, I_m, and $\Theta = \Sigma \cup \Gamma$, it is to find a *repair* I_r of I.

Data cleaning rules. As remarked earlier, dependencies studied so far for data repairing are good at determining whether our data are dirty or not, i.e., whether errors are present in our data, but they do not tell us how to correct the errors.

To make effective use of dependencies in data cleaning, we define *cleaning rules*, to tell us what attributes should be updated and to what value they should be changed. More specifically, for each MD in Γ and each CFD in Σ, we derive a cleaning rule, by giving an operational semantics for the dependencies. As will be seen in Section 7.2.3, we use these rules to find repairs. These rules also update the *confidence* in the accuracy of attributes, initially placed by the user (see the cf rows in Figure 7.3(b)). We use t^I and $t^{I'}$ to denote the tuple t in instances I and I', respectively, carrying the same tuple id. For each tuple $t^I \in I$ and each attribute A of t^I, we use $t^I[A].\text{cf}$ to denote the confidence in $t^I[A]$ in instance I.

We say that an instance I' of R is a *result of enforcing a rule* $\varphi \in \Theta$ on I w.r.t. master data I_m, denoted by $I \rightarrow_{(\varphi, I_m)} I'$, if one of the following conditions holds.

(1) MDs. If φ is an MD $R[X_1] \approx R_m[X_2] \rightarrow R[Y_1] \rightleftharpoons R_m[Y_2]$, then there exist a master tuple $s \in I_m$ and a tuple $t^I \in I$ such that (a) in I, $t^I[X_1] \approx s[X_2]$ but $t^I[Y_1] \neq s[Y_2]$, (b) in I', $t^{I'}[Y_1] = s[Y_2]$, and for all $C \in Y_1$, $t^{I'}[C].\text{cf}$ is the minimum $t^I[A].\text{cf}$ for all $A \in X_1$, and (c) I' and I agree on every other tuple and attribute value, carrying the same confidence.

That is, φ is enforced on (t^I, s) as a cleaning rule by letting $t^{I'}[Y_1] := s[Y_2]$ to correct $t^I[Y_1]$ with the master data $s[Y_2]$, and by inferring the new confidence $t^{I'}[Y_2].\text{cf}$. Intuitively, the confidence of an attribute value is about how certain a variable is correct (i.e., in the concept of fuzzy set membership), instead of how probable one thinks that a variable is correct (i.e., in the concept of subjective probability). Hence, following fuzzy logic [Klir and Folger, 1988], we define $t^{I'}[Y_2].\text{cf}$ by taking the minimum confidence of attributes in $t^I[X_1]$, rather than the product of the confidences of all the attributes in $t^I[X_1]$.

(2) Constant CFDs. If φ is a CFD $R(X \rightarrow A, t_{p_1})$, where $t_{p_1}[A]$ is a *constant*, then there exists a tuple $t^I \in I$ such that (a) $t^I[X] \asymp t_{p_1}[X]$ but $t^I[A] \neq t_{p_1}[A]$, (b) $t^{I'}[A] = t_{p_1}[A]$ and $t^{I'}[A].\text{cf} = d$, where d is the minimum $t^I[A'].\text{cf}$ for all $A' \in X$, and (c) I' and I agree on every other tuple and attribute value, carrying the same confidence.

As a cleaning rule, φ updates t^I by letting (a) $t^{I'}[A] := t_{p_1}[A]$, to correct $t^I[A]$ with the constant $t_{p_1}[A]$, and (b) $t^{I'}[A].\text{cf}$ be the minimum confidence in the attributes of $t^I[X]$.

(3) Variable CFDs. If φ is a CFD $R(Y \rightarrow B, t_{p_1})$, where $t_{p_2}[B]$ is a wildcard "_", then there exist tuples $t_1^I, t_2^I \in I$ such that (a) $t_1^I[Y] = t_2^I[Y] \asymp t_{p_2}[Y]$ but $t_1^I[B] \neq t_2^I[B]$, (b) $t_1^{I'}[B] = t_2^I[B]$, and $t_1^{I'}[B].\text{cf}$ is the minimum of $t_1^I[B'].\text{cf}$ and $t_2^I[B'].\text{cf}$ for all $B' \in Y$, and (c) I' and I agree on every other tuple and attribute value, sharing the same confidence.

That is, the rule derived from φ is used to *apply* a tuple $t_2^I \in I$ to another tuple $t_1^I \in I$, by letting $t_1^{I'}[B] := t_2^I[B]$ to update $t_1^I[B]$ with the value $t_2^I[B]$, and by letting $t_1^{I'}[B].\text{cf}$ take the minimum confidence in all attributes of $t_1^I[Y]$ and $t_2^I[Y]$.

Example 7.23 Example 7.20 demonstrates how the MD ψ and the CFDs φ_2, φ_3 and φ_4 are enforced as cleaning rules, to repair the transaction data given in Figure 7.3(b). □

As shown by Example 7.20, by treating CFDs and MDs as cleaning rules, we can integrate data repairing and record matching in a uniform process. More specifically, we can use a chase-like procedure to clean data, along the same lines as the one given in Definition 4.21. It differs from the chase procedure given there in that it fixes errors by interleaving repair (enforcing CFDs) and match (enforcing MDs) operations.

Definition 7.24 Given an instance I_0, master data I_m, and a set $\Theta = \Sigma \cup \Gamma$, where Σ is a set of CFDs and Γ is a set of MDs, a *chasing sequence* of I_0 by Θ w.r.t. I_m is a sequence of instances $I_1, \ldots, I_\ell, \ldots$, such that for each $i \geq 1$, $I_{i-1} \rightarrow_{(\varphi_i, I_m)} I_i$ for some $\varphi_i \in \Theta$.

We say that a chasing sequence $I_1, \ldots, I_k$ is *terminal* if it is finite and moreover, $I_k \models \Sigma$ and $(I_k, I_m) \models \Gamma$. We refer to such an I_k as a *stable* instance. □

The procedure starts with I_0, and repeatedly enforces CFDs in Σ and MDs in Γ until it reaches a "clean instance" to which no more cleaning rule can be applied. This instance is *stable* since it cannot be further changed by enforcing CFDs and MDs in Θ. We will study the termination and Church-Rosser property of this chase-procedure in Section 7.2.4.

Remarks. Compared to the editing rules of Section 7.1.2 for fixing a *single* tuple via matching with master data, here we target repairing a *database* via *both* matching (MDs) and repairing (CFDs); in particular, we enforce CFDs as cleaning rules to repair a tuple in a relation with either the constants in a CFD, or (more accurate) values of the corresponding attributes from another tuple in the same relation, without referencing master data.

The rule derived from MDs have an operational semantics similar to the one given in Definition 4.20. Nevertheless, the cleaning rules use master data when updating tuples, instead of invoking matching functions. Moreover, we use cleaning rules derived from CFDs.

7.2.3 A FRAMEWORK FOR DATA CLEANING

Based on cleaning rules, we outline a data cleaning system, referred to as UniClean. It takes as input a dirty relation I, a master relation I_m, a set Σ of CFDs and a set Γ of MDs. It generates a repair I_r of I with a small cost(I_r, I), such that $I_r \models \Sigma$ and $(I_r, I_m) \models \Gamma$.

As opposed to the repairing methods described in Section 3.3, UniClean generates fixes by unifying matching and repairing processes. Furthermore, it stresses the accuracy by distinguishing these fixes with three levels of accuracy. Various fixes are found by executing three algorithms consecutively, as shown in Figure 7.4 and illustrated below.

7.2. UNIFYING DATA REPAIRING AND RECORD MATCHING

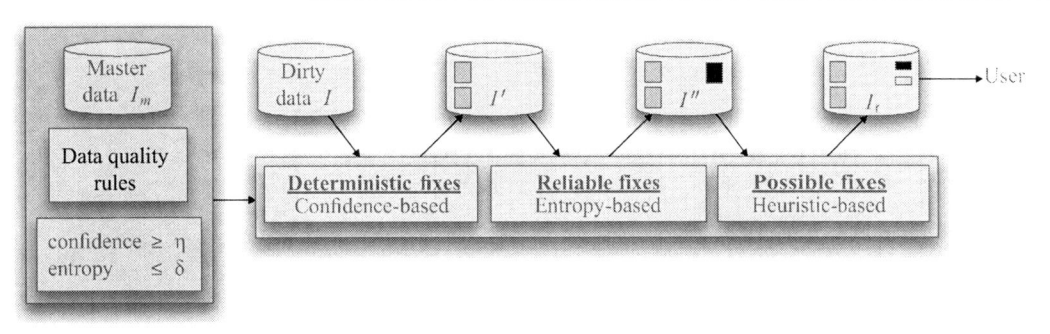

Figure 7.4: Overview of UniClean.

(1) Deterministic fixes based on confidences. We define deterministic fixes *w.r.t.* a *confidence threshold* η set by domain experts. When η is sufficiently high, e.g., if it is close to 1, an attribute $t[A]$ is considered correct if $t[A].\text{cf} \geq \eta$. We refer to such attributes as *asserted* attributes. In the first phase of UniClean, we enforce a cleaning rule $\varphi \in \Theta = \Sigma \cup \Gamma$ on tuples in I only when their attributes in LHS(φ) are all asserted (see below). Hence, the fixes generated are accurate up to η, and are marked as *deterministic fixes*.

(2) Reliable fixes based on entropy. Deterministic fixes may not exist for those attributes with *low or unavailable confidence*. In the second phase of UniClean, we correct such attributes based on the relative certainty of the data, measured by entropy, which has proved effective in data transmission [Hamming, 1950] and compression [Ziv and Lempel, 1978], among other things. We apply a cleaning rule φ to update an erroneous attribute $t[A]$ only if the entropy of φ for certain attributes of t is below a given threshold δ (see below). Fixes generated via entropy are accurate to a certain degree, and are marked as *reliable fixes*.

(3) Possible fixes. Not all errors can be fixed in the first two phases. For the remaining errors, we use heuristic methods to generate fixes, referred to as *possible fixes*. To this end, we extend the methods given in Section 3.3 by supporting both CFDs and MDs. It can be verified that the heuristic method always finds a repair I_r of I such that $I_r \models \Sigma, (I_r, I_m) \models \Gamma$, while keeping all the deterministic fixes produced earlier *unchanged*.

At the end of the process, fixes are marked with three distinct signs, indicating *deterministic*, *reliable* and *possible*, respectively. Below we present the methods underlying each phase of UniClean, and refer the reader to [Fan et al., 2011e] for detailed algorithms.

Deterministic fixes. We say that a fix is *deterministic* by a rule $\varphi \in \Theta$ *w.r.t.* a given threshold η if it is generated as follows, based on what φ is.

(1) When φ is an MD $R[X_1] \approx R_m[X_2] \rightarrow R[Y_1] \rightleftharpoons R_m[Y_2]$. By enforcing φ on a tuple $t \in I$ and a master tuple $s \in I_m$, it generates a fix $t[Y_1] := s[Y_2]$ (see Section 7.2.2 for cleaning rules). Then the fix is *deterministic* if $t[A].\text{cf} \geq \eta$ for all $A \in X_1$ and if $t[B].\text{cf} \leq \eta$ for all $B \in Y_1$. That is, $t[Y_1]$

is changed to the master value $s[Y_2]$ only if (a) all the premise attributes $t[A]$'s are asserted, and (b) none of the attributes in $t[Y_1]$ is yet asserted.

(2) When φ is a constant CFD $R(X \rightarrow A, t_{p_1})$. By enforcing φ on a tuple $t \in I$, it generates a fix $t[A] := t_{p_1}[A]$. Then the fix is *deterministic* if $t[B].\text{cf} \geq \eta$ for all $B \in X$ and if $t[A].\text{cf} \leq \eta$. That is, all the attributes in $t[X]$ are asserted, but $t[A]$ is not.

(3) When φ is a variable CFD $R(Y \rightarrow B, t_p)$. For each $\bar{y}$ in $\pi_Y(\rho_{Y \asymp t_p[Y]} I)$, let $\Delta(\bar{y})$ denote the set $\{t \mid t \in I, t[Y] = \bar{y}\}$, where π and ρ are the projection and selection operators, respectively. That is, for all t_1, t_2 in $\Delta(\bar{y}), t_1[Y] = t_2[Y] = \bar{y} \asymp t_p[Y]$. Suppose that φ is enforced on tuples $t_1, t_2 \in I$, and it generates a fix $t_1[B] := t_2[B]$. Then the fix is *deterministic* if (a) for all $A \in Y$, $t_1[A].\text{cf} \geq \eta$ and $t_2[A].\text{cf} \geq \eta$, (b) $t_2[B].\text{cf} \geq \eta$, and moreover, (c) t_2 is the only tuple in $\Delta(\bar{y})$ with $t_2[B].\text{cf} \geq \eta$ (hence, $t_1[B].\text{cf} \leq \eta$). That is, for all the attributes A in LHS(φ), $t_1[A]$ and $t_2[A]$ are asserted, and moreover, $t_2[B]$ is *the only B-attribute value* in $\Delta(\bar{y})$ that is asserted, while $t_1[B]$ is suspected erroneous.

By the definition of cleaning rules (Section 7.2.2), when attribute $t[A]$ is updated by a deterministic fix, its confidence $t[A].\text{cf}$ is upgraded to be the minimum of the confidences of the premise attributes of the rule used. As a result, $t[A]$ is also asserted, since all premise attributes have confidence values above η. In turn $t[A]$ can be used to generate deterministic fixes for other attributes in the *recursive* cleaning process.

Example 7.25 Consider the master relation I_m and relation I of Figure 7.3 with the confidence rows. Let Θ be the set consisting of the CFDs φ_1, φ_3 and the MD ψ given in Example 7.20. Consider a threshold $\eta = 0.8$. Using Θ and I_m, one can find deterministic fixes for t_1 and t_2 in I w.r.t. η by letting $t_1[\text{city}] := \text{EDI}, t_1[\text{city}].\text{cf} := 0.9, t_1[\text{FN}] := s_1[\text{FN}], t_1[\text{FN}].\text{cf}:=0.9, t_1[\text{phn}] := s_1[\text{tel}], t_1[\text{phn}].\text{cf} := 0.9, t_2[\text{street}] = t_1[\text{street}] := 10 \text{ Oak St}, t_2[\text{street}].\text{cf} := 0.8$, and $t_2[\text{post}] := t_1[\text{post}], t_2[\text{post}].\text{cf} := 0.8$. Similarly, for tuples $t_3, t_4 \in I$, we can find a deterministic fix by letting $t_3[\text{city}] := \text{LDN}$ and $t_3[\text{city}].\text{cf} := 0.8$. □

An algorithm for finding deterministic fixes can be found in [Fan et al., 2011e], which is in $O(|D||D_m|\text{size}(\Theta))$ time, where size(Θ) is the length of Θ.

Reliable fixes. For the attributes with *low or unavailable confidence*, UniClean looks for evidence from the data itself *instead of confidence*, using entropy to measure the degree of certainty. The entropy of a discrete random variable $\mathcal{X}$ with possible values $\{x_1, \ldots, x_n\}$ is defined as follows [Cover and Thomas, 1991; Srivastava and Venkatasubramanian, 2010]:

$$\mathcal{H}(\mathcal{X}) = \Sigma_{i=1}^{n}(p_i \cdot \log 1/p_i),$$

where p_i is the probability of x_i for $i \in [1, n]$. It measures the degree of the certainty of the value of $\mathcal{X}$: when $\mathcal{H}(\mathcal{X})$ is sufficiently small, it is highly accurate that the value of $\mathcal{X}$ is the x_j with the largest probability p_j. The less $\mathcal{H}(\mathcal{X})$ is, the more accurate the prediction is.

We use entropy to resolve data conflicts. Consider a variable CFD $\varphi = R(Y \rightarrow B, t_p)$ defined on a relation I. For $\bar{y}$ in $\pi_Y(\rho_{Y \asymp t_p[Y]} I)$, a deterministic fix may not exist when, e.g., there are

7.2. UNIFYING DATA REPAIRING AND RECORD MATCHING

	A	B	C	D	E	F
t_1:	a_1	b_1	c_1	d_1	e_1	f_1
t_2:	a_1	b_1	c_1	d_1	e_2	f_2
t_3:	a_1	b_1	c_1	d_1	e_3	f_3
t_4:	a_1	b_1	c_1	d_2	e_1	f_3
t_5:	a_2	b_2	c_2	d_1	e_2	f_4
t_6:	a_2	b_2	c_2	d_2	e_1	f_4
t_7:	a_2	b_2	c_3	d_3	e_3	f_5
t_8:	a_2	b_2	c_4	d_3	e_3	f_6

Figure 7.5: Example relation of schema R.

$t_1, t_2 \in \Delta(\bar{y})$ such that $t_1[B] \neq t_2[B]$ but both have high confidence. Indeed, using the cleaning rule derived from φ, one may either let $t_1[B] := t_2[B]$ or let $t_2[B] := t_1[B]$.

To find accurate fixes, we define the entropy of φ for $Y = \bar{y}$, denoted by $\mathcal{H}(\varphi|Y = \bar{y})$:

$$\mathcal{H}(\varphi|Y = \bar{y}) = \Sigma_{i=1}^{k} \left(\frac{\mathcal{C}_{YB}(\bar{y}, b_i)}{|\Delta(\bar{y})|} \cdot \log_k \frac{|\Delta(\bar{y})|}{\mathcal{C}_{YB}(\bar{y}, b_i)} \right),$$

where (a) $k = |\pi_B(\Delta(\bar{y}))|$, the number of distinct B values in $\Delta(\bar{y})$, (b) for each $i \in [1, k]$, $b_i \in \pi_B(\Delta(\bar{y}))$, (c) $\mathcal{C}_{YB}(\bar{y}, b_i)$ denotes the number of tuples $t \in \Delta(\bar{y})$ with $t[B] = b_i$, and (d) $|\Delta(\bar{y})|$ is the number of tuples in $\Delta(\bar{y})$.

Intuitively, we treat $\mathcal{X}(\varphi|Y = \bar{y})$ as a random variable for the value of the B attribute in $\Delta(\bar{y})$, with a set $\pi_B(\Delta(\bar{y}))$ of possible values. The probability for b_i to be the value is $p_i = \frac{\mathcal{C}_{YB}(\bar{y}, b_i)}{|\Delta(\bar{y})|}$. When $\mathcal{H}(\varphi|Y = \bar{y})$ is sufficiently small, it is highly accurate to resolve the conflict by letting $t[B] := b_j$ for all $t \in \Delta(\bar{y})$, where b_j is the one with the highest probability, i.e., $\mathcal{C}_{YB}(\bar{y}, b_j)$ is the maximum among all $b_i \in \pi_B(\Delta(\bar{y}))$. Hence given an entropy threshold δ, we generate a fix by letting $t[B] := b_j$ only if $\mathcal{H}(\varphi|Y = \bar{y}) \leq \delta$, and refer to such fixes as *reliable fixes*. In particular, $\mathcal{H}(\varphi|Y = \bar{y}) = 1$ when $\mathcal{C}_{YB}(\bar{y}, b_i) = \mathcal{C}_{BA}(\bar{y}, b_j)$ for all distinct $b_i, b_j \in \pi_B(\Delta(\bar{y}))$. Note that if $\mathcal{H}(\varphi|Y = \bar{y}) = 0$ for all $\bar{y} \in \pi_Y(\rho_{Y \bowtie t_p[Y]}I)$, then $I \models \varphi$.

Example 7.26 Consider an instance of schema $R(A, B, C, D, E, F)$ shown in Figure 7.5, and a CFD $\phi = R([A,B,C] \to [D], t_{p_1})$, where t_{p_1} consists of wildcards only, i.e., ϕ is an FD. Observe that (a) $\mathcal{H}(\phi|ABC = (a_1, b_1, c_1)) \approx 0.8$, (b) $\mathcal{H}(\phi|ABC = (a_2, b_2, c_2))$ is 1, and (c) $\mathcal{H}(\phi|ABC = (a_2, b_2, c_3))$ and $\mathcal{H}(\phi|ABC = (a_2, b_2, c_4))$ are both 0.

From these we can see the following. (1) For $\Delta(ABC = (a_2, b_2, c_3))$ and $\Delta(ABC = (a_2, b_2, c_4))$, the entropy is 0; hence these sets of tuples do not violate ϕ, i.e., there is no need to fix these tuples. (2) The fix based on $\mathcal{H}(\phi|ABC = (a_1, b_1, c_1))$ is relatively accurate, but not those based on $\mathcal{H}(\phi|ABC = (a_2, b_2, c_2))$. In light of these, UniClean will only changes $t_4[D]$ to d_1, and marks it as a reliable fix. □

An algorithm is given in [Fan et al., 2011e] for finding reliable fixes in $O(|D|^2 \text{size}(\Theta))$ time, which keeps the deterministic fixes found earlier by UniClean unchanged in the process.

Possible fixes. The outcome of the first two phases of UniClean is a "partial repair" I' of I, which may still contain errors that are not corrected by deterministic fixes or reliable fixes. In light of these, we need to fix the remaining errors in I' and produce a repair I_r of I such that $I_r \models \Sigma$, $(I_r, I_m) \models \Gamma$, and moreover, I_r preserves the deterministic fixes generated earlier, i.e., such fixes remain unchanged since they are assured to be correct. In contrast, reliable fixes may not be 100% correct and hence, we allow them to be changed.

To produce I_r, we extend the repairing method described in Section 3.3 by (a) supporting matching with master data I_m and MDs, (b) preserving the deterministic fixes generated earlier, and (c) keeping reliable fixes generated as many as possible. Such an algorithm has been developed by Fan et al. [2011e], which guarantees to find a repair I_r of I such that $I_r \models \Sigma$, $(I_r, I_m) \models \Gamma$, and I_r preserves all the deterministic fixes in I'.

Example 7.27 Recall the relation I, CFDs φ_1–φ_4 and the MD ψ from Example 7.20. As shown in Example 7.25, the first two phases of UniClean identify several fixes for I. However, the data still have errors, e.g., tuple t_3 in I does not satisfy the CFD φ_4 even after t_3[city] is fixed. To this end we find possible fixes: (a) t_3[FN] := Robert by enforcing CFD φ_4, (b) t_3[phn] := 3887644 by matching s_2 with the MD ψ, and (c) t_4[street, post] := t_3[street, post] by enforcing φ_3 with t_3. After these steps we get a repair of I that satisfies both the CFDs and MDs, and moreover, retains the deterministic fixes generated earlier. □

7.2.4 STATIC ANALYSES OF DATA CLEANING WITH CFDS AND MDS

To reveal insights into the interaction between data repairing and record matching, we next identify fundamental problems associated with data cleaning in this setting. We provide the complexity of these problems, and refer to [Fan et al., 2011e] for their proofs. We show that these problems are intractable and hence, the algorithms underlying UniClean are heuristic.

Satisfiability and implication. As remarked earlier, there are two central problems associated with dependencies, namely, the satisfiability problem and the implication problem. We have studied these problems for CFDs in Chapter 2. We now revisit these problems for CFDs and MDs taken together. The satisfiability problem for CFDs and MDs is as follows.

- INPUT: A master relation I_m of schema R_m, a set Σ of CFDs defined on relations of schema R, and a set Γ of MDs defined on instances of (R, R_m).
- QUESTION: Does there exist a nonempty instance I of R such that $I \models \Sigma$ and $(I, I_m) \models \Gamma$?

Intuitively, this is to determine whether the cleaning rules in $\Theta = \Sigma \cup \Gamma$ are consistent with each other. The practical need for the consistency analysis is evident.

We say that Θ *implies* another CFD (resp. MD) ξ, denoted by $\Theta \models \xi$, if for any instance I of R, whenever $I \models \Sigma$ and $(I, I_m) \models \Gamma$, then $I \models \xi$ (resp. $(I, I_m) \models \xi$). For MDs, we use the notion of

7.2. UNIFYING DATA REPAIRING AND RECORD MATCHING

$(I, I_m) \models \Gamma$ given in Definition 7.21, focusing on stable instances. For stable instances, the notions of deduction (Definition 4.11) and implication coincide.

The *implication problem* for CFDs and MDs is stated as follows.
- INPUT: I_m, Σ and Γ as in the satisfiability problem, and another CFD or MD ξ.
- QUESTION: Does $\Theta \models \xi$?

As mentioned earlier, we want to use the implication analysis to remove redundant rules from Θ, i.e., those that are a logical consequence of other rules in Θ. For CFDs and MDs, the implication problem has two settings: when ξ is a CFD and when ξ is an MD.

Theorems 2.14 and 2.22 tell us that for CFDs alone, the satisfiability problem is NP-complete and the implication problem is coNP-complete. The result below shows that these problems for CFDs and MDs put together have the same complexity as their counterparts for CFDs. That is, adding MDs does not make our lives harder.

Theorem 7.28 For CFDs and MDs put together
1. the satisfiability problem is NP-complete, and
2. the implication problem is coNP complete, when ξ is either a CFD or an MD for deciding $\Theta \models \xi$.

The lower bounds remain unchanged when master data are fixed.

Crux. (1) Lower bounds. The lower bound for the satisfiability problem immediately follows from Theorem 2.14, since the satisfiability problem for CFDs is a special case of the satisfiability analysis of CFDs and MDs taken together. Similarly, when ξ is a CFD, the lower bound of the implication problem follows from Theorem 2.22. When ξ is an MD, one can verify that the complement of the implication problem is NP-hard by reduction from 3SAT. The proofs use a fixed master relation, which is independent of input 3SAT instances.

(2) Upper bounds. There exists an NP (resp. coNP) algorithm for deciding the satisfiability (resp. implication) of CFDs and MDs taken together. The algorithms are also based on the small model properties of these problems, which are verified along the same lines as the small model properties of their counterparts for CFDs given in Theorems 2.14 and 2.22. □

Data cleaning. Recall the data cleaning problem stated in Section 7.2.2. One wants to know how costly it is to compute a repair I_r. Below we show that its decision problem is NP-complete: it is intractable to decide whether there exists a repair I_r with cost(I_r, I) below a predefine bound. Worse still, it is infeasible in practice to find a PTIME approximation algorithm with performance guarantee. Indeed, the problem is not in APX, the class of problems that allow PTIME approximation algorithms with approximation ratio bounded by a constant. In the sequel we consider only satisfiable collections Θ of CFDs and MDs.

Theorem 7.29 (1) The data cleaning problem is NP-complete. (2) Unless P = NP, for any constant ϵ, there exists no PTIME ϵ-approximation algorithm for DCP.

Crux. (1) The NP lower bound follows immediately from Theorem 3.11, which shows that the repairing problem for a fixed set of FDs is already NP-complete, which is a special case of the cleaning problem. The upper bound is verified by providing an NP decision algorithm.

(2) The approximation hardness is verified by reduction from 3SAT, using gap techniques (see, e.g., [Wegener and Pruim, 2005]). We show that given any constant $\epsilon \geq 1$, there exists an algorithm that finds a repair I_r of an input relation I such that $\text{cost}(I_r, I) \leq \epsilon \cdot \text{cost}(I_o, I)$, where I_o is a repair of I with optimal cost, if and only if there exists a PTIME algorithm to decide whether 3SAT instances are satisfiable. From these it follows that unless P = NP, for any constant ϵ, there exists no PTIME ϵ-approximation algorithm for the cleaning problem. Here $\epsilon \geq 1$ since the cleaning problem is a minimization problem. □

Termination and the Church-Rosser property. There are two questions about the chase-like procedure given in Definition 7.24. One is the *termination problem*.

- INPUT: I_m and $\Theta = \Sigma \cup \Gamma$ as in the satisfiability problem, and a relation I.
- QUESTION: Does there exist a terminal chasing sequence of I by Θ w.r.t. I_m?

It is to determine whether the chase process stops, i.e., it reaches a fixpoint such that no more cleaning rules in Θ can be further enforced.

The other one is the *determinism problem* about the Church-Rosser property of the chase procedure (see Section 4.5), which asks whether all terminal chasing sequences end up with the same fixpoint no matter in what order the rules in Θ are enforced.

- INPUT: I_m, Θ and I as in the termination problem.
- QUESTION: Do all terminal chasing sequences of I by Θ w.r.t. I_m lead to the same *unique* fixpoint?

The need for studying these problems is evident. A rule-based process is typically *non-deterministic*: multiple rules can be applied at the same time, and the output of the process may be dependent on the order of the rules enforced. Worse still, even for data repairing, Example 3.12 tells us that a rule-based method may lead to an *infinite* process.

No matter how important, these problems are rather challenging.

Theorem 7.30 *The termination and determinism problems are both PSPACE-complete for CFDs and MDs taken together, and remain PSPACE-hard even in the absence of MDs.*

Crux. The lower bounds of both problems are verified by reduction from the halting problem for linear bounded automata, which is PSPACE-complete [Aiken et al., 1993]. A linear bounded automaton is a 6-tuple $\langle Q, \Upsilon, \Lambda, q_0, F, \delta \rangle$, where (a) Q is a finite set of states, (b) Υ is a finite tape alphabet, (c) blank $\in \Upsilon$ is the blank symbol, (d) $\Lambda \subseteq \Upsilon \setminus \{\text{blank}\}$ is a finite input alphabet, (e) $q_0 \in Q$ is the start state, (f) $F \subseteq Q$ is the set of halting states, and (g) $\delta : Q \times \Upsilon \to Q \times \Lambda \times \{\text{Left, Right}\}$ is the next move function. Given such an automaton M and a string $x \in \Lambda^*$, the halting problem asks whether M halts on input x.

The upper bounds are proved by providing non-deterministic polynomial-space decision algorithms to check whether there exists a terminal chasing sequence of a given relation, and whether all terminal chasing sequences for an input relation lead to the same repair. Since PSPACE = NPSPACE, the problems are in PSPACE. □

7.3 RESOLVING CONFLICTS

We have seen how we can benefit from integrating data repairing and record matching for data monitoring and cleaning. As another case study, we next show how we can capitalize on the interaction between data consistency and data currency, for conflict resolution.

Conflict resolution is also known as data fusion. Given tuples that pertain to the same real-world entity and are possibly from different sources, it aims to combine these tuples into a single tuple and resolve conflicts. The need for studying this problem is evident in data integration and exchange, among other things. Moreover, as remarked in Chapter 6, we often find multiple values of the same entity residing in a database. While these values were *once* the true values of the entity, some of them may have become *stale* and *inconsistent*. These also highlight the need for conflict resolution, to improve the quality of our data and to answer queries using the true values of the entity. Conflict resolution has been a longstanding issue. Traditional methods typically resolve conflicts by taking, e.g., the max, min, avg, any of attribute values (see [Bleiholder and Naumann, 2008] for a survey).

We can do better by taking data consistency and data currency together. We first give an overview of the approach (Section 7.3.1). We then introduce a model for conflict resolution (Section 7.3.2), based on techniques we have seen for improving data consistency (Chapter 2) and data currency (Chapter 6). Finally, we present a framework for conflict resolution (Section 7.3.3) and study its associated fundamental problems (Section 7.3.4).

7.3.1 CONFLICT RESOLUTION: AN OVERVIEW

We study the following *conflict resolution problem*. Given a set I_e of tuples pertaining to the same entity, it is to identify the *true values* of the entity *relative to the set*, i.e., a single tuple in which each attribute has consistent and the most current value taken from I_e.

This problem is rather challenging. Indeed, Chapter 3 tells us that it is already highly nontrivial to find consistent values for an entity. Moreover, Chapter 6 shows that it is hard to identify the most current entity values since in the real world, reliable timestamps are often absent [Zhang et al., 2010]. Add to this the complication that when resolving conflicts, one has to find the entity values that are *both* consistent *and* most current.

Example 7.31 Consider the photo "V-J Day in Times Square" that portrays an American sailor kissing a nurse in Times Square, New York City, on August 14, 1945. The nurse and sailor in the photo are identified as Edith Shain and George Mendonça, respectively, and their information is collected in sets E_1 and E_2 of tuples, respectively, shown in Figure 7.6.

164   7. INTERACTIONS BETWEEN DATA QUALITY ISSUES

		name	status	job	kids	city	AC	zip	county
E_1	r_1:	Edith Shain	working	nurse	0	NY	212	10036	Manhattan
	r_2:	Edith Shain	retired	n/a	3	SFC	415	94924	Dogtown
	r_3:	Edith Shain	deceased	n/a	null	LA	213	90058	Vermont
E_2	r_4:	George Mendonça	working	sailor	0	Newport	401	02840	Rhode Island
	r_5:	George Mendonça	retired	veteran	2	NY	212	12404	Accord
	r_6:	George Mendonça	unemployed	n/a	2	Chicago	312	60653	Bronzeville

Figure 7.6: Instances E_1 for entity Edith and E_2 for George.

Currency constraints:	$\varphi_1 : \forall t_1, t_2 \ (t_1[\text{status}] = \text{"working"} \wedge t_2[\text{status}] = \text{"retired"} \rightarrow t_1 \prec_{\text{status}} t_2)$ $\varphi_2 : \forall t_1, t_2 \ (t_1[\text{status}] = \text{"retired"} \wedge t_2[\text{status}] = \text{"deceased"} \rightarrow t_1 \prec_{\text{status}} t_2)$ $\varphi_3 : \forall t_1, t_2 \ (t_1[\text{job}] = \text{"sailor"} \wedge t_2[\text{job}] = \text{"veteran"} \rightarrow t_1 \prec_{\text{job}} t_2)$ $\varphi_4 : \forall t_1, t_2 \ (t_1[\text{kids}] < t_2[\text{kids}] \rightarrow t_1 \prec_{\text{kids}} t_2)$ $\varphi_5 : \forall t_1, t_2 \ (t_1 \prec_{\text{status}} t_2 \rightarrow t_1 \prec_{\text{job}} t_2)$ $\varphi_6 : \forall t_1, t_2 \ (t_1 \prec_{\text{status}} t_2 \rightarrow t_1 \prec_{\text{AC}} t_2)$ $\varphi_7 : \forall t_1, t_2 \ (t_1 \prec_{\text{status}} t_2 \rightarrow t_1 \prec_{\text{zip}} t_2)$ $\varphi_8 : \forall t_1, t_2 \ (t_1 \prec_{\text{city}} t_2 \wedge t_1 \prec_{\text{zip}} t_2 \rightarrow t_1 \prec_{\text{county}} t_2)$
CFDs:	$\psi_1 : ([\text{AC}] \rightarrow [\text{city}], (213 \| \text{LA}))$; $\psi_2 : ([\text{AC}] \rightarrow [\text{city}], (212 \| \text{NY}))$;

Figure 7.7: Currency constraints and constant CFDs.

We want to find their true values, i.e., a tuple t_1 for Edith (resp. a tuple t_2 for George) such that the tuple has the most current and consistent attribute values for her (resp. his) status, job, the number of kids, city, AC (area code), zip, and county in E_1 (resp. E_2). However, the values in E_1 (E_2) have conflicts, and carry no timestamps. They do not tell us, for instance, whether Edith still lives in NY, or even whether she is still alive. □

The situation is not hopeless. As we have seen in Chapter 6, we can often deduce certain currency orders from the semantics of the data. In addition, Chapter 2 tells us that CFDs can be used to improve data consistency. When these are taken together, we can often infer some true values from inconsistent tuples, even in the absence of timestamps.

Example 7.32 From the semantics of the data of Figure 7.6, we can deduce the *currency constraints* (Chapter 6) and constant CFDs (Chapter 2) shown in Figure 7.7.

(1) Currency constraints. We know that for each person, status only changes from working to retired and from retired to deceased, but not from deceased to working or retired. These can be expressed as currency constraints φ_1 and φ_2 given in Figure 7.7. Similarly, we know that job can only change from sailor to veteran but not the other way around. We can express this as φ_3. Moreover, the number of kids typically increases monotonically. This is expressed as φ_4, assuring that t_2 is more current than t_1 in attribute kids if $t_1[\text{kids}] < t_2[\text{kids}]$.

7.3. RESOLVING CONFLICTS

In addition, we know that for each person, if $t_1 \prec_{status} t_2$, then t_2 is also more current than t_1 in job, AC and zip. Furthermore, if t_2 is more current than t_1 in city and zip, it also has more current county than t_1. These are expressed as φ_5–φ_8.

(2) *Constant CFDs*. In the U.S., if the AC is 213 (resp. 212), then the city must be LA (resp. NY). These are expressed as CFDs ψ_1 and ψ_2 in Figure 7.7.

We can enforce these constraints on E_1, given in Figure 7.6, to improve the currency and consistency of the data. By *interleaving* the inferences of data currency and consistency, we can actually identify the true values of entity Edith, as follows:

(a) from the currency constraints φ_1 and φ_2, we find that her latest status is deceased;

(b) by φ_4, we find that her true kids value is 3 (assuming null $< k$ for any number k);

(c) from the outcome of step (a) above and φ_5–φ_7, we can conclude that her latest job, AC and zip are n/a, 213 and 90 058, respectively;

(d) after the currency inference steps (a) and (c), we can apply the CFD ψ_1 and find her latest city as LA; and

(e) after the consistency inference step (d), from the outcome of steps (c) and (d) we get her latest county as Vermont, by applying φ_8.

Now we have identified a single tuple t_1 = (Edith Shain, deceased, n/a, 3, LA, 213, 90085, Vermont) as the true values of Edith in E_1 (the address is for her cemetery). □

This example suggests the following. (1) Data currency and data consistency interact with each other, and should be taken together when resolving conflicts. Indeed, not only deducing currency orders helps us *improve the consistency* (e.g., from steps (a), (c) to (d)), but data consistency inferences also help us *identify the most current values* (e.g., step (e) is doable only after (d)). (2) By specifying data currency and consistency in terms of constraints, we can deal with both issues in a uniform logical framework.

7.3.2 A MODEL FOR CONFLICT RESOLUTION

We now introduce a model for conflict resolution based on both data currency and data consistency. We resolve conflicts by reasoning about available currency information (partial currency orders and currency constraints) and about data consistency (CFDs).

Data currency. Recall the notions of normal instances, temporal instances with currency orders, completions of temporal instances, currency constraints and current instances from Section 6.2. We revise some of these notions for conflict resolution.

Consider a relation schema $R = (A_1, \ldots, A_n)$. We focus on *entity instances* I_e of R, which are sets of tuples of R all pertaining to the *same* real-world entity as identified by data deduplication (Chapter 4). For example, two entity instances are given in Figure 7.6: $E_1 = \{r_1, r_2, r_3\}$ for entity "Edith," and $E_2 = \{r_4, r_5, r_6\}$ for "George."

We revise currency orders $\prec_{A_i}$ of Section 6.2 to represent *available* temporal information about an entity instance. We define a partial order $\preccurlyeq_{A_i}$ on I_e, referred to as *currency order for attribute* A_i, such that for all tuples $t_1, t_2 \in I_e$, $t_1 \preccurlyeq_{A_i} t_2$ if and only if either $t_1[A_i] = t_2[A_i]$ or $t_1 \prec_{A_i} t_2$. In contrast to the currency order $\prec_{A_i}$ defined in Chapter 6 that is a strict partial order, here $\preccurlyeq_{A_i}$ is reflexive: if t_1 and t_2 share the same A_i-attribute value then t_1 is as current as t_2 in their A_i-attribute. In particular, $t_1 \preccurlyeq_{A_i} t_2$ if $t_1[A_i]$ is null, i.e., an attribute with value missing is ranked the lowest in the currency order.

Using currency orders $\preccurlyeq_{A_i}$, a *temporal instance* I_t of I_e is given as $(I_e, \preccurlyeq_{A_1}, \ldots, \preccurlyeq_{A_n})$. We remark that each $\preccurlyeq_{A_i}$ is partial and can be even empty. For example, for E_1 above, we only know that $r_3 \preccurlyeq_{\text{kids}} r_1$ and $r_3 \preccurlyeq_{\text{kids}} r_2$ since $r_3[\text{kids}]$ is null, which are in $\preccurlyeq_{\text{kids}}$, while the currency orders for other attributes are empty excluding the case when $t_1[A] = t_2[A]$. For E_2, we assume that no temporal information is available, and hence all currency orders are *empty* in its temporal instance excluding the case when tuples carry the same attribute value.

We define *completions* I_t^c of I_t and the *current tuple* $\mathsf{LST}(I_t^c)$ of I_t^c as in Section 6.2. For conflict resolution we use a simple form of currency constraints defined on I_t^c:

$$\forall t_1, t_2 \; (\varphi \to t_1 \prec_{A_r} t_2).$$

In contrast to their general form given in Section 6.2, a currency constraint here is defined on two tuples in I_t^c. We find that this simple form of currency constraints suffices to specify currency information commonly found in practice, and can be automatically discovered along the same lines as CFD discovery (Section 3.1). Furthermore, as will be seen in Section 7.3.4, such currency constraints simplify the analyses of data currency.

Example 7.33 Recall the entity instances E_1 and E_2 from Figure 7.6. Currency constraints on these instances include φ_1–φ_8 as specified in Figure 7.7 and interpreted in Example 7.32.

It is readily verified that for any completion E_1^c of E_1, if it satisfies these constraints, it yields $\mathsf{LST}(E_1^c)$ of the form (Edith, deceased, n/a, 3, x_{city}, 213, 90 058, x_{county}) for Edith, in which the most current values for attributes name, status, job, kids, AC, and zip are deduced from the constraints and remain unchanged, while x_{city} and x_{county} are values determined by the total currency order given in E_1^c. Observe that the values of the current tuple are taken from *different tuples* in E_1, kids = 3 from r_2 and AC = 213 from r_3. Similarly, for any completion of E_2 that satisfy these constraints, their current tuple has the form (George, x_{status}, x_{job}, 2, x_{city}, x_{AC}, x_{zip}, x_{county}). These tell us that currency constraints help us find the most current values of entities for some but not necessarily *all* of its attributes. □

Data consistency. To express when current data are consistent we use constant CFDs $\psi = R(X \to A, t_p)$, where pattern tuple t_p consists of constants only (see Section 2.1). Such a CFD is defined on *the current tuple* $t_e = \mathsf{LST}(I_t^c)$ of a completion I_t^c. It assures if $t_e[X] = t_p[X]$ and if $t_e[X]$ contains the consistent and most current X-attribute values, then the most current value for $t_e[B]$ is $t_p[B]$ in the pattern.

7.3. RESOLVING CONFLICTS   167

Observe that a constant CFD is defined on a *single tuple* $t_e = \mathsf{LST}(I_t^c)$. In light of this, we do not need general CFDs here, which are typically defined on *two tuples*.

Example 7.34 Consider the constant CFDs ψ_1 and ψ_2 given in Figure 7.7. From the analysis of Example 7.33 it follows that for all completions of E_1 that satisfy ψ_1, they yield the same current tuple (Edith, deceased, n/a, 3, LA, 213, 90 058, Vermont), in which x_{city} is instantiated as LA by ψ_1, and as a result, x_{county} can in turn be instantiated as Vermont by the currency constraint φ_8 of Figure 7.7. □

Conflict resolution. We are now ready to specify entities by taking currency and consistency together. Extending Definition 6.3 by incorporating constant CFDs, we define a *specification of an entity* as $S_e = (I_t, \Sigma, \Gamma)$, where $I_t = (I_e, \preceq_{A_1}, \ldots, \preceq_{A_n})$ is a temporal instance, Σ is a set of currency constraints, and Γ is a set of constant CFDs. A completion $I_t^c = (I_e, \preceq_{A_1}^c, \ldots, \preceq_{A_n}^c)$ of I_t is called a *valid completion* of S_e if $I_t^c \models \Sigma$ and $I_t^c \models \Gamma$. We say that S_e is *valid* if there exists a valid completion I_t^c of S_e. For example, the specification consisting of E_1 (or E_2) and the constraints given in Figure 7.7 is valid.

Conflicts and true values. There may exist many valid completions I_t^c for a specification S_e, each leading to a possibly different current tuple $\mathsf{LST}(I_t^c)$. When two current tuples differ in some attribute, there is *a conflict*. We aim to resolve such conflicts by identifying the true values of the entity. If all such current tuples agree in *all* attributes then the specification is conflict-free, and a *unique* current tuple exists for the entity specified by S_e. In this case, we say that this tuple is the true value of the entity derived from S_e, defined as follows.

The *true value* of S_e, denoted by $\mathsf{T}(S_e)$, is the *single* tuple t_c such that for *all valid* completions I_t^c of S_e, $t_c = \mathsf{LST}(S_e)$, if such a tuple exists. For each attribute A_i of R, $t_c[A_i]$ is called the *true value* of A_i in S_e.

In other words, S_e is deterministic if $\mathsf{T}(S_e)$ exists, in the terms of Section 6.3.

The conflict resolution problem. Given a specification S_e of an entity, conflict resolution is to find the minimum amount of additional information such that $\mathsf{T}(S_e)$ exists.

The additional currency information is specified in terms of a *currency order* $O_t = (I', \preceq'_{A_1}, \ldots, \preceq'_{A_n})$ defined in Section 6.3. We use $S_e \oplus O_t$ to denote the extension $S'_e = (I'_t, \Sigma, \Gamma)$ of S_e by enriching I_t with O_t, where $I'_t = (I_e \cup I', \preceq_{A_1} \cup \preceq'_{A_1}, \ldots, \preceq_{A_n} \cup \preceq'_{A_n})$. We consider such currency orders O_t that $\preceq_{A_i} \cup \preceq'_{A_i}$ is a partial order for all $i \in [1, n]$. We use $|O_t|$ to denote the size of O_t, defined by $\Sigma_{i \in [1,n]} |\preceq'_{A_i}|$, i.e., the sum of the sizes of all the partial orders in O_t, where $|\preceq'_{A_i}|$ is the cardinality of binary relation $\preceq'_{A_i}$.

Given a valid specification $S_e = (I_t, \Sigma, \Gamma)$, the *conflict resolution problem* is to find a partial currency order O_t such that (a) $\mathsf{T}(S_e \oplus O_t)$ exists and (b) $|O_t|$ is minimum.

Example 7.35 Recall from Example 7.33 the current tuples for George. Except for name and kids, we do not have a unique current value for its attributes. However, if a currency order O_t with, e.g.,

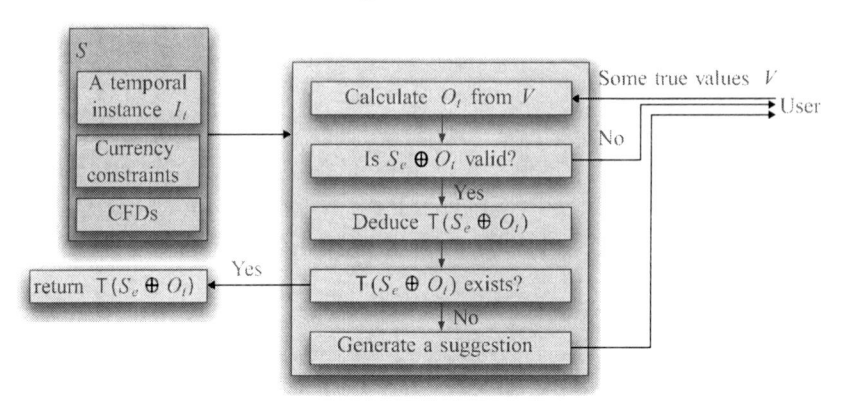

168 7. INTERACTIONS BETWEEN DATA QUALITY ISSUES

Figure 7.8: A framework for conflict resolution.

$r_6 \prec_{\text{status}} r_5$, is provided by the users (i.e., status changes from unemployed to retired), then the true value of George in E_2 can be derived as (George, retired, veteran, 2, NY, 212, 12 404, Accord) from the currency constraints and CFDs of Figure 7.7. □

7.3.3 A FRAMEWORK FOR CONFLICT RESOLUTION

We now outline a framework for finding the true value of an entity. As depicted in Figure 7.8, given a specification $S_e = (I_t, \Sigma, \Gamma)$ of an entity, the framework is to find $\mathsf{T}(S_e)$ by interacting with the users. Along the same lines as the framework for finding certain fixes (Section 7.1.4), the framework provides the users with suggestions. A *suggestion* is a minimum set $\mathcal{A}$ of attributes of the entity such that as long as the true values of these attributes are provided by the users, $\mathsf{T}(S_e)$ is automatically deduced from the user input, Σ, Γ and the partial currency information in I_t. The true values for $\mathcal{A}$ are represented as a currency order O_t. More specifically, the framework deduces $\mathsf{T}(S_e)$ as follows.

(1) *Validity checking.* It inspects whether $S_e \oplus O_t$ is valid, via automated reasoning, where O_t is a currency order provided by the users (see step (4) below), *initially empty*. If so, it follows the "Yes" branch. Otherwise the users need to revise O_t by following the "No" branch.

(2) *True value deducing.* After $S_e \oplus O_t$ is validated, it derives the true values for as many attributes as possible, again via automated reasoning.

(3) *Finding the true value.* If $\mathsf{T}(S_e \oplus O_t)$ exists, it returns the true value and terminates, by following the "Yes" branch. Otherwise, it follows the "No" branch and goes to step (4).

(4) *Generating suggestions.* It computes a suggestion $\mathcal{A}$ along with their candidate values from the active domain of S_e, such that if the users pick and validate the true values for $\mathcal{A}$, then $\mathsf{T}(S_e \oplus O_t)$ is warranted. The users are expected to provide V, the true values of some attributes in $\mathcal{A}$, either by

taking candidate values for the attributes or choosing some *new* values not in the active domains. Note that the users do not have to enter values for all attributes in $\mathcal{A}$. These true values in V are automatically converted to a currency order O_t. Given O_t, $S_e \oplus O_t$ is constructed and the process goes back to step (1).

The process proceeds until $T(S_e \oplus O_t)$ is found, or when the users opt to settle with true values for a subset of the attributes of the entity in question.

As will be seen in Section 7.3.4, each step of the analysis is nontrivial, from NP-complete and coNP-complete to Σ_2^p-complete. Nevertheless, efficient heuristic algorithms underlying the framework have been developed (see [Fan et al., 2012a] for details).

7.3.4 FUNDAMENTAL PROBLEMS FOR CONFLICT RESOLUTION

To understand the challenges introduced by the interaction between data currency and data consistency, we revise some fundamental problems for data currency and consistency we have seen earlier, in the context of conflict resolution. We provide their complexity bounds, and refer the interested reader to [Fan et al., 2012a] for the proofs of the results.

Consistency. We start with the *consistency problem for entity specifications*.
- INPUT: A specification $S_e = (I_t, \Sigma, \Gamma)$ of an entity.
- QUESTION: Is S_e valid? That is, does there exist a valid completion of S_e?

This problem extends the satisfiability problem for constant CFDs (Corollary 2.15) and the consistency problem for data currency (Theorem 6.10) by asking whether currency constraints, constant CFDs and partial currency orders, when put together, have conflicts with each other. This problem is important to conflict resolution: step (1) of the framework given in Section 7.3.3 checks the consistency of entity specifications.

Recall from Theorem 6.10 that the consistency problem for data currency is Σ_2^p-complete for currency constraints defined on an unbounded number of tuples. The result below tells us that for simple currency constraints defined on two tuples (Section 7.3.2), the problem becomes NP-complete even when constant CFDs are present. We have seen from Corollary 2.15 that the satisfiability problem for constant CFDs is NP-complete. The result is rather robust: it remains in NP when simple currency constraints are taken into account.

Theorem 7.36 The consistency problem for entity specifications is NP-complete. It remains NP-complete for valid specifications $S_e = (I_t, \Sigma, \Gamma)$ of an entity when:
(1) both Σ and Γ are fixed, i.e., its data complexity;
(2) $\Gamma = \emptyset$, i.e., when only currency constraints are present; or
(3) $\Sigma = \emptyset$, i.e., when only constant CFDs are present.

Crux. The upper bound is verified by giving an NP decision algorithm for the consistency analysis. The lower bounds are shown by reductions from 3SAT when Σ is a fixed set of currency constraints

170 7. INTERACTIONS BETWEEN DATA QUALITY ISSUES

and the set Γ of CFDs is empty (for (1) and (2) above), and by reduction from the non-tautology problem [Garey and Johnson, 1979] when $\Sigma = \emptyset$ (for (3)). □

Certain currency orders. Recall the *certain ordering problem* from Section 6.3. We revisit the problem for entity specification, when constant CFDs are present and when we adopt a simple form of currency constraints. The analysis of certain ordering is conducted at step (2) of the framework of Section 7.3.3, for deducing true values of attributes.

Recall from Theorem 6.13 that for general currency constraints, the problem is Π_2^p-complete. We show below that for simple currency constraints, the analysis becomes easier.

Theorem 7.37 The certain ordering problem is coNP-complete for valid specifications $S_e = (I_t, \Sigma, \Gamma)$ of an entity. It remains coNP-hard when:

(1) both Σ and Γ are fixed;
(2) $\Gamma = \emptyset$, i.e., with only currency constraints; or
(3) $\Sigma = \emptyset$, i.e., when only constant CFDs are present.

Crux. The upper bound is shown by providing an NP decision algorithm for the complement of the certain ordering problem. The lower bounds are verified by reductions to the complement of the problem, from 3SAT when $\Gamma = \emptyset$ and Σ is fixed (for (1) and (2)), and from the non-tautology problem when $\Sigma = \emptyset$ (for (3)). □

True value deduction. Recall the *deterministic current instance problem* from Section 6.3. We revise this problem to determine, given a valid specification $S_e = (I_t, \Sigma, \Gamma)$ of an entity, whether $T(S_e)$ exists. That is, whether there exists a tuple t_c such that for all valid completions I_t^c of S_e, $\mathsf{LST}(I_t^c) = t_c$. This analysis is needed by step (3) of the conflict resolution framework of Section 7.3.3, to decide whether S_e has sufficient information to deduce $T(S_e)$.

Theorem 6.13 shows that for data currency specifications, the problem is Π_2^p-complete. Nonetheless, the result below shows that simple currency constraints make our lives easier. The proof is similar to the one for Theorem 7.37 sketched above.

Theorem 7.38 The deterministic current instance problem is coNP-complete for valid specifications $S_e = (I_t, \Sigma, \Gamma)$ of an entity. It remains coNP-hard when

(1) both Σ and Γ are fixed;
(2) $\Gamma = \emptyset$, i.e., with only currency constraints; or
(3) $\Sigma = \emptyset$, i.e., when only constant CFDs are present.

Coverage analysis. The last problem is referred to as the *minimum coverage problem*.
- INPUT: A valid specification $S_e = (I_t, \Sigma, \Gamma)$ of an entity and a positive integer k.
- QUESTION: Does there exist a currency order O_t such that (1) $T(S_e \oplus O_t)$ exists, and (2) $|O_t| \leq k$?

This is to check whether one can add a partial currency order of a *bounded* size to S_e such that the enriched specification has sufficient information to deduce all the true values of the entity. The ability to solve this problem helps us identify what *minimum* additional currency information is needed to deduce the true value. The analysis is required by step (4) of the framework of Section 7.3.3. This problem has not been studied for currency analysis in Chapter 6.

This problem is, unfortunately, Σ_2^p-complete. Unless P = NP, there exist no PTIME exact algorithms that compute a minimum currency order O_t such that $T(S_e \oplus O_t)$ exists.

Theorem 7.39 The minimum coverage problem is Σ_2^p-complete. It remains Σ_2^p-hard for valid specifications $S_e = (I_t, \Sigma, \Gamma)$ of an entity even when:

(1) both Σ and Γ are fixed;

(2) $\Gamma = \emptyset$, i.e., with only currency constraints; or

(3) $\Sigma = \emptyset$, i.e., when only constant CFDs are present.

Crux. The upper bound is verified by giving an NP^{coNP} algorithm for deciding whether there exists a partial currency order O_t of size $|O_t| \leq k$ such that $T(S_e \oplus O_t)$ exists. The lower bounds are proven by reductions from the $\exists^*\forall^*3\text{DNF}$ problem [Stockmeyer, 1976] when Σ is fixed and $\Gamma = \emptyset$ (for (1) and (2)), and when $\Sigma = \emptyset$ (for (3)). □

7.4 PUTTING THINGS TOGETHER

We have seen that there are intimate connections between data consistency and data deduplication, and between data consistency and data currency. Capitalizing on these we can substantially improve the quality of our data. Nevertheless, the interactions between various data quality issues are an area that has been largely overlooked. Among other things, there are strong connections between the following issues, which have not been explored.

(1) Information completeness and data currency. This is obvious: the challenges introduced by data currency stem from missing temporal information. On the other hand, to determine relative information completeness it is a must to keep our master data current.

(2) Information completeness and data consistency. On one hand, to repair the values of an entity we have to make sure that its true values are not missing from our database. On the other hand, for information completeness we have to maintain consistent master data.

(3) Data deduplication and data currency. As remarked earlier, to find the true values of an entity we need to identify all tuples that pertain to the entity. This requires data deduplication. On the other hand, currency information helps us effectively detect duplicates, as demonstrated by Li et al. [2012b]. Therefore, no matter whether we want to improve data currency or detect duplications, we have to take both into account.

Putting things together, a data quality management system should aim to improve all five aspects of data quality: data consistency, data accuracy, data deduplication, information completeness and data currency, by making maximum use of their interactions.

Data quality is widely perceived as one of the most important issues for data management. The need for studying data quality cannot be overstated. In particular, the emergence of big data has placed increased demand on techniques for improving the quality of the data, which are as important as techniques for coping with the sheer size of the data.

Data quality is a rich source of questions and vitality for researchers. Indeed, the study of data quality management has raised as many questions as it has answered. Among the five central aspects of data quality, while there has been extensive work on data consistency and data deduplication, the study of the other issues is still rather preliminary, let alone their interactions. Even for data consistency and deduplication, a number of questions still need to be settled. Below we address some open issues in connection with data quality.

Data consistency. As examples, we highlight two open issues in connection with data consistency. One concerns CFD discovery. As shown in Section 3.1, algorithms have been developed for automatically discovering CFDs. These methods, however, often find an excessive amount of CFDs for users to inspect and investigate for classifying data errors. This calls for the development of a metric for ranking representative CFDs, and top-k algorithms for discovering high-quality representative CFDs. The other issue is about the quest for effective and efficient methods to find certain fixes to large collections of critical data. As remarked in Section 7.1, this is very important yet very challenging.

Data deduplication. This remains by far the most popular topic of data quality. A long-standing issue is object identification, for identifying data with complex structures that refer to the same real-world entity. There is tremendous need for this in Web page clustering, schema matching, pattern recognition, and spam detection, among other things, and recently social network analysis has generated a renewed interest in the topic for graph structured data. While there has been a host of work on the topic (see, e.g., [Bhattacharya and Getoor, 2006] for a survey), effective algorithms are yet to be developed.

Data accuracy. In contrast to data consistency and deduplication, the study of data accuracy is still in its infancy, from theory to practical methods. One of the most pressing issues concerns how to determine whether one value is more accurate than another. As remarked in Chapter 1, this issue is quite challenging when reference data are not available. This calls for the development of models, quantitative metrics, and effective algorithms for assessing the relative accuracy of data, in the absence of reference data. We believe that appropriate dependencies can be developed for specifying relative accuracy, and hence, data accuracy can be handled in the same rule-based logical framework as the other issues.

Information completeness. The study of this issue is still preliminary. The model of relative information completeness (Chapter 5) allows us to determine whether a database has complete information to answer our queries. However, quantitative metrics and practical algorithms are not yet in place for us to conduct the evaluation in practice.

Data currency. Similar remarks apply to the study of data currency. The results in this area are mostly theoretical (Chapter 6). Effective algorithms for evaluating the currency of our data and for deriving current values from a database are yet to be developed.

Quality of distributed data. Already hard to improve the quality of data in a centralized database, it is far more challenging to efficiently detect and fix errors in distributed data. For instance, as we have seen in Chapter 3, error detection is straightforward in a centralized database, but the problem becomes intractable for distributed data when either minimum data shipment or minimum response time is requested [Fan et al., 2010a, 2012d]. When it comes to data repairing, effective and scalable methods have not been studied for distributed data. The quality of distributed data is, however, a topic of great interest to big data, which are typically partitioned and distributed. This requires that we revisit the five central data quality issues for distributed data, and give them a full treatment in that context.

The quality of Web data. The study of data quality has mostly focused relational data. However, data quality issues are on an even larger scale for data on the Web, e.g., XML data and social graphs. Needless to say, these issues are far more intricate than their relational counterparts. These open up a new frontier for data quality research.

BIBLIOGRAPHIC NOTES

The editing rules, methods, framework, and complexity results for finding certain fixes (Section 7.1) are taken from [Fan et al., 2010b, 2012c]. A prototype system, CerFix [Fan et al., 2011d], has been developed to find certain fixes based on the methods of Section 7.1, and has proven effective and efficient in data monitoring. The need for finding such fixes has long been recognized [Giles, 1988; Herzog et al., 2009]. Indeed, prior repairing methods (Chapter 3) do not always guarantee that repairs (fixes) are correct, and moreover, new errors may be introduced while attempting to fix existing ones in the repairing process.

While the dynamic semantics of editing rules (eRs) resembles that of matching dependencies (MDs) (Chapter 4), they are quite different: MDs are for record matching, not for data repairing. Furthermore, in the absence of matching functions, MDs only specify what attributes should be identified, but do not tell us how to update them. Even when matching functions are present, it is not clear how such functions could be represented or obtained. Instead of using matching functions, we leverage consistent and reliable master data to find correct values. Indeed, both editing rules (Section 7.1) and data cleaning rules (Section 7.2) are defined in terms of master data and dynamic semantics.

A method for matching input tuples with master data was presented by Chaudhuri et al. [2003], without repairing the tuples. It should also be remarked that editing rules and data cleaning rules are quite different from edits studied for census data repair [Fellegi and Holt, 1976; Giles, 1988; Herzog et al., 2009]. Indeed, edits are conditions defined on single records in a single relation, and are used to localize errors rather than to fix errors. In other words, edits do not have a dynamic semantics. For the same reason, editing rules and data cleaning rules are also different from CFDs. A dynamic (or active) semantics of rules has been considered in the more general setting of active databases (see [Widom and Ceri, 1996] for a survey). In that setting, rules are far more general than the editing rules and cleaning rules considered here: they are used to specify events, conditions and actions. As a result, even the termination problem for those rules is undecidable, as opposed to the coNP and PSPACE bounds for editing rules and data cleaning rules, respectively.

The approach to cleaning data by integrating data repairing and record matching (Section 7.2) is taken from [Fan et al., 2011e], in which the system UniClean was also proposed. One of the main differences between the framework for finding the certain fixes and the system UniClean is whether they clean data one tuple at a time (data monitoring), or clean sets of tuples all together (data cleaning). It was noted by Sauter et al. [2007] that it is far less costly to correct a tuple at the point of entry than to fix it afterward. This kind of data monitoring was advocated by Chaudhuri et al. [2003], Faruquie et al. [2010], Sauter et al. [2007] and Chen et al. [2010], and is considered in Section 7.1. In contrast, the system UniClean described in Section 7.2 aims to repair a database rather than individual tuples. This is often needed when we have to clean a database that has already been used for years, and has collected a large amount of (possibly dirty) data.

Another difference between the two approaches is that certain fixes are based on one kind of constraints, namely, editing rules, whereas UniClean attempts to unify CFDs for repairing and MDs for matching. Similar efforts to combine merge and match operations were made by Dong et al. [2005], Whang et al. [2009] and Weis and Naumann [2005]. The previous work focused on record matching but advocated the need for data repairing to match records. The merge/fusion operations adopted there were more restrictive than updates (value modifications) suggested by cleaning rules in UniClean. Furthermore, when no matches are found, no merge or fusion can be conducted there, whereas UniClean still repairs data by using CFDs. There has also been a host of work on ETL tools (see [Herzog et al., 2009] for a survey), which support data transformations, and can be employed to merge and fix data [Naumann et al., 2006], although they are typically not based on a constraint theory and are specific to a particular application domain [Rahm and Do, 2000].

One of the distinguishing features of the repairing methods for certain, deterministic, reliable and possible fixes is the incorporation of confidence and reliability information. Most repairing methods return candidate repairs without any information about their validity, confidence or accuracy (Chapter 3). The system UniClean uses confidence to derive deterministic fixes, and employs master data and entropy to improve the accuracy of repairs. Entropy has been proved effective in, e.g., database design, schema matching, data anonymization, and data clustering [Srivastava and Venkatasubramanian, 2010]. As explained in Chapter 3, the methods of Cong et al. [2007] and Bohannon et al. [2005] employ confidence to guide a repairing process. These confidences, however, are placed by users. A general statistical method was studied by Mayfield et al.

[2010] to derive missing values. Decision theory was used to rank possible repairs (*a.k.a.* preferred repairs [Greco et al., 2003b]) by Yakout et al. [2010b]. To ensure the accuracy of repairs generated, the methods of Mayfield et al. [2010] and Yakout et al. [2010b] require to consult users.

Conflict resolution (data fusion) has been studied in data integration, starting with Dayal [1983]. The problem studied there is to combine and fuse data from different data sources into a single representation (see [Bleiholder and Naumann, 2008; Dong and Naumann, 2009] for surveys). In that context, inconsistencies are typically resolved by selecting the max, min, avg, any value [Bleiholder and Naumann, 2008], giving higher priority to data from reliable data sources [Papakonstantinou et al., 1996]. In that line of work, including the system UniClean, the currency of data was not considered. The need for current values is, however, widely recognized [Dong and Naumann, 2009; Motro and Anokhin, 2006; Subrahmanian et al., 1995]. As remarked earlier, prior work on data currency is based on timestamps. However, reliable timestamps may not be available in practice. Indeed, we have seen that timestamps are often missing, among other things [Zhang et al., 2010].

To make use of data currency in the absence of reliable timestamps, we present the conflict resolution method (Section 7.3) based on the currency model of Chapter 6. This allows us to infer true values needed to resolve conflicts from available information, by unifying data currency and data consistency, and by employing *automated reasoning*. This method and its complexity results for conflict resolution are taken from [Fan et al., 2012a].

There have been different approaches to discovering true values from data sources, based on the following: vote counting and probabilistic computation [Blanco et al., 2010; Galland et al., 2010; Wu and Marian, 2011; Yin et al., 2008]; source dependencies to find copy relationships and reliable sources [Dong et al., 2009a,b]; and lineage information and probabilistic methods [Widom, 2005]. No information about the reliability of data sources is assumed in the conflict resolution framework presented in this chapter, but the information can be readily incorporated into the framework upon its availability. Guo et al. [2010] proposed using uniqueness constraints to cluster objects from multiple data sources, and to employ machine learning techniques to discover the true values of the objects. They considered different kinds of rules, however, and did not support data repairing in the clustering process. Record linkage techniques were recently proposed by Li et al. [2012b], by using temporal information to identify records that refer to the same entity. These techniques again assume the availability of timestamps, and focus on record matching only. In other words, the consistency of the matches found is not guaranteed there.

List of Symbols

$\mathcal{R}$	Relational schema	10
R	Relation schema	10
attr(R)	The set of attributes in schema R	10
dom(A)	The domain of attribute A	10
CQ	The class of conjunctive queries	10
UCQ	Union of conjunctive queries	10
$\exists$FO$^+$	Positive existential FO queries	10
FO	First-order logic queries	10
FP	Datalog	10
CFD	Conditional functional dependency	15
$\eta_1 \asymp \eta_2$	η_1 matches η_2 for CFD pattern checking	16
CIND	Conditional inclusion dependency	19
$\Sigma \models \varphi$	Σ implies φ	25
$\Sigma \vdash_\mathcal{I} \varphi$	A dependency φ is provable from Σ using inference rules in $\mathcal{I}$	28
$\Sigma \models_\sigma \varphi$	A dependency φ is propagated from Σ via view σ	31
SC, PC, SP	Fragments of CQ queries	34
supp(φ, I)	Support of dependency φ in a relation I	40
supp(X, t_p, I)	Support of itemset (X, t_p) in I	41
$\preceq$	Partial order on itemsets	41
clo(X, t_p)	Closed itemset of (X, t_p)	41
t^D	Tuple t in instance D, carrying a temporary tuple id	53
cost(D, D')	The differences between a database D and a repair D' of D	54
$\approx$	Similarity predicate	74
MD	Matching dependency	74
$\rightrightarrows$	Matching operator	74
$\Sigma \models_d \varphi$	An MD φ is deduced from a set Σ of MDs	79
RCK	Relative candidate key	81
$(D, D')_{[t_1, t_2]} \models_o \varphi$	Enforcing MD φ on tuples (t_1, t_2) in instance D, yielding D'	86
$\preceq_A$	Semantic dominance	89
CC	Containment constraints	96
RCQ	The set of complete databases	97
RCDP	The relatively complete database problem	100
RCQP	The relatively complete query problem	100
(T, ξ)	A c-table	106

$\text{Mod}(T, \xi)$	The set of instances represented by (T, ξ)	107
T	A c-instance	107
EID	Entity id	121
$\prec_A$	Partial currency order for attribute A	121
I	Normal instance of relation schema R	121
I_t	Temporal instance of R with partial currency orders	121
I_t^c	A completion of partial currency orders in I_t	122
$\mathbf{S}$	A specification of data currency	123
$\text{LST}(I_t^c)$	The current instance of I_t^c	124
$\text{Mod}(\mathbf{S})$	The set of all consistent completions of $\mathbf{S}$	123
CPS	The consistency problem for data currency specifications	126
O_t	A currency order	126
COP	The certain ordering problem	126
DCIP	The deterministic current instance problem	127
CCQA	The certain current query answering problem	128
$\bar{\rho}$	A collection of copy functions	133
$\bar{\rho}^e$	An extensions of copy functions in $\bar{\rho}$	133
$\text{Ext}(\bar{\rho})$	The set of all extensions of $\bar{\rho}$	133
I_t^e	An extension of a temporal instance I_t by $\bar{\rho}^e$	133
$\mathbf{S}^e$	An extension of $\mathbf{S}$ by $\bar{\rho}^e$	133
CPP	The currency preservation problem	135
ECP	The existence problem for currency preserving copy functions	135
BCP	The bounded copying problem	136
I_m	A master relation	142
eR	Editing rule	142
$t[X_p] \simeq t_p[X_p]$	Tuple t matches the pattern t_p in an eR	142
$t \to_{(\varphi, t_m)} t'$	An eR φ and a master tuple t_m apply to a tuple t, yielding t'	143
(Z, T_c)	Region	144
$t \to_{((Z,T_c),\varphi,t_m)} t'$	Applying (φ, t_m) to t w.r.t. region (Z, T_c), yielding t'	145
$t \to^*_{((Z,T_c),\Sigma,I_m)} t'$	Tuple t' is a fix of t by (Σ, I_m) w.r.t. (Z, T_c)	145
$I \to_{(\varphi, I_m)} I'$	Enforcing a cleaning rule φ on I with I_m, yielding instance I'	155
η	Confidence threshold	157
δ	Entropy threshold	157
I_e	Entity instance	165
$\preccurlyeq_A$	Currency order for attribute A, in conflict resolution	166
S_e	A specification of an entity	167
$T(S_e)$	The true value of S_e	167
$S_e \oplus O_t$	The extension of S_e with the partial currency order O_t	167

Bibliography

Serge Abiteboul and Oliver M. Duschka. Complexity of answering queries using materialized views. In *Proc. 17th ACM SIGACT-SIGMOD-SIGART Symp. on Principles of Database Systems*, pages 254–263, 1998. DOI: 10.1145/275487.275516 Cited on page(s) 117

Serge Abiteboul, Paris C. Kanellakis, and Gösta Grahne. On the representation and querying of sets of possible worlds. *Theor. Comp. Sci.*, 78(1):159–187, 1991. DOI: 10.1016/0304-3975(51)90007-2 Cited on page(s) 108, 117

Serge Abiteboul, Richard Hull, and Victor Vianu. *Foundations of Databases*. Addison-Wesley, 1995. Cited on page(s) 4, 5, 9, 10, 11, 13, 21, 25, 26, 27, 28, 29, 31, 33, 35, 36, 38, 55, 74, 80, 86, 88, 102, 106, 108, 117, 125

Foto N. Afrati and Phokion G. Kolaitis. Repair checking in inconsistent databases: Algorithms and complexity. In *Proc. 12th Int. Conf. on Database Theory*, pages 31–41, 2009. DOI: 10.1145/1514894.1514899 Cited on page(s) 68

Rakesh Agrawal and Ramakrishnan Srikant. Fast algorithms for mining association rules in large databases. In *Proc. 20th Int. Conf. on Very Large Data Bases*, pages 487–499, 1994. Cited on page(s) 65

Alexander Aiken, Dexter Kozen, Moshe Y. Vardi, and Edward L. Wimmers. The complexity of set constraints. In *Proc. 7th Workshop on Computer Science Logic*, pages 1–17, 1993. DOI: 10.1007/BFb0049320 Cited on page(s) 162

Noga Alon and Joel Spencer. *The Probabilistic Method*. John Wiley, 1992. Cited on page(s) 67

Rohit Ananthakrishna, Surajit Chaudhuri, and Venkatesh Ganti. Eliminating fuzzy duplicates in data warehouses. In *Proc. 28th Int. Conf. on Very Large Data Bases*, pages 586–597, 2002. DOI: 10.1016/B978-155860869-6/50058-5 Cited on page(s) 71, 89

Musbah M. Aqel, Nidal F. Shilbayeh, and Mohammed S. Hakawati. CFD-Mine: An efficient algorithm for discovering functional and conditional functional dependencies. *Trends in Applied Sciences Research*, 7(4):285–302, 2012. DOI: 10.3923/tasr.2012.285.302 Cited on page(s) 65

Arvind Arasu, Surajit Chaudhuri, and Raghav Kaushik. Transformation-based framework for record matching. In *Proc. 24th Int. Conf. on Data Engineering*, pages 40–49, 2008. DOI: 10.1109/ICDE.2008.4497412 Cited on page(s) 89

180 BIBLIOGRAPHY

Arvind Arasu, Christopher Ré, and Dan Suciu. Large-scale deduplication with constraints using Dedupalog. In *Proc. 25th Int. Conf. on Data Engineering*, pages 952–963, 2009. DOI: 10.1109/ICDE.2009.43 Cited on page(s) 89, 90

Marcelo Arenas, Leopoldo Bertossi, and Jan Chomicki. Consistent query answers in inconsistent databases. In *Proc. 18th ACM SIGACT-SIGMOD-SIGART Symp. on Principles of Database Systems*, pages 68–79, 1999. DOI: 10.1145/303976.303983 Cited on page(s) 11, 53, 67

Marcelo Arenas, Leopoldo Bertossi, and Jan Chomicki. Answer sets for consistent query answering in inconsistent databases. *Theory and Practice of Logic Programming*, 3(4-5):393–424, 2003a. DOI: 10.1017/S1471068403001832 Cited on page(s) 67

Marcelo Arenas, Leopoldo Bertossi, and Jan Chomicki. Consistent query answers in inconsistent databases. *Theory and Practice of Logic Programming*, 3(4-5):393–424, 2003b. DOI: 10.1145/303976.303983 Cited on page(s) 118

David Aumueller, Hong Hai Do, Sabine Massmann, and Erhard Rahm. Schema and ontology matching with COMA++. In *Proc. ACM SIGMOD Int. Conf. on Management of Data*, pages 906–908, 2005. DOI: 10.1145/1066157.1066283 Cited on page(s) 90

Carlo Batini and Monica Scannapieco. *Data Quality: Concepts, Methodologies and Techniques*. Springer, 2006. Cited on page(s) 10

Marianne Baudinet, Jan Chomicki, and Pierre Wolper. Constraint-generating dependencies. *J. Comp. and System Sci.*, 59(1):94–115, 1999. DOI: 10.1006/jcss.1999.1632 Cited on page(s) 37

Roberto J. Bayardo, Bart Goethals, and Mohammed J. Zaki, editors. *Proc. 2nd IEEE ICDM Workshop on Frequent Itemset Mining Implementations*, volume 126 of *CEUR Workshop Proceedings*, 2004. Cited on page(s) 42

Catriel Beeri and Moshe Y. Vardi. A proof procedure for data dependencies. *J. ACM*, 31(4):718–741, 1984. DOI: 10.1145/1634.1636 Cited on page(s) 11

Radim Belohlávek and Vilém Vychodil. Data tables with similarity relations: Functional dependencies, complete rules and non-redundant bases. In *Proc. 11th Int. Conf. on Database Systems for Advanced Applications*, pages 644–658, 2006. DOI: 10.1007/11733836_45 Cited on page(s) 90

Omar Benjelloun, Hector Garcia-Molina, David Menestrina, Qi Su, Steven Whang, and Jennifer Widom. Swoosh: A generic approach to entity resolution. *VLDB J.*, 18(1):255–276, 2009. DOI: 10.1007/s00778-008-0098-x Cited on page(s) 89

Laure Berti-Equille, Anish Das Sarma, Xin Dong, A Marian, and Divesh Srivastava. Sailing the information ocean with awareness of currents: Discovery and application of source dependence. In *Proc. 4th Biennial Conf. on Innovative Data Systems Research*, 2009. Cited on page(s) 6, 120, 130, 138

Leopoldo Bertossi. Consistent query answering in databases. *ACM SIGMOD Rec.*, 35(2):68–76, 2006. DOI: 10.1145/1147376.1147391 Cited on page(s) 138

Leopoldo Bertossi. *Database Repairing and Consistent Query Answering*. Morgan & Claypool Publishers, 2011. DOI: 10.2200/S00379ED1V01Y201108DTM020 Cited on page(s) 10, 11, 38, 53, 67, 138

Leopoldo Bertossi, Loreto Bravo, Enrico Franconi, and Andrei Lopatenko. The complexity and approximation of fixing numerical attributes in databases under integrity constraints. *Inf. Syst.*, 33(4-5):407–434, 2008. DOI: 10.1016/j.is.2008.01.005 Cited on page(s) 38

Leopoldo Bertossi, Solmaz Kolahi, and Laks V. S. Lakshmanan. Data cleaning and query answering with matching dependencies and matching functions. In *Proc. 14th Int. Conf. on Database Theory*, pages 268–279, 2011. DOI: 10.1145/1938551.1938585 Cited on page(s) 75, 86, 87, 88, 89

Leopoldo Bertossi, Solmaz Kolahi, and Laks V. S. Lakshmanan. Declarative entity resolution via matching dependencies and answer set programs. In *Proc. 15th Int. Conf. Principles of Knowledge Representation and Reasoning*, pages 380–390, 2012a. Cited on page(s) 89

Leopoldo Bertossi, Solmaz Kolahi, and Laks V. S. Lakshmanan. Data cleaning and query answering with matching dependencies and matching functions. *Theor. Comp. Sci.*, 2012b. DOI: 10.1145/1938551.1938585 Cited on page(s) 88

George Beskales, Ihab F. Ilyas, and Lukasz Golab. Sampling the repairs of functional dependency violations under hard constraints. *Proc. VLDB Endow.*, 3:197–207, 2010. Cited on page(s) 68

Indrajit Bhattacharya and Lise Getoor. Entity resolution in graphs. In Diane J. Cook and Lawrence B. Holder, editors, *Mining Graph Data*. John Wiley & Sons, 2006. DOI: 10.1002/0470073047 Cited on page(s) 172

José A. Blakeley, Neil Coburn, and Per-Åke Larson. Updating derived relations: Detecting irrelevant and autonomously computable updates. *ACM Trans. Database Syst.*, 14(3):369–400, 1989. DOI: 10.1145/68012.68015 Cited on page(s) 117

Lorenzo Blanco, Valter Crescenzi, Paolo Merialdo, and Paolo Papotti. Probabilistic models to reconcile complex data from inaccurate data sources. In *Proc. 22nd Int. Conf. on Advanced Information Systems Eng.*, pages 83–97, 2010. DOI: 10.1007/978-3-642-13094-6_8 Cited on page(s) 175

Jens Bleiholder and Felix Naumann. Data fusion. *ACM Comput. Surv.*, 41(1):Paper 1, 2008. DOI: 10.1145/1456650.1456651 Cited on page(s) 72, 89, 163, 175

Philip Bohannon, Wenfei Fan, Michael Flaster, and Rajeev Rastogi. A cost-based model and effective heuristic for repairing constraints by value modification. In *Proc. ACM SIGMOD Int. Conf. on Management of Data*, pages 143–154, 2005. DOI: 10.1145/1066157.1066175 Cited on page(s) 55, 57, 67, 174

Philip Bohannon, Eiman Elnahrawy, Wenfei Fan, and Michael Flaster. Putting context into schema matching. In *Proc. 32nd Int. Conf. on Very Large Data Bases*, pages 307–318, 2006. Cited on page(s) 36

Philip Bohannon, Wenfei Fan, Floris Geerts, Xibei Jia, and Anastasios Kementsietsidis. Conditional functional dependencies for data cleaning. In *Proc. 23rd Int. Conf. on Data Engineering*, pages 746–755, 2007. DOI: 10.1109/ICDE.2007.367920 Cited on page(s) 36

Agnes Boskovitz, Rajeev Goré, and Markus Hegland. A logical formalisation of the fellegi-holt method of data cleaning. In *Proc. 5th Int. Symp. on Intelligent Data Analysis*, pages 554–565, 2003. DOI: 10.1007/978-3-540-45231-7_51 Cited on page(s) 38, 68

Loreto Bravo, Wenfei Fan, and Shuai Ma. Extending dependencies with conditions. In *Proc. 33rd Int. Conf. on Very Large Data Bases*, pages 243–254, 2007. Cited on page(s) 24, 26, 28, 29, 36

Loreto Bravo, Wenfei Fan, Floris Geerts, and Shuai Ma. Increasing the expressivity of conditional functional dependencies without extra complexity. In *Proc. 24th Int. Conf. on Data Engineering*, pages 516–525, 2008. DOI: 10.1109/ICDE.2008.4497460 Cited on page(s) 37, 66

Renato Bruni and Antonio Sassano. Errors detection and correction in large scale data collecting. In *Proc. 4th Int. Symp. on Intelligent Data Analysis*, pages 84–94, 2001. DOI: 10.1007/3-540-44816-0_9 Cited on page(s) 68

Michael J. Cafarella, Alon Y. Halevy, and Nodira Khoussainova. Data integration for the relational web. *Proc. VLDB Endow.*, 2(1):1090–1101, 2009. Cited on page(s) 11

Toon Calders and Bart Goethals. Non-derivable itemset mining. *Data Min. Knowl. Discov.*, 14(1): 171–206, 2007. DOI: 10.1007/s10618-006-0054-6 Cited on page(s) 42

Toon Calders, Raymond T. Ng, and Jef Wijsen. Searching for dependencies at multiple abstraction levels. *ACM Trans. Database Syst.*, 27(3):229–260, 2003. DOI: 10.1145/581751.581752 Cited on page(s) 65

Andrea Cali, Domenico Lembo, and Riccardo Rosati. On the decidability and complexity of query answering over inconsistent and incomplete databases. In *Proc. ACM SIGACT-SIGMOD Symp. on Principles of Database Systems*, pages 260–271, 2003. DOI: 10.1145/773153.773179 Cited on page(s) 118

Diego Calvanese, Giuseppe De Giacomo, Maurizio Lenzerini, and Moshe Y. Vardi. View-based query processing: On the relationship between rewriting, answering and losslessness. *Theor. Comp. Sci.*, 371(3):169–182, 2007. DOI: 10.1016/j.tcs.2006.11.006 Cited on page(s) 117

Bogdan Cautis, Serge Abiteboul, and Tova Milo. Reasoning about XML update constraints. *J. Comp. and System Sci.*, 75(6):336–358, 2009. DOI: 10.1016/j.jcss.2009.02.001 Cited on page(s) 90, 91

Surajit Chaudhuri, Kris Ganjam, Venkatesh Ganti, and Rajeev Motwani. Robust and efficient fuzzy match for online data cleaning. In *Proc. ACM SIGMOD Int. Conf. on Management of Data*, pages 313–324, 2003. DOI: 10.1145/872757.872796 Cited on page(s) 140, 173, 174

Surajit Chaudhuri, Bee-Chung Chen, Venkatesh Ganti, and Raghav Kaushik. Example-driven design of efficient record matching queries. In *Proc. 33rd Int. Conf. on Very Large Data Bases*, pages 327–338, 2007a. Cited on page(s) 89

Surajit Chaudhuri, Anish Das Sarma, Venkatesh Ganti, and Raghav Kaushik. Leveraging aggregate constraints for deduplication. In *Proc. ACM SIGMOD Int. Conf. on Management of Data*, pages 437–448, 2007b. DOI: 10.1145/1247480.1247530 Cited on page(s) 89, 90

Kuang Chen, Harr Chen, Neil Conway, Joseph M. Hellerstein, and Tapan S. Parikh. USHER: Improving data quality with dynamic forms. In *Proc. 26th Int. Conf. on Data Engineering*, pages 321–332, 2010. DOI: 10.1109/ICDE.2010.5447832 Cited on page(s) 68, 174

Wenguang Chen, Wenfei Fan, and Shuai Ma. Incorporating cardinality constraints and synonym rules into conditional functional dependencies. *Inf. Proc. Letters*, 109(4):783–789, 2009a. DOI: 10.1016/j.ipl.2009.03.021 Cited on page(s) 37

Wenguang Chen, Wenfei Fan, and Shuai Ma. Analyses and validation of conditional dependencies with built-in predicates. In *Proc. 20th Int. Conf. Database and Expert Systems Appl.*, pages 576–591, 2009b. DOI: 10.1007/978-3-642-03573-9_48 Cited on page(s) 37, 52, 66, 67

Fei Chiang and Renée J. Miller. A unified model for data and constraint repair. In *Proc. 27th Int. Conf. on Data Engineering*, pages 446–457, 2011. DOI: 10.1109/ICDE.2011.5767833 Cited on page(s) 67

Fei Chiang and Renée J. Miller. Discovering data quality rules. *Proc. VLDB Endow.*, 1(1):1166–1177, 2008. Cited on page(s) 65

Bogdan S. Chlebus. Domino-tiling games. *J. Comp. and System Sci.*, 32(3):374–392, 1986. DOI: 10.1016/0022-0000(86)90036-X Cited on page(s) 26

Jan Chomicki. Consistent query answering: Five easy pieces. In *Proc. 11th Int. Conf. on Database Theory*, pages 1–17, 2007. DOI: 10.1007/11965893_1 Cited on page(s) 118, 138

Jan Chomicki and David Toman. Time in database systems. In Michael Fisher, Dov Gabbay, and Lluis Víla, editors, *Handbook of Temporal Reasoning in Artificial Intelligence*, pages 429–467. Elsevier, 2005. Cited on page(s) 11, 137

Peter Christen. Febrl -: An open source data cleaning, deduplication and record linkage system with a graphical user interface. In *Proc. 14th ACM SIGKDD Int. Conf. on Knowledge Discovery and Data Mining*, pages 1065–1068, 2008. DOI: 10.1145/1401890.1402020 Cited on page(s) 89

James Clifford, Curtis E. Dyreson, Tomás Isakowitz, Christian S. Jensen, and Richard T. Snodgrass. On the semantics of "now" in databases. *ACM Trans. Database Syst.*, 22(2):171–214, 1997. DOI: 10.1145/249978.249980 Cited on page(s) 138

Edgar F. Codd. Extending the database relational model to capture more meaning. *ACM Trans. Database Syst.*, 4(4):397–434, 1979. DOI: 10.1145/320107.320109 Cited on page(s) 121

Edgar F. Codd. A relational model of data for large shared data banks. *Commun. ACM*, 13(6): 377–387, 1970. DOI: 10.1145/362384.362685 Cited on page(s) 11

Edgar F. Codd. Relational completeness of data base sublanguages. In Randall Rustin, editor, *Data Base Systems: Courant Computer Science Symposia Series 6*, pages 65–98. Prentice-Hall, 1972. Cited on page(s) 8, 11

Edgar F. Codd. Understanding relations (installment #7). *FDT - Bulletin of ACM SIGMOD*, 7(3): 23–28, 1975. Cited on page(s) 107

William W. Cohen. WHIRL: A word-based information representation language. *Artif. Intell.*, 118 (1-2):163–196, 2000. DOI: 10.1016/S0004-3702(99)00102-2 Cited on page(s) 89

William W. Cohen and Jacob Richman. Learning to match and cluster large high-dimensional data sets for data integration. In *Proc. 8th ACM SIGKDD Int. Conf. on Knowledge Discovery and Data Mining*, pages 475–480, 2002. DOI: 10.1145/775047.775116 Cited on page(s) 71

Gao Cong, Wenfei Fan, Floris Geerts, Xibei Jia, and Shuai Ma. Improving data quality: Consistency and accuracy. In *Proc. 33rd Int. Conf. on Very Large Data Bases*, pages 315–326, 2007. Cited on page(s) 52, 55, 57, 60, 67, 174

Graham Cormode, Lukasz Golab, Korn Flip, Andrew McGregor, Divesh Srivastava, and Xi Zhang. Estimating the confidence of conditional functional dependencies. In *Proc. ACM SIGMOD Int. Conf. on Management of Data*, pages 469–482, 2009. DOI: 10.1145/1559845.1559895 Cited on page(s) 66

Thomas M. Cover and Joy A. Thomas. *Elements of Information Theory*. Wiley-Interscience, 1991. DOI: 10.1002/0471200611 Cited on page(s) 158

Evgeny Dantsin and Andrei Voronkov. Complexity of query answering in logic databases with complex values. In *Proc. 4th Int. Symp. Logical Foundations of Computer Science*, pages 56–66, 1997. DOI: 10.1007/3-540-63045-7_7 Cited on page(s) 104

Anish Das Sarma, Jeffrey Ullman, and Jennifer Widom. Schema design for uncertain databases. In *Proc. 3rd Alberto Mendelzon Workshop on Foundations of Data Management*, 2009. Cited on page(s) 90

Umeshwar Dayal. Processing queries over generalization hierarchies in a multidatabase system. In *Proc. 9th Int. Conf. on Very Data Bases*, pages 342–353, 1983. Cited on page(s) 175

Paul De Bra and Jan Paredaens. Conditional dependencies for horizontal decompositions. In *10th Int. Colloquium on Automata, Languages, and Programming*, pages 67–82, 1983. DOI: 10.1007/BFb0036898 Cited on page(s) 37

Marc Denecker, Alvaro Cortés-Calabuig, Maurice Bruynooghe, and Ofer Arieli. Towards a logical reconstruction of a theory for locally closed databases. *ACM Trans. Database Syst.*, 35(3):Paper 22, 2010. DOI: 10.1145/1806907.1806914 Cited on page(s) 118

Alin Deutsch, Bertram Ludäscher, and Alan Nash. Rewriting queries using views with access patterns under integrity constraints. *Theor. Comp. Sci.*, 371(3):200–226, 2007. DOI: 10.1016/j.tcs.2006.11.008 Cited on page(s) 117

Xin Dong, Alon Y. Halevy, and Jayant Madhavan. Reference reconciliation in complex information spaces. In *Proc. ACM SIGMOD Int. Conf. on Management of Data*, pages 85–96, 2005. DOI: 10.1145/1066157.1066168 Cited on page(s) 174

Xin Dong, Laure Berti-Equille, Yifan Hu, and Divesh Srivastava. Global detection of complex copying relationships between sources. *Proc. VLDB Endow.*, 3(1):1358–1369, 2010. Cited on page(s) 6, 120, 130, 138

Xin Luna Dong and Felix Naumann. Data fusion - resolving data conflicts for integration. *Proc. VLDB Endow.*, 2(2):1654–1655, 2009. Cited on page(s) 175

Xin Luna Dong, Laure Berti-Equille, and Divesh Srivastava. Truth discovery and copying detection in a dynamic world. *Proc. VLDB Endow.*, 2(1):562–573, 2009a. Cited on page(s) 6, 11, 120, 130, 138, 175

Xin Luna Dong, Laure Berti-Equille, and Divesh Srivastava. Integrating conflicting data: The role of source dependence. *Proc. VLDB Endow.*, 2(1):550–561, 2009b. Cited on page(s) 6, 175

Burton Dreben and Warren D. Goldfarb. *The Decision Problem: Solvable Classes of Quantificational Formulas*. Addison Wesley, 1979. Cited on page(s) 27

Allen Dreibelbis, Eberhard Hechler, Bill Mathews, Martin Oberhofer, and Guenter Sauter. Information service patterns, part 4: Master data management architecture patterns. IBM, 2007. Cited on page(s) 94

Curtis E. Dyreson, Christian S. Jensen, and Richard T. Snodgrass. Now in temporal databases. In Ling Liu and M. Tamer Özsu, editors, *Encyclopedia of Database Systems*, pages 1920–1924. Springer, 2009. DOI: 10.1007/978-0-387-39940-9 Cited on page(s) 138

Wayne W. Eckerson. Data quality and the bottom line: Achieving business success through a commitment to high quality data. In *The Data Warehousing Institute*, 2002. Cited on page(s) 2, 119

Mohamed G. Elfeky, Vassilios S. Verykios, and Ahmed K. Elmagarmid. TAILOR: A record linkage toolbox. In *Proc. 18th Int. Conf. on Data Engineering*, pages 17–28, 2002. DOI: 10.1109/ICDE.2002.994694 Cited on page(s) 89

Charles Elkan. Independence of logic database queries and updates. In *Proc. 9th ACM SIGACT-SIGMOD-SIGART Symp. on Principles of Database Systems*, pages 154–160, 1990. DOI: 10.1145/298514.298557 Cited on page(s) 117

Ahmed K. Elmagarmid, Panagiotis G. Ipeirotis, and Vassilios S. Verykios. Duplicate record detection: A survey. *IEEE Trans. Knowl. and Data Eng.*, 19(1):1–16, 2007. DOI: 10.1109/TKDE.2007.250581 Cited on page(s) 6, 11, 71, 72, 74, 89

Larry English. Plain English on data quality: Information quality management: The next frontier. *DM Review Magazine*, April 2000. Cited on page(s) 2

Ronald Fagin. A normal form for relational databases that is based on domains and keys. *ACM Trans. Database Syst.*, 6(3):387–415, 1981. DOI: 10.1145/319587.319592 Cited on page(s) 11

Ronald Fagin. Horn clauses and database dependencies. *J. ACM*, 29(4):952–985, 1982. DOI: 10.1145/322344.322347 Cited on page(s) 38

Ronald Fagin and Moshe Y. Vardi. The theory of data dependencies - an overview. In *11th Int. Colloquium on Automata, Languages, and Programming*, pages 1–22, 1984. DOI: 10.1007/3-540-13345-3_1 Cited on page(s) 21, 25, 26, 27, 36

Wenfei Fan. Dependencies revisited for improving data quality. In *Proc. 27th ACM SIGACT-SIGMOD-SIGART Symp. on Principles of Database Systems*, pages 159–170, 2008. DOI: 10.1145/1376916.1376940 Cited on page(s) 89

Wenfei Fan and Floris Geerts. A uniform dependency language for improving data quality. *Q. Bull. IEEE TC on Data Eng.*, 34(3):34–42, 2011. Cited on page(s) 38

Wenfei Fan and Floris Geerts. Capturing missing tuples and missing values. In *Proc. 29th ACM SIGACT-SIGMOD-SIGART Symp. on Principles of Database Systems*, pages 169–178, 2010a. DOI: 10.1145/1807085.1807109 Cited on page(s) 103, 112, 116

Wenfei Fan and Floris Geerts. Relative information completeness. *ACM Trans. Database Syst.*, 35(4):Paper 27, 2010b. DOI: 10.1145/1862919.1862924 Cited on page(s) 101, 116

Wenfei Fan, Floris Geerts, and Xibei Jia. Semandaq: a data quality system based on conditional functional dependencies. *Proc. VLDB Endow.*, 1(2):1460–1463, 2008a. Cited on page(s) 68

Wenfei Fan, Floris Geerts, Xibei Jia, and Anastasios Kementsietsidis. Conditional functional dependencies for capturing data inconsistencies. *ACM Trans. Database Syst.*, 33(2):Paper 6, 2008b. DOI: 10.1145/1366102.1366103 Cited on page(s) 22, 25, 28, 31, 36, 52, 55, 66

Wenfei Fan, Shuai Ma, Yanli Hu, Jie Liu, and Yinghui Wu. Propagating functional dependencies with conditions. *Proc. VLDB Endow.*, 1(1):391–407, 2008c. DOI: 10.1145/1453856.1453901 Cited on page(s) 33, 34, 38

Wenfei Fan, Floris Geerts, Shuai Ma, and Heiko Müller. Detecting inconsistencies in distributed data. In *Proc. 26th Int. Conf. on Data Engineering*, pages 64–75, 2010a. DOI: 10.1109/ICDE.2010.5447855 Cited on page(s) 66, 67, 173

Wenfei Fan, Jianzhong Li, Shuai Ma, Nan Tang, and Wenyuan Yu. Towards certain fixes with editing rules and master data. *Proc. VLDB Endow.*, 3(1):173–184, 2010b. Cited on page(s) 139, 148, 173

Wenfei Fan, Hong Gao, Xibei Jia, Jianzhong Li, and Shuai Ma. Dynamic constraints for record matching. *VLDB J.*, 20(4):495–520, 2011a. Cited on page(s) 37, 75, 80, 83, 84, 89

Wenfei Fan, Floris Geerts, Jianzhong Li, and Ming Xiong. Discovering conditional functional dependencies. *IEEE Trans. Knowl. and Data Eng.*, 23(5):683–698, 2011b. DOI: 10.1109/TKDE.2010.154 Cited on page(s) 43, 44, 46, 47, 65

Wenfei Fan, Floris Geerts, and Jef Wijsen. Determining the currency of data. In *Proc. 30th ACM SIGACT-SIGMOD-SIGART Symp. on Principles of Database Systems*, pages 71–82, 2011c. DOI: 10.1145/1989284.1989295 Cited on page(s) 137

Wenfei Fan, Jianzhong Li, Shuai Ma, Nan Tang, and Wenyuan Yu. Cerfix: A system for cleaning data with certain fixes. *Proc. VLDB Endow.*, 4(12):1375–1378, 2011d. Cited on page(s) 68, 173

Wenfei Fan, Jianzhong Li, Shuai Ma, Nan Tang, and Wenyuan Yu. Interaction between record matching and data repairing. In *Proc. ACM SIGMOD Int. Conf. on Management of Data*, pages 469–480, 2011e. DOI: 10.1145/1989323.1989373 Cited on page(s) 89, 139, 151, 157, 158, 159, 160, 174

Wenfei Fan, Floris Geerts, Nan Tang, and Wenyuan Yu. Conflict resolution with data currency and consistency. Unpublished manuscript, 2012a. Cited on page(s) 139, 169, 175

Wenfei Fan, Floris Geerts, and Jef Wijsen. Determining the currency of data. *ACM Trans. Database Syst.*, 37(3):Paper 4, 2012b. DOI: 10.1145/1989284.1989295 Cited on page(s) 37, 125, 137

Wenfei Fan, Jianzhong Li, Shuai Ma, Nan Tang, and Wenyuan Yu. Towards certain fixes with editing rules and master data. *VLDB J.*, 21(2):213–238, 2012c. Cited on page(s) 68, 139, 148, 149, 150, 173

Wenfei Fan, Jianzhong Li, Nan Tang, and Wenyuan Yu. Incremental detection of inconsistencies in distributed data. In *Proc. 28th Int. Conf. on Data Engineering*, 2012d. DOI: 10.1109/ICDE.2012.82 Cited on page(s) 66, 67, 173

Tanveer A. Faruquie, K. Hima Prasad, L. Venkata Subramaniam, Mukesh K. Mohania, Girish Venkatachaliah, Shrinivas Kulkarni, and Pramit Basu. Data cleansing as a transient service. In *Proc. 26th Int. Conf. on Data Engineering*, pages 1025–1036, 2010. DOI: 10.1109/ICDE.2010.5447789 Cited on page(s) 174

Ivan Fellegi and David Holt. A systematic approach to automatic edit and imputation. *J. Am. Stat. Assoc.*, 71(353):17–35, 1976. DOI: 10.1080/01621459.1976.10481472 Cited on page(s) 11, 38, 52, 68, 82, 174

Ivan Fellegi and Alan B. Sunter. A theory for record linkage. *J. Am. Stat. Assoc.*, 64(328):1183–1210, 1969. DOI: 10.1080/01621459.1969.10501049 Cited on page(s) 71, 89

Peter A. Flach and Iztok Savnik. Database dependency discovery: A machine learning approach. *AI Commun.*, 12(3):139–160, 1999. Cited on page(s) 65

Sergio Flesca, Filippo Furfaro, Sergio Greco, and Ester Zumpano. Querying and repairing inconsistent XML data. In *Proc. 6th Int. Conf. on Web Information Systems Eng.*, pages 175–188, 2005. DOI: 10.1007/11581062_14 Cited on page(s) 11

Enrico Franconi, Antonio Laureti Palma, Nicola Leone, Simona Perri, and Francesco Scarcello. Census data repair: A challenging application of disjunctive logic programming. In *Proc. 8th Int. Conf. on Logic for Programming, Artificial Intelligence, and Reasoning*, pages 561–578, 2001. DOI: 10.1007/3-540-45653-8_39 Cited on page(s) 68

Helena Galhardas, Daniela Florescu, Dennis Shasha, and Eric Simon. Ajax: An extensible data cleaning tool. In *Proc. ACM SIGMOD Int. Conf. on Management of Data*, page 590, 2000. DOI: 10.1145/335191.336568 Cited on page(s) 68, 90

Helena Galhardas, Daniela Florescu, Dennis Shasha, Eric Simon, and Cristian-Augustin Saita. Declarative data cleaning: Language, model and algorithms. In *Proc. 27th Int. Conf. on Very Large Data Bases*, pages 371–380, 2001. Cited on page(s) 54, 89, 90

Helena Galhardas, Antónia Lopes, and Emanuel Santos. Support for user involvement in data cleaning. In *Proc. 13th Int. Conf. Data Warehousing and Knowledge Discovery*, pages 136–151, 2011. DOI: 10.1007/978-3-642-23544-3_11 Cited on page(s) 68

Alban Galland, Serge Abiteboul, Amélie Marian, and Pierre Senellart. Corroborating information from disagreeing views. In *Proc. 3rd ACM Int. Conf. Web Search and Data Mining*, 2010. DOI: 10.1145/1718487.1718504 Cited on page(s) 11, 175

Jaffer Gardezi and Leopoldo Bertossi. Tractable cases of clean query answering under entity resolution via matching dependencies. In *Proc. Int. Conf. on Scalable Uncertainty Management*, 2012a. Cited on page(s) 89

Jaffer Gardezi and Leopoldo Bertossi. Query rewriting using datalog for duplicate resolution. In *The 2nd Workshop on the Resurgence of Datalog in Academia and Industry*, 2012b. Cited on page(s) 89

Jaffer Gardezi, Leopoldo Bertossi, and Iluju Kiringa. Matching dependencies: Semantics and query answering. *Frontiers of Computer Science*, 6(3):278–292, 2012. DOI: 10.1007/s11704-012-2007-0 Cited on page(s) 89

Michael Garey and David Johnson. *Computers and Intractability: A Guide to the Theory of NP-Completeness*. W. H. Freeman and Company, 1979. Cited on page(s) 22, 35, 55, 126, 170

Robert S. Garfinkel, Anand S. Kunnathur, and Gunar E. Liepins. Optimal imputation of erroneous data: Categorical data, general edits. *Operations Research*, 34(5):pp. 744–751, 1986. DOI: 10.1287/opre.34.5.744 Cited on page(s) 68

Gartner. Forecast: Enterprise software markets, worldwide, 2008-2015, 2011 update. Technical report, Gartner, 2011. Cited on page(s) 3

Floris Geerts and Bruno Marnette. Static analysis of schema-mappings ensuring oblivious termination. In *Proc. 13th Int. Conf. on Database Theory*, pages 183–195, 2010. DOI: 10.1145/1804669.1804694 Cited on page(s) 116

Philip Giles. A model for generalized edit and imputation of survey data. *The Canadian J. of Statistics*, 16:57–73, 1988. DOI: 10.2307/3315216 Cited on page(s) 173, 174

Seymour Ginsburg and Edwin H. Spanier. On completing tables to satisfy functional dependencies. *Theor. Comp. Sci.*, 39:309 – 317, 1985. DOI: 10.1016/0304-3975(85)90145-8 Cited on page(s) 67

Seymour Ginsburg and Sami Mohammed Zaiddan. Properties of functional-dependency families. *J. ACM*, 29(3):678–698, 1982. DOI: 10.1145/322326.322331 Cited on page(s) 38

Bart Goethals, Wim Le Page, and Heikki Mannila. Mining association rules of simple conjunctive queries. In *Proc. 8th Int. SIAM Conf. on Data Mining*, pages 96–107, 2008. Cited on page(s) 66

Bart Goethals, Dominique Laurent, and Wim Le Page. Discovery and application of functional dependencies in conjunctive query mining. In *Proc. 12th Int. Conf. Data Warehousing and Knowledge Discovery*, pages 142–156, 2010. DOI: 10.1007/978-3-642-15105-7_12 Cited on page(s) 66

Lukasz Golab, Howard Karloff, Flip Korn, Divesh Srivastava, and Bei Yu. On generating near-optimal tableaux for conditional functional dependencies. *Proc. VLDB Endow.*, 1(1):376–390, 2008. Cited on page(s) 37, 66

Lukasz Golab, Howard Karloff, Flip Korn, Avishek Saha, and Divesh Srivastava. Sequential dependencies. *Proc. VLDB Endow.*, 2(1):574–585, 2009. Cited on page(s) 37

Lukasz Golab, Flip Korn, and Divesh Srivastava. Efficient and effective analysis of data quality using pattern tableaux. *Q. Bull. IEEE TC on Data Eng.*, 34(3):26–33, 2011. Cited on page(s) 66

Georg Gottlob. Computing covers for embedded functional dependencies. In *Proc. 6th ACM SIGACT-SIGMOD-SIGART Symp. on Principles of Database Systems*, pages 58–69, 1987. DOI: 10.1145/28659.28665 Cited on page(s) 38

Georg Gottlob and Roberto Zicari. Closed world databases opened through null values. In *Proc. 14th Int. Conf. on Very Large Data Bases*, pages 50–61, 1988. Cited on page(s) 116

Gösta Grahne. *The Problem of Incomplete Information in Relational Databases*. Springer, 1991. DOI: 10.1007/3-540-54919-6 Cited on page(s) 11, 100, 106, 107, 108, 109, 117

Gianluigi Greco, Sergio Greco, and Ester Zumpano. A logical framework for querying and repairing inconsistent databases. *IEEE Trans. Knowl. and Data Eng.*, 15(6):1389–1408, 2003a. DOI: 10.1109/TKDE.2003.1245280 Cited on page(s) 67

Sergio Greco and Cristian Molinaro. Towards relational inconsistent databases with functional dependencies. In *Proc. 12th Int. Conf. on Knowledge-Based Intelligent Information and Engineering Systems*, pages 695–702, 2008. DOI: 10.1007/978-3-540-85565-1_86 Cited on page(s) 67

Sergio Greco and Francesca Spezzano. *Incomplete Data and Data Dependencies in Relational Databases*. Morgan & Claypool Publishers, 2012. Cited on page(s) 86

Sergio Greco, Cristina Sirangelo, Irina Trubitsyna, and Ester Zumpano. Preferred repairs for inconsistent databases. In *Proc. 7th Int. Conf. on Database Eng. and Applications*, pages 202–211, 2003b. DOI: 10.1109/IDEAS.2003.1214927 Cited on page(s) 175

Sudipto Guha, Nick Koudas, Amit Marathe, and Divesh Srivastava. Merging the results of approximate match operations. In *Proc. 30th Int. Conf. on Very Large Data Bases*, pages 636–647, 2004. Cited on page(s) 71, 89

Songtao Guo, Xin Dong, Divesh Srivastava, and Remi Zajac. Record linkage with uniqueness constraints and erroneous values. *Proc. VLDB Endow.*, 3(1):417–428, 2010. Cited on page(s) 175

Richard W. Hamming. Error detecting and error correcting codes. *Bell System Technical Journal*, 29 (2):147–160, 1950. Cited on page(s) 157

Mauricio A. Hernández and Salvatore J. Stolfo. Real-world data is dirty: Data cleansing and the merge/purge problem. *Data Mining and Knowledge Discovery*, 2(1):9–37, 1998. DOI: 10.1023/A:1009761603038 Cited on page(s) 89

Mauricio A. Hernández and Salvatore J. Stolfo. The merge/purge problem for large databases. In *Proc. ACM SIGMOD Int. Conf. on Management of Data*, pages 127–138, 1995. DOI: 10.1145/568271.223807 Cited on page(s) 71, 73, 82, 89

Thomas N. Herzog, Fritz J. Scheuren, and William E. Winkler. *Data Quality and Record Linkage Techniques*. Springer, 2009. Cited on page(s) 4, 10, 11, 68, 71, 72, 89, 173, 174

Ykä Huhtala, Juha Kärkkäinen, Pasi Porkka, and Hannu Toivonen. TANE: An efficient algorithm for discovering functional and approximate dependencies. *Comp. J.*, 42(2):100–111, 1999. DOI: 10.1093/comjnl/42.2.100 Cited on page(s) 39, 44, 47, 65, 66

Richard Hull. Finitely specifiable implicational dependency families. *J. ACM*, 31(2):210–226, 1984. DOI: 10.1145/62.2162 Cited on page(s) 38

Ihab F. Ilyas, Volker Markl, Peter J. Haas, Paul Brown, and Ashraf Aboulnaga. Cords: Automatic discovery of correlations and soft functional dependencies. In *Proc. ACM SIGMOD Int. Conf. on Management of Data*, pages 647–658, 2004. DOI: 10.1145/1007568.1007641 Cited on page(s) 65

Tomasz Imieliński and Witold Lipski Jr. Incomplete information in relational databases. *J. ACM*, 31(4):761–791, 1984. Cited on page(s) 11, 100, 106, 107, 108, 109, 117

Matthew A. Jaro. Advances in record-linkage methodology as applied to matching the 1985 census of Tampa Florida. *J. American Statistical Association*, 89:414–420, 1989. DOI: 10.1080/01621459.1989.10478785 Cited on page(s) 71, 81, 89, 90

Ronald S. King and James J. Legendre. Discovery of functional and approximate functional dependencies in relational databases. *Journal of Applied Mathematics and Decision Sciences*, 7(1):49–59, 2003. DOI: 10.1155/S117391260300004X Cited on page(s) 65

George J. Klir and Tina A Folger. *Fuzzy sets, Uncertainty, and Information*. Englewood Cliffs, N.J: Prentice Hall, 1988. Cited on page(s) 155

Anthony C. Klug. Calculating constraints on relational expressions. *ACM Trans. Database Syst.*, 5(3):260–290, 1980. DOI: 10.1145/320613.320615 Cited on page(s) 32, 33, 35, 38

Anthony C. Klug and Rod Price. Determining view dependencies using tableaux. *ACM Trans. Database Syst.*, 7(3):361–380, 1982. DOI: 10.1145/319732.319738 Cited on page(s) 32, 33, 35, 38

Knowledge Integrity. Two sides to data decay. *DM Review Magazine*, 2003. Cited on page(s) 119

Solmaz Kolahi and Laks V. S. Lakshmanan. Exploiting conflict structures in inconsistent databases. In *Proc. 14th east European conf. on Advances in databases and information systems*, pages 320–335, 2010. DOI: 10.1007/978-3-642-15576-5_25 Cited on page(s) 67

Solmaz Kolahi and Laks V. S. Lakshmanan. On approximating optimum repairs for functional dependency violations. In *Proc. 12th Int. Conf. on Database Theory*, pages 53–62, 2009. DOI: 10.1145/1514894.1514901 Cited on page(s) 67

Manolis Koubarakis. Database models for infinite and indefinite temporal information. *Inf. Syst.*, 19(2):141–173, 1994. DOI: 10.1016/0306-4379(94)90008-6 Cited on page(s) 138

Manolis Koubarakis. The complexity of query evaluation in indefinite temporal constraint databases. *Theor. Comp. Sci.*, 171(1-2):25–60, 1997. DOI: 10.1016/S0304-3975(96)00124-7 Cited on page(s) 138

Nick Koudas, Avishek Saha, Divesh Srivastava, and Suresh Venkatasubramanian. Metric functional dependencies. In *Proc. 25th Int. Conf. on Data Engineering*, pages 1275–1278, 2009. DOI: 10.1109/ICDE.2009.219 Cited on page(s) 37, 90

Alon Y. Levy. Obtaining complete answers from incomplete databases. In *Proc. 22nd Int. Conf. on Very Large Data Bases*, pages 402–412, 1996. Cited on page(s) 100, 117

Alon Y. Levy and Yehoshua Sagiv. Queries independent of updates. In *Proc. 19th Int. Conf. on Very Large Data Bases*, pages 171–181, 1993. Cited on page(s) 117

Alon Y. Levy, Inderpal Singh Mumick, Yehoshua Sagiv, and Oded Shmueli. Equivalence, query-reachability, and satisfiability in datalog extensions. In *Proc. 12th ACM SIGACT-SIGMOD-SIGART Symp. on Principles of Database Systems*, pages 109–122, 1993. DOI: 10.1145/153850.153860 Cited on page(s) 103

Chen Li. Computing complete answers to queries in the presence of limited access patterns. *VLDB J.*, 12(3):211–227, 2003. Cited on page(s) 117

Jinyan Li, Haiquan Li, Limsoon Wong, Jian Pei, and Guozhu Dong. Minimum description length principle: Generators are preferable to closed patterns. In *Proc. 21st National Conf. on Artificial Intelligence and 18th Innovative Applications of Artificial Intelligence Conf.*, pages 409–414, 2006. Cited on page(s) 42

Jinyan Li, Guimei Liu, and Limsoon Wong. Mining statistically important equivalence classes and delta-discriminative emerging patterns. In *Proc. 13th ACM SIGKDD Int. Conf. on Knowledge Discovery and Data Mining*, pages 430–439, 2007. DOI: 10.1145/1281192.1281240 Cited on page(s) 42

Jiuyong Li, Jiuxue Liu, Hannu Toivonen, and Jianming Yong. Effective pruning for the discovery of conditional functional dependencies. *Comp. J.*, 2012a. to appear. DOI: 10.1093/comjnl/bxs082 Cited on page(s) 43, 65

Pei Li, Xin Dong, Andrea Mauricio, and Divesh Srivastava. Linking temporal records. *Frontiers of Computer Science*, 6(3):293–213, 2012b. DOI: 10.1007/s11704-012-2002-5 Cited on page(s) 138, 171, 175

Ee-Peng Lim, Jaideep Srivastava, Satya Prabhakar, and James Richardson. Entity identification in database integration. *Inf. Syst.*, 89(1-2):1–38, 1996. Cited on page(s) 71, 89, 90

Jixue Liu, Jiuyong Li, Chengfei Liu, and Yongfeng Chen. Discover dependencies from data - a review. *IEEE Trans. Knowl. and Data Eng.*, 24(2):251–264, 2012. DOI: 10.1109/TKDE.2010.197 Cited on page(s) 65, 66

Stéphane Lopes, Jean-Marc Petit, and Lotfi Lakhal. Efficient discovery of functional dependencies and armstrong relations. In *Advances in Database Technology, Proc. 7th Int. Conf. on Extending Database Technology*, pages 350–364, 2000. DOI: 10.1007/3-540-46439-5_24 Cited on page(s) 65

David Loshin. *Master Data Management*. Knowledge Integrity, Inc., 2009. Cited on page(s) 3, 94, 100, 101

Claudio L. Lucchesi and Sylvia L. Osborn. Candidate keys for relations. *J. Comp. and System Sci.*, 17(2):270–279, 1978. DOI: 10.1016/0022-0000(78)90009-0 Cited on page(s) 83, 84, 90

Michael J. Maher. Constrained dependencies. *Theor. Comp. Sci.*, 173(1):113–149, 1997. DOI: 10.1016/S0304-3975(96)00193-4 Cited on page(s) 37

Michael J. Maher and Divesh Srivastava. Chasing constrained tuple-generating dependencies. In *Proc. 15th ACM SIGACT-SIGMOD-SIGART Symp. on Principles of Database Systems*, pages 128–138, 1996. DOI: 10.1145/237661.237693 Cited on page(s) 37

David Maier. *The Theory of Relational Databases*. Computer Science Press, 1983. ISBN 0-914894-42-0. Cited on page(s) 11

Heikki Mannila and Kari-Jouko Räihä. Dependency inference. In *Proc. 13th Int. Conf. on Very Large Data Bases*, pages 155–158, 1987. Cited on page(s) 65, 90

Heikki Mannila and Kari-Jouko Räihä. On the complexity of inferring functional dependencies. *Discrete Applied Mathematics*, 40(2):237–243, 1992. DOI: 10.1016/0166-218X(92)90031-5 Cited on page(s) 65

Chris Mayfield, Jennifer Neville, and Sunil Prabhakar. ERACER: a database approach for statistical inference and data cleaning. In *Proc. ACM SIGMOD Int. Conf. on Management of Data*, pages 75–86, 2010. DOI: 10.1145/1807167.1807178 Cited on page(s) 174, 175

Raoul Medina and Lhouari Nourine. A unified hierarchy for functional dependencies, conditional functional dependencies and association rules. In *Proc. 7th Int. Conf. on Formal Concept Analysis*, pages 98–113, 2009. DOI: 10.1007/978-3-642-01815-2_9 Cited on page(s) 65

Donald W. Miller Jr., John D. Yeast, and Robin L. Evans. Missing prenatal records at a birth center: A communication problem quantified. In *AMIA Annu Symp Proc.*, pages 535–539, 2005. Cited on page(s) 2, 93

Amihai Motro. Integrity = validity + completeness. *ACM Trans. Database Syst.*, 14(4):480–502, 1989. DOI: 10.1145/76902.76904 Cited on page(s) 100, 116, 117

Amihai Motro and Philipp Anokhin. Fusionplex: Resolution of data inconsistencies in the integration of heterogeneous information sources. *Information Fusion*, 7(2):176âĽ"196, 2006. DOI: 10.1016/j.inffus.2004.10.001 Cited on page(s) 175

Felix Naumann and Melanie Herschel. *An Introduction to Duplicate Detection*. Morgan & Claypool Publishers, 2010. DOI: 10.2200/S00262ED1V01Y201003DTM003 Cited on page(s) 10, 11, 71, 89

Felix Naumann, Alexander Bilke, Jens Bleiholder, and Melanie Weis. Data fusion in three steps: Resolving schema, tuple, and value inconsistencies. *Q. Bull. IEEE TC on Data Eng.*, 29(2):21–31, 2006. Cited on page(s) 89, 174

Noel Novelli and Rosine Cicchetti. Fun: An efficient algorithm for mining functional and embedded dependencies. In *Proc. 8th Int. Conf. on Database Theory*, pages 189–203, 2001. DOI: 10.1007/3-540-44503-X_13 Cited on page(s) 65

Dan Olteanu, Christoph Koch, and Lyublena Antova. World-set decompositions: Expressiveness and efficient algorithms. *Theor. Comp. Sci.*, 403(2-3):265–284, 2008. DOI: 10.1016/j.tcs.2008.05.004 Cited on page(s) 117

Boris Otto and Kristin Weber. From health checks to the seven sisters: The data quality journey at BT. Technical Report BE HSG/ CC CDQ/ 8, University of St. Gallen, St. Gallen, Switzerland, 2009. Cited on page(s) 3

Christos H Papadimitriou. *Computational Complexity*. Addison Wesley, 1994. Cited on page(s) 10, 113, 128, 135, 149, 150, 151

Yannis Papakonstantinou, Serge Abiteboul, and Hector Garcia-Molina. Object fusion in mediator systems. In *Proc. 22nd Int. Conf. on Very Large Data Bases*, pages 413–424, 1996. Cited on page(s) 175

Nicolas Pasquier, Yves Bastide, Rafik Taouil, and Lotfi Lakhal. Discovering frequent closed itemsets for association rules. In *Proc. 7th Int. Conf. on Database Theory*, pages 398–416, 1999. DOI: 10.1007/3-540-49257-7_25 Cited on page(s) 41, 42

John Radcliffe and Andrew White. Key issues for master data management. Gartner, 2008. Cited on page(s) 94

Erhard Rahm and Philip A. Bernstein. A survey of approaches to automatic schema matching. *VLDB J.*, 10:334–350, 2001. DOI: 10.1007/s007780100057 Cited on page(s) 71, 90

Erhard Rahm and Hong Hai Do. Data cleaning: Problems and current approaches. *Q. Bull. IEEE TC on Data Eng.*, 23(4):3–13, 2000. Cited on page(s) 174

Vijayshankar Raman and Joseph M. Hellerstein. Potter's wheel: An interactive data cleaning system. In *Proc. 27th Int. Conf. on Very Large Data Bases*, pages 381–390, 2001. Cited on page(s) 68

Ran Raz and Shmuel Safra. A sub-constant error-probability low-degree test, and a sub-constant error-probability PCP characterization of NP. In *Proc. 29th Annual ACM Symp. on Theory of Computing*, pages 475–484, 1997. DOI: 10.1145/258533.258641 Cited on page(s) 151

Simon Razniewski and Werner Nutt. Completeness of queries over incomplete databases. *Proc. VLDB Endow.*, 4(11):749–760, 2011. Cited on page(s) 117

Thomas Redman. The impact of poor data quality on the typical enterprise. *Commun. ACM*, 2: 79–82, 1998. DOI: 10.1145/269012.269025 Cited on page(s) 2

Fatiha Saïs, Nathalie Pernelle, and Marie-Christine Rousset. L2r: A logical method for reference reconciliation. In *Proc. 22nd National Conf. on Artificial Intelligence*, pages 329–334, 2007. Cited on page(s) 90

Emanuel Santos, João Pavão Martins, and Helena Galhardas. An argumentation-based approach to database repair. In *Proc. 19th European Conf. on Artificial Intelligence*, pages 125–130, 2010. Cited on page(s) 68

Sunita Sarawagi and Anuradha Bhamidipaty. Interactive deduplication using active learning. In *Proc. 8th ACM SIGKDD Int. Conf. on Knowledge Discovery and Data Mining*, pages 269–278, 2002. DOI: 10.1145/775047.775087 Cited on page(s) 71, 89

SAS, 2006. http://www.sas.com/industry/fsi/fraud/. Cited on page(s) 4

Guenter Sauter, Bill Mathews, and Ostic Ernest. Information service patterns, part 3: Data cleansing pattern. IBM, 2007. Cited on page(s) 68, 140, 141, 174

Luc Segoufin and Victor Vianu. Views and queries: Determinacy and rewriting. In *Proc. 24th ACM SIGACT-SIGMOD-SIGART Symp. on Principles of Database Systems*, pages 49–60, 2005. DOI: 10.1145/1065167.1065174 Cited on page(s) 117

Warren Shen, Xin Li, and AnHai Doan. Constraint-based entity matching. In *Proc. 20th National Conf. on Artificial Intelligence and 17th Innovative Applications of Artificial Intelligence Conf.*, pages 862–867, 2005. Cited on page(s) 89, 90

Christopher C. Shilakes and Julie Tylman. Enterprise information portals. Technical report, Merrill Lynch, Inc., New York, NY, November 1998. Cited on page(s) 2

Parag Singla and Pedro Domingos. Object identification with attribute-mediated dependencies. In *Principles of Data Mining and Knowledge Discovery, 9th European Conf.*, pages 297–308, 2005. Cited on page(s) 89, 90

Yannis Sismanis, Paul Brown, Peter J. Haas, and Berthold Reinwald. Gordian: Efficient and scalable discovery of composite keys. In *Proc. 32nd Int. Conf. on Very Large Data Bases*, pages 691–702, 2006. Cited on page(s) 90

Richard T. Snodgrass. *Developing Time-Oriented Database Applications in SQL*. Morgan Kaufmann, 1999. Cited on page(s) 11, 137

Shaoxu Song and Lei Chen. Differential dependencies: Reasoning and discovery. *ACM Trans. Database Syst.*, 36(3):16:1–16:41, 2011. DOI: 10.1145/2000824.2000826 Cited on page(s) 37, 83, 90

Shaoxu Song and Lei Chen. Discovering matching dependencies. In *Proc. 18th ACM Conf. on Information and Knowledge Management*, pages 1421–1424, 2009. DOI: 10.1145/1645953.1646135 Cited on page(s) 83, 90

Marc Spielmann. *Abstract state machines: Verification problems and complexity*. PhD thesis, RWTH Aachen, 2000. Cited on page(s) 102

SQL Standard. International Standard ISO/IEC 9075-2:2003(E), Information technology: Database languages, SQL Part 2 (Foundation, 2nd edition), 2003. Cited on page(s) 17

Divesh Srivastava and Suresh Venkatasubramanian. Information theory for data management. In *Proc. ACM SIGMOD Int. Conf. on Management of Data*, pages 1255–1256, 2010. DOI: 10.1145/1807167.1807337 Cited on page(s) 158, 174

Larry J. Stockmeyer. The polynomial-time hierarchy. *Theor. Comp. Sci.*, 3(1):1–22, 1976. DOI: 10.1016/0304-3975(76)90061-X Cited on page(s) 102, 105, 126, 128, 135, 136, 171

V.S. Subrahmanian, Sibel Adali, Anne Brink, J.ames J. Lu, Adil Rajput, Timothy J. Rogers, Robert Ross, and Charles Ward. HERMES: A heterogeneous reasoning and mediator system. Technical report, University of Maryland, 1995. Cited on page(s) 175

Ron van der Meyden. Logical approaches to incomplete information: A survey. In Jan Chomicki and Gunter Saake, editors, *Logics for Databases and Information Systems*, pages 307–356. Kluwer, 1998. DOI: 10.1007/978-1-4615-5643-5 Cited on page(s) 11, 106, 117, 138

Ron van der Meyden. The complexity of querying indefinite data about linearly ordered domains. *J. Comp. and System Sci.*, 54(1):113–135, 1997. Cited on page(s) 11, 138

Moshe Y. Vardi. The complexity of relational query languages. In *Proc. 14th Annual ACM Symp. on Theory of Computing*, pages 137–146, 1982. Cited on page(s) 55, 101, 125

Moshe Y. Vardi. Fundamentals of dependency theory. In Egon Börger, editor, *Trends in Theoretical Computer Science*, pages 171–224. Computer Science Press, 1987. Cited on page(s) 11

Moshe Y. Vardi. On the integrity of databases with incomplete information. In *Proc. 5th ACM SIGACT-SIGMOD Symp. on Principles of Database Systems*, pages 252–266, 1986. DOI: 10.1145/6012.15419 Cited on page(s) 116

Vassilios S. Verykios, Ahmed K. Elmagarmid, and Elias Houstis. Automating the approximate record-matching process. *Inf. Sci.*, 126(1-4):83–89, 2002. Cited on page(s) 71, 89

Victor Vianu. Dynamic functional dependencies and database aging. *J. ACM*, 34(1):28–59, 1987. DOI: 10.1145/7531.7918 Cited on page(s) 90, 91

Loan Vo, Jinli Cao, and Johanna Rahayu. Discovering conditional functional dependencies in XML data. In *Proc. 22nd Australasian Database Conference*, pages 143–152, 2011. Cited on page(s) 66

Jianyong Wang, Jiawei Han, and Jian Pei. CLOSET+: searching for the best strategies for mining frequent closed itemsets. In *Proc. 9th ACM SIGKDD Int. Conf. on Knowledge Discovery and Data Mining*, pages 236–245, 2003. DOI: 10.1145/956750.956779 Cited on page(s) 42

Junhu Wang. Binary equality implication constraints, normal forms and data redundancy. *Inf. Proc. Letters*, 101(1):20–25, 2007. DOI: 10.1016/j.ipl.2006.07.004 Cited on page(s) 90

Ingo Wegener and R. Pruim. *Complexity Theory: Exploring the Limits of Efficient Algorithms*. Springer, 2005. Cited on page(s) 162

Melanie Weis and Felix Naumann. DogmatiX tracks down duplicates in XML. In *Proc. ACM SIGMOD Int. Conf. on Management of Data*, pages 431–442, 2005. DOI: 10.1145/1066157.1066207 Cited on page(s) 11, 90, 174

Melanie Weis, Felix Naumann, Ulrich Jehle, Jens Lufter, and Holger Schuster. Industry-scale duplicate detection. *Proc. VLDB Endow.*, 1(2):1253–1264, 2008. Cited on page(s) 89, 90

Steven Whang and Hector Garcia-Molina. Entity resolution with evolving rules. *Proc. VLDB Endow.*, 3(1):1326–1337, 2010. Cited on page(s) 89

Steven Whang, Omar Benjelloun, and Hector Garcia-Molina. Generic entity resolution with negative rules. *VLDB J.*, 18(6):1261–1277, 2009. Cited on page(s) 89, 174

Jennifer Widom. Trio: A system for integrated management of data, accuracy, and lineage. In *Proc. 2nd Biennial Conf. on Innovative Data Systems Research*, pages 262–276, 2005. Cited on page(s) 175

Jennifer Widom and Stefano Ceri. *Active Database Systems: Triggers and Rules for Advanced Database Processing*. Morgan Kaufmann, 1996. Cited on page(s) 174

Jef Wijsen. Database repairing using updates. *ACM Trans. Database Syst.*, 30(3):722–768, 2005. DOI: 10.1145/1093382.1093385 Cited on page(s) 67

William E. Winkler. Methods for evaluating and creating data quality. *Inf. Syst.*, 29(7):531–550, 2004. DOI: 10.1016/j.is.2003.12.003 Cited on page(s) 52, 68, 82, 89

William E. Winkler. Set-covering and editing discrete data. In *Proc. of the Section on survey research methods, American statistical association.*, pages 564–569, 1997. Cited on page(s) 68

William E. Winkler. Overview of record linkage and current research directions. Technical report, U.S. Census Bureau, 2006. Technical report, Statistical Research Division. Cited on page(s) 89

William E. Winkler. Methods for record linkage and bayesian networks. Technical Report RRS2002/05, U.S. Census Bureau, 2002. Cited on page(s) 71, 89, 90

Minji Wu and Amélie Marian. A framework for corroborating answers from multiple web sources. *Inf. Syst.*, 36(2):431–449, 2011. DOI: 10.1016/j.is.2010.08.008 Cited on page(s) 175

Catharine M. Wyss, Chris Giannella, and Edward L. Robertson. Fastfds: A heuristic-driven, depth-first algorithm for mining functional dependencies from relation instances. In *Proc. 3rd Int. Conf. Data Warehousing and Knowledge Discovery*, pages 101–110, 2001. DOI: 10.1007/3-540-44801-2_11 Cited on page(s) 65

Mohamed Yakout, Ahmed K. Elmagarmid, and Jennifer Neville. Ranking for data repairs. In *Proc. 13th Int. Conf. on Database Theory*, pages 23–28, 2010a. DOI: 10.1109/ICDEW.2010.5452767 Cited on page(s) 68

Mohamed Yakout, Ahmed K. Elmagarmid, Jennifer Neville, and Mourad Ouzzani. GDR: A system for guided data repair. In *Proc. ACM SIGMOD Int. Conf. on Management of Data*, pages 1223–1226, 2010b. DOI: 10.1145/1807167.1807325 Cited on page(s) 68, 175

Mohamed Yakout, Ahmed K. Elmagarmid, Jennifer Neville, Mourad Ouzzani, and Ihab F. Ilyas. Guided data repair. *Proc. VLDB Endow.*, 4(5):279–289, 2011. Cited on page(s) 68

William Yancey. BigMatch: A program for extracting probable matches from a large file. Technical Report Computing 2007/01, U.S. Census Bureau, 2007. Cited on page(s) 71, 89

Peter Z. Yeh and Colin A. Puri. Discovering conditional functional dependencies to detect data inconsistencies. In *Proc. 8th Int. Workshop on Quality in Databases*, Paper 8, 2010. Cited on page(s) 65

Peter Z. Yeh and Colin A. Puri. An efficient and robust approach for discovering data quality rules. In *Proc. 22nd IEEE Int. Conf. on Tools with AI*, pages 248–255, 2010. DOI: 10.1109/ICTAI.2010.43 Cited on page(s) 65

Peter Z. Yeh, Colin A. Puri, Mark Wagman, and Ajay K. Easo. Accelerating the discovery of data quality rules: A case study. In *Proc. 23rd Conf. on Innovative Applications of Artificial Intelligence*, 2011. Cited on page(s) 65

Xiaoxin Yin, Jiawei Han, and Philip S. Yu. Truth discovery with multiple conflicting information providers on the web. *IEEE Trans. Knowl. and Data Eng.*, 20(6):796–808, 2008. DOI: 10.1109/TKDE.2007.190745 Cited on page(s) 11, 175

Mohammed J. Zaki. Mining non-redundant association rules. *Data Min. Knowl. Discov.*, 9(3): 223–248, 2004. DOI: 10.1023/B:DAMI.0000040429.96086.c7 Cited on page(s) 65

Mohammed J. Zaki and Ching-Jui Hsiao. Efficient algorithms for mining closed itemsets and their lattice structure. *IEEE Trans. Knowl. and Data Eng.*, 17(4):462–478, 2005. DOI: 10.1109/TKDE.2005.60 Cited on page(s) 42

Haopeng Zhang, Yanlei Diao, and Neil Immerman. Recognizing patterns in streams with imprecise timestamps. *Proc. VLDB Endow.*, 3(1-2):244–255, 2010. Cited on page(s) 6, 119, 138, 163, 175

Jacob Ziv and Abraham Lempel. Compression of individual sequences via variable-rate coding. *IEEE Trans. Inf. Theory*, 24(5):530–536, 1978. DOI: 10.1109/TIT.1978.1055934 Cited on page(s) 157

Authors' Biographies

WEIFEI FAN

Wenfei Fan is the (Chair) Professor of Web Data Management in the School of Informatics, University of Edinburgh, UK. He is a Fellow of the Royal Society of Edinburgh, UK, a National Professor of the 1000-Talent Program, and a Yangtze River Scholar, China. He received his Ph.D. from the University of Pennsylvania, U.S.A., and his M.S .and B.S. from Peking University, China. He is a recipient of the Alberto O. Mendelzon Test-of-Time Award of ACM PODS 2010, the Best Paper Award for VLDB 2010, the Roger Needham Award in 2008 (UK), the Best Paper Award for IEEE ICDE 2007, the Outstanding Overseas Young Scholar Award in 2003 (China), the Best Paper of the Year Award for Computer Networks in 2002, and the Career Award in 2001 (USA). His current research interests include database theory and systems, in particular data quality, data integration, database security, distributed query processing, query languages, social network analysis, Web services, and XML.

FLORIS GEERTS

Floris Geerts is Research Professor in the Department of Mathematics and Computer Science, University of Antwerp, Belgium. Before that, he held a senior research fellow position in the database group at the University of Edinburgh, UK and a postdoctoral research position in the data mining group at the University of Helsinki, Finland. He received his Ph.D. in 2001 from the University of Hasselt, Belgium. His research interests include the theory and practice of databases and the study of data quality, in particular. He is a recipient of the Best Paper Awards for IEEE ICDM 2001 and IEEE ICDE 2007.